Andrew Marr is currently the chief political commentator for the *Independent*, and he has been political editor of both the *Economist* and the *Scotsman*. In 1994 he was voted 'Columnist of the Year' by the BBC's *What the Papers Say* and also in the British Press Awards. He is a regular television and radio broadcaster, whose recent work includes BBC Television's *The Battle of Ideas*. His first book, *The Battle for Scotland*, is also published by Penguin.

Andrew Marr is married with three children and lives in East Sheen, London.

RULING BRITANNIA

The Failure and Future of British Democracy

ANDREW MARR

PENGUIN BOOKS

PENGUIN BOOKS

Published by the Penguin Group
Penguin Books Ltd, 27 Wrights Lane, London w8 5TZ, England
Penguin Books USA Inc., 375 Hudson Street, New York, New York 10014, USA
Penguin Books Australia Ltd, Ringwood, Victoria, Australia
Penguin Books Canada Ltd, 10 Alcorn Avenue, Toronto, Ontario, Canada M4V 3B2
Penguin Books (NZ) Ltd, 182–190 Wairau Road, Auckland 10, New Zealand

Penguin Books Ltd, Registered Offices: Harmondsworth, Middlesex, England

First published by Michael Joseph 1995
This revised edition published in Penguin Books with a new Afterword 1996
3 5 7 9 10 8 6 4 2

The author and publishers would like to thank Faber & Faber Ltd
for permission to use the following copyright material:
'Homage to a Government' by Philip Larkin from
Collected Poems edited by Anthony Thwaite.

The moral right of the author has been asserted

Typeset by Datix International Limited, Bungay, Suffolk
Printed in England by Clays Ltd, St Ives plc

321.8043

For Donald and Valerie Marr,
my parents

Contents

Unacknowledgements

This book was possible thanks to the great generosity and kindness of many politicians, including ministers; civil servants; fellow journalists; city and business types and others who gave me, wittingly or otherwise, important insights. I am not going to list them. The politicians, many of them, will probably object to my conclusions and would be mortified to be associated with them. Officials don't like being named as sources. Nor do most business people. And fellow hacks mostly get their names in print enough anyway. But to you all: ta.

Acknowledgements

I would like to thank some people by name, though. I want to thank *The Independent* collectively, which is a wonderful place to work, and to Hamish McRae, Mary Dejevsky and Jane Taylor in particular for giving me ideas and (in the case of the latter two) editing embarrassing bits out of my columns. I want to thank Jackie for not divorcing me while I was babbling incoherently about judicial review or hunched over the desk. I want to thank Harry and Isabel for tolerating my curious behaviour too, and Jack and Pauline Ashley for helping us so generously. And Emily for sleeping through the night. And Gina Ford for getting her to. And I want to thank Tony Bevins, who read the proposal and scribbled question-marks all over it. And Cat Ledger, my agent, who sold the book for £250,000* to Michael Joseph, where I want to thank Louise Haines, the editor.

* Joke.

INTRODUCTION

Generous Plans of Freedom

A WORD FROM THE BOOK

Welcome, friend. Come in. Sit down, sprawl, flop.
(Unless still fumbling me in the bookshop.)
Cup of tea? KitKat? Something stronger? Fine.
Comfort's the thing. Take a sip. Recline.
For I am not a comfortable read. By most yardsticks
I cannot not sell. In Britain, anything on politics
Gets quickly pulped to make room for the twenty-sixth
Biography of Eustace Mimsy-Splodge
The Bloomsbury potter who knew Blodge
Who lived with someone dull but sex-obsessed
Who met, however briefly, Vita Sackville-West;
I'll be done for by *Confessions* (Rita Chevrolet)
And travel yarns – *A Vicar's Girl in Hudson Bay*
Or the collected cheque-book stubs of Archer, J.
The stone-faced man from W.H. Smith
Will say: 'We need the space for *Urban Myths*'
And then I'll be no more. But until I'm nixed
I am the story of our modern politics,
Told by a 'pundit' – (which means his special vice is
Pestering folk with his advices).
Walt Lippmann, the grand-dad of pundits, said
More newspapermen had been ruin-ed
By self-importance than by booze
And this author, as you'll shortly see,
Gets through his day on nips of neat pomposity.
Forgive him. If you can't, fling me aloft –
But aim me, please, at something soft.

The Time

This is a book about British democracy in the last years of the century. It asks how much political power we have as voters and party supporters; how our government really operates; and how, in simple and practical ways, we can restore our most important national inheritance to full strength. The timing is no coincidence. Quite soon, there will be a general election which will offer the British the clearest and most important constitutional choice since the arrival of mass democracy here. In previous such elections, the main parties have largely agreed about the rules and nature of the political system. That is not true this time. The result, either way, will mould our country for the next millennium. It offers one serious choice which even the millions of Britons fed up to the back teeth with politics need to chew over and think about before swallowing.

If, after seventeen or eighteen years of continuous Conservative rule, despite the party's civil war over European Union, and facing a popular young Labour leader, the Conservatives achieve a fifth successive parliamentary majority – well then, we will be living in something very close to a one-party system of government. The question of whether the broad Conservative coalition can ever be beaten will become a serious one. Such an event will change the underlying assumptions about the British system and thus – since the constitution is a bundle of acts and assumptions – the constitution too. The pendulum will have fallen off its hinge. Tories tend to shy away from this conclusion. They prefer to suggest that they stand for business-as-usual, the old ways. When, today, the Conservatives choose to fight on 'the constitution', they imply they want to stop or reverse change. They oppose any further powers passing to Brussels and allege that to give Scotland or Wales a measure of self-control over their own affairs would break up the United Kingdom. They stand for the Old Constitution. But in truth there have been huge changes to our political system; the Old Constitution has crumbled away long ago. Local government, parliamentary behaviour, the civil service, the judiciary, the power of the

Treasury and the Foreign Office, the use of unelected committees – all have changed radically, beyond the scope of the
textbooks. There has been no business-as-usual.

So, faced with the choice, every British voter needs to be
aware of the constitutional audit of the Conservative years, to
know about their stewardship of our democracy and to have
thought about the consequences of going on into the early
2000s as we have been. Many of the questions raised over these
past few years about the new corporatism, corruption, the rise
of unaccountable quangos, the feebleness of Parliament, the role
of ministers and journalists and pressure groups, must now
return with redoubled force. These are matters which have hit
the headlines repeatedly, producing a vague but general feeling
of political decay. Giving evidence to a committee on public
standards in 1995, David Hunt, a leading cabinet minister, said
that such standards in Britain were among the highest in the
world and had been considered so through most of his lifetime.[1]
Then, in somewhat histrionic terms, he announced:

The events of the past eighteen months or so, however, with the
public breakdown of that consensus, have been traumatic for many of
us, with colleagues and revered institutions being defamed and attacked with slurs, innuendo and downright lies. It seems that nothing
is sacred, and even that nothing can ever be the same again.

I hope to have avoided innuendo in what follows and, as a
general rule, lies. But, at the same time, I hope to demonstrate
to the open-minded reader that not only will nothing be the
same ever again – David Hunt was right about that – it
shouldn't be and mustn't be, either.

Many people, conservatives of a different stripe from Hunt,
assume that a Labour or Liberal-Labour administration could
sweep in and return us to something like the post-war political
settlement. They hope that, by voting for the opposition, they
will be, in effect, pressing the nation's rewind button. It won't
necessarily be a land of beige Morris Minors and the first Beatles
LP, but it will return Britain to nice, traditional social-demo-
cratic politics, as half-remembered from the fifties and sixties.

There will be dull but honest politicians, a consensus about welfare and employment. It will be a Britain in which Keynesian economists and large manufacturing combines ensure that everyone has a nine-to-five job – a land in which benign Whitehall mandarins with BBC voices plan fairly for everyone. This is not an ignoble vision but it is a hopelessly sentimental and unrealistic one. It tries to blank out the international background of modern politics. It won't happen. In fact, an opposition victory would give us even more cause to think about our political system than a Tory one. Labour and the Liberal Democrats are committed to a wide range of reforms which, if carried together, would amount to a revolution. There are the Scottish Parliament and the Welsh Assembly,[2] which, however impeccably democratic their credentials, pose questions for the future running and composition of the mainly English Westminster Parliament. There is the possibility of deeper integration in a European Union. There is the reform or abolition of the House of Lords, the matters of a Bill of Rights and a Freedom of Information Act. There is the matter too of the Monarchy's powers. If the Liberal Democrats hold the balance of power, there may even be reform of the voting system. There is the question of which, if any, of the above should be sanctioned by a national referendum. And the more one looks at the list, the more one wonders about whether the time is not finally ripe to thoroughly reorder our affairs with a new settlement, a written constitution, as the reformers' organization, Charter 88, wants. Thus the accumulated political frustration and depression of the left, the bar-room and dinner-table conversations of years, piled up into pre-legislative form and ready for blast-off. But what it might actually mean; how it would work; whether it would produce a new pride in our institutions – all that is unknowable, a matter of faith now which may be a matter of law.

Some of these issues – the Union, devolution, a Bill of Rights, power-sharing, proportional representation, referendums – have been gingerly placed on the national agenda by the Conservatives in their search for a settlement to the Ulster conflict. But, applied to the mainland by left-of-centre reformers, they would transform the heart of the British political landscape. We would become less centralized, less easily controlled from London. Some think we would slowly resolve ourselves back into our historic nations, liquidating the Britishness that was born in the seventeenth century and which found its most intense modern expression in the two world wars. Less dramatically, voting reform and reform of party funding would threaten to push the Tories out of power for a long time – perhaps ensuring that one of the modern world's most successful political parties never again governed alone – and end the 'Conservative century' in a final, door-slamming way. One can be cynical about the ability of a Labour or Lib–Lab government to deliver as much as it promises. But even some of these reforms would change our country. So it seems a good time to give an account of what our current 'real constitution' consists of. If we do not know where we are, it is hard to talk about where we should be going. And the startling truth is that, however great the political changes awaiting us after the next election, the pace of economic and social change has been so great that we have lived through a ragged political revolution already. A Labour revolution may loom; but a Tory one has already been accomplished.

For post-war Britain is dead. There is an end-of-century feeling about, a great uprooting of institutions and assumptions. For most of us, there is less security, less feeling of control. 'Life seems to be speeding up' is a common, if indistinct, way of expressing a common, if indistinct, feeling. The changes, though, are real enough. What have been the biggest political events of the post-Cold War world so far? There have been two, but they are so closely intertwined that they seem like one. They are the arrival of a global free market and the new information technologies – respectively, the extreme logical developments of the liberalism and science of the eighteenth-century Enlightenment. Bigger, more volatile markets and newer technologies need one another, and always have. They embrace. The British imperial trade and the tea clipper, then the flying-boat, were part of a single, world-changing technopolitical velocity. The same is true today of the satellite and the bond market, the fibre-optic cable and the transnational company. Just as population growth has accelerated, so too have the effects of these leaps in inter-connectedness, and the markets they create. The modern global economy and the so-called information superhighway have already produced huge flows of people, money and power. They are the giant motors of the speeding up that we all notice in our everyday lives. And they have consequences for democracy too.

Both drive away power and authority from the institutions that ran the old world. In particular, they leave behind the national governments. These once had huge direct economic power, through controls on money, and state industries, and the ability to set wage rates, and so on. And, almost as important, they had the authority which comes from knowing more than their populations – these were the governments of specialists and bureaucrats and scientists who believed, with some justifica-tion, that they could 'run' their societies almost like children running train-sets. It was a simple, top-down world, in which political parties competed to take their turn at flicking and jerking the levers of power. The global markets and the democra-tizing power of technology have blown this world away. It's gone, and our political imaginations have hardly begun to cope with the change. Of course, this toppling of the old order faces every developed and open country. But it is perhaps particularly difficult for Britain.

The Place

Why? Because the British are getting accustomed to seeing themselves almost as a forgotten people, a brushed-aside nation. At a big conference in London in 1995, a range of speakers, from the Prince of Wales to German and Japanese commenta-tors, urged the British to cheer up, buck up and stop whingeing. Good advice; but in this new global system, great events seem to bypass Britain. Typhoon Thatcher blasted across these islands and disappeared somewhere off into a mid-Atlantic haze. The most impressive events in technology, politics and culture, which once upon a time seemed to happen here, or at least in Europe, are now occurring elsewhere, mostly on either side of the Pacific. History is no longer made in Britain. Like so many other commodities, it comes stamped with the words 'Made in China'. The Asian miracle may merely repeat what happened in Britain first; but its scale is vastly bigger – China is currently seeing the biggest migration in human history, and grows each year by a staggering amount. Once the British, like other European nations, prided themselves on being a people with power, with control over their own destiny. The British statesman spoke and things happened across the world. The British thought up steam-engines and liberalism, free trade and spinning machines, and exported these, and the world was changed. The British, in short, happened to other people. Now the world happens to Britain.

In many ways, this withdrawal of influence is a liberation. The modern British have nothing to feel guilty about. We have escaped most of our imperial history and are living in a world no longer dominated by dark ideological battles. If liberty means only the freedom to get on with our lives without being frightened of the state, or of invasion by a rival state, then our liberties seem pretty secure. If power has shifted away from politicians to markets and bureaucrats, so that things that are central to our lives – the cost of money, the availability of work, the regulations that govern our leisure and our countryside – are decided without political discussion, plenty of people will be unworried by that. It could be called the final victory of paternalism and liberalism over politics, a condition in which the great clashes between socialism and capitalism are over and, with all that past brouhaha pushed to one side, there is simply less need for politics: a world in which the awkward machinery of ballot boxes, parties and parliaments can be allowed to dwindle into unimportance. Shop, don't vote: you get far more choice, you have more control and the makers of commodities lie less often than the makers of laws.

And, for many Britons, today's heroes are more likely to be

business gurus with attitude, like Richard Branson or Anita Roddick, or the leaders of environmental campaigns, than politicians. Private companies are taking over more and more of things that were once the state's – healthcare, prisons, training. Some refer ironically to their higher status – as the AA calls itself 'the fourth emergency service' and its rival, the RAC, says, 'it isn't the car that's broken down, it's law and order.' This is a worldwide phenomenon, though where the encroachment of the private sector on politics has gone to the logical extreme (with the calamitous election of a media tycoon as Italian prime minister, or the candidacy of Ross Perot, an American businessman, for the US presidency) it has ended in tears. We have seen nothing like that here and have a party political system which makes it unlikely – Alan Sugar or Sir John Harvey-Jones cannot 'run' for prime minister. But, in Britain, politics has become a pretty despised business. It attracts fewer people than ever before; millions of people have left the parties and the brightest graduates are less likely than before to look to Westminster for their careers. People coming out of schools and colleges see more glittering prizes, including power, in the City, or journalism, or a big multinational than in dusty ministries and the cosy incompetence of Parliament. And the voters? They are recording greater levels of cynicism than pollsters can remember about the whole political trade. It has all led some observers to talk of a 'post-political age', even the death of politics.

But if this is all a benign development, why are so many of us feeling so depressed about the state of the state? The victory of the market has hardly been paralleled by a growth in national confidence or happiness. We seem to be losing something we valued. The Britain inherited from the great struggles of the mid-century, with its particular securities and inefficiencies, is slipping away. The symbols of its retreat infest our everyday lives, our newspapers, our imaginations. In a nation once known for its indomitably self-assured middle classes, even the middle classes are insecure. A parliamentary system once regarded as utterly clean and respectable is held up across the country as stinkingly corrupt. (The assumption being wrong in both cases, but never mind.) A Welfare State which young Britons were once brought up to venerate as this country's great domestic achievement is sneeringly accused of feeding the social decay it was meant to stop: New Jerusalem as a shabby, jerry-built and generally provisional suburb of the rest of the world, in which children murder children and generations pass without knowing a proper job. A Royal Family which was once (though it seems hard to believe) a symbol of hope, slithers and sinks in a rubbish-tip of sexual self-revelation. You'd almost expect to hear that Westminster Palace is falling down – and in fact Big Ben, old Britain's chief political symbol, has slipped very slightly sideways, undermined by a tunnel to the new Docklands London, symbol of the rising global economy. Let us admit it. Most of us have been, for some of the time, ashamed of what our country has become, even when that shame is tempered by defiant patriotism.

So it might seem logical, even sensible, to approach this question of our political future in a mood of some gloom. The current writer yields to no one (except Will Hutton) in fashionable gloom but was much struck by a coincidence. I was passing time one night in the Press Gallery library of the House of Commons when I found and flicked open a dusty book. It looked as if it hadn't been touched since it was first placed in the glass-fronted cabinet with a dedication from its proud author some time before the First World War. Charles Masterman was exactly my age when he wrote, in 1909, *The Condition of England* – a liberal newspaper hack then, though later a Treasury minister. Reflecting on the Sunday newspapers – the tabloids of his day – Masterman mourned that they reflected a world

of violence and madness. Men and women knife each other in the dark. Children are foully butchered by unknown assailants. Suicides sprinkle every page: now that a girl may die with another woman's husband; now that a family may escape the hell of unemployment; now simply for weariness, because the whole effort of life has lost significance and crumbled into dust and ashes. The most insistent noise which reverberates through their pages is the clicking of the huge machine of English justice, as couples once married in affection are torn apart, or a long procession of murderers, thieves, absconding solicitors, fraudulent company promoters, are swept into the cold silence of the penal system.

And I thought . . . Oh

That, after all, was the England celebrated today in Merchant Ivory films, the alleged Golden Age of decency, national prosperity and optimism before the First World War. So what does one conclude? Perhaps that despair about the condition of the country, including its political culture, is a rather limp reaction to our current troubles. Deep pessimism has been refuted too regularly by human ingenuity and reformist energy. There is no pre-ordained cycle of decline, nothing irreversible about what has happened. Today, any 'audit of peace' would give post-Cold War Britons a balance-sheet which included huge advantages and offered new chances. Much of the insecurity of our times derives from just the same factors which, seen differently, could help build a fizzing future. These cloudy, work-scarred islands are unusually agape to the rest of the world, making them vulnerable but also sensitive to change. The sharing of a global language and a very open economy mean that Britons are early guinea-pigs for globalization – its victims, yes; but its potential opportunists too.

The Reason

So we are at a time when there is a great choice to be made about our political system. And we live in a country which needs to keep its nerve and think clearly about the opportunities and dangers ahead. But many people will ask why the two things should be assumed to be connected – why the political system still matters to the rest of our lives. The British are supposed to be 'pragmatic' and hostile to abstract theorizing; and perhaps there is something in the character that refuses to take words like democracy and politics entirely seriously until convinced that they connect to other words like jobs, security and income. Making a living is the basic business of life and many people will see any political argument as secondary, even faintly frivolous, unless it links firmly to that basic business. Today they may say, 'Ah, power has moved to the markets; the politicians can't deliver the jobs they used to promise us; we might as well forget that stuff.'

They would be wrong. The defeat of politics means, in the end, the triumph of anarchy, and its retreat has already been an agonizing business for millions. The shrinking of the political world hits the poor first, for they are the ones who rely most heavily on benefits, on state schooling, on the NHS, on the police: there are no private security companies patrolling Wine Alley in Govan, or Chapeltown in Leeds, or the Blackbird Leys estate in Oxford. In the whirlwind of the global market, it is the political state which provides the first and sometimes only educational and economic protection for millions of people. They may be disillusioned by politics; they may be ceasing to vote; they may be wholly outside the main political conversation. But they are the object, the acted-upon human clay, of much of what we call politics. The middle classes too, facing the same global economic pressures that hit British manufacturing in the early eighties and then the service sector a few years later, have found that the shrinking power of the state has not cut them off from politics. It has certainly not brought a shrinking tax bill.

Even the wealthiest are far less robustly independent of the state, and thus of politics, than the myth suggests. Britain has a comparatively huge private education sector, but there are still some 180,000 children from what might be called upper-class and middle-class families attending state schools.[3] Though many middle-class people do use private healthcare schemes, when it comes to big, expensive operations they still turn to the NHS – as do, more regularly, the increasing numbers outside full-time employment and the old. And there are large cohorts of Britons who know the cost of politics when it goes wrong – the families hit by injustices in the Child Support Act; the nurses and others who were sold rubbishy pensions; small company owners who have been driven out of business by grossly onerous or daft regulations; villagers who suspected (rightly) that they were being served with compulsory purchase orders to build a new road based on bogus economics and faulty logic; doctors and prison managers who find a tide of paperwork overwhelming their proper jobs. There are plenty of concrete, matter-of-fact reasons to reassert the political part of our lives. But there are deeper reasons too, not unimportant to our economy because they are a little more abstract.

For as long as history records the story of societies, one important human need has been a feeling that we have some communal (and latterly, national) control over our destinies. Without that basic security, we cannot think far ahead; we lose ourselves. Prosperous and decent survival in a much more numerous and closely-connected world will require economic adaptability and flexibility. But it will also require a culture which keeps nourishing and sustaining people for that competition. Many countries, not just Britain, have managed a short sprint, and then become exhausted. The real challenge is to evolve a society which replicates, generation after generation, well-educated, adaptable and secure people who can think long and plan carefully. And that long-termism requires successful politics. It requires a belief in things being well-ordered enough to make saving rational; a trust that taxes will pay their predictable and sure social dividend; an expectation that investments will not be robbed by greedy middlemen or devoured by inflation; an assumption that the administration is tolerably clean and effective, so that it is worth planning for the future; and an assurance that the national and local bureaucracies are not too onerous but are efficient and reliable, so that citizens will be treated fairly by the 'system'. It needs rootedness, a nourishing culture.

Only on the basis of what we might call good political husbandry can there be a long-term economic success. We need a politics which helps ensure that the things we have learned as a country can be handed on to a generation which will keep those social and political instincts in good repair. Our recent national weaknesses for short-term investments; for bricks-and-mortar, not industry; for high annual dividends, rather than capital-building stocks; and for inflation are signs of lack of confidence in politics, at its widest – a lack of belief in the rules about how we get on together. Take it now, because you don't know what might happen tomorrow. Consume it yourself, because otherwise somebody else will. Grab what you can, from whom you can, while you can. When someone suggests sacrificing something for the common good, curl your lip and ask yourself, 'What's his game?' There is a relationship between the long-term economic success of a country and its political self-confidence which is not mathematical, but which certainly, and uncomfortably, exists. Britain's political autonomy is limited by, among other things, its people's relative incompetence at making money. Similarly, its economic record has been damaged by its centralist, decaying and mistrusted political culture.

Visiting London, the great Voltaire told his Parisian readers: 'Commerce, which has enriched English citizens, has helped to make them free, and this freedom in turn has extended commerce, and that has made the greatness of the nation.' The link between wealth and freedom remains as real today as it was in the 1720s, certainly for individuals and still too for nations: Voltaire's virtuous circle, reversed, becomes a vicious one. The poorer we get, relative to other countries, the less bargaining power we will have over terms of trade, the price of our money, the environmental regulations which affect us, the conditions of our employment, and many other matters up to and including military defence. And our relative position has been worsening for over a century. Is the 'nourishing culture' still available as an option in this less powerful Britain? I believe it is, but it won't be the centralist paternalism of old and the case must be argued through. We cannot break away from our past, but we cannot return to it, either. If we are to survive and thrive in the new world, we need to be confident about our institutions and our politics, and thus about ourselves. We need a sense of gravity. At the moment, we are losing it.

The Trouble

So there is as near as I can get to a stolidly pragmatic, British, gumboots-on-the-ground sort of explanation as to why politics matters to our prosperity. (And – oh, jings – I had to quote a Frenchman to do it.) But this book isn't simply about politics; it is about democracy, and its condition in Britain now. So the next question is, does better politics necessarily involve a more effective democracy? Or is it, perhaps, just about better administration? While it is true that countries can be democratic and badly run, or authoritarian and efficiently run, any check-list of the most successful countries has tended to match fairly closely to the democracies. Efficient but undemocratic countries eventually become inefficient because they stifle the ingenuity and creativity of their people; without diversity and experiment, economies rot.

Does it follow that the more democracy, the better? Only up to a point. There is a limit. Making direct democratic choices, rather than subcontracting them to professionals, is a time-consuming and distracting thing. Democratic idealists have followed the great American writer Henry Thoreau, who asked: 'Must the citizen ever for a moment, or in the least degree, resign his conscience to the legislator? Why has every man[4] a conscience then? I think that we should be men first and subjects afterwards.'[5] But the majority has taken a different view, accepting that, in a busy and complex world, we have to let legislators get on and take some decisions for us. Politicians are nothing but specialist social choosers – people who have 'gone into decisions' rather than going into teaching, or the City, or whatever. As for the rest of us, we have followed Oscar Wilde, who complained that the trouble with socialism (and the same goes for politics generally) is that it takes too many evenings.

Between Thoreau's idea of everyone being his or her own ruler; and Wilde's belief that life is too short and interesting for politics, modern liberal societies negotiate a trade-off. Popular democracy and government-by-experts are forever in a state of tension which needs to be continuously adjusted and negotiated over. That might sound a Frenchly theoretical thing to say, but most of us recognize it in practice. We don't want a say about everything, all the time; but where we know about something, or have an interest in it, then we do want a say. We become aware, pretty quickly, when the amount of say we have got is too little; then we get steamed up and want to do something to assert ourselves again. We write to our MP, or bother our councillor, or vote, or attend a protest meeting. And this instinctive stroppiness is a social good because where the maximum number of knowledgeable and interested people have a chance to express their views and talk about them, testing them one against another, big mistakes are generally avoided. There is a further advantage on the side of democracy. The more we are democratically involved, the more we are implicated, too: when mistakes do happen, as they must, we cannot simply blame them upon some anonymous or high-up booby. Instead of seething and feeling put-upon, we take some responsibility, and perhaps learn from them and so grow up a little. Being able to do this growing up is the difference between the political childishness of being a subject, slave or servant of the state – and the condition of political adulthood, or citizenship.

Now, a main point of what follows is simply that we do not have enough of this basic grown-upness in our British system today. Power has moved from people connected to the democratic machine, to people who aren't. It has moved from local councillors to quangos; and from national politicians to the markets or supranational bodies, particularly to Brussels. Furthermore, these shifts are connected: it is because London politicians have lost so much 'posh' power (over currencies, trade, defence) that they have been sweeping up for themselves, and their appointees, more down-to-earth or 'common' powers over schools, training and so on, which local communities could reasonably expect to have for themselves. There has been plenty of constitutional change, as we shall see, but it hasn't tended to increase the adult democracy. It hasn't focused on where power is going, whether to the markets, or the European Union, or to quangos, and then tried to pursue those powers and mark them with open, democratic processes. Instead, the political changes we have had have tended to disguise the new sources of power, and muffle democratic involvement in them.

Indeed, if there is one unmistakable signal of degeneration now, it is fuzziness and confusion, the destruction of clear lines of responsibility and blame. Whether this is because power has been privatized, or the civil service reformed by devolving power, or local services handed over to private and unelected boards, the loss of clarity and simplicity is a real problem. You could describe this as 'post-modern politics'*, an inevitable and even virtuous product of a more complex and intertwined world. But what does it say to voters? It says: you don't know who is to blame any more. You won't find out. And, even if you did, my friend, there's nothing you can do. This mentality has been described by Kingsley Amis as 'sodding the public'. And a sodded public is not a happy one.

The story is told of the great Labour politician Nye Bevan that he, like so many sodded Britons today, was engaged in a search for power long before he finally reached the British cabinet. He started young: 'Very important man. That's Councillor Jackson,' his father had said to him. 'What's the Council?' he asked. 'Very important place indeed and they are very powerful men,' his father had replied. Bevan continued:

When I got older I said to myself: 'The place to get to is the Council. That's where the power is,' so I worked very hard and . . . I got on the Council. I discovered when I got there that power *had* been there, but it had just gone. So I made some inquiries, being an earnest student of social affairs, and I learned that the power had slipped down to the County Council. That was where it was and where it had gone to. So I worked very hard again and I got there and it had gone from there too.[6]

Were Bevan alive today he would have found the power had gone not just from all the local councils, but from Parliament,

---

* Though you'd be a wally if you did.

and would have worked hard, as before, and been surprised how little was left in Cabinet, and would have worked still harder, perhaps, and lost an election or two, and found himself on the European Commission. And he would have inquired after power, and he would have discovered that a lot of it had gone somewhere called the market and more to organizations like the GATT, which he couldn't be elected to, however hard he worked. And he would have sat down and laughed, and then wept fat salt tears for the days of innocence, when democracy seemed a straightforward thing.

British democracy is not extinct, nor have the recent failures produced an intolerable situation. Most people don't feel oppressed by their politicians, merely a bit contemptuous of them. If things carry on as they are, we shall jog along, no doubt. But we will slowly become angrier about small things for which there seems no remedy and no excuse – the pig-troughs of privatisation, and the evil incompetence of some local councils – and notice ever more starkly that the country is divided into the powerful and the rest, and this discontent will spread and fester. And, without being alarmist, I think that, were we to slink away from the search for a better democracy, we would eventually pay a heavy price. We would make our country nastier, excluding more and more people from the condition of true belonging. It is not necessarily the case that the system would become intolerable; but it would be wrong to make the just-tolerable the enemy of the realistically-better. The democratic tradition is held in trust, by each generation for the next, and there are certain duties of repair and maintenance involved.

There's nothing new about this. It has been so from the first days that a system of voting developed. As early as 1806, long before parliamentary reform, the great Tory radical, William Cobbett, had a few earthy comments about people who allow politics to decay. He was talking of voters at Westminster who took bribes, but his lash reaches the apathetic and indolent of all times, all those inclined to leave the bother of reform until there's a crisis that forces it. Electors in small boroughs, who depended on a few rich men, had some excuse, Cobbett reckoned:

Their crime is indeed detestable . . . their names ought to be inscribed upon the gallows-tree, after their carcasses have therefrom been carried piecemeal by the fowls of the air; 'BE SUCH THE FATE OF THE VENDORS OF THEIR CHILDREN'S LIBERTIES AND HAPPINESS' ought to be uttered from the lips of every honest man; but still *they* have some excuse; they have the excuse of the hungry robber . . . But for you, electors of Westminster, what excuse shall be made for *you*, if you fail in the performance of your duty; if you violate so sacred a trust? If you, who have all the political advantages that time and place can give; who well understand what is right, and who have no temptation to do what is wrong; who can plead neither ignorance nor want; who are, in short, as free as you could possibly be made by any scheme of liberty that human art is capable of devising; what shall be said for you if, setting at nought all considerations of country and of individual honour, you should become the passive instruments, the down-trodden things, of some half-dozen opulent men.[7]

And he said too that someone holding the vote, who neglects it or lets the franchise decay, is guilty of 'an act of baseness, not merely a degradation of himself, but a crime against others.' Phew. But the man cannot be denied. Like the electors of Westminster, we have no excuses.

The Book

Given the time, the place, the reason for being worried and the present trouble, I concluded there was a case for a fairly straight-forward attempt to record the reality of our political system today. There have been many excellent books about the British constitution. Walter Bagehot is the Homer of these matters and was followed by an array of eminent Victorians, Edwardians and others. Most recently, the Conservative writer Ferdinand Mount produced a work of great freshness, force and clarity and the estimable Sir Alan Watkins, the last man to live in Grub Street, is currently at work on another, which cannot help but make us think. Two high-browed and down-to-earth professors, Anthony King and Peter Hennessy, produce superb essays and books on the subject regularly, and I have learned a lot from both of them. Too late to be taken account of here, Will Hutton produced his neo-Keynesian bestseller, *The State We're In*. Still, because I hadn't yet read a description of the messy, rambling, inconsistent political system I have spent the last decade tramping around as a reporter, and because of the constitutional debate today, it seemed to me there was a reason to have another go. Though there is a huge literature of political biography and memoirs, relatively few books attempt to draw general lessons. And I discovered a large body of academic writing about democratic theory which was glitteringly clever but mostly extremely silly. That leaves political journalism, which has earned me a good living, but which was fairly compared by one of its giants[8] to writing upon water. Unless you fill your house and head with yellowing cuttings, it is hard to remember what the papers were saying about who, when, and how it connects to the next thing. So this is meant to help plug a gap. I have tried to pull together and set in order. In doing so, I have stolen sentences from better writers and rifled through cleverer people's heads, and I have stitched insights together and misheard and no doubt misunderstood and perhaps, though I hope not, misrepresented. But there we are.

As the reader will have noticed already, the result isn't just a description. It is humanly impossible to describe our current mess without lurching at times into polemic, and wondering always about how it could be reformed. The detailed work of reform is for policy wonks and politicians and others, but I have added a few small stones to the pile. Well, they will be something to argue with. Finally, though the tone of this book is critical of the British constitution, by which I mean nothing more or less than the system of authority, law and practice under which political power is exercised in daily life, I would not like it to be supposed that I want it overthrown. Our institutions, some of them, are reformable and have a robustness which, even now, can be returned to full strength with some doctoring. The Commons, which will get a good kicking later in this book, still manages to produce serious confrontations and arguments about real ideas and, for all its faults, I would hate to swap it for a boring Continental semi-circle with buttons for voting and a single podium from which speakers read out prepared texts to silent, somnolent representatives. Nor, in general, would I want to import somebody else's constitution. The German one is fine for Germans but would not suit us; the American one is sadly decayed and in need of almost as radical reform as our own; the French constitution is an autocratic abomination; the Italian one is an entertainment. Just because the British one is in bad shape doesn't mean that we are unique in having problems or that our problems are worse. They may even be lesser. But that is about the worst reason I can think of for slumping back with a self-satisfied grin. It doesn't seem that constitutions are easy things to pack into boxes and air-freight from one culture to another. The best constitutions are rooted in the history, prejudices, modern myths and geography of the people concerned. We need to rethink and reform ours, but we cannot merely look abroad and import fresh ideas, as we do for most other things. We have real problems which nobody else can help us with.

The pattern of the book is as follows. I start at the 'bottom', looking at the voter, then the local party and local government, including the rise in unelected local government. Then we move to Parliament. At the centre of the book is an investigation of the British State, both as a player in the world, and as something we live under. Then there comes a concluding chapter, which contains reasons to be cheerful, and things to do.

CHAPTER ONE

The British Voter

'The English People believes itself to be free; it is gravely
mistaken; it is free only during the election of Members of
Parliament; as soon as the Members are elected, the people is
enslaved; it is nothing.' – Jean Jacques Rousseau (1712–78)

The Glorious Privilege

What is it to vote? It is to speak. It is to judge the powerful. It is
to connect oneself, even in a small way, to the direction of the
nation. To vote may also be to protest. It may be to celebrate;
to give thanks for the past few years by choosing more of the
same. To vote may be to express fear or optimism. It may be an
act of wild, poetic idealism or a cold calculation of personal
benefit. To vote may be to conform, either to a neighbourhood
('the folk around here tend to be Tories') or to a group
('teachers are Labour'). To vote may to be to hold hands with
the past ('we've always been Liberals') or to consciously break
with a family past ('Mum was Labour; I'm not going back to
that'). To vote may be an act of faith or of apostasy. It may be a
confirmation of one's deepest political identity ('I just *am* a
Conservative'). For an eighteen-year-old, to vote is part of our
tribal initiation into adulthood – a rite of passage granted only
in 1969. For the old, to vote may be an act of defiance, an
assertion, against the odds, of still mattering ('I may be stuck
away in this rancid backwater of a nursing-home but I've got
my opinion'). For those of us in between, voting may, however
modestly, help mark a life-change, as it can often mark a change
in the country's political life. Voting may be all, or none, of this
perhaps rather personal, quirky list. There are other ways of
having a voice – writing to the newspapers, scrawling graffiti,
boycotting products, calling a late-night phone-in show – but

21

voting precedes them as a basis of citizenship. If in the modern world you lack the right to a vote you are in some sense a diminished creature.

It is a great thing to have a vote, in historical terms a rare privilege, and in geographical terms a thing even now denied across great swathes of the world. If many of us in Britain, whose forebears marched and fought and shouted and threw themselves under horses for such an abstract-seeming right, have forgotten its specialness, others can rebuke our ignorance. Hear Rich Mkhondo, a Reuters journalist in South Africa, describing a day in April 1994:

Voting in my township began with whistles by men, ululations by women, and a three-and-a-half hour wait to end apartheid and usher in democracy. As a thirty-eight-year-old black South African, I had never until today had any voice in the affairs of my country. I awoke at 5 a.m. to be in the front seat of history. It was like getting ready for baptism as a new congregation member. Hours later, tense and excited while inscribing a long-denied 'X' on the ballot-paper, it was like a heady first romance. It ended what once seemed an impossible journey . . . my dignity and self-worth had finally been restored. I am keeping my political choice secret . . .

Mr Mkhondo's ecstatic tone is worth bearing in mind when we debate the condition of democracy in Britain. Our people, whether Victorian artisans voting for the first time, or matrons queuing to mark their cross in 1929, once felt like he did. The vote was fought for, and for good reasons, and it is our badge of belonging.

It is, moreover, a power still used by the vast majority of Britain in the most important elections, however low the turn-out may be at local and European parliamentary elections. A reasonably public-minded person, who voted as a sixty-eight-year-old in the 1992 general election, and who hopes to do so next time, might well have clocked up thirty visits to the polling station – 14 general election votes, three in European elections, one in a referendum (or two, if the voter is Scottish or Welsh) plus, perhaps, 12 sets of local elections. If we reckon it takes about five minutes to actually vote, that only comes to two-and-a-half hours of voting activity in a lifetime. But add in the thought and the reading of newspapers and watching of television bulletins and the family arguments and the conversations in the pub that may have preceded those thirty quick pencil-flicks and our voter could claim that a meaningful proportion of time and mental activity had gone into it. And yet . . . however punctiliously keen on our status as voters and however civic-minded, we British have come a long way from Mr Mkhondo's excitement. In my tribal township, East Sheen in West London, I was taking my two small children to buy ice-cream on the same weekend as he was voting in South Africa. Here, there was an election too, as locally mundane and unhistoric as the other one was neither, and our sticky journey past front gardens and shop windows was punctuated by orange Liberal Democrat posters and pink-and-blue Tory ones, with only the occasional flare of Labour scarlet. The children were asking about them, and I wasn't very successful at explaining the differences, but I did get over the message that voting allowed you to decide who 'made the rules'.

But was this wild simplification so extreme that it was actually a lie? Plenty of British voters would say so. The level of cynicism and depression about the reality of modern democracy suggests that something has happened to us that goes beyond mere weariness or complacency about the great privilege. In terms of the participation of citizens and the power of politicians, the heyday of British democracy came only after the Second World War. It is new. Yet we speak about our democracy with the apathy of ancients. These are not only casual impressions. In a poll by ICM for Channel Four in April 1994,[1] 30 per cent of the respondents went as far as to claim that Britain was 'not a democracy'. Among younger voters, aged eighteen to thirty-nine, the figure was even higher, 35 per cent. Asked whether Britain was getting more or less democratic, 39 per cent said less. And 71 per cent agreed with the statement: 'The voting system produces governments which do not represent the views of most ordinary people.' Since an even higher percentage, 83 per cent, thought that if one party held power for long enough 'they can get away with anything', this mood may partly reflect the irritation of voters about the performance of a fourth successive Tory government. But these are remarkably high levels of rejection for a country which has so long boasted of being among the first and most stable of parliamentary systems. One Conservative minister privately responded that such polls were merely grumbling, and meant nothing: people still turned out in their millions when it actually came to a general election. This is poor logic: the very people who feel most strongly that the democracy isn't functioning may still be motivated to take whatever chance they get to protest at the ballot-box.

Not that we should be complacent about the numbers who do vote. True, the turnout at post-war general elections has been roughly similar, ranging from highs of 84 per cent and 82.5 per cent in 1950 and 1951 to a low of 72 per cent in the 1970 election. (The highest turnout this century was actually in the first 1910 election, when nearly 87 per cent of those eligible to vote did so: but those who see Edwardian Britain as a glorious noon of democracy should remember that relatively few people were allowed to vote, including no women.) Some 7.7 million people voted in 1910, on those high turnouts. In the 1918 election, based on a wider franchise, only 59 per cent voted – but that meant more than 21 million people. At the last general election, in 1992, the turnout was relatively good, at 77.7 per cent, perhaps reflecting the expected photo-finish between the main parties. Even so, and with a record number of candidates, 9.6 million British citizens – far more than the population of Scotland and Northern Ireland put together, more than the population of Greater London, too – didn't vote. When it comes to our attenuated local democracy, the position is of course far worse. Just 44 per cent of people voted in the local elections of 1994, and this was in line with the majority of post-war local contests. The four European elections have seen the lowest turnouts of all – 36 per cent in 1989 and 32.6 per cent in 1994. Despite the frantic efforts of all parties to whip up public interest, all they did was, in the immortal words of Willie Whitelaw on another occasion, go about the country stirring up apathy. It is true that around a quarter of voters claim to have contacted their MP at some stage, and that two-thirds have signed a petition, showing some interest in the process of decision-making. All in all, however, British voters seem at best coolly sceptical, and at worst dismissive, about the democratic system.

The Snarl of Paper Tigers

There are excellent reasons for this scepticism. The ability of the modern voter to help change national policies by the exercise of a vote is terribly slim. We drop our ballot papers like feathers into the void and somewhere, sometimes, they accumulate to tip a giant scale and eject or elect an Honourable Member. But for our feathers to make a difference is rare. The accidents of neighbourhood play a big part in how much influence an individual voter can hope to have. In most post-war elections there have been a number of swing constituencies, the ones that actually do change their allegiance, whilst most of the country remains divided into loyal blocks, within which nothing much changes. For much of the 1980s and into the current decade, Labour has been forced back into its Celtic and northern redoubts and the Conservatives have governed happily as the party of the English south. This leaves certain areas, including much of the Midlands, parts of the North-east and the English West country, where the swing constituencies are concentrated. And, of course, inside those swing constituencies, there are still a majority of voters whose allegiances are firmly fixed for most of the time. That leaves relatively few people – the 'floaters' in the right places – who can usually be expected to determine which party wins. One estimate bandied around by party strategists is that only around 500,000 people, that is, the uncommitted ones in the constituencies which are genuinely in the balance, 'matter' in a general election. The rest of us may contribute to the overall national total of votes cast, but so long as we behave in character, our direct influence on the shape of the House of Commons is negligible. It is possible that an education in the potential of tactical voting would make more voters matter; and a change in the system of voting certainly would. But, in the meantime, most of us comprise silent, loyal stage armies.

Because of this, party leaders respond by targeting ever more closely those groups of voters at the sharp end of the battle – classically, the lower middle classes of the Midlands, and the southern aspirational working-class voter, 'Basildon man' – and tailoring their agendas to what pollsters tell them such people want. If you live elsewhere, or if your views are firmly to the left or right of the centre, then you are not likely to be at the forefront of the minds of the politicians drawing up their national manifesto ideas. This in turn narrows the political debate. The Labour politician Bryan Gould quit Britain for his native New Zealand when his brand of macro-economics moved off the scale of the politically respectable. Part of the reason for that was the perception in his party that it too needed to compete on a narrow stretch of ideological turf for the cautious and easily-scared souls of the swing voters. People who are not so cautious, or more robust – traditional socialists, anti-European English nationalists – have long noticed this timidity and concluded that the political system is not tailored for them. They are, of course, absolutely right. Given how many voters are effectively marginalized by the terms of a national campaign, perhaps it is surprising that such a large proportion regularly assert their existence through the ballot-box.

But even if the lucky voter is in a position of electoral power, ready to be swayed by the arguments and living in a marginal constituency, how is he or she to make a rational decision? John Major's post-1992 administration was savagely castigated for breaking its manifesto and campaign promises on taxation. But the sad truth is that the manifestos of the winning parties are only a rough guide to how they will behave in government. An audit of the broken promises and betrayed manifesto visions of the past twenty-five years, all those world-class education systems and robustly successful economic models, the Heath government's promised Edinburgh Convention and

Labour promises in the sixties and seventies to halt the rise in crime, would make the thoughtful voter weep. Take just one issue, the great failure through most of modern British history to deal with inflation. You might have thought the issue never cropped up in manifestos. But every winning party in modern times promised to deal with it as a priority. The 1959 Tory manifesto promised that 'Our paramount aim' would be a stable international pound and that monetary and other measures would be used to 'keep the cost of living as steady as possible'. Inflation rose. In 1964 Labour promised 'new and more relevant policies to check the persistent rise in prices'. Inflation rose faster. In 1966 Labour boasted the 'first serious attack on the rising cost of living'. If so, that attack was humiliatingly repulsed – inflation rose. In 1970, the victorious Tories promised to 'give overriding priority to bringing the present inflation under control'. In its February 1974 manifesto the Tory government admitted that its warning that it would be a slow, hard job 'proved even truer than we had feared at the time' and blamed world prices. Inflation was starting to get out of control. Labour savaged the record and promised tough price controls. In its October 1974 election manifesto Labour promised, 'The first priority must be a determined attack on inflation . . .' This 'priority' led to a situation described in the 1979 manifesto of the successful Tories: 'Under Labour prices have risen faster than at any peacetime period in the three centuries in which records have been kept . . .' and more promises. Under Thatcher, at least for a while, inflation was tamed. The 1987 Tory manifesto crowed of 'success in the battle against inflation . . . There is no better yardstick of a party's fitness to govern than its attitude to inflation. Nothing is so politically immoral as a party that ignores that yardstick . . . We will not be content until we have stable prices.' Yet it was that 1987–1992 administration which allowed inflation to start to rise dangerously again, requiring painful and deflationary measures to curb it. Not very moral.

The debate about the deep-rooted causes of post-war British inflation need not detain us here: my point is simply that, for a shrewd and economically literate voter worried about the great

evil of inflation, there was no point in deciding which way to vote
by reading the party manifestos: it was almost all hot air
for thirty years. At press conferences during the campaign,
reporters strive to pin down the party leaders on this policy or
that. But little of the result filters back to the voters, and we are
long past the time when a broken promise, exposed on the floor
of the Commons, caused any frisson of outrage after the event.
Politicians' readiness to treat their own manifestos as acts of party
propaganda, rather than as pledges offered to voters, makes a
nonsense of the idea of proper representative democracy. Yet this
argument has now virtually gone by default.

But the thing is worse than that. The biggest problem with
party manifestos is that they are disparate bundles of policies
from which voters may not pick and choose. Some people
may approve everything in the Labour or the Liberal Democrat
agenda; others may be so committed to the Tory cause that
they regard the five-yearly assortment of assertions and wheezes
from Conservative Central Office as an unimprovable distilla-
tion of human wisdom. But most people will find some
fragments of gold here, a few shards of silver there, and
mountains of unappealing dross everywhere. This doesn't stop
us taking all things into account and deciding which is the
least worst jumble of promises and ideas: we still have *some*
choice. But it forces voters to make ridiculous decisions about
their personal priorities. What, for instance, about the voter
who wants to see an end to nuclear power but who also
strongly believes in the need for lower income tax? That
is hardly an implausible combination, indeed it probably reflects the views of millions of people. But there is no way
you can vote for both those things under the British system.
What if you are passionately in favour of private schooling
but also rather worried about the effect on the Constitution
of fifteen years of Conservative rule? Again, a perfectly plausible
position. In some places, you might vote Liberal Democrat.
But in most of the swing constituencies, you would have
to choose – little Amelia's place at St Ethelberta's, or the reform
of the political system. You can't have both. Sorry, pal. Either, or.

We have the garment in black, Modom – and if you don't like black, there's only white.

Such starkly Hobsonian choices are hardly new. But, as fewer people vote automatically on class or family grounds, and are better informed about more things than ever before, this lack of choice dressed up as 'the nation chooses' seems increasingly absurd. The grand clash of ideologies and allegiances, left or right, for labour or capital, once disguised the problem. You might not like much of the manifesto but you knew which side you were on. But, if that was ever sufficient, it looks a lot less so in this more consumerist and un-ideological age. The rust-stained political Dreadnoughts, glaring across the water at one another, devised in an earlier age to change Britain decisively one way or another, now seem ill-equipped to provide the more complex and responsive political options that modern voters want. Again, people notice. They have been noticing the lack of choice and the fundamental fraud of manifestos. They have spotted that general elections are becoming heavily focused on specialized battlegrounds and 'swing voters' that exclude most of the nation. And they are becoming aware, in a general way, that politicians may not have nearly as much power as they claimed. Representative democracy requires a measure of expectation which our system now lacks.

Of the mechanical answers to the lack of choice confronting British voters at the moment, none is better known, or in principle stronger, than the introduction of proportional voting, PR. These initials make most followers of politics yawn. This is not because a voting system which allowed the number of MPs to roughly reflect the numbers of votes cast for each party is a bad idea. Nor is it an impractical one – Britain is in a relatively small minority of democratic countries which reject it. The trouble is that no subject in politics is more caked in hypocrisy and self-interest than the electoral system, and no reform is harder to envisage passing through the Commons than voting reform. Proportional representation has been advocated plenty of times in the past, and for the obvious reason that it is 'fairer', it reflects more closely the wishes of the voters, which is what

democracy is all about. But it has always been rejected by a
Commons elected on the first-past-the-post system. The explana-
tions for rejecting it have generally been that the current
'winner-takes-all' method of voting produces a clear result and
hence 'strong government'; and that it allows a close, absolute
relationship between the MP and his or her constituency
voters.

It is true that PR systems are likelier to require coalition
governments, and hence deals between politicians of different
parties, to produce compromise agendas which have not themselves been chosen. But we have already seen the alternative
drawbacks of the current system, which are less discussed.
Under our system, both the big parties are in fact sprawling
coalitions anyway. In Britain, you don't get the choice of
voting for a moderate social democrat, or a red-hot fundamentalist socialist – you just get a Labour candidate, who might be
either, depending upon the seat. You don't get the choice, if
you tend to the right, of either a staunchly pro-European
MP or, if you prefer, a crisply right-wing Tory nationalist.
You just get a Conservative Party candidate, who might be
either. Tory pro-Europeans are invited, if they live in Stafford,
to vote for Mr Bill Cash, who does not represent their views;
Tory Euro-sceptics, if they live in Harrow, are forced to vote
for the arch-Europeanist Hugh Dykes, or waste their vote. In
other words, coalition politics exists already, but it is camou-
flaged by the big parties. (Providing, incidentally, one reason
why British journalism is so obsessed with 'split' stories in the
major parties – often these are nothing more than the teasing
out and discussion of policy differences which would, under a
system involving more, smaller, parties, be argued between
parties, not between factions inside one party. As politics becomes less ideological and fixed, the British system virtually
guarantees the impression of party division and thus the weakness of leaders, a by-product of the determination to have
'strong government'.) Here, the compromises are achieved internally by the sprawling coalitions called Labour and Tory, and
then put to the voters without choice. At least with conventional

coalitions, the fact of compromise is built into the system, takes place under the glare of publicity and is well understood.

At this point, the MP favouring the current system will talk rhapsodically about the importance of North-east Oatcake being represented by a single Member, who has a special relationship with the Oatcakeians, no matter what their and his political stripe. There is some truth in the romance: it is undoubtedly a good thing that a left-wing Labour MP is forced to try to resolve problems with bureaucrats that are plaguing a local business, and that a right-wing MP is forced to confront, week by week, the poorest and most desperate recipients of welfare. Neither can retreat entirely into a mental and political ghetto, and this is a genuine bonus. On the other hand, the numbers of people who actually go and see their MP are relatively modest, and it is not clear that an individual wouldn't prefer to be able to choose the Member in a multi-MP seat who seemed closest to his or her own views. If the voter with a leaking roof and a thuggish landlord could take the matter to a leftish MP known for her interest in housing matters, as against a traditional Conservative who specialized in the defence of the realm, that might well be a liberation, and good for the parliamentary system generally. In Ireland, there is considerable evidence of a sort of market in MPs, with constituents trying out and comparing the services of the two or three TDs (as they call them) and later voting for the most effective. This, perhaps, is partly what worries the Westminster variety. Competition and the market are fine things. But dash it, chaps; there is a limit. The multi-member system of proportional representation is, it should be noted, far more democratically appealing than the idea of a 'list' which tops up the numbers elected by constituencies with extra MPs nominated by the parties to ensure the final totals in Parliament roughly match the proportion of votes won by the parties. This gives huge power to the party machines to reward toadies and dreadful people of all sorts: we already have enough charmed circles in this country of people giving one another favours to make us revolt at the prospect of another, and certainly charmless, one.

However, I am allowing myself and the reader to be ensnared by the *arguments* for and against voting reform. These are much beside the point. The fundamental reason that the Commons votes against changing the voting system is that the MPs in it were elected under the current system. Both the government of the day and its backbenchers are the grateful winners of our winner-takes-all system who have duly taken all. People who have scrambled to the top of the apple-tree aren't going to vote for the orchard to be grubbed up. Labour was for voting reform itself, until it started winning first-past-the-post elections, and then it hurriedly revised its opinion. Similarly, the Liberal enthusiasm for proportional representation, however noble and righteous, only blazed forth once that great party found itself unable to win general elections under the present system. Only the Tories have been consistent; but then, only the Tories have been consistent winners. There have been signs of a growth in pro-PR sentiment in the Labour Party as direct result of the long Thatcher-Major era – pro-reform MPs, like Robin Cook, make no secret of the fact that they want change in the voting system so that 'Margaret Thatcher can never happen again'. But if Labour wins outright next time do we think they will change the voting system that brought them to power? There is room, as they say, for rational doubt.

All the rest, all the high-minded arguments either way, are so much pious blather wrapped around naked self-interest. Similarly, the reason MPs are against that 'list system' of PR discussed above is not that it breaks the spirit of the link between all Members and their seats, or because it encourages party patronage. It is because they are frightened of letting in a class of MPs who don't have to hare up and down to their constituencies, open bags of mail and listen to whingeing pensioners, and who are therefore likelier to have the time to make clever speeches, get the foreign trips and become ministers. Damn them, they might even have time to think a bit, and make everyone else look dim by comparison. It wouldn't do, would it? Even those MPs who have genuinely convinced themselves of the case against PR, or for PR and argue it with shining eyes, are rationalizing after the event. They are no more to be trusted than a man on £400,000 a year arguing against supertax or the dairy farmer who disagrees with the margarine adverts. Generally speaking, it is pretty safe advice to listen to no politician's arguments about the voting system unless the politician concerned is a Tory MP in favour of proportional representation or a Liberal Democrat who believes in the current system.

It follows from this that the voting system Britain has today is the voting system Britain is stuck with, unless it should happen that a general election produces a hung Parliament, in which Labour is dependent upon Liberal Democrat support, and in which the Lib-Dems ruthlessly and successfully black-mail Labour into conceding and implementing a bill to change the system. Even then, a lot of conservative-minded and self-interested Labour MPs would have to vote for a measure which they thought would lose them their careers. (During this process, there would of course be a huge uproar; hundreds of angry, bespittled red political faces would appear on television screens roaring about the constitution and democracy. But these would be merely the pips squeaking and could be safely ignored. The public-spirited viewer could hop to another channel to watch murders or a gardening programme.) Voting reform with multi-member constituencies would, I think, be a worthwhile and welcome change in the British system, making our politics noticeably more voter-friendly. But, since it depends on one sequence of events and no other, all one can do is point this out before, in a philosophical spirit, moving on.

Of Activists and Passivists

So let us go from the individual to the next, most primitive, level of political organization, the friendly, neighbourhood politi-cal party. To turn from voter to party member is at once to exclude forty-nine out of every fifty Britons: even at the most generous measure, there are far fewer than a million individual party activists in this country, out of an electorate of 43.2

million. Most members do little if anything beyond writing a cheque and carrying a card. Yet party membership, and the more assertive democratic involvement that goes with it, remains extremely important to our system. If to have the vote is to have a voice, however weak, then to be actively political is to train that voice – even, occasionally, to sing. The first models of democracy assumed that citizens would stand and speak and argue. Few of us now do. But those who choose to do so are the anonymous heroes of the democratic way. This may sound an odd thing to say. Readers of this book will fall into two categories: members of political parties, and people who think that anyone in a party is wasting their time and would be better advised to 'get a life'. But activists aren't to be pitied. They should be admired. For, without them, the workers and followers, the system which is meant to guard our liberties and guarantee our political adulthood, would have no chance of working. The wiser leaders have always known it. Clem Attlee, turned from a right-wing upper-middle-class dilettante into a socialist by working at a boys' club in the East End of London, praised 'those who did the tedious jobs, collected our exiguous subscriptions, trying to sell literature, and carrying the improvised platform from one street to another. They got no glamour. They did not expect to live to see victory, but, uncomplainingly, they worked to try to help on the cause.'[2] All the political parties have similar modest legions at work, even now. Parties are, in a parliamentary democracy, the transmission belt of the system. To change the metaphor, they are also a filter, however crude. As a newspaper writer, I can confirm from my postbag that there are far worse loonies and charlatans out there than the ones who get into full-time politics.

Historically, local parties were pretty exciting places. Before democracy, they really were parties – the wild political orgies of drunkenness and bribery that were commonplace when small groups of electors were pawed over by rival aristocrats are one of the abiding images of early British politics. The local activists were the ones carrying round the beer and the bribes, and the party 'members' were the ones lying snoring on the tavern flagstones. A good election might involve a fair amount of violence, too, of course, this being an ancient British hobby. There exists an anonymous poem called 'Election Day, A Sketch from Nature', which describes the scene around 1817:

> . . . all is riot and confusion,
> Fraud, friendship, scandal, and delusion;
> Now houses stormed, and windows broken . . .
> Now greeting, hooting and abuse,
> To each man's party prove of use;
> And mud, and stones, and waving hats,
> And broken heads, and putrid cats,
> Are offerings made to aid the cause
> Of order, government and laws . . .
> And elbowing, jostling and cajoling,
> And all the jockeyship of polling,
> And deep manoeuvre and duplicity
> Prove all elections fair and free.[3]

Sad to report, even the more rumbustious of today's by-elections, preferably with a Liberal Democrat surge and a stroppy press corps, do not quite live up to this. We may retain a certain robustness in political argument, but democracy has proved a politer, more pallid system. Folding leaflets, jamming them into envelopes and applauding a complacent young barrister from London in hair gel is the lot of the party worker these days.

Mass democracy may have diminished the market for dead cats, but it did bring in the first of the real local parties by the middle of the Victorian period. The Conservative associations, set up after Disraeli extended the franchise in the 1860s, allowed tradesmen and farmers, squat squires in remote shires and local yokels alike, to hear and (almost as important) see the Great Men whose speeches and doings they read about in the fast-expanding press. Money was collected, the People were roused, though not too much, and the Leader was exhibited. Arguments and arch jokes at the expense of the enemy, however stale in the Imperial Parliament, bloomed afresh in the provinces. The same was true for the Liberals, with their nonconformist followers, thirsty for righteous rhetoric. The Tories formed the Primrose League for women supporters and their rivals countered with the Women's Liberal Federation. The first truly disciplined and effective party in the modern sense were perhaps the Irish Home Rulers under Parnell. But the roots of modern mass politics were certainly taking hold of the country a century ago, in the great age of meetings and public organizations and marching.

Thousands turned out, packing urban halls and assembling on hillsides, when the parliamentary orators went on tour. The best, the Chamberlains and the Gladstones, the Churchills and the Parnells, attracted vast crowds. Heckling was regarded as almost essential, part of the entertainment and part of the politics. At a much humbler level, the local Member could count on a good and usually respectful turnout at the village or town hall. The local party organized these primitive acts of democratic involvement and was rewarded not with the power to tell their MP what to do – that had been conveniently vetoed more than a century earlier by the political philosopher Edmund Burke – but with the gentler balm of social contact – teas and polite questions and hearty handshakes. The business was by all accounts a patronizing and even naïve transaction. In some parts of the country, particularly at election time, the role of party member and partisan was rougher: stone-throwing, fighting and crimes against property were far from unknown even during Edwardian parliamentary contests. As Emmeline Pankhurst put it in 1914: 'Window-breaking, when Englishmen do it, is regarded as an honest expression of political opinion.' By the standards of the time, membership of the local party probably seemed pretty good free entertainment. Once the Labour movement came on to the scene there was a new motive for joining and attending local parties. The socialist gospel was fresh and not readily available, as the civic and religious authorities banned agitators from their premises. If you wanted to hear it, you had to go. Across Britain, people formed branches of the Independent Labour Party and numerous other socialist clubs to educate themselves in a new kind of politics. In his biography of

Nye Bevan, Michael Foot tells the story of the Tredegar Query Club, which had a question-mark as its button-hole emblem and whose members were young miners 'in revolt against the coalowners, the local preachers, the union leaders, the Band of Hope, the local Council, Parliament, God and every other established authority open or concealed.'[4] There were many such. For decades, socialism was argued through in local halls and meeting-places throughout Britain by a rising class which was high on self-education and arguing itself into a different way of looking at the world.

But these glory days of local politics have faded to sepia tedium. National politicians are familiar from television and we no longer follow their lengthier arguments with close attention. When leaders travel the country, or make themselves available to be cross-questioned by listeners or viewers, the local parties are rarely involved. These things are done from the centre. The local Member, unless he or she happens to be a big national figure, is rarely much of a draw for uncommitted voters – and even Foreign Secretaries and Chancellors are gratified to find forty or fifty people waiting for them in a sports centre hall when they do their local round. Local parties are generally poor as a source of entertainment and ideas. In the early eighties, I endured many nights of tedium in an Edinburgh Labour branch. The people were good but the experience of venomous arguments about whether we should nationalise the top 200 companies before or after we had toppled world capitalism eventually palled. On the Conservative side, MPs say that two or three times a year these days they will get a good-going argument about some aspect of government policy. In some places, no doubt, this happens more often, but in others, less. That leaves the yawning O, Organization, and on all sides MPs agree that the great or glamorous issues of the day are ousted by fund-raising, the tedium of rambling 'report-backs' from other meetings, and the painful deliberations of innumerate treasurers and their confused assistants. Then there is the real politics, the politics of who gets to be secretary, and the dramas of local faction. The local parties are, like many local institutions, always at the mercy of the personal feud or the tyranny of a power-crazed inadequate — there have been associations torn asunder over some imagined slight to the branch secretary's spouse, or thrown into turmoil by a single obnoxious organizer. This kind of politics is more often the triumph of hope over experience than something that brings obvious rewards. The almost comically dismal self-assessment by Leonard Woolf, Labour activist and husband of Virginia, is worth quoting as a warning to all who are drawn to the activity.

Looking back at the age of eighty-eight over the fifty-seven years of my political work in England, knowing what I aimed at and the results . . . I see clearly that I achieved practically nothing. The world today and the history of the human anthill during the last fifty-seven years would be exactly the same as it is if I had played pingpong instead of sitting on committees and writing books and memoranda. I have therefore to make the rather ignominious confession . . . that I must have in a long life ground through between 150,000 and 200,000 hours of perfectly useless work.[5]

Most of us, perhaps, are neither quite so rigorously self-scrutinizing nor so ambitious as to expect to change human history. For all their failings, local parties are still, in the mid-1990s, more than a century after they first sprang up across the nation, the place where most politically active people learn the basics of the trade — how to speak in front of others, how to organize successful campaigns or cabals, how to keep lists of supporters that actually work, how to communicate the message to apolitical neighbours. They go on from there, perhaps, to become councillors and even MPs. They are both nursery and family. Parties provide the comradeship and support which enable politically committed people to keep the faith during the bad times. They can, working at their best, alert their national political leaders to policies that are unpopular or silly — that happened during the poll tax disaster, when local Conservative associations, having been militantly in favour of replacing the rates, then campaigned ferociously and successfully for the replacement of the replacement, assisting, whether wittingly or not, in the fall of Margaret Thatcher. In return, local parties can provide an essential sounding-board and reality-bath for the MPs. Most political memoirs have a tribute by the Great Personage to some unknown figures, local party workers, chairmen, agents or whatever. These are the people 'without whom' . . . Doubtless, some of these tributes are merely there for form's sake, rather as smirking actors thank the director they couldn't stand for making it all possible. There are plenty of examples of politicians who regard the local party as a bore and a nuisance. Tom Driberg, chairman of the Labour Party in the 1950s, and a florid fellow, condescended to represent the outer London constituency of Barking on the basis that 'the Barking people would only expect him to come to one meeting a year.'[6] More recently, the Conservative MP Julian Critchley, also a florid specimen, treated some members of his local Aldershot party with such open contempt in print that the rift became unbridgeable. Critchley is both knowing – 'Some of my best friends are Tories. Thank God it is still more important in the Tory party to turn up on time, be polite and assiduous than it is to hold a set of political opinions . . .' but also too satirically observant for his own good – '(at elections) the evenings are spent preaching to the converted, or to their Labradors, which, on issues such as Rhodesia, were better behaved than their owners . . .'[7]

But neither the Driberg approach nor the Critchley one is a good long-term bet for the aspirant MP. In the majority of cases, successful politicians rely a lot on the folks back home. Tony Blair is untypical in having such a large and motivated local Labour party at Sedgefield, his home base, but he is pretty typical in going back and chewing the cud with local workers at least occasionally. A young Conservative MP puts it thus: 'On our side, Conservative associations are still much less political than socialist ones, so there is more of a cross-section of the local community. The vast majority of them have no professional ambitions in politics. So you can talk to them and carry messages back to Westminster with some idea that you are passing on the views of real people.' It works both ways. If you attend any social function given by a local political party featuring the local Member, you will find a curious mix of pride in ownership and acerbic shafts of insight, not dissimilar to mutual criticism round a family table. These local parties are, it turns out, rather more important to the system than a mere collection of envelope-stickers and free delivery-persons whose role is swiftly being ousted by the mass media. They are, even now, the fecund bottom-layer of the democratic way.

They have also been quite clearly in decline, for the reasons given above. Let's start with the crudest measurement of all, membership. As with so many aspects of post-war British democracy, a high point came in the 1950s, a decade now glibly dismissed as the era of complacent and consensual 'Butskellism' which nonetheless saw levels of participation in politics not matched since. The Conservative Party boasted a membership of around 2.8 million people in 1952; although the party is notoriously secretive about its current membership, and keeps no central lists, the most careful study suggests that numbers are down to around three quarters of a million.[8] Some insiders say the figure is even lower. The same study suggests that the Tory party 'has been losing, on average, about 64,000 members a year since 1960 . . . if nothing is done to halt this decline, the party will fall to below 100,000 members by the end of the century.'[9] That seems a precipitous enough decline, but the gross membership numbers heavily overstate the actual activity. A survey of Conservative members suggested that 68 per cent of them had attended no party meeting in the previous year, 78 per cent had devoted no time at all to party activities in the previous month, and 83 per cent considered themselves either not very active or inactive. Nearly half the Tory membership was aged sixty-six or more and just 5 per cent were under thirty-five. It may be that the Conservatives are near their base figure, but a decline of this magnitude, if it continued, would imply that, by the year 2000, there would be only around 20,000 active Tories in the entire country, of whom the vast majority will be very old!

Tory MPs will privately make the point that their associations are run largely by retired people with more time on their hands who spend quite a lot of that time complaining about how old the membership is. But, says one, that was always the case: in his constituency a decade ago, there were a collection of people in their seventies, and few others. Now they are all dead . . . but the constituency association still comprises a collection of people in their seventies. And so it goes on. On the Labour side, you find the same phenomenon. 'The biggest group are still folk who came in during the 1930s, though they're rarely able to get to meetings nowadays,' says one Labour MP of his city-centre constituency. 'My old people are the ones who still believe in turning up and doing the work,' says another. The younger Labour members are often middle-class people in their thirties and forties, but from working-class families. The paucity of the young and angry may be something to do with the lack of appeal of a politics which is nationally influenced by opinion polling rather than ideology. Certainly, party headquarters have spent a lot of time agonizing about youthful extremism – while the Young Conservatives have shrivelled as an organization, the hard-line Federation of Conservative Students was closed down by Conservative Central Office during Norman Tebbit's tenure as party chairman for the sin of embarrassingly extreme displays of punk Thatcherism in the late 1980s. He reckoned some of their libertarian ideology was nearer anarchism than Toryism. The Labour Party Young Socialists suffered the same fate at the hands of Neil Kinnock after years of Trotskyist infiltration.[10]

And what of Labour? On a long historical perspective, its membership decline has been nearly as disastrous as the Conservative Party's. In 1952 it had an individual membership of 1.01 million, excluding the millions of trade unionists 'counted in' as part of the block vote. That million-plus party had declined to around 240,000-plus at its low point in the early nineties. But the arrival of Tony Blair as Labour leader in 1994 has provoked a revival of the party at grass-roots level which has surprised commentators. Within nine months of his election as leader – an exercise in democracy that involved 925,109 votes being cast, including those of levy-paying trade unionists and members of socialist clubs – Labour's individual membership had climbed by nearly 100,000 to 330,000. Of course, this is a short period and the gap between Labour under Blair in the nineties and Labour under Attlee in the fifties remains huge and, perhaps, unbridgeable. Nevertheless, the Blairite restoration of Labour may well be sustained. For one thing, the party's new system of taking the views of members through policy forums involves them more. For another, Blair's leadership seemed to strike a chord with ordinary party members as distinct from the minority of hard-core activists. When Labour voted to abandon its old 'common ownership' Clause IV commitment in April 1995, for instance, the constituency parties backed their leader by an average majority of 85 per cent. Given that Labour leaders have historically been either scared of the leftist 'extremism' of party activists, or contemptuous of it, this suggests a remarkable turnaround. If Labour leaders no longer have to depend on the backing of conservative trade union bosses to protect them from the instincts of their own supporters, then the possibility of a revival of mass-membership politics must be taken seriously. This model depends hugely on a rapport between leader and led and would therefore appear vulnerable to a falling-out of love, as inevitably happens with nine out of ten leaders. We shall see. Of the other electoral parties, the Liberal Democrats, with a membership of just over 100,000, probably have a higher activism level than either of their bigger rivals, partly because of their proportionally strong base in local government. The Scottish National Party has around 20,000 members, though it uses lotteries and other devices to spread its network; Plaid Cymru has around 9,000, the Greens around 5,000; and the others are even smaller.

Thus far, the appeal of party politics has been hard to sell to the rising generation of potential activists. Instead, many have migrated to the booming single-issue campaigns, of which some, like Greenpeace and Friends of the Earth, boast memberships bigger than that of the Labour Party. Again, anecdotal and personal experience strongly confirms the statistics. I know, and perhaps the reader does too, several examples of people in their late teens and twenties who focus their political attention on environmentalism (if they are emotionally of the left) and hostility to the European Union (often, if they are of the right) who, perhaps twenty years ago, would have been party-political activists. But saving the whale is now preferable to saving the working class or the middle class. At least it is surer: the single-issue pressure group offers a much clearer idea of political success. If you join a political party then your chances of altering society by doing so seem remote and at several removes. A pressure group has a chance of real, if limited, achievements: a live whale is a live whale, and a bypass that isn't built is a field or a wood that remains.

If local parties are declining numerically and also ageing, can we at least say that they retain their influence and importance vis-à-vis national politics? It is a mixed picture, and it is worth reiterating that individual MPs may be strongly influenced by individual party contacts back home. But overall the message is of loss of influence rather than rising influence. Organizationally, the influence of party activism may seem quite strong in the 1990s. Conservative activists have become more assertive at party conference, as the party's European factionalism tears it apart. Despite attempts by Central Office to control them more tightly, Tory associations remain legally, financially and to some extent politically separated from the centre: they cannot, for instance, have candidates forced upon them.[11] Yet the loss of party membership has been mirrored by a loss of local funds flowing upwards to Tory Central Office in recent years and this has been only partly because of disillusion with government policies. The internal reformers of the Conservative Charter Group blame the secrecy and top-down approach of the party machine nationally − a machine which both managed to take money from a range of crooks, and still ran up huge overdrafts. Just before the 1993 Conservative conference one reformer, John Stafford, a member of the National Union executive, argued that members were 'walking out of the constituencies because they feel they have no influence on events . . . It never seems to have occurred to those at the top that they owe loyalty too downwards, to party members. If the people doing these things were dismissible by the constituencies, in democratic elections, their disloyalty would be brought to an end. But sadly, that sanction is not available.' Tory membership may well revive if the party is driven into opposition; fear is a great recruiting-sergeant. But, to do so, the Conservatives may need to emulate Blair's New Labour in rethinking its attitude to the ordinary party foot soldiers.

These formal influences are only a small part of the picture. For all the big parties, policy is still made at the top, heavily influenced by private polling, by national pressure groups and by 'policy wonks' – pebble-glassed youths and twin-suited young women sitting in offices in central London. Labour may have its policy commissions and its rolling policy review, but final decisions on policy are kept well away from the grassroots activists. After the bruising experiences of Trotskyist entryism during the eighties, the party leadership wants its members' advice, rather than their orders. The Conservatives are, as Mr Stafford noted, even more robustly elitist about these things. They have always made policy at Smith Square and Downing Street, not at Brighton or Blackpool or in the hundreds of local Conservative clubs: the role of the party's local associations is to squeal with pain, several years too late, as a policy failure is doggedly implemented. Annual conferences have some influence, reminding the party leaderships of the broad views of those activists who come – boosting the standing of this leader, helping slow the career of that minister. But no leadership of a large party would nowadays consider the views of the conference absolutely binding. More generally, as national leaderships are able to gather more and more detailed information on the views of the public through polling, so the special role of the activist as a reporter of the feeling on the street is squeezed. Simultaneously, the drop in numbers of people in local parties undermines their usefulness as a sample of local opinion: the activists become even more isolated as a specialist group, and national leaders become ever more wary of their views. With some justice: Labour was damaged as an effective electoral machine by its two great upsurges of activist rebellion, the Bevanite revolt of the early 1950s and the Bennite one of the early 1980s. Both of these fundamentalist uprisings underlined the point that local activists are not necessarily in touch with their neighbours. Living in an area doesn't guarantee that you represent it. And even the majority views and the political priorities of one area – whether Welsh mining town or Surrey commuter suburb – may be alien to the electorate as a whole, and so dangerous for the party which listens to them too intently.

That isn't the whole story, however. Academic research has shown that both the Conservatives and Labour did better in those marginal constituencies in the 1992 general election where they had strong local parties, compared to the marginals where the local parties were weak. Patrick Seyd, a politics lecturer at Sheffield University, whose research was quoted earlier, has concluded:

We estimated that a 10 per cent rise from the 1987 general election level of campaigning will increase the party's share of the vote by 1 per cent. Such a figure may sound small but it could make the difference between winning and losing a general election. It is roughly the same figure, for example, as the latest British General Election Study attributes to the 'leadership effect': the greater appeal of John Major to voters against Neil Kinnock in 1992. So more election posters, election leafleting and canvassing do pay electoral dividends.

The tricky message for national leaderships is that local parties need to be encouraged, without activists being given the whip hand over policy. It may seem that Tory and Liberal Democrat activists are more 'ordinary', more likely to be representative of some general will than socialists, but, here again, the evidence suggests otherwise. It was local Scottish Conservatives who pushed hardest for the abolition of the rating system and its replacement by the poll tax, while Tory activists throughout Britain wanted to stick with Margaret Thatcher even when it was obvious that doing so would make their party less likely to win the subsequent election. Lib-Dems, as any attender at their conferences will testify, are no more typical of the wider electorate. Their enthusiasms for land-value-tax and close interest in waste-disposal techniques mark them out, however subtly, from the mass of their fellow citizens.

So there is a paradox and a problem for representative democracy here. On the one hand, local parties are important for our democratic system as we have inherited it. They are a training ground, a political family, a support-mechanism for MPs and councillors, the essential first layer for traditional political activity – and, in marginal seats, a vital part of the battle. Yet they are also fading in strength and real influence at national level for perfectly logical reasons. A party without a vocal local membership would have sold its soul unequivocally to the opinion-formers and mood-manipulators of the metropolis. Yet a party which hands real power to its local adherents often lands in trouble with the nation as a whole. The self-obsessed political classes of London SW1 look out at their presumed supporters across the land with a mixture of bafflement and suspicion. Fewer and fewer 'supporters' look back at them. Party connections, which are central to a functioning democracy, are in poor repair.

Politics Without Parties?

To recap: our voting and party system today is giving us vastly less choice than we are accustomed to in other parts of life. It offers lucky-dip manifestos; limits the number of 'swing', government-making voters to a minority; and depends upon parties – sort of national political clubs – which have become unpopular with the public and uninfluential with their leaders. Not a very promising start in this journey through our political system, is it? So do we need this cumbersome early twentieth-century system of balloting and party bureaucracy in order to enjoy democracy? In recent years, there has been growing interest in one of the oldest political notions of all – direct democracy, in which we all take part in discussing the issues and deciding them. As we've seen, this has always had its champions, but now there is a growing feeling that technology may be about to flick the switch on a democratic transformation. This is a book of description, not prophecy, but, even so, it's worth pausing to consider whether we need to stick with the traditional political base described so far.

The Trouble With Athens

Up to now, the biggest bar to direct democracy has been the assumption among the ruling group that the majority of people are too ignorant, busy or thoughtless to take part in political decision-making themselves. Parties and professional leaders are therefore necessary to organize the choices, advertise them, make sense of them. These assumptions, it is fair to point out, have underpinned government throughout most of recorded history. Whenever some idealistic proponent of direct democracy starts talking about Athens, it is worth recalling that this experiment in direct, mass decision-making (which nevertheless excluded women, slaves and immigrants) lasted a mere 130 years before the idea was chucked aside by Greek civilization as a failure – monarchy, autocracy, oligarchy and totalitarianism all apparently seemed more sensible. Between Athenian times and modern times, democracy was more regularly a term of abuse than a serious proposition, even when liberal and representative government began to evolve.

Even the creators of the United States regarded the proponents of democracy as mad, bad and dangerous to know. One of those early American democrats, the writer and politician Melancton Smith, sounds appealingly modern when he argued that representatives should 'resemble those they represent. They should be a true picture of the people, possess a knowledge of their circumstances and wants, sympathize in all their distress, and be disposed to seek their true interests.' But he lost that argument. The far more famous James Madison, writing as Publius in the *Federalist Papers*, spoke for the majority of educated and politically-conscious America when he explained that pure democracy would result in 'the mischiefs of faction . . . such democracies have ever been spectacles of turbulence and contention; have ever been found incompatible with personal security or the rights of property; and have in general been as short in their lives as they have been violent in their deaths.' More tersely still, the great early US statesman John Adams senior exclaimed that democracy was 'the most ignoble, unjust and detestable form of government.' America had representative government, but managed to avoid democracy until the passage of the Voting Rights Act in 1965.

In Europe, cartoons of an evil, drunken and murderous Parisian mob provided a dominant image of democracy in action for decades following the French Revolution. Britain was a legal and liberal state for centuries before it was a democratic one. The mass franchise came about because of the requirements of industrialization, and the need to incorporate an increasingly threatening and militant working class, not because of democratic theory. Even then, there was little belief among the rulers that the ruled should be admitted as more than audiences and occasional voters. As two recent writers on democracy have pointed out, 'Gladstone, the great Liberal prime minister to whose genius Britain's smooth progress to representative government can largely be attributed, doubted in the 1890s whether even a Wolverhampton solicitor was fit to sit in the Cabinet.'[12] Today, it is thought impolite for the ruling group to make their feelings so explicit. Instead of treating the masses as incapable of political decision-making on grounds of class or education, the modern establishment reassures itself that the citizenry are too busy getting on with their own lives. The small self-selected groups of political activists in parties are one thing – they are held and directed within hierarchical organizations ultimately controlled by the politicians themselves. But the ability of the voters *en masse* to take decisions is something quite else. Occasionally, politicians let the mask slip: when John Major was explaining during the Maastricht controversy on European Union why he was against a referendum, he said that the matter was 'highly complex' and people might be influenced by all sorts of 'irrelevant' things when trying to decide. Yet his own Home Secretary had not bothered to read the treaty under discussion; and his own MPs were more influenced by 'outside' matters (the pressure of government whips, the future of their own careers) than most voters would have been. And after Norman Lamont, the then Chancellor, who had helped negotiate the treaty, left the government, he raised the question of whether or not the whole game was worth a candle: 'I cannot pinpoint a single concrete economic advantage that unambiguously comes to this country because of our membership.' In such circumstances, for politicians to say that there could not be a referendum because the matter was too sophisticated for the ordinary voter was . . . well, pretty impertinent. No?

This traditional hostility among politicians to the idea of people participating directly in decision making has been strengthened most recently by the apparent irresponsibility of voters' views as reflected in opinion polls. People choose both better public services and much lower taxes; they want 'greener' transport policies but oppose higher petrol prices. Their knowledge of individual politicians or party policies is scanty. They prefer media which give them little politics and lots of sport, sex and soap. 'The people' are, in short, selfish, ignorant and hypocritical dunderheads who cannot be allowed to decide the important stuff. This is the rarely stated but common assumption of political élites everywhere. As one American writer has said of his country.

When there are problems to discuss, élites discuss them exclusively with other élites. Political leaders talk among themselves or with business leaders, with educators, with lawyers, with economists, with lobbyists. It is against the American credo to stratify people by social class, but one of the most rigid barriers in today's America is the barrier that separates the men and women who 'serve' the public from the public itself.[13]

The élites here too no longer justify themselves in terms of their family background or personal wealth – John Major came from a lower-middle-class and relatively poor family – but they justify their power as deriving from their expertise, their knowledge. The same American writer labelled this 'the Culture of Technical Control', the use of expert thinking to control as many aspects of the human environment as possible. Specialism is ultimately incompatible with full democracy – it assumes that the average individual knows too little about almost everything to be able to make a serious and informed choice about almost anything. It is this attitude that has left the British voter with so few choices and made joining a party (a supporters' club for the social policy specialists) so unappealing.

There are some fairly obvious logical objections to all this. First objection: if the people are so hopelessly inexpert, why should they be expected to be good at choosing between the highly complex mix of individuals and policies offered by political parties – a choice that is considered almost sacred, the centre and meaning of our whole political system? If they can't be trusted to decide whether or not Britain should be part of a new European Union, why can they be trusted to decide whether or not the Conservative or Labour case for government is the better one? Second objection: if the political leaders are so expert, if they are initiates in some hidden science of choosing, why are they so bad at it, and why do they disagree about so many basic questions? These questions surely suggest that political choice is ultimately about values, not technical detail. Should gas pricing be altered by the monopoly supplier to lock in big corporate users, helping ensure its prosperity in a more competitive market, but at the cost of higher bills for small users like pensioners? Is it worth building that road through that wood in order to save ten minutes' driving time and twenty accidents per year? Is the continuance of a deep-mined coal industry of such social value to the country that we should continue to subsidize it by X amount? Is it worth British soldiers dying in Bosnia? These are typically complicated questions that deserve long discussion and require further information before they can be fairly answered. But, in the end, they are about values, balancing goods and bads and coming down in a personal way on one side or the other for reasons that are not technical. And values are something we are all competent to talk about. Indeed, whenever we think our choices are really meaningful, most of us are pretty good at the technical stuff: when it comes to choosing mortgage products, cars, gadgets, schooling and cosmetics, we are a sophisticated lot. The real difference is we don't think about politics because we don't think that thinking will make any difference. This state of mind has been well-described as 'rational ignorance'.

If that disposes of the theoretical objections to more direct democracy, what about the practical objections? What about the fact that people often don't have time to think about such things, or sufficient information? What about the thoughtlessness and confusion in thinking revealed by opinion polls? What about the sheer volume of decisions to be made? These are all serious and real objections to a wider notion of democracy. But, before going further, it is worth remembering that some of them apply to the current system of representative democracy too. The average MP doesn't, in fact, have a huge amount of time for thinking about policy either: the demands of the constituency postbag, of the administrative side of the job, the need to act as voting fodder on a wider range of issues than he or she can be fully informed about, all help keep many legislators in a state of more or less willing ignorance. Ministers are generally too deeply buried in the affairs of their own departments to have particularly detailed knowledge about the whirring mass of decision making going on elsewhere. And as for information, though MPs have special resources like the Commons Library and the ability to put down questions to government departments, it is clear from the amount of use that MPs make of newspapers and television programmes that many of their facts derive from exactly the same sources as their constituents use daily.

The practical difficulties about expanding the role of the voter in a democracy are currently the subject of great academic and political discussion. How, for instance, to get beyond the thoughtless, knee-jerk opinions which make up opinion polls? How to move from off-the-cuff responses to considered judgement? One answer, 'citizens' juries', takes the old English tradition of the jury in legal matters and tries to apply it to political affairs. If a randomly-chosen cross-section of the British is thought capable of deciding the guilt or innocence of accused people in complex financial or murder cases, why should they not be capable of deciding arguments about the national debt, or the ownership of the railways? If 200,000 people a year are involved this way in the justice system, spending days, weeks or months arbitrating on the freedom or incarceration of their fellows, why can a similar number of people not be involved in the political system, arbitrating on lesser matters? Now, it is true that our current system of juries, involving almost everyone, is rather newer than most people realize[14] and that there have been moves to get rid of juries from the more complex financial fraud cases precisely because of the weight of expertise and information involved. But juries retain widespread support as a system and, frankly, few political issues are as complex as the trial of a City fraudster.

There have been attempts to see how such a system might operate in practice, including in the United States, where the Jefferson Center has organized fourteen such exercises on 'America's Tough Choices'; a 'consensus conference' on plant biotechnology organized by the Science Museum in London, and the Channel Four 'People's Parliament' exercise. Another version of the same idea was hatched in the United States by a professor called James Fishkin who devised what he called 'deliberative polling'. His idea was that ordinary opinion polls merely measure people's kneejerk responses to simple and some-times loaded questions, when what we really want to know is what they would choose, had they sufficient time, access to the arguments, facts and the ability to cross-question the experts. He suggested finding several hundred people, or more, selected by the same criteria as pollsters use to cover the ages, incomes, sex balance and so on; then persuading them to come together for several days and argue the propositions through. For such a poll, you make sure they have all the information they need and you bring in outside experts, including politicians, to be cross-examined by them. Finally, you put to them again the propositions you put originally, to discover their 'deep' or 'thought-through' opinions. This was tried, under the direction of Professor Fishkin, for *The Independent* newspaper and Channel

Four on the subject of crime, and produced high-quality debate and sophisticated results. (Though liberals should note that this spectrum of British opinion was in favour of the death penalty when first polled and then, after taking time to think through all this consequences . . . was firmly still in favour of the death penalty.) The same technique, somewhere between a jury and a poll, is likely to be used during the 1996 presidential election in the US.

The final version of direct democracy is, naturally, the referendum. Britain has seen few referendums. There have been the June 1975 referendum on British membership of the Common Market (as it was then known); the 1973 Northern Ireland border poll referendum; the Scottish and Welsh devolution referendums of March 1979; and various smaller-scale local referendums, often organized by local authorities. For mainstream British politics, the referendum has been the device of the seventies, another decade when Westminster leaders were struggling with divided parties and small majorities. Since then, the Establishment has dismissed referendums, considering them a way of evading tough decisions. That hasn't been the public view: polls have suggested that three-quarters of British voters would like referendums and that two-thirds would use local referendums if they had the chance. Meanwhile, the European Union has brought referendums back to centre-stage; the dramatic Danish 'no' and the close-fought French referendum of 1992 made many British people wonder why they too could not have a direct say on Maastricht. But, despite the fact that Parliament was no longer, as it were, *virgo intacta*, the government said no. The most familiar arguments against more referendums are that they would substitute media-dominated hysteria for serious, responsible deliberation. We will look at the role of Parliament later, but, for now, the best response is to suggest that anyone who seriously believes this should spend half an afternoon in the visitors' gallery of the House of Commons.

Referendums have, in fact, become fairly common in many developed countries. Switzerland is famously referendum-mad. The Swiss had their first direct citizen vote in the canton of

Schwyz in 1294 and celebrated seven hundred years later with another cantonal referendum which threw the entire EU trunk-road planning into frenzy by voting against allowing heavy lorries to carry on rumbling through an Alpine valley. No other Europeans would have been able to do that, except possibly the few citizens of Liechtenstein. Since 1848, when the Swiss referendum went national, they have had some 414 state-wide referendums, and the average Swiss is asked to decide upon up to a dozen national issues a year, plus the local and cantonal ones.[15] One commentator on Swiss politics has ob-served that, 'It is no exaggeration to say that Swiss citizens are called to the polls more times in one year than most Europeans are in a lifetime.'[16] Just over half of the states of the US allow some form of referendum or citizen initiative-proposed laws, covering issues as wide-ranging as gun control and rent control, gay rights and welfare rights, the use of drugs, whether non-dentists in Idaho should be allowed to fit dentures, whether self-service petrol stations should be allowed in Oregon – and, of course, the electric chair. These initiatives typically have to attract signatures of between 3 and 10 per cent of the voters in order to be put to the whole state. The Californians are particu-larly keen on referendums, and have scared the pants off establish-ment politicians with their radical government-limiting and anti-immigrant views. There have been more than 130 such initiatives in California since 1950; and the 1990 California ballot pamphlet contained 221 pages of proposals.[17] But plenty of other countries have gone for the increased use of referendums, including Italy (everything from hunting laws to the abolition of the Enterprise Ministry), Ireland (abortion, divorce and Maastricht), Australia (treatment of aborigines, judges' retire-ment, local government), New Zealand (closing hours for bars, the electoral system) and many more.

Yes, referendums can produce the 'wrong' result. But so can Parliaments and elections. Yes, they are less effective in produc-ing deep thought and judgement than the more gimmicky-sounding wheezes, such as voter juries. But a referendum campaign shakes the place up; it confronts voters with real choices; it educates the country in democracy. And this would be no mean achievement for a country like ours where we are not only cynical about our current politics, but increasingly ignorant of our own democratic history and theory. Addressing his fellow Americans a few years back, the poet, farmer and ecologist Wendell Berry warned them: 'Our most serious problem, perhaps, is that we have become a nation of fantasists. We believe, apparently, in the infinite availability of finite resources ... We believe that democratic freedom can be preserved by people ignorant of the history of democracy and indifferent to the responsibilities of freedom.'[18] We have the same fantasies here, and they are no less dangerous: the hard-won privilege of voting is something we need to think rather harder about. It will no longer do for the British legislators to treat referendums as an untried, suspicious and unwholesome device, tainted by the way the Nazis used them in the thirties. Voting, on rare occasions, for people about whom one knows little and whose powers are anyway debatable, is not the only possible form of voting; and one day, even we may discover that.

We started this chapter by talking of the vote as a glorious privilege, a great thing, a badge of belonging. So it is. But we've also seen how it is today a much lesser deal than the democratic rhetoric makes out. The greatness of the vote was its efficiency, its power to transmit views and force change. If that power is failing, then there's a duty to search for ways of recovering it – different forms of voting. Otherwise the privilege becomes a dead ritual and democrats find themselves shrivelling again into falsetto-voiced midget subjects.

CHAPTER TWO

Down the Local

'Obscure to London buzz, and wayward bee
The squat Bastilles of British Liberty – '
– George Jones, 'British Idylls', 1810

The earliest ideas about democracy were about local democracy, in the sense of near-at-hand events and processes. It was assumed that to participate you had to be able to physically attend meetings and vote, and perhaps speak there. Democratic politics first meant local politics, whether it was in ancient Athens or Geneva or New England. In Old England, too, there had been at least local meetings, going back to Anglo-Saxon times, which developed a tentative relationship with the central power in London. There were parishes, borough meetings, assemblies of the various guilds and the courts leet. In Scotland, the post-reformation Kirk offered a similar forum for the discussion of local issues during the years when that nation was close to being a theocracy. Local politics, though far from inclusive, remained an important part of British life until the Industrial Revolution. The historians of modern local government relate that,

A traditional part of the British constitution is the right of the people to assemble to discuss matters of common interest. In the eighteenth and early nineteenth century, county meetings of the freeholders of the county, assembled in the open air under the sheriff, were common events. They would debate matters of local or national interest, and would often send petitions to Parliament. In the towns, the mayors would call similar meetings, which also were exempt from the restrictions of the Seditious Meetings Act and enjoyed a clear but undefined constitutional status. So too, at the parish level, the open vestries, though sometimes riotous and usually inefficient, provided a form of direct democracy.[1]

This looks, at first sight, not a world away from the New England townships described with such delight in 1839 by the thirty-four-year-old French writer Alexis de Tocqueville. He enthused that 'the strength of free peoples resides in the local community. Local institutions are to liberty what primary schools are to science; they put it within the people's reach . . . without local institutions a nation may give itself a free government, but it has not got the spirit of liberty.'[2] The question of how much local autonomy actually existed in Britain itself long ago became a subject of political controversy: romantic socialists tended to emphasize a happy, lost country of sturdy peasant meetings, while Conservative writers pooh-poohed the existence of any local politics. But history lessons aside, de Tocqueville's words are worth dwelling on. The spirit of liberty, like charity, does begin at home. Near-at-hand power can feel as strong as power exercised at higher removes: for the homeless family, the decision of local politicians, bureaucrats or government appointees can make the difference between a tolerable existence and an intolerable one. Life-chances can depend on local schools. Local decisions about roads, policing or parks make a more immediate impact on families than most Acts of Parliament. As children abused in Islington could confirm, bad local government can be more oppressive than most of the wickedness of Westminster; and well-exercised local power can mitigate the follies of the centre.

These points are essential to the non-totalitarian state, which rests on a multiplicity of centres of authority. It is no coincidence that the Eastern European countries emerging from the communist ice-age seized on the idea of civil society, intermediate institutions between citizen and state, as one of the great inventions of the West. A country which prizes and defends a high degree of independence in its churches, schools, towns and regions cannot be totalitarian, and probably cannot be oppressive either. The political and philosophical writer Ernest Gellner, one of the unpolished ornaments of modern Britain, has pointed out that civil society depends upon a separation of different ideas about mankind – economic, political, moral and so forth – and that this is one of its main glories:

The price of liberty may once have been eternal vigilance: the splendid thing about Civil Society is that even the absent-minded, or those preoccupied with their private concerns or for any other reason ill-suited to the exercise of eternal and intimidating vigilance, can look forward to enjoying their liberty. Civil Society bestows liberty even on the non-vigilant.[3]

For we British, so far, so good. Rhetorically, at least, all our main parties and politicians are firm believers in civil society and the spread of powers. The trouble has been that we suffer from a highly centralized and jealous political tradition which has been unwilling in practice to protect what it celebrates in principle. Generations of socialists, who cut their teeth in local politics, turned into ruthless centralizers when they reached London. The reasoning always sounded impeccable. Sidney and Beatrice Webb, the Fabian intellectuals and early historians of local government, believed that, 'We cannot afford to let a town have what police it wishes, what trade regulations it prefers . . . what highways, markets or sanitation it elects, or what degree of physical health, of education and of social order it happens to appreciate . . .' There must be enforced, they said, so 'that National Minimum of efficiency without which the well-being of the whole will be impaired.'[4] Eighty years later, Conservative radicals in the Thatcher government were using almost identical language against socialist local councils, as we shall see. Efficiency has always been emblazoned on the black flag of the centralists.

On this question, the difference between left and right has come to be primarily about the nature of local institutions. The dominant Tory argument has been in favour of self-run, un-elected schools, hospitals and so on, largely because of the political behaviour of elected local authorities. The left, after years of bitter exile from central power, has started to proclaim the need for self-sufficient, entrenched local democracy. The Liberal Democrats, meanwhile, have become so firmly the party of local government that many of their members seem disdainful about the national contest for Parliament – to the intense irritation of Lib-Dem leaders. The problem the Tories face is that local power without local democracy becomes corrupt and is hardly a good way of teaching de Tocqueville's 'spirit of liberty' – where, in a world of private bodies and closed meetings, are local people supposed to pick up the habits of speaking out, comparing arguments and making choices? But the problem for left-wing and liberal advocates of local government is that their logic, as we shall see, directly challenges the British political system itself. To speak of entrenched powers for local government in a centralized state whose Parliament claims absolute sovereignty is little short of revolutionary. And yet these are such mild-mannered revolutionaries one cannot quite believe that they have the backbone to follow through the consequences of their arguments.

The History of Local Government in just a few Pages

In the beginning there was mayhem. There were Royal Charters for boroughs and Justices of the Peace, and vestries and presbyteries and parishes and manorial rights and Corporations and Quarter Sessions. A Britain of rutted tracks, of local dialects and obscure customs, was also a country whose shires and towns and villages itched under different forms of governance. No Napoleonic vision of order and rationality had penetrated to the crannies and folds of pre-nineteenth-century Britain. Across this disorganized map the real rulers were, in the main, local oligarchies of merchants and landowners, though county meetings, grand juries and so on could, from time to time, draw in the alehouse equivalent of the chattering classes, too. The JPs or magistrates who in pre-industrial England exercised a very wide range of powers, were often Anglican clergy or landowners. They dealt with petty crime, the destitute, roads, taxes, licences, even some wages. They had by law to be gentry – the poor, or 'persons of Mean Estate' were specifically excluded – and they were chosen by word of mouth, co-optation and family or political connection. The fellow-feeling of local magistrates and parliamentarians meant institutional conflict was unlikely. What we would today call 'the different tiers of government' hunted foxes and shot pheasant together. Often, the older brother might be the local MP and younger brothers or cousins the local magistrates. The JPs and the borough grandees were in some sense agents of the Crown, and thus working on behalf of the London politicians. But even if London had wanted to come down heavily, the primitive administration and slow communications of that era meant that a fair degree of local autonomy was the only practicable option: if efficiency has been the battle cry of centralizers, bad roads have been the defensive rampart for a thousand quiet communities.

That confused and private world of clique and jobbery was finally stormed and transformed by the rise of the state in industrial Britain. First, a new Victorian Magistracy sprang up, involving the establishment of more boards and committees and appointed bodies of all kinds. There was, initially, little democracy about the process; central-government 'doers' are always in a hurry. It was de Tocqueville, again, who noted that, 'Of all forms of liberty, that of a local community, which is so hard to establish, is the most prone to the encroachments of authority. Left to themselves, the institutions of a local community can hardly struggle against a strong and enterprising government.' And the late Victorian governments which swept away the old systems of local power and established a new, if haphazard series of arrangements, were nothing if not strong and enterprising. Commissioners of baths and wash-houses and burial boards were scattered across the Victorian nation. Generally, one good reforming idea merely opened up the need for more – an historian relates the case of the 1833 statute banning the employment of children aged under the age of nine in some factories. But which rickety urchin was nine and which eight? The lack of any formal registration of births for the urban poor then needed to be dealt with. While that was being done it had to be left up to doctors to work out the child's likely age for the purposes of the act. But just who was a real doctor – who could be trusted? This helped fuel concern, talk and finally remedy about the absence of formal medical qualifications.[5]

So one reform was midwife to the next. Bureaucracy –

efficient, uncorrupt, predictable – was the social invention of the age. As the social machinery spread, shadowing the industrial machinery, the burden fell more heavily on ratepayers to fund the necessary new bureaucracies. Thus, the machinery of election – for the new health boards, for the guardians of the Poor Law, for school boards – spread too. This evolving local democracy quickly developed a franchise larger than for Westminster (female householders, for instance, could vote in some local elections a full century before women got the vote for Parliament). But in other respects, the local franchise was a democratic scandal, with some ratepayers getting up to six votes, while those too poor to pay rates got none. Astonishingly, paupers – or, in today's language, people 'on welfare' – were kept off the local electoral roll until 1948. But, by the final decades of the last century, the rising political challenge of the working classes had convinced even powerful Tory reactionaries like Lord Salisbury of the case for widespread local democracy. Against the danger of 'spendthrift demagogues' winning power, that Prime Minister placed his hope on consolidating the power of the landed classes through elections, and, crucially, on balancing the rising power of the state with local power.[6]

So local government was modernized and democratized in order to act as the agent for national change. But, in the Victorian century, something else which was novel and important to the story started to happen. Local government, using its steadily-accumulating new powers ever more vigorously in the race to modernize and regulate the industrial nation, began to outstrip the parliamentarians. Water and sewerage came first, then gas, then municipal trams and the first electrical companies, all done on the rates and borrowed money, all without much more than worried acquiescence from London. Joseph Chamberlain built a national reputation by gassing and watering and lighting and paving Birmingham, using a Liberal machine in the city that had transformed local politics by the 1870s. Glasgow claimed to be the first city in the post-Roman world to pipe clean water to its citizens, destroying the scourge of cholera. It later went on to diversify into a vast range of modernizing activity, including the creation of its own telephone system – as did, at the other end of the country, Tunbridge Wells. Hull's municipal telephones, too, were famous into modern times. By the First World War, socialist councils in Scotland and the North of England were enthusiastically throwing themselves into a flood of municipal enterprises – buying up baby food and men's suits and selling them on at cost price, building civic washhouses and even cinemas, encouraging the local people to study mathematics and music. Doncaster ran its racecourse and Rochdale controlled the ice-cream trade. Bath acquired powers to regulate tea houses and Wolverhampton ran a cold-store. Sidney Webb, writing over a century ago, celebrated this flowering of local reform:

The Individualist Town Councillor will walk along the municipal pavement, lit by municipal gas and cleansed by municipal brooms with municipal water, and seeing by the municipal clock in the municipal market that he is too early to greet his children coming from the municipal school, will use the national telegraph system to tell them not to walk through the municipal park but to come by the municipal tramway, to meet him in the municipal reading-room, by the municipal art gallery, museum and library . . . 'Socialism, sir,' he will say, 'don't waste the time of a practical man by your fantastic absurdities. Self-help, sir, individual self-help, that's what's made our city what it is.'[7]

The satirist in Webb was right: this explosion of local activity helped fill the yawning gaps left by a national politics that was still focused on foreign affairs, above all the Empire, and was, until the arrival of the New Liberalism, deeply suspicious of the growth of state activity. But the growth of local democracy is more than the accumulation of tales of provincial make-do while the Imperial Parliament was looking elsewhere. The mushrooming of the great cities, Manchester and Birmingham, Glasgow and Leeds, Belfast and Cardiff, marked the character of Britain during her years of triumph. Their rise was the rise of this country; their decline has been a national fall. Local capital, local self-esteem and local public-mindedness built commercial and political centres which proved, once and for all, that democracy does not have to be focused on the nation-state to achieve things. Pace through their marbled, mahogany-panelled city halls, saunter through their municipal art galleries, packed with glorious things, go in search of what remains of their nineteenth-century infrastructure, the monuments, the parades, the Turkish bath-houses, the grand bridges and viaducts – indeed, look at these things in scores of lesser towns and cities, too – and you find almost heartbreaking evidence of vanished local supremacies throughout the land.

We are today almost in the position of the anonymous Anglo-Saxon poet wandering through the ruins of the Roman city of Bath during the Dark Ages and trying desperately to understand what manner of people might have lived there with the confidence and knowledge to build such a place:

> Wondrous is this stone-wall, wrecked by fate;
> the city-buildings crumble, the works of the giants decay
> . . . The earth's embrace,
> Its fierce grip, holds the mighty craftsmen . . .
> A man's mind quickened with a plan;
> Subtle and strong-willed, he bound
> the foundations with metal rods – a marvel.
> Bright were the city halls, many the bath-houses,
> lofty all the gables . . .[8]

For us, too, these people, the tobacco lords, the jute barons, the steel magnates and, in every case, the regiments of reformers and do-gooders, too, seem as long gone as the Romans did in the eighth century. They were not conquered or removed by plague, but merely bankrupted by their inability to pass their enterprise down generation by generation, and by two world wars. After those wars, unlike earlier ones, the state did not contract but vastly expanded its ambition in a way that forced back all power centres outside the few square miles of the City, Whitehall and Westminster.[9] The local civic commanders fell prey to an unimaginative and haughty centralism, the possessiveness of a nation-state which had less to be proud about than it admitted. True, their wealth had been won by the nation; it was the wealth of empire and of early triumphs in the industrial race. True, these cities built up political machines that could be oppressive and corrupt and which, eventually, squandered their own recent inheritance. But that is not the whole truth. There was a local pride and enterprise, a home-grown ingenuity which was precious. When we think about local government in our own time, it would be a terrible mistake to concentrate only on the attenuated, beaten-down and rather dreary institutions which only a minority of us bother to vote for. We should remember what was once accomplished by local enterprise and vision. We should, just sometimes, raise our eyes to the finely-chiselled pediments that still adorn corners of our crumbling and vandalized cities.

Blame the Politicians – all of them

Why did we lose the local constitution that helped build the nation during its period of greatness? The story is partly industrial but there are strong constitutional lessons too, and they do not reflect well on either of the parties which has dominated modern Britain. Essentially, local power became increasingly party-political, and thus an ever-sharper threat to the party in power at Westminster; and the doctrine of absolute parliamentary sovereignty meant such a threat could be all too easily destroyed. The lack of a single constitutional settlement for Britain meant that local democracy was struggling for power in a Darwinian jungle dominated by the giant, carnivorous state. As soon as they asserted themselves, or seemed even mildly irritating, local autonomies were hunted down by the big beasts of Westminster. The less power and wealth the great cities were able to use for their own ends, the fewer ambitious and talented people went into local politics, and a cycle of decline began. But it was our old friend the party system which linked local democracy to national democracy and so made the hunting-down inevitable.

The nationalization of local politics can be seen by looking at the London-based press. In 1901 at the start of the modern era the local elections, which were for comparatively important councils, steadily accumulating more powers, were not considered interesting enough to be recorded or discussed in serious newspapers – not one word appeared in *The Times*. In 1995, the local elections were discussed obsessively by such papers. Not, though, because London was any more interested in who would provide the best park service in Birmingham or use local taxes most efficiently in Rutland: the actual merits of the councils and councillors were largely ignored. Instead, the elections were treated as a kind of giant referendum or opinion-poll on the prime minister and national government, which wasn't up for election. A malign dynamic is at work in British politics. The more unpopular a national government becomes, the more voters, egged on by the national media, use local elections to express national protest. Local politics is relegated to a passing verdict on national politics and the local contest is mindlessly appropriated by the centralized party debate. In its hurry and pain, the centre reacts by punishing local governance, now in the hands of its enemies, by removing more powers. So local voters treat the next elections even more casually. By 1995, this dynamic had left Britain with few Tory councillors and almost-powerless local councils. The previous chapter has given a hint of why modern parties have found it so important to move into local government. They were stepping-stones, and the more ambitious politicians have always hoped to move on from a council leadership to a parliamentary candidacy.[10] National parties regarded local politics rather as military commanders regard territory: swathes of the country were 'ours'; great cities were 'taken'; the capture of one shire provided a home base for further advances. Parties had to build support and then move onwards and upwards for the national prize.

But there has always been an element of genuine local do-goodery coexisting with the national struggle. The Liberal machine in Birmingham was an engine of reform before it became a national politician's 'base'. The London County Council, established in 1889, had active and well-organized party groupings from the early days, while the Independent Labour

Party was organizing across industrial Britain by the outbreak of the First World War. But it was only really in the 1920s that Labour started to establish versions of municipal socialism that worried Westminster Conservatives and Liberals at the national level. They in turn allied and set up local front organizations to combat the socialist peril. There were 'Progressives' in Edinburgh, 'Independents' and 'Ratepayers' everywhere and a London Municipal Society that was hard to distinguish from the Conservative Party. In some places the anti-Labour fronts, playing on local pride, went further: the Southampton Independent Party was launched in 1920 and there was a Bristol Citizens' Party, too. After the Second World War, the Conservatives organized more openly, as local government became a mimicry of the national struggle. From then on, the actions of Tory councillors were a fit subject for civil servants of Labour ministers to worry about; and the doings of left-wing local authorities were regularly discussed round Conservative cabinet tables.

Perhaps it was inevitable. Local politics could develop independently of the national struggle for only so long. The most famous confrontations involved socialist councils taking on the authority of the state. The best-known of all was the Poplar rebellion, when Labour councillors from the impoverished East End London borough of Poplar defied the post-war Lloyd George coalition government in 1921 over the operation of the Poor Law benefits and the unfair system of paying for London services. The councillors, led by the future Labour Party leader and Christian socialist George Lansbury, deliberately refused to pay for police, water and other services, using the money to provide a more generous system of outdoor relief for local people. They were imprisoned at Brixton and Holloway, where crowds gathered and sang the Red Flag to them. Though this was a clear confrontation between local and central government, it was essentially a socialist rebellion against financial orthodoxy, imposed through the Poor Law, which had originated in Elizabethan times and been regularized in 1834. The Poplar council was a classic exponent of municipal socialism, opening wash-houses, swimming baths, libraries and parks, building council houses and establishing a minimum wage in the borough – thoroughly against the spirit of pre-Keynesian Westminster. Their rebellion was meant to be a big one, and to spread. The councillors' defiant attitude to the sovereignty of Parliament is well caught by the title of their explanatory pamphlet – *Guilty and Proud of It*.

The actions of the Poplar councillors were followed by other Labour Poor Law Guardians from Wales to County Durham. But, though the Poplar rebellion helped destroy the Poor Law, no localist uprising since has really dented the self-confidence of central government. By the end of the Second World War, with the hardening of a straight left-right political competition, local government was largely party-politicized and, from then on, there was no mainstream dissent about its subordinate role. The Labour governments were composed partly of the same men who had tried to build municipal socialism earlier in the century – Attlee, Bevan, Tom Johnston, Herbert Morrison – but they had long ago transferred their visions from the local to the national scale, and retained little enthusiasm for local autonomy. They were the masters then, and had no time for myopic municipal doubters. They pursued a policy of centrally-organized welfarism – removing voluntary hospitals from local control, for instance – and national economic management that left little room for local variation. It was resented in Scotland, among other places; enough so to allow Winston Churchill in the 1950 election campaign to play on the patriotic hostility among businessmen and many voters to nationalization, a form of 'serfdom' which Churchill argued was taking economic power out of Scotland and handing it to London pen-pushers. Conservative governments were, if anything, rather less impatient about local councils until the Thatcher revolution, whose energy, pulsing out from that famous brick tardis between Whitehall and St James's Park, acknowledged no rivals. But that was because, from 1945 to 1979, the Tories were essentially followers rather than leaders of the domestic agenda: for them, the growth of a hugely ambitious post-war state was something to be civilized and reined in – and local autonomy was a rein.

There have always been soft words about local democracy, throughout modern times, as if the national politicians felt a little guilty about their compulsive centralism. Harold Wilson, for instance, was inclined to bang on about 'the fundamental and growing importance of local government . . . there will always be things which are best decided by people on the spot . . .' Even Margaret Thatcher, who found so many local authorities deeply irritating, and abolished some of the bigger ones, nevertheless mumbled pious phrases about its enduring value (she, of course, like the other party leaders, had her own army of councillors to consider). Independent studies commissioned by central government, like the 1969 Redcliffe-Maud Commission and the 1976 Layfield report, also assumed that there was something called local democracy which was a valuable part of the constitution. But in the case of both the Wilson and Thatcher governments, the true power relationship was never in doubt. Here, for example, is Wilson addressing the Commons in 1969 on the subject of those Tory councils who had refused to follow the minister Tony Crosland's insistence that 'every fucking grammar school in England' was to be destroyed, eventually via a Whitehall circular to local authorities:

The majority of authorities are, in fact, cooperating with national policy . . . but the completion of the task and the availability of comprehensive education in significant areas of the country are held back by the opposition of a small minority of local education authorities . . . there are those who will want to fight this on partisan and doctrinaire grounds.

If the authorities failed to take the hint of the circular, Wilson went on, he would legislate to force them to. So much for 'people on the spot'. In the tone of his menacing message, Wilson can hardly be distinguished from Nicholas Ridley, nearly twenty years later, telling the Commons that localism must bow to the wisdom of the centre:

We issued a consultative paper over two years ago warning local authorities that we might have to force them to expose their activities to competition if they did not choose to do that themselves. A few authorities responded but the vast majority continued to increase the burdens that they were imposing on their ratepayers ... The bill requires compulsory competitive tendering.

Opposite ideologies; identical reflexes.

The almost-obliterated memory of direct democracy and the achievements of Victorian local government are a reminder that not all our history has been centralist and contemptuous of local popular power – a fact that has escaped the leader-writers of some eminent newspapers. 'Tis now, but 'twas not always or absolutely thus. But there are no heroes in this story: it is too easy to look at the assault on local democracy since 1979 and suffer false memory syndrome about its condition under previous Labour administrations. That said, it is time to turn to the follies and miseries of the recent past.

Margaret Thatcher's Wee Mistake

Margaret Thatcher did not set out to 'smash' local government. Before she came to power, her associates on the right of the Tory party had evolved a powerful critique of oppressive centralism, ranging from derision of the post-war assumption that 'the man in Whitehall knows best' to attacks on undemocratic rule by unelected bodies, or Quangos. When the Conservatives arrived in office they were seen as champions of the shires and the local. The party was strongly represented in local government which hadn't had such a bad record through the seventies, and seemed in less urgent need of reform than national governance. Halfway through the Thatcher period, the Widdicombe Committee set up to inquire into local government produced a report which confirmed that, for all its faults, the town hall was still thriving: it found that nearly a third of the voters were able to name at least one of their councillors and a fifth had had contact. More than three quarters were satisfied with their local council's services, a higher proportion than were satisfied with central government.[11] And, although Lady Thatcher later came to be seen as an arch-enemy of local autonomy, that has never been how she saw herself. She had been attracted by local referendums.

Her poll tax, the flagship that became an uncontrollable fire-ship, was often spoken of by its critics as being inherently centralist. Well, it was a badly thought-out, crazily introduced and thoroughly inequitable tax, but it had been conceived as the opposite of a centralist measure. By her own account:

The community charge offered a last chance of responsible, efficient local democracy in Britain. Its abandonment will mean that more and more powers will pass to central government, that upward pressure on public spending and taxation will increase accordingly, and that still fewer people of ability will become local councillors.

Starting with good intentions and carrying on as someone who thought herself a champion of the local against the central, Lady Thatcher presided over a government which, with its successor, has proved an implacable enemy to democracy as practised in the towns and shires of Britain. Why?

Having known most of the ministers responsible, I am sure there was no blueprint for what happened. Everything in the British system conspires to ensure that a radical or even a strong-minded government is likely to diminish local autonomy. The Conservatives had no philosophy of local government, at any rate nothing strong enough to make them, in power at the centre, self-aware about the wider consequences. Constitution-ally, they were all over the place. Here, for instance, is Norman Tebbit having a go at his old Tory sparring-partner:

In his March 1991 statement concerning local government structure and finance, Mr Heseltine made up an entirely new and quite false constitutional theory, when he said: 'We need responsible elected local authorities *not only* to provide a check and a balance to Westminster . . .' That is not true. Local government is not to be used or seen as a way of frustrating the outcome of general elections. It has only those powers given to it for the time being by Parliament, which is itself the main check or balance upon central government . . . In general we suffer from too much government – especially local government.[12]

But yet another senior figure of Thatcherite Toryism, Nigel Lawson, talked of the 'constitutional principle of local autonomy', though he also complained about 'the collapse of the traditional understanding that, irrespective of the colour of the Party in power at local level, a local authority would conduct its affairs in more or less conformity with the economic policy of the government of the day.'[13]

It hadn't been *that* traditional, as we have seen. And Lawson, probably the cleverest of the big names of the Thatcher administrations, finally went public about the philosophical muddle when speaking to MPs in the mid-eighties:

We suffer from an unfortunate constitutional set-up in this country as a result of our consistent pursuit in every way of the middle way. There are countries like West Germany and the United States which have a genuine federal constitution and where local authorities . . . are genuinely held to account. They are independent authorities and the electorate understands the responsibilities that these authorities have for managing their own affairs. That does not work too badly. You also have the opposite. The French, very logically, have a unitary constitution and carry it to the extreme where nearly every decision is dictated from the centre – Paris . . . That works out not too badly. We have a curious mixture because our constitution is midway between the two: we have a unitary constitution but nevertheless the local authorities have considerable autonomy.[14]

The confusion pointed out by the then Chancellor mattered terribly for local government because, as we shall see, it allowed the national government to set about trying to solve a series of national problems without any clear belief in the role or legitimacy of the local level of democracy. As a result we travelled further in the direction of centralist France (which has, however, pursued a modest decentralist agenda in recent years) and further away from a federal model.

Against this background of a nationalized local politics and muddled constitutional thinking, the political situation when Lady Thatcher came to power was stoked for conflict. In the eighties there was an ideological edge to the local-versus-central battle that had hardly been quite so present before. If the Thatcherites had broken the old centrist consensus from the right, then many local Labour authorities, particularly in London and Liverpool, were trying to break it from the left. Either there were Trotskyists (as in Lambeth and Liverpool) committed to a 'transitional programme' of raising demands that the capitalist system could not satisfy. Or they had been happily captured by the rainbow coalition of pressure groups in the metropolis. In most cases, no doubt, the councillors were trying defiantly to better the lot of people in their patch, but they were doing so in ways calculated to produce the maximum fury and contempt from a right-wing administration at Westminster. The 'people's republic of South Yorkshire' and the Greater London Council, even though its support for Sinn Fein and gay rights made most of the headlines, were basically trying to pursue the same agenda of municipal socialism – public housing, cheap fares and spending policies which directly challenged the ruling financial orthodoxy – which formed the programme of the Poplar councillors. But the Thatcher government was far less pliable than the Lloyd George one. Despite its high-profile, expensive and imaginative campaign reminding people of its democratic mandate ('say no to no say'), the abolition of the GLC was final proof that Britain was too small for politicians like Thatcher and Livingstone to share any power inside it. Livingstone and the London left had asked for it. And she was not the lady to refuse them.

Had the early 1980s seen a handful of high-profile, high-spending local authorities go Tory and stay Tory, the assault on local democracy under the Conservatives might have been less severe. But it would probably still have happened, simply because of the central commitment of the Thatcher governments to reducing the size of the state. Yet, as Nigel Lawson put it,

Although it accounted for about a quarter of total public spending, the constitutional principle of local autonomy meant that in practice the Government had no direct control over local government current expenditure . . . The battle for control of local government spending between the Treasury and the local authorities – which were supported increasingly by successive Secretaries of State for the Environment – became one of the perennial themes of the Thatcher years.[15]

This financial imperative was the most important single factor.

And there certainly was terrible waste and incompetence at local level. It drove some thoughtful Tories, including Lord Lawson and various ministers in John Major's administrations, to conclude that local services should be limited, but funded almost fully from local taxation, so ending the connection with the Treasury. This proved a blown-up bridge too far: a residual belief in local government prevented – only just – the final nationalization of British administration. Instead, in pursuit of financial control, Michael Heseltine tried a whole range of curbs and bridles, including fiendishly complicated block-grant systems, the formation of the Audit Commission and, in 1984, ratecapping. There followed, after the 1987 election, new powers to cap local-authority spending, the taking of the local business rate under national Treasury control and the compulsory tendering policy mentioned above. There was a further political problem for the Conservatives, however, which none of these mechanisms really dealt with, which was that the rating system excluded many people from contributing – of the thirty-five million local electors in England, only twelve million were liable for full rates. Thus, it could be argued, financial irresponsibility could be indulged in by Labour councillors without incurring the electoral penalty.

For Margaret Thatcher, it all hung together:

Many people had no direct reason to be concerned about their council's overspending, because somebody else picked up all or most of the bill. Worse still, people lacked the information they needed to hold their local authority to account . . . It is not surprising that many councillors felt free to pursue policies which no properly operating democratic discipline would have permitted. This lack of accountability lay behind the continued overspending.[16]

Her argument is crucial to understanding what happened to local government: the centre saw the local as not only wasteful and incompetent but, at some politically subliminal level, illegitimate. Local authorities may have had the trappings of democracy – ballot boxes in polling-stations, canvassers and results published in the newspapers – but they lacked, in her view, the extras that made democracy live – proper and public measurements of their effectiveness, and a call on every voter's pocket. No taxation without representation; but no representation without taxation. This logic, which led to the poll tax, suggests that anyone who is not a net contributor should not be a democratic participant – the logic behind the old property qualifications progressively dismantled in the nineteenth century. It also, more attractively, takes for granted that performance measurement and free information is essential to full democracy. These are, the reader may recall, conspicuously lacking when it comes to national government.

What lessons does the history of our local democracy have for us at the end of this century, after several decades of almost perpetual reform, controversy and argument? The first lesson is that local government can work, and be liberating, providing it has proper democratic accountability and – for the two go together – responsibility. It hasn't had these, for the second lesson is that, under our unbalanced and fluid constitution, the place of local government has never been decided. It grew because there were jobs for it to do. Under constitutional theory, Parliament has merely loaned power and permitted local bodies to act as its agents. Council powers could be granted and taken away at a moment's notice, and often were. Where new duties were given them, this generally happened because the centre had failed, or the job was too unglamorous and onerous, as with the recent example of community care. Local authorities' boundaries were insecure, their money-raising ability imprisoned by a possessive, not-to-be-mocked Treasury, the follies of one authority being quickly broadcast to the rest of the nation, tarnishing scores of others. Whereas the central government could swell the national debt to alarming proportions and call in grand-sounding economic theories to its defence, local government was quickly collared for extravagance. In the early years of John Major's government, local authorities were routinely attacked by ministers for running debts which compared to some Third World nations. The ministerial worry was fair enough but central government was itself borrowing some £50 billion at the time, a huge total in historic terms which, had a Labour government been in office, it might well have been unable to fund. Centralism has been a hypocritical and pompous doctrine, as well as a blundering one.

Centralism is not enough even for those who practise it. As we shall see, community is the watchword of the nineties and a mood of something like remorse is discernible among some of the leading ideologues of the Thatcher years. Today's Liberal Democrats are passionately, if unsurprisingly, in favour of local democracy. The Labour Party says it has reformed, and makes much of pluralism, and the need to respect local decision-making. It has proposed a system of annual elections for a third of councillors at budget time to improve local accountability and its former constitutional affairs spokesman, Graham Allen, has even been inclined to talk late at night about giving local government entrenched powers, thus breaking the ikon of parliamentary sovereignty. Faced with the implications of Scottish Home Rule for England, Labour has experimented with a range of ideas designed to pass power from Westminster back to locally-chosen bodies. But in this respect Labour is an association of recently reformed alcoholics and we must wait cautiously to see how they behave if they take over the distillery.

As for the Conservatives, they have made at least one discovery of huge value to local government, which is that the politicians don't have to run things themselves; and mostly shouldn't. They can operate highly effectively by contract and regulation – in the jargon of the management revolution, 'steering' rather than 'rowing'. This is a genuine breakthrough and opens the way to a new kind of politics, as we shall see later. But the Tories have a serious and special problem. They speak passionately about Burke's small platoons, they still talk of local 'democracy', not just local services, they still pay lip-service to the idea of an autonomous civil society. (Lip-service is also a kind of service; this is not all cynicism; the Tory case for independent institutions has been too long held to be mere camouflage.) But when one considers what they have actually done, a pattern emerges which contradicts all these fine words.

The Conservatives have disconnected the ideas 'local' and 'democracy'

The first phase, until the mid-1980s, involved on the one hand those financial curbs and, on the other, an attempt by Michael Heseltine to find new ways of reinvigorating local democracy. These were local referendums and directly elected mayors and both were shot down. The second phase, from 1987–90, saw more curbs and the arrival of the poll tax, intended to revitalize local democracy and make it more responsive. That failed, too. Then came the third phase, which originated in 1988 in piecemeal form but has become more blatant and thought-out since. This started from the assumption that local democracy (by now, because of the malign dynamic, heavily in the hands of anti-Conservative groups of councillors) was a complete failure. Instead there would be a system of local administration that bypassed the ballot-box, devolving power to consumer and user-groups (parents, patients, businesses) rather than local authorities. This is another version of the deal which says: 'shopping, not voting'. Or, to put it in the more elegant language of William Waldegrave, High Tory theorist and author of the poll tax, 'The key point . . . is not whether those who run our public services are elected, but whether they are producer-responsive or consumer-responsive. Services are not necessarily made to respond to the public simply by giving citizens a democratic voice, and a distant and diffuse one at that, in their make-up.'[17] The Conservative revolution has not been seriously or properly thought through – as is the way with revolutions. For Waldegrave's argument applies with as much, or as little, force to Westminster, which is more 'distant and diffuse' for many of us than the town hall. In which case, why bother with politics at all? These are cold, deep waters, into which we must now take a short but bracing plunge.

Quangos: Or, Dispensing with the Voter

The direct assault on local autonomy, carried on for a variety of reasons by a variety of ministers, might have left the system a little bruised but not fundamentally weaker than after previous periods of strong central government. But what has made local democracy a joke in Britain – and not a very funny one – has been this third phase, the slick substitution of appointees for councillors. The use of committees of state-appointed people, generally meeting in private, to run large swathes of public life is a story which, in strict logic, could be left to a later section of this book which deals with the state machine itself. But the impact of what are popularly known as quangos is today most controversial and serious at the local level; and the subject might as well be dealt with now.

There has been terrible confusion over the word quango, some of it caused by genuine doubt about which bodies should and should not be included, some of it the result of deliberate obfuscation. The academic Anthony Barker minted the acronym (which stands for quasi-autonomous non-governmental organization) at the beginning of the seventies. It is a broad term for the large range of bodies of appointed, non-elected, non-civil service people running things, overseeing things, or advising about things, and usually spending or controlling public money. Perhaps the most important thing about the acronym is its negative connotation. Despite sounding vaguely like a fruit drink or a friendly marsupial, quangos have been regarded as a Bad Thing. In the seventies this was because they were seen as a symptom of the bloated and sluggish state bureaucracy of the period. More recently, it was because they were seen as symbols of jobs-for-the-boys under Conservative rule. Because of this, ministers have tried to find substitute abbreviations, preferably as dull-sounding as possible. Non-Governmental Organizations (NGOs) and Non-Departmental Public Bodies (NDPBs) have been two examples of the poetic spirit of Whitehall. NGOs, which refers largely to charities and state-funded pressure groups, are reminiscent of the Flanders and Swann song about gnus – 'I'm a Ngo; another Ngo'. NDPB sounds like something you put on in case of nuclear or biological warfare. Neither abbreviation, for different types of bodies, has had anything like the public resonance of quangos.

I may seem to be making a bit of a meal of the naming of parts, but the political battle over quangos is inextricably tied up with names and numbers. For instance, the biggest growth by far in unelected, government-appointed committees is in the National Health Service Trusts, Training and Enterprise Councils, City Technology Colleges and Grant-Maintained Schools. A Conservative government committed to reducing the numbers of quangos has dealt with this embarrassment by the happy expedient of trying to exclude most of the above from its list of NDPBs. Bodies running schools and other educational institutions 'are not part of the processes of national government', according to the Cabinet Office, despite the fact that school curriculums, numbers and funding are all dictated by Whitehall. Training and Enterprise Councils don't count either because these are 'non-profit-making private sector companies . . . working under contract to the Employment Department Group.'[18] Etcetera. Partly as a result of such creative verbal accounting, ministers have been able to announce great successes in culling public bodies – there were, by their counting methods, forty-four fewer in 1994 than in 1993, and a total of 1,345. Yet, at exactly the same time, outside observers have detected a huge rise in quangos. The first serious analysis of the problem in the mid 1990s, 'The Democratic Audit of the United Kingdom',[19] asserted that there were 5,521 non-elected bodies carrying out executive functions on behalf of the government. The vast majority of these bodies, 4,723, were operating at local level. Just to complicate things finally, this report coined another acronym, EGOs, standing for Extra-Governmental Organizations, and with a clear verbal message of its own.

So what are we really talking about – quangos, NDPBs or EGOs? How many of whatever they are, are there? And why is everybody so cross? As I have suggested already, this is a field of British government where the confusion is deliberate. The commonsense approach is to include the widest range of unelected and appointed public bodies with real powers, and only then to subdivide them into national or local, executive or merely advisory. If we follow this line, then it is clear that overall numbers have indeed grown substantially, and that the main trend has been to create a new system of local rule. It is the replacement of local democracy by centrally-controlled committees that has caused the political kerfuffle. And ministerial embarrassment about it derives from the Tories' own hostility to committees when they were in opposition in the seventies. In those days, 785 quangos were assiduously hunted down and held up by their heels for public ridicule in right-wing pamphlets and newspaper articles and Thatcherite think-tanks, like the Adam Smith Institute, inveighed against them. The Conservative polemicists Michael Fallon, later a Thatcherite minister, and Philip Holland MP, two eminent fence-takers in the quango-hunt, complained in one pamphlet that: 'Local government is being deprived of more and more of the functions it used to be thought capable of fulfilling.'[20] In the early years of the Thatcher government there was an attempt to lead quangos round to the back of the bicycle shed and apply the humane killer: in 1979, one of the great radical civil servants of post-war Whitehall, Sir Leo Pliatsky, ended the lives of 240 or so committees and organizations dependent on the state, out of more than 2,000 at that time – but saved the public purse only 250 jobs.

Yet today, after so many years of Thatcher and Thatcherite government, the replacement of local government by quangos is immeasurably more advanced than when she came to power. Unelected governance has pushed itself into what Douglas Hurd (in another context) described as 'the nooks and crannies of everyday life'. The Democratic Audit mentioned above said that local quango-type organizations included a complex jumble of public bodies, private companies, voluntary outfits and others, operating under 'no consistent regime of constitutional or legal accountability'. These local bodies

act under the direction of government ministers and their departments and major executive bodies under government control, like the Housing Corporation or the Funding Agency for Schools. They are responsible for social housing, schools, further education, training for employment, hospitals and health care – public services of great importance to people at local level, some of which until recently were mainly the preserve of local authorities.

Stuart Weir, the writer who has been researching the subject most carefully, estimated during 1994 that only a third of them were accountable to either of the main auditing bodies, the National Audit Office (which reports to Parliament) or the Audit Commission (set up by the Thatcher government to oversee local authorities, and lobbying to take quangos under its remit too). Only 14 per cent were under an ombudsman. Only 2 per cent were covered by open-government codes. Only half published a register of their members' interests. Only 5 per cent allowed a member of the public to attend their board or committee meetings. It amounts to a quiet and anti-democratic revolution which has rightly moved high up the agenda of the political parties.

National and Regional Quangos: Rule by 'Good Chaps'

Before describing the local quango revolution, however, it is right to briefly describe the national situation, which is less controversial, older and which has seen less recent change. Ministers haven't been able to do everything themselves or directly through civil servants for ages. There were quangos in the 1890s and throughout the modern era committees of unelected 'great and good' have proliferated. These committees can broadly be split into two kinds. There are the ones to advise ministers about things they don't have time for themselves – which architects should be chosen for a big public contract; what does Government need to know about the latest developments in gene therapy; which Scottish historic buildings should be listed? And there are the ones that run things – the BBC Board of Governors, the Sports Council, the various research councils, English Heritage, the Nature Conservancy Council, the National Rivers Authority and the committee overseeing the national curriculum for schools. They maintain the old British tradition of 'good chaps' at the top running things through an old boys' (with token girls) network.

Each year, the Cabinet Office produces a book simply called *Public Bodies* which lists most of these organizations, under the department of government which sponsors them. Even now that the nationalized industries have largely been sold back to the private sector again, it is a bewilderingly long, and occasionally weird, list. Here is a flavour of the latest one, which includes: the Apple and Pear Research Council; the Nuclear Powered Warships Safety Committee; the Advisory Council on Conscientious Objectors; the Consultative Panel on Badgers and Tuberculosis; Investors in People UK; the Black Country Limestone Advisory Panel; the Indian Family Pension Funds Body of Commissioners; the Committee on Mutagenicity of Chemicals in Food, Consumer Products and the Environment; the National Breastfeeding Working Group; the Football Licensing Authority; the Welsh Office's Place Names Advisory Committee; the Poisons Board; the Advisory Committee on Novel Foods; the . . . well, you get the general picture. Many, clearly, do useful and non-controversial work, though some seem a bit-outdated. (For example, is it really necessary to maintain a UK Polar Medal Assessment Committee, and isn't it increasingly likely that the Advisory Committee on Coal Research might well outlast the actual British coal industry?) Others are formed for a specific purpose and have a short, high-profile life – like the Millennium Commission, charged with choosing ideas for celebrating the year 2000. Many run grants and policies for specific areas, such as the Scottish Crofters Commission, run national museums and parks, or were clearly set up in response to a press furore – there is, for instance, a Northern Ireland Advisory Committee on Travellers.

Some are big spenders with a big national profile. The Housing Corporation spends around £1.8 billion and the educational funding councils around £3 billion. Some are large and figure regularly on the television news: the National Rivers Authority has a staff of 7,550. Some aren't and don't: you rarely hear reports about the ten-strong Advisory Committee on Historic

Wreck Sites. All, though, are part of the government of the country, in however obscure a way, and all come under some kind of political control. It is hard, even for the most paranoid of journalists (present writer included), to discern an oppressive state bearing down on the citizenry through the malign agency of, say, the Consultative Committee on Badgers. But some of the time, the political composition of such committees, which report to ministers rather than directly to Parliament, is a source of real concern, for the line between advice and policy-making is a notoriously blurred one. So the composition of the Board of Governors of the BBC has been a matter of controversy, particularly during the period when the Thatcher government was determined to rein in the Corporation. The small groups of academics and political pamphleteers meeting in Notting Hill, at the headquarters of the School Curriculum and Assessment Authority, to plan what must be taught in schools, were widely accused by teachers of being excessively slanted towards right-wing or conservative interests. Some of their early proposals were then attacked by right-wing newspapers for being insufficiently patriotic and traditionalist. It was, at least, gin-clear that that particular quango was acting in a way that produced strong and political reactions.

Although many quangos, particularly the scientific ones, are there to give ministers unbiased advice, however unwelcome, ministers try to keep a close eye on any bodies whose role is likely to be controversial. The body theoretically overseeing appointments until 1996 was a group of civil servants in the Cabinet Office called the Public Appointments Unit (PAU). In an average year, ministers make a total of up to ten thousand such appointments. Traditionally, the lists of candidates have come from the political parties, MPs and personal contacts of ministers – stories of appointments made by ministers after chance meetings in taxis and on the golf course are rife. In a published report in 1995, the PAU itself listed how appointments were made to a range of high-spending executive bodies. Under 'sources of names', it frequently lists 'Department' (that is, people the ministers and top civil servants already know about). For Scottish and Welsh quangos it says: 'Names known to SO plus additional canvassing [whatever that means] ... Names known to WO ...'[21] Public concern about quangos and their political bias led John Major to encourage more advertising and more people to write directly, suggesting themselves or their friends for service on public bodies. When the Nolan Committee on standards in public life reported in May 1995, it called for a new independent Public Appointments Commissioner, who would publish a code of conduct for making appointments, and would replace the PAU. Sir Len Peach, a former IBM executive and NHS chief executive, duly took up the post just before Christmas 1995, promising to oversee a system of 'transparency, balance and merit'. Though ministers would remain responsible for the 9,000 jobs in more than a thousand public bodies that come under his remit, he will monitor and oversee the appointments – which could run to 2,000 a year. This must be an advance, but it was odd that in the early stages no attempt was made to set up the central database of appointments, political affiliations and so on without which proper analysis of jobs for the chaps will be very difficult. And we must not be naive about it: whenever a body is handling something politically sensitive, the intention will always be to have 'sound chaps' on board. Though the Government whips no longer keep their own separate list of reliable people, the PAU noted that 'they may suggest candidates who have come to their attention for one reason or another ... Increasingly, over the years, the Chief Whip's Office has made nominations direct to the PAU list ...'[22]

Some of the jobs are very well-paid indeed. For instance, Lord Wyatt of Weeford, a fervent supporter of Lady Thatcher, was appointed by her government to chair the Horserace Totalisator Board on a salary of £95,000 a year and then, after lavishing praise on ministers, reappointed by the Major government. Such examples have added to the atmosphere of mistrust and unease about patronage. In general, though, it is hard to argue with the right of a government to set up, maintain and control a certain number of advisory committees. Political reformers would be wise to deal with the issue of national quangos on a case-by-case basis. Some need to be killed off; some need to be made directly accountable to Parliament; but many may be left safely alone.

There is, however, one further issue concerning unelected governance above the most local level, and that is the covert creation of regional administration. When Labour launched its ill-thought-out ideas for regional parliaments across England, these were rightly attacked by Tories for having little public support. But the other side to the story is the creation of unelected regional government, both through government agencies and through quangos. Thanks to direct rule, Northern Ireland has been the part of the UK most burdened by unelected government, though the Scottish Office also supervises a huge array of quangos. But the Urban Development Corporations in Birmingham, the Black Country, Bristol, Manchester, Leeds, London Docklands, Merseyside, Plymouth, Sheffield, Teesside, Trafford Park and Tyne and Wear, each run by appointees chosen by the Cabinet Office, the Department of the Environment and local authorities, show that the system is no stranger to England either. Then there are the regional health authorities, the regionally-managed regeneration budgets and the regional system of allocating funds from the EU. In 1994, the government appointed ten senior civil servants, in charge of some £4 billion of public money, to act as regional directors, with the task of coordinating regional spending for the Environment, Employment, Trade and Industry and Transport departments. It was an attempt to devolve administration out of Whitehall itself and nearer to the people already running quangos in the English regions, but the appointment of the seven men and three women, all civil service high-fliers in their forties or early fifties, led to criticism that a covert system of 'viceroys' was being put in place – they were also compared to Roman proconsuls, British Imperial district commissioners and French prefects.[23] MPs suggested that the 'viceroys' would need monitoring, and one, Peter Kilfoyle, the Labour Member for Liverpool Walton, complained that his region was being administered secretively: 'I cannot even discover how the structure works, and who gives the final nod.' While regional parliaments or assemblies for England may be an excessive reaction, the spread of 'good chaps' governance from Whitehall right across the country smells more of patronizing paternalism than a functioning democracy.

Local Quangos: above Politics?

Up and down the country, week after week, in the administrative offices of hospitals, in schools, in local business centres, in their own premises and in private houses, thousands of people gather privately to spend our money on training programmes, schools, colleges, hospitals and regeneration schemes. Decent types, most of them, no doubt, but their names are unknown to the wider public, their views and arguments are unreported and their stewardship is opaque. There is no central list of this new administrative class, but anecdotage from around the nation suggests that many are retired or part-time businessmen, often supporters or members of the local Conservative association, who find themselves helping to run education for youngsters, organize the clearing of land in town centres, oversee institutions for the mentally ill and reorganize the local hospital. Some business organizations are privately expressing worry about the time all this takes, and the justness of unelected power. 'I'm happy to give my time, but I don't want to be seen as some sort of unelected interloper', was one not untypical comment. And the quango-member with such qualms is right to worry: in many cases, it seems that government by appointment has replaced elected local government merely because Tory councillors have lost at the ballot box and Tory ministers didn't want to share power with councils run by opposition parties.

Where have all these bodies come from? The short answer is, from the final wave of radical Thatcherite reform in the late 1980s and early 1990s. In any historical investigation into our times, great attention ought to be paid to the Year of Hubris, more commonly known as 1988, the high water mark of Thatcherite triumphalism and swagger. It not only saw the poll tax on to the statute book, but produced the new-model housing associations, the NHS trusts, the Training and Enterprise Trusts, the Local Enterprise Trusts, and the grant-maintained schools. Trusts had been used much earlier in the Thatcher years, notably in housing and urban policy. But it was the explosion in their numbers after 1988 that changed things dramatically. They are part of the state, but a part that was designed specifically for the delivery of Conservative policies, established without the general prior acceptance which most successful new institutions require. They imply that hospitals, training programmes, housing associations and schooling are all properly dealt with outside politics, or perhaps above politics. Is this reasonable?

Hospitals

The NHS has never been a bastion of local control: there was a complex and centralized management structure from the first. It was Nye Bevan, its founding political father, who switched policy at a late stage in 1948, only weeks before the Bill was due to be published, and decided to nationalize the 1,771 English and Welsh local authority hospitals, and the 1,334 voluntary hospitals, an act which infuriated the Conservative opposition and persuaded it to vote against the Bill (something the party lived long to regret). Typical centralism: Bevan was a self-certain figure in a great hurry, who was spending much of his emotional energy in fighting the doctors' trade union, the BMA. Exactly forty years later, another self-certain man in a great hurry, who was also spending most of his energy fighting the BMA, proved to be as little concerned for local democracy as Bevan. Kenneth Clarke, the originator of the current NHS reform programme, has many qualities, but a tender regard for local autonomy has never been among them. Indeed, his views on local councillors are not quotable in a volume of light family entertainment like this one. Working under great pressure from Margaret Thatcher, he devised a split between provider institutions (including the 495 NHS trusts and the buyers of services – the eight regional health authorities, and the district health authorities – which are also part of the quango system) and GP fundholders (often, your local doctor). The involvement of local councillors through the old health authorities, that had been part of the original NHS, was abruptly terminated.

The new trusts have wide powers to employ staff on their own terms, to deal in land and property, borrow some money and invest as they see fit. Their eleven-strong boards run hospitals, community services, services for the mentally ill and ambulances. The chairmen are appointed by the Secretary of State and paid, as are the directors. The process of appointment is being opened up but a complex sequence of word-of-mouth, personal recommendation and vetting remains, as I write, at the heart of it. The new managers have not been quick to ingratiate themselves with the doctors or nurses. In one celebrated case, following earlier clashes, the chairman of the Homewood NHS Trust in Surrey, Roy Lilley, attacked doctors for being 'stuck in a Sir Launcelot Spratt mode, where they think they can storm into a ward and . . . everyone is terrified of them.' Doctors' duties to their patients should come third, after their duties to the organizations which employed them and their duty to get themselves properly trained, he added. In another case, early in 1995, Southampton University Hospitals Trust caused comment by doubling the salary of its chief executive to nearly £100,000, while rewarding five thousand staff for a record-breaking year with a £5 Boots gift voucher. You do not have to be a defender of the consultant culture to see a serious clash between the ethos of the private sector and of the NHS at work here.

As to the Trust chairmen's politics, there was an embarrassing outburst of frankness from the junior minister Baroness Denton in 1993 when she admitted, 'I can't remember knowingly appointing a Labour supporter.' She was at the DTI and dealing with other quangos but she later explained, 'You don't put in people who are in conflict with what you are trying to achieve. It's no good going on an NHS trust board if you don't believe in the policy that the Department of Health is pursuing.' The following year, the Labour Research Department reported that 120 NHS Trusts had members who were either Conservative Party members or on the boards of companies which had paid money to the party, while this was true of Labour people in only twenty trusts. Tories or their business supporters held the chairmanship of sixty-six trusts; only four chairmen or chairwomen were connected with the Labour Party. Of the other members, health professionals are appointed, but so, in the search for reliability, are many sturdy amateurs. One further example must stand for many others: on April Fool's Day, 1994, the Dartford and Gravesham NHS Trust in Kent began work with its five newly-appointed non-executive directors, whose job was to represent the public. They were Janet Dunn, wife of the local Tory MP; Kenneth Maw, a retired banker and Tory councillor; Malcolm Nothard, former Tory leader of the district council; Eileen Tuff, chairwoman of the local Conservative association; and Professor Michael Kelly, a cardiac specialist. Four paid-up Conservatives out of five.[24]

Many trusts will allow members of the public to come to meetings, but this is largely up to them – they are not subject to the requirement to let press and public into their meetings which was imposed on local authorities and some other bodies by a 1960 Act sponsored by a young backbencher called Margaret Thatcher. They report instead to a little-known Leeds-based body, the NHS Management Executive. Though, in Clarke's words, the trusts are intended to see 'decision making devolved as far as possible to local level', this emphatically does not involve locally-chosen representatives. The results of the trusts' work are immediate, and dramatic, ranging from new parking arrangements to new pay deals, the closure of wards and a host of other changes. These trusts are accountable – but only up to Whitehall. Locally, they are obscure and their members little-known. As Dr Paddy Ross, a Hampshire surgeon who opposed the reforms and left Britain to work in the West Indies put it, 'The Government was determined that all hospitals would become trusts irrespective of the view of the local population or the staff concerned.' This process has been well described as a species of Thatcherite nationalization.[25]

It has produced an NHS aware of its costs; but at a cost. There has been a grotesque rise in the number of bureaucrats and bitter accusations about profligacy. To take just one early and well-publicized case, the West Midlands regional health authority was attacked by MPs for wasting £10m thanks to 'serious shortcomings in the management, control and accountability' of services, and a senior civil servant described its behaviour as 'a shambles'. The market-mimicking system means that the various quangos running the NHS are judged on 'throughput' and are under pressure to pass patients about; and those most in danger of being 'dumped' are the chronically sick, long-term cases which are, as it were, unprofitable. In the longer term, there is a problem about mixing a market system, designed to encourage competition between units for cash, with the cooperative ethos of the old NHS which worked as a single entity. Although the official line was the Orwellian one that 'competition enhances cooperation' between hospitals, even ministers would speak privately of their bafflement about how such opposite cultures were supposed to be compatible. The logic of the system was clearly to privatize the providers of services, the hospitals and ambulance fleets. This 'hidden agenda' has been repeatedly and convincingly denied by the post-Thatcher Conservative leadership. But there was little doubt that the original Thatcherites had privatization and the much wider use of private medicine as an aim: in his memoirs, Nicholas Ridley, one of Lady Thatcher's closest confidants, says that she saw state provision in health and education 'as a free service necessary for those who could not afford higher standards, but she hoped that their numbers would dwindle as more and more families became able to afford to choose those higher standards in the private sector for themselves.'[26] But the post-Thatcher Tories regarded health privatization as a piece of logic too far. They were left with a half-commercialized system which lacked local accountability but was nevertheless to remain a central state service. At least the message to local authorities was nice and clear: as the eminent Tory councillor and former leader of Glasgow City Council, John Young, put it,

The members of NHS Trusts have to attend eleven meetings a year and get £5,000. That is more than most councillors get, and councillors can often give more than three hundred days a year. The leader of Strathclyde [then Europe's largest local authority] is paid less than his secretary and the leader of the City of Glasgow District Council gets little more than an office cleaner, and to my mind that's quite insulting.[27]

Training

There are some striking parallels in the development of training quangos. Like health, training is fundamental to a decent and prosperous future and is a public function largely run outside democratic control. It has rarely had much local democratic input, being run centrally from Whitehall for most of the post-war period. The situation today, dominated by the eighty-two Training and Enterprise Councils (TECs) and, in Scotland, the twenty-two Local Enterprise Companies (LECs), originated at almost the same time as the NHS Trusts. The TECs were introduced by Norman Fowler, a contemporary of Clarke's at Cambridge, and they depended on the same market-mimicking rhetoric as the health reforms. The hospitals had their purchaser-provider split: training, said Fowler, would depend on 'new partnerships . . . between employers and government, customers and providers.' The TECs buy and supervise training in their area, including a wide range of youth training services once run by the government itself. Some 1,200 businessmen and community leaders are involved, and nearly eight hundred companies have senior directors on TEC boards of between eight and sixteen members. They run annual budgets of between £4m and £55m – in total, they are responsible for a budget of some £3 billion.[28] They are private companies, spending public money, and they are not responsible to any regulatory body. The 1994 Conservative Campaign Guide asserted that in England and Wales the TECs 'are publicly accountable to local people.'

They do indeed hold annual public meetings, publish business plans and meet councillors. They are heavily audited by central government. But accountability generally implies some ability to discipline those spending public money. And, by that measure, TECs are certainly not accountable to the communities they serve: the survey cited already discovered not a single TEC that had recruited through open advertisement. Instead, they relied upon the chairman's personal contacts, 'networking' and recommendations from other board members. Or, to put it more succinctly, the golf club. One historian described the situation in pre-modern Britain: 'Before the nineteenth century a good many local agencies were . . . "close" or "select", that is, they were oligarchies . . . who continually renewed their hold on office by a process of co-optation.'[29] It is not an entirely cheap point to ask how far the system of the 1990s differs from that of the 1790s. There is another reason for being worried about this way of running training. The most persuasive modern economists argue that national prosperity depends heavily on the local and regional level where, ideally, many similar small companies are competing to excel in local specialisms – textiles, or watchmaking, or electronics or whatever – and are thus able to develop into world-class centres. For this to work well, as it does in Northern Italy, most of Germany and much of France, it is important that the local banking, training and educational infrastructures are working efficiently together for the benefit of the local lead industries. That does imply an element of golf-club networking, but it also suggests that there needs to be a bigger and more open local strategy, involving schools and colleges and planners, than can be provided by TECs and LECs alone.

Housing

Another form of quango spending large sums of public money locally is the housing association – ancient institutions whose public role has been transformed by Conservative governments' determination to get them to take on the role of public housing once provided largely through local authorities. The relevant act (1988 again) was described by the National Federation of Housing Associations. It was intended to roll back 'the frontiers of council housing to allow privatization in an area previously thought to be sacrosanct: and gives housing associations the opportunity to replace local authorities . . .' Well, why not?

One of the greatest successes of early Thatcherism was to give council house owners the right to buy; and one of the biggest stains on local democracy has been the stinking, inhuman or sometimes just dreary public housing that was provided from the fifties onwards. Though local authorities began relatively recently to provide neighbourhood offices, through most of the post-war period the distance between the town hall and the housing estate seemed too great to provide a sense of common ownership by tenants. There was too little community pride. This may have been partly because of brutalist architecture and lousy administration, but it was also to do with ownership. Not everyone, though, either could or wanted to buy their flat or house.

The first attempt at dealing with this had come in 1986–87 and was not one of Nicholas Ridley's better ideas. Housing Action Trusts, or HATs, were meant to transfer ownership of a housing estate from the local authority to a private landlord or a housing association, with central government offering taxpayers' money to renovate the homes as part of the deal. But for this to happen the tenants had to vote in favour; and the combination of the words 'private landlord' and Margaret Thatcher was enough to put off most council tenants from considering the idea. This was so despite a rigged voting system; many council tenants in the relevant areas had seen private developers moving in around them and, in the Yuppie boom years, didn't like the results. Others felt that a government whose welfare and employment policies were impoverishing them couldn't possibly have their best interests at heart. At any rate, HATs never took off. Nearly a decade after the late Nicholas Ridley had thought the idea up, only four are operating.

Turning directly to housing associations to try to rebuild a sense of genuine common interest and ownership was a reaction to the failure. It is hard to argue that this is an area where the rights of town hall democracy must be paramount, particularly given their record. Every member of a community has a common interest in local hospitals, the environment, transport and schools. But this is not so clearly the case with housing, except where the common interest in offering decent accommodation to the poorest and most helpless comes in. There is, though, one familiar problem: it again involves the spending of large sums of taxpayers' money without local political accountability – taxes which once went to the town hall now go to private housing associations. Today these have nearly 900,000 houses, get around £3 billion a year from the taxpayer and, in the six years after the act, invested some £8.5 billion in new housing. The author of the most recent investigation into their accountability noted that,

Housing associations, unlike some other publicly funded bodies, are not under a contractual obligation to hold public meetings, or to make copies of their annual reports or corporate plans widely available. However, it is clear that about half the respondents hold regular [public or semi-public] meetings.[30]

So half don't. MPs speak with despair about the quality of management in some inner-city housing associations. In the housing association world the biggest worry is the pressure on their board members, who are heavily audited by central government and have financial liabilities in a more entrepreneurial system, yet are unpaid and under-trained. If, one day, a national scandal breaks out in the booming housing association movement then, Reader, don't be too surprised.

Schools

But it is the arrival of quangos in the educational system, particularly for schools, that has caused the most public discussion, with the possible exception of the Hospital Trusts mentioned above. Local management of schools, giving them much more autonomy from the council, has been widely welcomed. But the core of political controversy centres on the one thousand or so grant-maintained schools which have so far opted out of local control altogether. They are supposed to be the forerunners for the whole taxpayer-funded secondary schooling system. Parents ballot to take 'their' school – more properly, the school in which their children were being taught for a certain time –

out of local political control, and get higher funding from central political control in return. This is reminiscent of the deal offered to tenants of HATs – money for improvements in return for opting out of local authority ownership – and has been similarly opposed by local campaigns, often led by Labour councillors.

If it opts out, the school is then controlled by its governors and, in strategic terms, by a new quango, the York-based Funding Agency for Schools (FAS). Over time, the idea is that this national quango will take over authority for more and more schools. It starts by working alongside the local education authorities, but only, like a pushy new executive, to elbow them out. Eventually, it takes total control over the provision of places. It will be able to close schools, enlarge them, propose a change in their character and open new schools without any reference to local wishes. Together with the Secretary of State's new powers, these have been described by one free-market academic analyst as

an extraordinary range of dictatorial powers . . . The minister will have authority similar to Henry VIII's dissolution commissioners: he and his officials will be empowered to rove across the country drawing up plans for reorganizing schools to eliminate surplus places, and to impose these without the need to take account of the views of parents, schools or local authorities.[31]

The idea originated in the Education Reform Act (of . . . Year of Hubris, 1988) and was given a further push, because of its failure to catch on, in 1992. Again, the individual opted-out schools are run by bodies of unelected and self-appointing boards who are under no legal obligation to heed the wishes of parents, never mind of the wider local community. The boards deal with the FAS and the Education Secretary and consult parents but can ignore them.

There is merit in moving away from direct local education authority control – the headteachers and governors of schools that have broken away and run themselves show little desire to move back under the wing of the town hall. Nor are school governors generally turning out to be the subservient tools of ministerial diktat: when, in the spring of 1995, a furore arose over school budgets, it was the school governors of Oxfordshire who led the revolt, threatening to set illegal budgets. This led to the prospect of governors, including parent-governors, who are meant to be the apolitical good guys of the Tory reforms, being sacked by the local authorities who were supposed to have been the 'political' bad guys of the story, on the orders of ministers responsible for the reforms. But the resulting belly-laugh is not an adequate response to the core political issue. Governors are spending not their own money, not borrowed money, but taxpayers' money; and they are making decisions on behalf of towns, estates, villages and shires, without being accountable to them. The diffusion of responsibility in the education system effectively destroys the clarity which democratic accountability depends on. The point was made forcibly in 1993 by the Commons Education Select Committee:

The problem that faces us is that it is impossible to know which authority to hold accountable for any shortcoming in educational provision or use of resources. Should a parent aggrieved because the roof of his child's classroom leaks blame the governing body of the school for spending too much on (say) teachers' salaries and too little on repairs and maintenance? Or should he blame the LEA (Local Education Authority) for spending money on town halls and public relations rather than on the schools budget? Or is it the fault of the Secretary of State for the Environment in allocating insufficient revenue support grant or preventing the authority from levying the community charge or the council tax at the necessary level? Or the Secretary of State for Education for refusing to let the LEA borrow for capital spending?[32]

Yet ministers want to have it neither way. They neither want to admit that they are themselves then responsible for the performance of schools which are controlled through central quangos; nor to accept that there is anything 'political' for local communities to express a view on. Norman Tebbit has argued that 'education no more needs political control than does the provision of groceries'.[33] But this is false. These schools are public bodies: their budgets and intake are public matters, controlled centrally by national government; what they teach is also laid down centrally; and their performance, whether over truancy or educational standards, is a matter of public concern, both locally and nationally. Successive central governments have identified educational failure as central to Britain's relative economic decline. Where public money is being spent on public concerns, it is ultimately absurd to say that public policy – that is, politics – has no place. Nor is the new system necessarily producing stronger powers for parents. The idea behind the system is that parents can exercise choice as consumers rather than voters – they can move schools and allow the market to dictate change as the funding follows the pupil. But since the FAS, run by bureaucrats, is also intended to keep spare capacity to a minimum this is bound to be a nonsense: to have choice you need to tolerate some waste. No one denies that it is good to see local schools have more power over their own day-to-day running and use of their budgets. That has been a Conservative success. But the big stuff, including what they teach, where and how, and how much money they have . . . all that is now securely in the hands of anonymous quangos, cut off from the lives of the communities they serve. And that is a Conservative failure.

The Arc of Bureaucracy

So welcome to the 'patronage state'. Quangos cannot be properly scrutinized by the local newspapers. They began their lives with a closed culture. This secrecy, combined with the huge amounts of money involved and the strongly pro-Conservative bias of the appointment system has sent up the stink of suspicion against what the Labour Peer Baroness Hollis has called a cosy circle of perk and privilege. Scandals have emerged in many parts of the country; others are doubtless hiding in the darkness. The minister-appointed or self-appointed members of this vast network of unelected power have been dubbed 'the new magistracy', a conscious echo of the old magistracy of local worthies swept away by local democracy in the Victorian period. At local level, it has been estimated that there were in 1994 up to

63,120 non-elected 'new magistrates' as against just over 25,000 elected local councillors. The reorganization of local govern-ment into single tiers would strip away the ranks of the latter still further, while the arrival of new police authorities with appointed members will make the imbalance still worse in the years ahead. If things carry on like this, there won't be enough members of the Conservative Party — as we have seen, a dwindling band — to staff all the jobs the unelected state has for them. (Perhaps it would be sensible to offer them overtly as an incentive to join — buy a party card and win an NHS Trust chairmanship.) Reacting to public anger, John Major's 'chief of staff' in 1995 announced that the government would try to cast its net wider to find people of expertise and public spirit through advertising and so on. This represented an advance, certainly: but you don't turn an unelected administrator into an elected administrator simply because you find him, or her, through a newspaper advert.

And there is a bigger pattern. What unites these quango-run areas of policy — the schools, the urban clearance programmes, the hospitals and mental health services, the housing trusts, the training schemes? They are all indisputably local things, about which central government is often necessarily and inevitably ignorant. The man from Whitehall cannot know the best way to train people in a particular area — what jobs are available, which employers are most experienced, what is likely to happen to the local economy. He can't know about the details of local health care, nor about the culture of individual schools, however often he sends inspectors in from outside. And, what's more, the government has already admitted that it is ignorant, which is why it appointed tens of thousands of local quangocrats in the first place. Ministers didn't put it quite like that, of course. Kenneth Clarke didn't get up in the House of Commons and say, 'Well, guys, let's admit it, none of us have the faintest clue about hospitals, we've made a complete bog of it, so we're going to hand them over to local folks who might do better.' That is not the political way. They talked about 'the efficient delivery of services' instead. In fact, though, all this passing down of administrative power from the central bureaucracy was admission of incompetence – overdue and tacit, but greatly to be welcomed, nevertheless. But the ministeriate didn't have the courage to hand down the political power as well. They tried to devolve the work, while keeping the control. They recognized that unelected quangos couldn't be given utter freedom, so they piled on the national controls, still exercised privately through Whitehall. They managed to combine a lack of democracy with bureaucratic inertia, the worst of both worlds. So the effect has been most odd.

It is easiest to see if one imagines a pound leaving the pocket of the individual and joining all the other taxes from his or her local community. The pounds are passed up the system to the Inland Revenue, then to the Treasury and then to various departments – Health, Environment, Employment – before falling back towards the taxpayer again, first via intermediate bodies like the Funding Agency for Schools or the Housing Corporation, and then to the quangos. Because this is public money, and the central government system wants to keep its authority, a complex and onerous system of bureaucracy follows the money downwards from Whitehall. (Almost all quangos complain of the multiplication of forms and the persistence of officials from their funding agencies.) Then whatever is left of the money is spent, locally, right beside the taxpayer who started the process, on his or her health care, training, housing or whatever. The pound has, as it were, passed high into the air, disappeared into a large centralized bureaucracy, and fallen to earth again nearby (or some of it has – pennies from heaven).

The arc upwards is golden, the arc downwards is dark with audit and bureaucracy. But what is missing? Obviously, any local political say. It is, on the face of it, an extraordinary way to spend money, for the state to gather it all up, pass it around, eventually confess that it doesn't really know how to spend it, and then pass it back, but only to be spent by people who are locally anonymous, and operate in small discrete groups, pursuing a relatively narrow agenda, and divorced from any more general debate about local priorities. The commonsense thing to do would seem to be to raise the money near at hand and then spend it locally, too, after a discussion at the level of the town, estate or village as to what the priorities were. Or would it?

Local Oppression; Local Revival

The trouble is, local government on the traditional model has had such a rotten record. Far too often for comfort, wherever one party is firmly embedded in power, political incompetence, arrogance and even outright corruption have followed. The allegations about the cynical use of council flat sales in Tory-run Westminster borough to create loyal Conservative-voting areas were among the worst levelled at any British politicians in the early nineties. Even that, however, was put into the shade by the failure of the nearby London borough of Islington, under Labour control, to stop suspected paedophiles and child-abusers attacking children in council care. Journalists from the London *Evening Standard* uncovered the massive scandal after a tip-off about a boy who had endured months of violent buggery. Yet, despite more than sixty articles and a stream of inquiries, the allegations about the experiences of many other children were dismissed by the then council leader Margaret Hodge (later a Labour MP) as 'a sensationalist piece of gutter journalism'. She later said she had been misled by Islington Council officers and denied that a culture of 'political correctness', which frightened people from making complaints about homosexual staff, was to blame for the council's unforgivably lazy and smug behaviour.

This Islington story was unusually horrific. We will probably never know how many vulnerable people were wounded for life by what happened in those children's homes. But the failure of councillors to keep a proper eye on their sprawling local empires is not unusual. Nor is the existence of a smug, defensive culture when one party enjoys unchallenged local dominance. British local government has in recent years been disfigured by arrogant and incompetent officialdom, unchecked by effective politicians and seemingly beyond the easy reach of local voters. The patronage state, however, isn't the answer. The problem of out-of-control bureaucracies is not, as we shall see, limited to local government. Nor is corruption there unanswered by sleaze higher up. We would be outraged were anyone to suggest that a series of scandals in Parliament, and Whitehall abuses of power, meant that democracy had failed and should be replaced by a permanent ruling committee appointed by the Queen. It is no more attractive to use the blights on local government as a reason for closing it down. Indeed, as I have suggested, the stripping-away of local powers discourages good people from going into local politics and helps undermine its effectiveness. What is needed is a mix of reforms, including annual voting; perhaps directly-elected mayors or provosts; the decentralisation and contracting-out of services; the referendums discussed earlier; and a vigorous, aggressive local press.

We must, in short, repair and restore our near-at-hand democracy, not shrug and leave it to disappear. Reforms to the current local authorities would, however, only be the start. There is growing and irrefutable evidence of the rise of a new kind of community politics in Britain, a phenomenon which is both important and largely ignored when we talk about 'politics'. This local activity fails to follow the conventions that stimulate the national media – the political parties are only vaguely involved, or not involved; it is unglamorous; it throws up no nationally-known leaders or personalities; it is confusing. The array of self-help groups, community schools, neighbourhood schemes, voluntary organizations and devolved local authorities that have started to criss-cross housing estates, boroughs and villages are beyond the imagination of Westminster. They are baggy and ordinary and seem shapeless, even meaningless, to those used to national parties and parliamentary careers. Only rare outsider-politicians, like the Liberal Democrat leader Paddy Ashdown, whose book *Beyond Westminster*[34] described examples of it, have really noticed the change.

Yet those who have looked have been astonished by the pullulating activity going on, as it were, 'below' the level of the town halls. There are community schools, urban villages, self-help groups of all kinds, neighbourhood patrols, housing cooperatives and associations, credit unions, local campaigning organizations, all of them meaning more to many middle- and working-class communities than traditional politics has realized. This is reminiscent of the Liberal dream of twenty or thirty years ago of 'a society with an infinity of centres of power, expressing the principles of mutual aid and mutual cooperation . . .'[35] But things have changed since then. Shifting employment patterns, higher levels of information technology, a wider awareness of the failures of centralized state (and town hall) bureaucracy and the growing ideology of 'community' have tilted the atmosphere further back towards the local. And, as that happens, there are just the first, faint signs of national politics taking note. On the left, for instance, the think-tank, the Institute for Public Policy Research, produced a report on self-help groups in 1995 which described a renaissance of such activity at the end of the twentieth century coming at:

a time of crisis and reappraisal for post-war welfarism, and with a time of diminishing public confidence in traditional representative democracy. It can be seen as a response to the failure of centralism and paternalism, two powerful tendencies which have helped to shape Western welfare democracies.[36]

On the surface, that analysis from the left is strikingly similar to much thinking from the right. David Green of the freemarket Institute of Economic Affairs, in a pamphlet mourning the death of the Friendly Societies and the pre-Welfare State network of mutual insurance and medical aid, wrote that the answer might involve 'leaving as little as possible to central government, and as much as possible to localities, financed by local taxes with free movement of people, goods and money to allow wide experimentation . . .' and called for more voluntarism and mutual aid outside the state.[37] Peter Lilley, the radical Tory Social Security Secretary, raised the possibility of passing responsibility for some welfare provision down the line, perhaps to local councillors, perhaps to some other local bodies. Occupying the new political ground known as 'communitarianism', writers like Dick Atkinson, who has worked in the ten-thousand-strong community village of Balsall Heath in Birmingham, share a general fed-upness with centralised services. He too finds 'a remarkably complex, vibrant life of mutual help and civic activity' across Britain and sees it as a reaction to the failures of centralism:

Much of the structure of the modern state has been shaped by a steady nationalization of power. Instead of local or regional health services we have a national health service. Instead of local agencies with some discretion over welfare, we have national, standardized systems that find it easier to distribute resources than to find the means for self-reliance. And, increasingly, instead of local government we have agencies working under contract for Whitehall.[38]

Something is stirring in the shrubbery. We have a left-right-centre reappraisal of the importance of localism, and the failures of centralism, coming at the same time as a growth in community organizations of all kinds. Where does this lead? Not, clearly, to a Britain of happy urban peasants in self-ruling communes. Any passing of power and money to small organizations will be a slow, ragged and complicated process, particularly while they lack strong advocacy at the political centre. Nor does it lead to political consensus there, or anything like it. The left, right and centre have profound differences to argue through about the nature and culture of local politics; the scope of transfers of wealth; whether any body smaller than the state can or should combat gross inequalities, and so on. The apparent agreement marked out above looks like the beginning of something new in the politics of the local: but it represents the start of fresh debates, not the end of argument. All that said, there are glimmerings of a rebirth of the local in a way that hasn't happened since the heyday of municipal activism nearly a century ago.

And a rebirth is needed: the only alternative left to us now is the quango system, designed to allow deferential and untroublesome local activity while keeping as much power as possible with the Court Party in London. The scandals about trips on Concorde, cars, perks and waste, and the taunts about patronage are inevitable effects of the state's attempt to keep its hands on power that it doesn't deserve. The system isn't only offensive, but can be just as wasteful as the worst local councils; the twelve urban development corporations set up as early as 1981 by Michael Heseltine, spent more than £30,000 to create each of the 162,000 jobs they brought to inner-city Britain. That is three times as much as regional programmes spend to create jobs and government-sponsored research suggested that, often, two out of every three jobs 'created' had simply been moved from a neighbouring area not covered by the programme. Some UDCs, such as Birmingham Heartlands, spent much more – more than £48,000 per job in that case – while Merseyside splashed out £400,000 on a concert to celebrate the five hundredth anniversary of Columbus.[39] This is just the kind of misbehaviour local authorities were lambasted for ten years earlier.

But the cost of government by quango is not to be measured primarily in pounds. The triumph of this system would have serious effects for almost anyone who pays taxes or uses local services, which is almost everyone. It is no good saying that greater parent involvement in a school managing board, or the involvement of local businessmen in inner-city redevelopment, or of party-political worthies on police committees, closes the democratic gap left by the decline of local councils. Modern life is complex enough without it becoming even harder to discover just who is responsible for local services – who can be blamed, or written to, who can be sacked, or praised. In the past, we may have tut-tutted about the local big wheels who carved up council contracts, bought land which was shortly to be developed, and got their children into the best schools. But at least there was the chance of their being exposed in the council chamber and kicked out of office. Before, admittedly, most of us didn't actually know who was running what in our area (though more people go to councillors with their problems than any other group). Now, though, we take it for granted that we don't know, and probably can't find out. All this has been happening at a time when many other locally-based utilities –water, gas, electricity – have passed into private hands, introducing the same values, and rows about salary levels and perks, into the politics and local newspapers of towns and counties across Britain. Though the two processes, privatization and quango-ization, are different, their effects and impact are not so dissimilar when the privatized utility has a monopoly, just like the TEC and the NHS Trust does. Monopolies are not susceptible to consumer power. We are back to Sir Kingsley Amis's sodded public.

Authority at the local level is an important fixture in our lives, something to hang on to, inveigh against, telephone or petition. When the local centres of power are made obscure and slippery, the individual loses a certain purchase on society. The citizen mentally shrugs, feeling that 'they' have won another of their mysterious victories. This has been going on remorselessly, year after year. Since 1979, there have been more than 150 Acts of Parliament diminishing the powers of local authorities, while some £24 billion of spending a year has been shifted to quangos. There has been little public debate about this huge shift, though it is belatedly beginning. It has not featured in Conservative manifestos or in party political broadcasts. It has not been proclaimed in ministerial speeches. Contrary to the professed intentions and prejudices of the party in power, this quiet anti-democratic revolution has 'just happened'. Lacking any firm philosophy of local government, the Conservatives did not have the foresight or will to prevent the disorientating consequences of policies they intended to be liberating. It is a shaming failure. We once drew much of our national energies, for construction and reform, from our local democracy. We deserve a little better than the democratic ruins today's national politicians have left us.

CHAPTER THREE

Westminster

O! Sordid den beneath whose Spires
Dull squinting Squires from Cloudy Shires
Contest th'Accounts which Publick work requires
And not all Ministers prove knaves and liars . . .
– T. Kavanagh, from 'Phoebus', 1827

All nations, all political systems, need theatre. Unless the rituals
and contests of power are at times acted out openly where
people can see them, democracy must fail. Unless the state's
principles are embodied in well-known places and events, and
unless the struggle between competing groups and rival ideas is
made flesh in known individuals, whether loved or hated, then
the whole business of government becomes too abstract to
engage the attention and commitment of the people. Our
theatre is the House of Commons and it is a finer theatre than
almost any other. During the eighties and nineties, as in many
previous periods, it has provided a tumultuous cascade of spec-
tacle, from the emotional debates on the Falklands War, to the
Westland crisis, the Howe and Lawson resignations, the fall of
Thatcher, the knife-edge votes over Maastricht, the stripping of
the Tory whip from dissident MPs, the confrontations between
Blair and Major. It has seen political assassinations, dramatic
expositions of belief, gentle accusations of betrayal and sour
declarations of support. On key issues, such as the single currency, it has seen excellent probing and challenging of quite
difficult arguments and the teasing-out of nuances and subtleties
in a refined and wholly serious way.

So in what follows now, a largely hostile critique of the
Commons today, I do not forget the importance and value of
the human melodrama it provides – the sick-looking faces
of ministers as they listen to resignation speeches from their

colleagues, the foaming wave of order-papers as votes are won and lost, the glimpses of backbenchers being harried by whips, the revealing body-language of Cabinet ministers as they sit squashed together on the front bench. I do not forget the lucid arguments, the shrewdly probing questions, the occasional genuinely sophisticated speeches. This is not mere democratic pageantry, or bad acting (though sometimes it's both) but the living and unpredictable story of power, transmitted contemporaneously to the living-rooms of millions of those affected by it. Ministers can, and do, make fools of themselves in front of the whole country. Opposition politicians hit home, or miss the point. Disgruntled local MPs deliver highly public and embarrassing rebukes. The immediacy of Parliament remains its single greatest asset. The Commons still dominates television and radio news bulletins, spreads itself across the front pages of newspapers and provides a vivid focus for the country's satirists, comics and novelists. Never in human history has part of a system of representative government been so exposed to so many people so regularly. This is a great thing, and a part of Parliament we must value and strengthen. No other European or American democracy has the silliness of our main chamber. But none of them has its virility either.

Self-congratulation is therefore in order. But that will do. For the most worrying single truth about the Westminster way is that this turbulent national drama has lost its capacity to really engage many millions of us. There is a glittering, splashy surface of crisis and resignation, confrontation and scandal. Below it, though, the public seem less interested than before, recording huge depths of cynicism and indifference about the views and actions of politicians. The parliamentary events are dramatic enough, in their own terms, and sometimes make good television. But they don't seem to connect strongly to other events. And as the surface activity has grown ever-more frenetic, with sexual and financial 'sleaze' and inter-party rows bubbling and erupting frequently, so that our remaining interest in Parliament is becoming tinged by distaste. And, despite its dramatic qualities, Parliament has become incompetent and irrelevant across many of its central functions. MPs rage at the loss of power to Brussels. But what is truly staggering is their own complacency and ineffectiveness when it comes to defending and servicing their central institution in its day-to-day existence.

It is not as if they themselves haven't noticed that something is wrong. Politicians go where power is. They have a third nostril, denied to the rest of us, which smells it out. At Westminster, they go through underpasses to ministerial offices. They queue up at Millbank, the refurbished Edwardian offices of the BBC, ITN and Sky News across the road from Parliament. They go, because they have to, to the committee corridor, where a coffee-trolley provides the only relief to sitting through dull deliberations on Bills. The alert ones get over to Brussels, and sometimes Washington; those who are ministers spend much of their time travelling abroad. In the mornings the Tories in particular go east to the City to find out about 'the real world'. But politicians go less and less to the chamber of the House of Commons. Granted, they turn up for the set-piece 'will the government fall?' occasions. Yes, most turn up for the twice-weekly bout of Prime Minister's questions, a kind of Punch-and-Punch show. It is one of the fixed social points in the political week. But when it comes to the pre-arranged debates, either on bills or on motions, then, as often as not, the casual visitor would be shocked to find that a chamber which cannot properly accommodate half the 650 elected Members looks ludicrously large for the score or so who have bothered to turn up. Are the absentees trying to tell us something?

Members of Parliament are the only constitutional link between the individual and the government, the human gate through which all complaint, interrogation and frustration must pass. We have already looked at the decline in the position of the voter, the local party and local government. We will turn in due course to the centre of traditional political power, the state itself. But if this corridor between people and state is not functioning freely and successfully, if it is not transmitting the views of the former to the latter, and correcting the behaviour of the rulers in accordance with the requirements of the ruled, then the whole system has failed at its most important link.

Let's start with the façade, the actual place. We are then going to go further in, scraping the immediate and familiar images away. But it is generally a mistake to ignore the obvious and tangible. Whatever its place in the real constitution, Parliament is also its own image – the building, the history. Like other Royal palaces, the democratic palace also maintains the formalities of power; this Gate too is guarded by suspicious policemen. Tourists cluster like crabs at Members' Entrance to watch the ministerial limousines whoosh in. Those who want to watch the MPs clash in a chamber not so different from the one in which Gladstone struggled with Disraeli, where Lloyd George spouted silvery derision and Churchill rumbled defiance, must patiently queue outside for hours, like humble petitioners at the portcullis. A century or so ago, visitors could come and go with relative ease, but in the 1880s Irish Fenian revolutionaries and Suffragette protesters gave the authorities the excuses that authorities always seek to close things off, erect barriers, turn people away. The IRA threat from the seventies onwards produced another lurch in the effective closure of the democratic temple to the people; and if peace continues to unfold in Northern Ireland there is little reason to hope that the buildings will become easier to enter. If there is one law of modern employment, it is that there is never a slump in the security business.

For most of its history after the Settlement of 1688, the Palace of Westminster has been the familiar club and talking-shop of a score or two of great families whose wealth, interests and rituals dominated Georgian and Victorian politics. It looks the part. The current edifice came a couple of generations before the mass franchise, or anything like it. In 1834, an older and chaotic collection of palace buildings was largely burned down amid great scenes of glee – it was the era before 'heritage' and, according to one observer, 'the jokes and radicalism were universal. If Ministers had heard the shrewd sense and intelligence of these drunken remarks!'[1] The old buildings were replaced by the current awesome structure, half-cathedral, half-grand country house. The palace, like its political function, echoes with ironies. This most aristocratic of buildings came about through free and open competition. It was chosen by modernizing City politicians who thought of themselves as landed countrymen. And this emblem of imperial world power, made possible by the factory system and naval force, was designed by spiritual dreamers, would-be medievalists. Physically, its scale and beauty, all Sir Charles Barry's rippling fantasies in soft yellow Yorkshire stone, the hierarchies of glass and slate and marble, are intended to overwhelm, rather than to reassure.

Politically too, Parliament has been a chameleon-institution, representing in succession kingly power, baronial power, the power of the aristocratic landed classes, the power of the Puritan revolution, the power of the industrial classes and the imperial civil service, and the power of the modern state. But it has rarely been a populist institution: whenever *demos* raised its hydra-heads, during the peasant and urban rebellions, or when democrats emerged among the Cromwellian soldiery, or when radicals, Chartists, Irish men and English women challenged during the past two centuries, Parliament has been solidly with the institutions of the Old Establishment on the other side. After the Second World War, Pathé newscasters took to describing it as the Parliament of a 'people's democracy' and today we may lazily think of 'parliamentary democracy' as a single concept. But parliamentary government – a sort of diffused and legalized absolutism – preceded parliamentary democracy by fully 250 years, and in many ways it is the absolutism, not the democracy, which remains the dominant influence in modern Britain.

It was a fanatical invalid Victorian writer, Albert Venn Dicey, who raised the doctrine of parliamentary sovereignty to its greatest height: 'Under all the formality, the antiquarianism, the shams of the British constitution, there lies an element of power which has been the true source of its life and growth. This secret source of strength is the absolute omnipotence, the sovereignty of Parliament.'[2] From the aristocratic age to the democratic one, he squeaked happily, the sacred, secret essence was unchanged: Parliament was omnipotent. Dicey, though, was confusing the institution which represented and justified power, with that interesting substance itself. Parliamentary sovereignty, or legal authority, was once the cloak behind which land-owning and business power operated its deal with the crown. In our century, it has been the cloak behind which the modern state has swollen and grown without overly alarming or shocking the people. It has delivered the assent of whatever portion of the nation needed to be kept on board – a portion which grew and grew until the final extension of the franchise. It has been a vital pressure-valve as one regime was replaced by another. But it has not therefore been the source of the power that the various forms of British government possessed.

In our age, those who competed to run the state organized themselves on the basis of mass parties, which effectively became part of the real constitution. The true power-dealers, the party leaderships, like the old ones, could conveniently slip below the old, glittering surface of 'Parliamentary sovereignty'. Agreements based on handshakes between Liberal intellectuals and union bosses, legislation based on the convictions of half a dozen key Tory leaders, and then implemented by party power, rigorously enforced, have been presented to the outside world as 'the will of Parliament', conjuring up confused but reassuring images of Cromwell, Pitt and Runnymede. The Commons has been a constitutional wand, able to transform the private party deal into something sweeping and inclusive, 'the people's will'. Or, as the Labour MP and academic Tony Wright has put it,

The model of disciplined parties using the opportunities afforded by a 'flexible' constitution to press their ideological purposes on the basis of transient electoral victories was a million miles away from Dicey's description of a constitution made democratic by a particular relationship between Commons and people. Yet Dicey's account of the constitution had opened a door through which others could eagerly and effortlessly pass.[3]

And pass they did. And now we are left with a yellow palace on a mudbank which is many things – legislative factory, television backdrop, collection of offices – but whose democratic parentage is at best doubtful and whose true significance is increasingly a matter for debate. What happens if and when the sources of power, the key interests, are no longer represented by politicians in the Commons? If, for instance, power moves to the European Union, or the global market? What does 'Parliamentary sovereignty' add up to then? It represents, at best, the right to say no, to withdraw, to justify a confrontation with whatever source of new power exists outside Parliament. As we shall see later, this seems an increasingly abstract and even unreal power. For certain people, parliamentary sovereignty is becoming something reassuring to suck when things look bad, the mental equivalent of a boiled sweet. If Parliament is powerful at a particular time, well then it is: if it no longer controls or connects to the sources of power, and is unwilling to shake the economic system by asserting its political authority, then to murmur happily that 'our Parliament is sovereign' is sloppy to the point of being meaningless.

The building itself still weaves a special spell, to be sure; once inside, the sheer weight of old stone arches and glittering mosaics and gilt wood, guarded by half-remembered statesmen's statues, presses down heavily upon those passing underneath. Its procedures and oddities accumulated over time – here, some lines painted on the floor of the chamber at two swords' length to prevent bloodshed during debate; there, paragraphs of debating rules introduced during the Irish Home Rule struggles of the 1880s – also murmur, continuity, integrity, accumulated wisdom, stored national power. These things particularly affect those working at Westminster, despite their pretence of worldly metropolitan sophistication when showing constituents and country cousins around. But this impression is a delusion. Outside, the place is taken ever less seriously. It is becoming ever more like a museum – the V&A of our political culture – and ever less powerful. Here is merely one institution among many, bobbing about on the tides of political and economic change. It is not magically sealed off from shifts in power around it, and it never was. In a world in which sovereigns are no longer sovereign, to call the British Parliament sovereign has become a way of avoiding uncomfortable questions about its practical power.

Inside the Palace

Having nodded at Parliament's ambiguous history – a long and magnificent sneer in stone – we can now enter the institution itself. And having done so we can mentally, at least, put to one side at least half of the huge palace, because it contains an institution so hopelessly anti-democratic and relatively powerless that it cannot be taken seriously in this account of the democracy. Though its origins go back to Anglo-Saxon times, the Lords has been in decline for so long that no one can remember when, or if, it was ever virile. The Victorian writer Walter Bagehot noted in the 1860s that the Lords was basically frightened of the rest of the country and because of that had only 'a sort of hypothetical veto' on the elected Commons: 'The House has ceased to be one of latent directors, and has become one of temporary rejectors and palpable alterers.'[4] And so it still is today. A few years later, Bagehot was declaring that the notion of aristocratic leadership 'is utterly dead' and ridiculing the idea that such a 'dully Conservative assembly' would be able to make itself popular again.[5] The notion of aristocratic leadership is no more popular today, and the Lords is scarcely less Conservative – at the beginning of 1994, there were 475 Tory peers and 275 crossbenchers, against a mere 115 Labour and 56 Liberal Democrats. Defeats inflicted on Tory governments in the Lords still tend to be victories of one type of conservative over another. Bagehot thought that the Lords would not be abolished –'Its danger is not in assassination, but in atrophy; not abolition, but decline' – and he has been right about that.

Let no one say that we British rush headlong to reform. The Lords came nearest to abolition as recently as 1911 after its confrontation with the reforming Liberal administration. Then its powers were further pruned back and the relevant act promised that, 'Whereas it is intended to substitute for the House of Lords as it at present exists a second chamber constituted on a popular instead of a hereditary basis . . .' But, despite occasional efforts, notably by the Labour politician Richard Crossman in 1968, nothing has ever been done to produce a second elected chamber. Even after the arrival of non-hereditary or 'life' peers in 1958, it remains, in central respects, much as it did in the Victorian era. Because of that, the Lords, despite its quite frequent anti-government rebellions, has its votes overturned with ruthless and unthinking regularity by modern administrations. Its committees produce reports which are intellectually admirable and which occasionally hit the headlines. It performs a modestly useful role in pointing out obvious errors and technical flaws in legislation, and in introducing subjects which the elected Commons is too timid to touch. Perhaps more significantly still, in its role as the highest court in England, it has become markedly more liberal in recent years. But its influence over policy is feeble and its debates, often fine, are rarely reported. Its ageing and feeble stars wink weakly in the constitutional murk. Labour again promise radical reform of the place, taking voting rights away from hereditary peers; but its aristocratic atrophy has lasted for so long that the old place almost begs for the application of the humane killer.

That won't be so easy. The Lords issue is likely to become live again if Labour win another election and try, not only to reform the Upper House, but to implement a Scottish Parliament. One senior Tory leader told me that he believed that with only 100 Opposition Conservative MPs and the House of Lords on his side, he could destroy the first two years of a Labour administration which dedicated itself to Scottish Home Rule. In that, the Lords would be essential because of their constitutional conservativism and residual powers of delay and amendment. Such a plan, if it came about, could not but make the Upper House highly controversial, just as it was before the First World War. But could it be destroyed? Ideas for its reform range from Labour's plan to limit voting and speaking to the life peers, who are the appointees of the political parties to the more thorough-going proposals for the creation of a directly elected second chamber, a sort of British senate, perhaps with elections by proportional representation held every seven years. The trouble with a minimal reform, though, is that it would merely entrench party patronage; while the use of any electoral system to reform the Lords would threaten the primacy of the Commons. There would then be two elected chambers and, arguably, if the Lords was elected by PR, it would be more representative of the nation than the Commons. Would the Commons allow such a threat to its status to be enacted? I think not. My instinct is that the reform of the Lords will either be a very modest measure, intended to reinforce the position of the governing party; or it will come about dramatically, because of a confrontation between the two Houses and, perhaps, an election. In the latter case, outright abolition is not impossible.

Pondering that, let us now turn and walk left instead of right out of the glittering central lobby of the Palace – according to the former minister Alan Clark, the third easiest place in Europe to get picked up, after Funland in Leicester Square and the arrivals lounge at Rome airport – and pass briskly, virtuously, to the Commons. It too is redolent of ancient deeds and aristocratic mores. But we could, in this account of the democracy, accept the doubtful parentage of the main chamber, were we sure that the place acted today as a properly functioning link in the democratic chain of command. If we thought it passed well-made, fully-considered laws on the people's behalf, held the government closely to account for its actions, and acted always to protect the liberties of the British people, then questions of its culture and history would be interesting but unimportant. It would be doing, as Scots put it, 'the business'. Dull business, much of the time – but then dull business, as Bagehot himself noted, is not necessarily something to complain of. 'Parliament,' he said, 'is a great thing, but it is not a cheerful thing . . . Life is short, but the forms of the House are long . . . Even in the dullest society you hear complaints of the dullness of Parliament – of the representative tedium of the nation.' But, argued Bagehot, the English (*sic*) were hardly a lively lot, and all the best business was a little dull.[6]

Oh, Mr B, were dullness merely the problem today! If only

we had a Parliament which was respected as a remorseless, quiet, effective machine. Here's a cheeky comparison which is nevertheless just a little more pertinent than impertinent. There was, a few years ago, an unintentionally hilarious moment at a Liberal Democrat conference. It was after the Iraqi invasion of Kuwait which led to the Gulf War. An obscure delegate came to the rostrum and said something along the following lines: 'I don't know whether Saddam Hussein is watching these proceedings or [seeming suddenly a little startled at her own thought] . . . er, has access to them by video, but the Liberal Democrats have a warning for you, Saddam Hussein . . .' Apparently unconscious of the idiotic and almost heroic self-importance of the words, assembled Lib-Dems sat solemn and nodding – even applauded. Well, hearing MPs in the Commons address themselves to the great issues of international trade, diplomacy or even monetary policy can sound almost as unreal. Government backbenchers can, at rare moments, exercise some leverage on the general drift of the executive policy which can, from time to time, help change the world beyond Westminster. But most of the time, frankly, it's more like children shouting at passing aircraft.

The Commons is alive with frantic activity every day of the session, of course – committees, debates, lobbies. Most MPs are creased and harassed individuals moving at a perpetual fast walk and straining the voice-box, memory and writing-hand during long working days (twelve or fourteen hours are not uncommon, day after day). They live, as do all the 3,500 Westminster village inhabitants, in a gossipy and self-obsessed world where sudden crises blow up, and there is always another tale ricocheting around the walls. But once the day is ended, it is often hard, standing back, to determine any good that has been done by the collective parliamentary class. In all the activity, there is at times a curious impression of deadness. The excitement is febrile. What seems at first sight to be important is revealed, at a second glance, to be merely self-important. The day dies, the 'whip' of business is over, and the flurries of activity are not transmitted to the wider world. Letters from constituents have been answered, tens of thousands of words exchanged, deals done. Ministers have been told a thing or two, and have replied on the late-evening news. Obscure parliamentary manoeuvres have been successfully brought off, privileges upheld, procedures sprung, whips confounded. But who else is listening? And why should they?

Whips, Priests, Principles and Power

The most basic and in theory the easiest job of the Commons in our system is of course to provide and sustain a government. This is done through the party system which, as we have noted earlier in the book, faces problems of its own. It is basically a simple, arithmetical task, based on the willingness of individual MPs to subdue their powers of thought and their consciences to the business of supporting the administration, or opposing it. Majority-making depends on treating individuals as neat, predictable, equally-sized units, as on an abacus, and MPs have never fully recovered their reputation with the public since this truth leaked out some time in the last century. But we live in interesting times, and the Conservative rebellion over Europe, which spread to other issues, means that this simple-seeming, administration-supporting function has looked rather less simple. It is possible that, over time, the breakdown of the old left-right ideologies, combined with the ubiquity of news outlets and the lowered status of government generally will produce a steadily less predictable, stormier Parliament of individuals. It's a heady thought.

Before thinking it through at greater length, though, it is necessary to analyse the daily reality of most backbenchers' lives. Do backbenchers matter? In any parliamentary day, some will feel that they have influenced the executive for good, either by getting a half-hour chat with a minister or a whip, or via some committee or other. This is sometimes called the 'trickle-up' effect. It is hard to separate propaganda from the truth: ministers always like to pretend they had the ideas first, and backbenchers like to think that they tipped off the minister to the value of monetarism, or the need for a health campaign about the dangers of baby-milk. Ministers do spend a fair amount of time around the House, though less and less, and there is two-way traffic. Backbench party committees can still be of great importance, particularly as places for ministers in trouble to vindicate or sink themselves. The private debates of these committees at times of national crisis have been almost as important as the public debates in the Chamber. They can unmake prime ministers but, when it comes to individual Members, the best MPs are mostly sucked up into the government itself, or the opposition shadow government, essentially switching allegiance from legislature to executive. From the point of view of the executive, this is necessary: the businessman and former adviser to Margaret Thatcher Sir John Hoskyns has noted that, 'For the purposes of government, a country of fifty-five million people is forced to depend upon a talent pool which could not sustain a single multi-national company.'[7] So much for the notion that the residue of backbench opinion is a daily nourishment to the government. Those not inside the government machine, or waiting to get inside, do not constitute a pool of wisdom as deep as they sometimes suppose. As the political writer Peter Riddell has demonstrated, more and more of the parliamentarians are a semi-professional political class without broad outside experiences to call on. These days, any middle-aged parliamentary failure with a gripe is described on television as a 'senior backbencher'. Mostly, this is just an attempt by the journalist to persuade the viewer that Sir Cornelius Bozo is on the programme because he represents some deep intellectual and political current, rather than because he happened to be the only bloke in the Commons lobby who didn't have a dinner engagement.

When it comes to the rougher influence of revolting MPs, in past times, there was just as much room for scepticism. For most of the time, the party machines have held such pressures securely in check. The real constitution of Parliament would make the small warrens of rooms off the Members' Lobby which house the party whips' offices a more important power-centre than the Chamber or the lobbies. Party discipline has been the foundation of modern British politics and those who wield the discipline have formidable power themselves. In 1869, the Victorian novelist Anthony Trollope put the case for dumb loyalty in the mouth of a fictitious forty-year-old Liberal MP called Barrington Erle, and it has not been put better since. Barrington

> hated the very name of independence in Parliament, and when he was told of any man, that that man intended to look to measures and not to men, he regarded that man as being both unstable as water and dishonest as the wind ... According to his theory of parliamentary government, the House of Commons should be divided by a marked line, and every Member should be required to stand on one side of it or on the other ... he did not think it possible that any vote should be given on a great question, either this way or that, as the result of a debate; and he was certainly assured in his own opinion that any such changing of votes would be dangerous, revolutionary and almost unparliamentary. A member's vote – except on some small crotchety open question thrown out for the amusement of crotchety members – was due to the leader of that member's party.[8]

It wasn't satire then, but a true description of how many respectable and successful parliamentarians thought. And it still is.

The whips' basic job is to make sure that the government of the day wins its votes; the name comes from the 'whippers-in' of the hunting field who round up straying hounds. But their role is far wider. They keep notes, both mental and pencil, of the performance of every MP, rating his or her punctuality, sobriety, intelligence, speaking ability, sex-life, honesty, financial liquidity and, of course, loyalty to the leadership. The squiggle of a whip's HB can ensure that someone who has spent half a lifetime slogging round backstreets and committee rooms to get into Parliament never makes it into government, and never quite knows why. When Bounderby's name is raised by the Prime Minister as a possible recruit the Chief Whip winces slightly and that is mostly that. Often rightly; David Waddington, who later became Governor of Bermuda, recalled that, as Chief Whip in the mid-1980s, he kept three MPs out of office. After his time, all made it in, and all subsequently had to resign in embarrassing circumstances. But the whips change too, and plenty of people work their passage back into favour. Some whips argue that the real pool of talent available at any one time is so small that their actual room for choice is very limited. 'Once you've excluded everyone who's incapable of turning up in the morning clean-shaven, and wearing a decent suit, and everyone who's a moron, and everyone who's totally disloyal, and everyone who hasn't already been sacked for one of the above reasons, there isn't a hell of a lot of choice,' one whip told me. But the mystique of the whips' office is not punctured by this reasoning: those who never make it are unlikely to consider themselves unemployable, and therefore blame unknown slanders noted down in the mysterious black notebooks kept in whips' locked drawers.

Whips are not only intelligence-gatherers. They are nannies, shoulders to cry on, spreaders of 'the government line', contact-points with other parties, recruiters of MPs to ask specific questions, or to barrack an opponent who is doing too well, and, of course, persuaders. The popular image of heavily-built men prepared to hold lighted cigarettes against the hands of dissidents is somewhat overdone, though both the Conservatives and Labour have employed sturdy gentlemen whom one would not wish to meet in a narrow Westminster passageway late at night. There have been cases of potential rebels being reminded by the whips of how they had so far managed to keep that extra-marital affair, or that boyfriend, or whatever, out of the newspapers. But there have also been cases of MPs in financial or personal trouble being helped out generously by the whips, being straightened out and – the word is not extreme – 'saved'. The most persistent rebels in the Major-Thatcher years were left alone by the whips, because they were regarded as hopeless cases: they were on the 'shits' list'. But when someone is proving seriously troublesome, the threats used against them tend to be political. Among the available carrots are knighthoods (or, as they nicely put it, 'a little something in front of your name') and even the possibility of a life peerage.

The most succulent carrots are promotions in and to the administration: the worst threats are the lack of such chances. The story is told of a rebel in the early 1990s who was brought into the office of the government Chief Whip, then Richard Ryder. The rebel explained in painful detail how his conscience would not allow him to support the government over such-and-such. Ryder was benign, inquired after the family, poured him a drink, and then asked him kindly whether he was looking forward to restarting his business career. The rebel looked puzzled. Well, said Ryder, it's very important to look after the family, find something to do with your life, and so on. The rebel looked even more puzzled. Well, Ryder is said to have continued, I mean, there's no point in continuing in politics, is there? Very good to be a man of conscience; terribly brave of you; full of admiration. But you don't seriously think you'll ever be a minister after this? You do understand that your political career is over? You don't really want to spend the rest of your life as a backbencher. Embittered – turn to booze? Might as well get out at the next election. At that, the rebel crumpled. Others, as we all know, did not. This combination of powers, and the access to Downing Street that goes with them, has helped ensure that the fame of the whips has risen in recent years. They have been flattered with demonic portrayals in television drama; they have produced two recent Tory prime ministers (Heath and Major); they have provided many of the fast-stream ministers. Bright Tories arriving at the Commons for the first time now quite often say that their main ambition is to spend a few years in the all-male whips' office. There, they hope, they will form the key relationships in the self-selecting 'staff college' which will bring them high office in due course. Actually helping run a department of state does not appear to be as glamorous these days as joining the political police.

If the whips exercise control over backbenchers, effectively tying the legislature to the executive, then day-to-day control over the proceedings of the Commons is partly in the hands of a man who controls the whips. Those who should know assert that among the fifty most powerful people in the country is the little-heard-of civil servant known as 'the usual channels'. This man, Murdo Maclean, is the private secretary to the government Chief Whip but his job is far more important than that suggests. He is the go-between among the whips' offices and in many ways the individual who does more than anyone to ensure that business continues. As one former whip puts it, the whips' office 'quite often make up the constitution as we go along; we are always trying out new ideas.' He means that the methods of getting business through and of allowing dissidents to let off steam without diverting the main task of the administration are always being slightly altered: during most sessions some new, if obscure, precedent is set for the next one. Often, of course, the government whips are trying to put one over on the opposition, or vice-versa. In serious cases, and regularly enough, these matters end up with the Speaker and her officials, who are the well-known and public face of parliamentary policing. The Speaker's power is formally acknowledged, not least by the magnificent suite of rooms she inhabits in the Palace, and where an array of celebrities, singers, politicians (and even journalists) are entertained. But Maclean, 'the usual channels', a genial, Garrick-clubby, ginger-haired Scotsman, is the man who can tell the whips that such-and-such would be overstepping the mark. As one whip explained: 'Murdo would say "no, I don't think that would be a good idea" and I would know perfectly well that he meant he thought I was infringing the rights of the opposition and, further, if I went ahead, he would blow the whistle on me.' Another senior parliamentarian describes him as the living Bible of the constitution, a walking repository of knowledge about the 'real rules of this place.'

He polices what both the main parties regard as the boundary-line between parliamentary democracy and parliamentary authoritarianism. That means he can make the difference between a legislative amendment succeeding and failing – true power indeed. Like many aspects of the real constitution, Murdo Maclean has been little noticed and his role developed almost by accident. The first holder of the job, Sir Charles Harris, arrived as a junior Conservative Party official at the door of Number

Ten in 1917 and was shown in by a butler straight to the bedroom where Lloyd George was addressing the war coalition whips. From the last two years of the First World War right through to 1961, this hugely influential and little-known man did the same job for all governments, accumulating a vast store of precedent and example in his head. He became, as it were, a flesh-and-blood storehouse of Parliament's own case-law throughout the rise of modern democracy. His formal appointment was originally a Conservative Party matter. He was paid for by Conservative Central Office to copy out the weekly 'whip' – confidential details of the business for the week, with the all-important voting instructions underlined – and circulate it to Tory MPs. When Labour won their first election in 1924, the new chief whip had no similar factotum, so the Tories 'lent' the new government Sir Charles. After a few months, the party began to protest that it was subsidizing the socialist administration, so by agreement the job was turned into a civil service one. In 1958, Sir Charles acquired a deputy, Freddie Warren, who took over the job three years later and lasted through most of the turbulent sixties and seventies. He was described by the Labour cabinet minister and diarist Richard Crossman as a man of 'astonishing' influence and he finally handed over, as Sir Freddie, to Murdo Maclean in 1978.

So Murdo is only the third holder of this job since the days of Kaiser Bill, his precedents and lines learnt and developed like the initiate of some intricate and private cult. He may be powerful and part of the Establishment, but this priesthood is not partisan. A former civil servant in Number Ten, Maclean found himself working frantic hours during the final year of the last Labour government, before switching overnight to serve the incoming Thatcher one. Maclean is on almost as friendly terms with the opposition as with his employer, the government chief whip: he is said to use the Tory whips' telephones to tip off the Labour ones about what is happening, and everyone pretends not to notice. He, and no one else, decides what one side of Parliament should know about the latest wheezes and devilment of the other; and everyone respects his judgement, while not really knowing the basis on which it works. It is all (short pause for self-congratulatory smile) very British. Maclean's importance to the Parliamentary process as it has developed under the party whips is well illustrated by the story of the committee that oversees party political broadcasts, ensuring that they don't overstep the line, keeping the parties in touch with what the others are doing, and so on. Given the importance of broadcasting in the political process, this is clearly big potatoes, and the committee includes senior figures from all the main parties, the Leader of the House, the Chief Whip and the Director-General of the BBC, as well as 'the usual channels', the self-effacing civil servant who chairs it. Except that it hasn't actually met since 1984: for all practical purposes, Murdo Maclean *is* the committee (and a busy committee he is).

His power, of course, depends on the greater and wider question of the power of the government and opposition 'business managers'. And the whips' power, very great, is nevertheless also an inverted complement to the submerged and reined-in power of backbench MPs. The party system, which has been with us for rather longer than democracy itself, is, like any autocrat, never quite sure of itself, always on the lookout for uprisings in the provinces. As noted earlier, both Labour and the Tories are wide coalitions of opinion: the former running from Marx to Social Democrats, and the latter from Continental-style Christian Democrats to (in the words of one eminent Tory) 'semi-fascists'. From the point of view of political leaderships, the job of holding these coalitions together despite their obvious and perpetual tensions, and so allowing the parliamentary system to function, is a high and noble calling: government whips admire their opposite numbers for doing a good job and the fellow-feeling between socialist and Tory 'men of business' is well known. But the system becomes vulnerable and open to criticism whenever a substantial view is not represented by the leaders of the coalitions – whether it be hostility to the European Union, or support for voting reform, or a conviction that nuclear weapons are immoral. Then, the coalitions face internal pressures at Westminster and, if these pressures are ignored, the eventual threat of electoral challenge outside. It is hardly surprising that there has always been vivid criticism of the party system, from Trollope onwards, and that it has tended to come from people of strong views, outside the party mainstream.

The Catholic writer and poet Hilaire Belloc, for instance, attacked the system savagely after serving as a Liberal MP in the early years of the century. He co-authored a book simply called *The Party System* in which the Tory and Liberal arrangements were satirically compared to a Shakespearean Verona where the Montagues and Capulets were intimately related and where 'the feud between the two houses was being kept up mainly for the dramatic entertainment of the people of Verona.'[9] Michael Foot published his attack on the same thing nearly forty years later ('ever more rigid party discipline is ... an engine for suppressing or at least hiding the very questions which need most to be discussed. Are we to tolerate a situation where the major parties become more and more monolithically united about less and less?'). The two men could hardly be more different. Yet both were writing as people on the Westminster margin – Belloc as a Roman Catholic radical and anti-semite, and Foot as left-wing socialist during the Cold War. Their attacks were similar and could be quoted approvingly by scores of political outsiders – Europhobes, communists, green radicals, racialists, animal rights activists. These are the people any natural whip dislikes and fears as 'unsound' and will try to do down should they by accident be elected to the House of Commons. Scattered enemies have been nothing to the power of the parties. But there have occurred moments when a group of dissident parliamentarians breaks through and the system suddenly seems to totter. And this is one such.

The Conservatives' long period in government from 1979 has been racked and dramatized by the divisions in the party over Europe, divisions which have at key moments produced the parliamentary crises mentioned earlier. Eventually, after the 1992 elections, the anti-Brussels Tories organized themselves with their own whips, their own private planning, their own spokesmen. A fine Queen Anne terraced house just over from the Lords, decorated with exquisite good taste and armed with rows of computers and intense young men, became the headquarters of the Maastricht rebellion, and continued to operate as a rival centre long afterwards. Finance came from well-known businessmen like Sir James Goldsmith. The rebels became a social group, a society of outcasts, an organization for individualists, a loners' club. One would see them trooping rather self-consciously into the back room of Westminster restaurants, trying to decide common lines on policies as different as rail privatization and fishing rights. Although they were, and are, a heterodox group, they acted as a highly influential party within a party – and then outside it, when eight of them were deprived of the whip by John Major in November 1994. This was an event without precedent in the modern Conservative Party and contributed to hardening the core of the rebel movement. Very occasionally, the odd maverick or crook had lost his right to be counted as one of the Conservative Party in Parliament; but for a prime minister to wipe out his paper majority by using this punishment on so many was a dramatic development.

It was also one which quickly proved self-defeating, since the expelled Tories promptly joined a rebellion over the imposition of value added tax on domestic fuel, helping to defeat the government over a central part of its November 1994 budget, and held together on other matters too, proclaiming their delight in being able to think things through for themselves and vote according to conscience. These rebels were not leading party figures, but they were able to use the media's enthusiasm for the story to take them into the living-rooms of the nation. They had the support of much of the Conservative press, and the parliamentary threat they represented both before and after losing the whip had a considerable influence on government policy. But by the time the cabinet sued for peace five months after the withdrawal of the whip, offering it back unconditionally, it seemed that the rebels had won. That led, in July 1995, to John Major's confrontation with his right-wing critics, when he resigned as Leader of the Conservative Party and beat off a challenge from the Thatcherite former Welsh Secretary, John Redwood. Major's extraordinary gamble, born of seething frustration, paid off, though a third of Tory MPs refused to support him.

By resigning, he was raising the question of whether the Conservatives could still function as a single party, and so radically entrenching his backbenchers. It had always been obvious that such a rebellion, if it spread widely enough, had the capacity to bring down an administration. John Major's earlier threat of a general election was and is the doomsday weapon of any government. It is akin to the mad scientist's threat to blow himself up along with the rest of the world. Major and his cabinet colleagues were using their own huge unpopularity in the country to threaten rebel MPs, thus turning lack of authority outside Westminster into a source of authority within it.

Rebels like Nicholas Budgen, the Wolverhampton MP, had argued that this was a barefaced attempt to deprive Parliament of its historic right to decide: 'When the House is told, "If you disagree with the expenditure of £75 million, there must be a general election", it makes those of us who are Conservatives and government supporters but who have the misfortune to disagree with extra expenditure in Europe ask, "What is our purpose in this place, and what is the purpose of this place?"' Mr Budgen went on to remind the Commons that the right to withhold assent for public spending was what it had fought the Stuart monarchs for – implying that the present-day corrupt olive-farmers of southern Europe were requiring unconstitutional imposts from the British taxpayer in rather the same way that Charles I had. 'It is disgraceful,' he continued, 'to threaten the House of Commons in this way so as to deprive us of our rights and emasculate us in our most important role . . .'[10]

The problem with Mr Budgen's logic was that there was in the Commons a substantial majority in favour of the EU and in favour of meeting Britain's treaty obligations to it: the possibility of the government being defeated, and the threats that resulted, came about only because the Labour and Liberal Democrat opposition were treating the relevant votes not as

European matters but as a vote of confidence in the government. They, in other words, were voting on the future of the Tory administration, not on the question of payments to the EU. On the matter of principle, there was not a division between the determination of the executive to pay the money, and the determination of the legislature not to. But Budgen's argument goes wider than the particular case which caused him to rebel: he was asking MPs to reconsider their priorities: how heavily does the job of supporting an administration weigh against the duties of individual reflection and conscience? The European issue is rare in its gravity, in the passions it arouses and in the way it unites the big parties, cutting out millions of anti-European voters from mainstream politics. And Nicholas Budgen is also rare in being a contented backbencher, without any desire to shin up the greasy pole. But the question raised by the collision of the issue and the man will not go away and is potentially a revolutionary one.

Administrations can, and have, given way on relatively minor matters and even make a show of allowing free votes on certain matters said to be of individual conscience. But this division between the essential and the inessential, the matter of conscience and the matter of high politics, has always been an unsatisfactory one, defined as much by the limits of party unity as by objective measures. It is curious that the legal age for gay sex or the Sunday opening hours for supermarkets are agreed to be issues which require MPs to agonize personally and act individually; while rights for disabled people or the workings of children's homes are not 'crockety members' and come under the party whip. The matter of when a government can allow itself to be defeated by a parliamentary vote is often as much about its authority in the country and the personal standing of its leader as about the issue itself. But there are ominous signs for the old ways. The huge range of issues bundled together in current party manifestos force voters, as we have already noted, to make ridiculous bulk purchases of policy. As the big left-right divisions melt away a little, they expose issues which are less amenable to decision-making by ideology (abortion, pollution, political reform, education). That means that MPs within parties are more likely to disagree, and that voters are going to be more interested in their individual views, since they may decide their vote on the basis of 'untraditional' issues, rather than old party allegiance. As the MPs see that there is political advantage for them in openly expressing their own range of views, they find a media which is keen to help them and expert in doing so. Where this leads is difficult to predict – perhaps nowhere much, perhaps to slimmed-down 'core manifestos' for parties, plus a wider scope for free votes. It is possible to imagine a system of government in which ministers regularly lost votes after fierce and well-informed debates; yet no election followed, because the executive considered that Parliament had spoken and that Parliament, as the source of political power, was properly sovereign. The unpredictability of such a system would make life harder for political leaders, but more interesting and democratically alive for the rest of us.

Under the party system, the ultimate logic of the Eurosceptic case would be for a new party, with its own discipline, to be formed and compete for seats. Only that would ensure that the anti-European voters would be practically re-enfranchised. The same is true on the left of politics for those who adhere to traditional socialist demand-management economics. The trouble is that under the first-past-the-post system, breaking away is politically suicidal – a lesson the Scottish Labour Party in the seventies and the Social Democratic Party in the eighties learned the hard way. A proportional voting system would almost certainly allow a UK nationalist party to emerge and win seats at Westminster. Then, instead of the submerged coalitions of today, held together by party whips within a large and sprawling party, we would have overt coalitions, operating programmes agreed between the parties. It is possible, at least, that this system would give backbenchers more real influence over the programme of government.

Soon after Major's resignation and re-election had officially settled the matter of Tory discipline, the party's left started to cause trouble. With brilliantly theatrical timing, just before the

1995 Conservative conference, Alan Howarth, the MP for Stratford-upon-Avon, defected to Labour, giving the Tories' loss of 'decency and fairness' as his reason. Then, at the New Year, Emma Nicholson, the MP for West Devon and Torridge, defected to the Liberal Democrats, mourning the loss of the Tories' 'One Nation' instincts. Conservative ministers denounced both defectors as perverse, piqued and treacherous, but to have defections following on so swiftly from the extraordinary events of summer 1995 was eloquent evidence of the difficulties facing the Tory coalition. As I write, more MPs are agonizing about whether they should defect and try to bring nearer a general election and the destruction of the Conservative government. Others, who won't leave, are looking further ahead to Opposition and contemplating a less party-driven attitude to the Commons. One highly respected minister confided privately that though he would not leave the party – 'I've been a Conservative too long to go now' – he would act as a disloyal member of the Opposition were it to be taken over by a right-wing leader like Michael Portillo. He would vote with a Labour or Lib-Lab government on issues about which he, as a centre-left Tory, felt they were right. Quite a few others, he said, would probably do the same. Beyond the mainstream, 1995–96 saw challenges which seem minor but are symptomatic of the frustration many people feel about the narrowness of the party agenda, concentrated on key voters as described earlier in the book. On the right, there was the announcement by the UK Referendum Party, funded by Sir James Goldsmith, that it would contest every parliamentary seat whose sitting MP was not in favour of a referendum on further European integration. As a party, it is a flea. But in a close election, this flea could bite, viciously enough, into the position of sitting Conservatives in marginal seats. On the left, the miners' leader Arthur Scargill called for the formation of a Socialist Labour Party to fight for traditional leftist policies, such as nationalization, hostility to the European Union, the absolution of private education and unilateral nuclear disarmament. He suggested that the party should be formed on 1 May

1996 and the idea was taken up by some activists and union leaders, including miners and railwaymen. Again, the longer-term chances of a leftist party depend heavily on the electoral system. In other EU countries, similar parties mostly gain below 10 per cent of the national vote. But in Germany, for instance, that won the Alliance 90/Green candidates 49 seats in the Bundestag in 1994. Whether or not such parties ever break into the British Parliament, however, the creaks, rebellions and defections of 1994–96 may well be harbingers of bigger changes to the old British party system in the next century.

Until then, the power of a British backbench MP to influence government, even if that MP is within a governing party, remains mostly potential power. He or she can on rare occasions act destructively, but most of the time this power is too impractical or drastic to use. It is analogous to the power that the British Parliament itself has over the European Union. It can always vote to pull out, and in that sense it remains sovereign, powerful, absolute. But this is a form of power so final and so sealed that it rarely affects daily issues. At Westminster, the possibility of a revolutionary revival of parliamentary power is always there, just as the revolutionary reassertion of national autonomy from the EU is always there. The difference is that at Westminster this revolution would be much easier to accomplish. It would require – what? – forty or so independent-minded Members on the majority side, who decided to shift the power-balance back against the executive. That's all. We can dream on. Meanwhile, the muscle-flexing of the Tory rebels stands as a giddy reminder of the coiled potency that lies in the fact of being elected to Parliament. The backbenchers' power has been dammed and diverted by party machines but it can always, in the right circumstances, break its banks.

Other instances of parliamentary power are more dubious. Making war is a Crown prerogative – one of those many executive functions in which, bizarrely, Parliament has no official role and which it seems rather pathetically careless of asserting its rights over. In practice, of course, it does have influence at moments of national crisis. The famous destruction of Chamberlain's premiership during the Norway debate in May 1940 is an obvious example. And the mood of the Commons steeled Margaret Thatcher in her determination to retake the Falkland Islands. But governments are far more often nudged by the Commons into doing what they are basically already in favour of, than they are persuaded to change their minds. 'Backbench pressure' is as often an excuse for ministerial actions as a real force. For instance, staying with the military theme, government ministers explained their lack of enthusiasm for intervention in the Bosnian war during 1992–93 by saying that 'the backbenches wouldn't wear it'. Some MPs certainly would have been unhappy. But it turned out that ministers had been telling the backbenchers that the generals wouldn't wear it; and some, at least, of the generals, that the MPs wouldn't wear it. It was hard to avoid the impression that the ministers had decided intervention was too risky, and were palming off the blame. Similarly, when Mrs Thatcher was putsched by her own party, it was true that Tory backbenchers had become frantic about the likelihood of her leading them to defeat at the polls; but it was the actions of her leading ministers, not Parliament, that were decisive in her downfall. Indeed, it is possible to argue that, since her leadership had been a powerful factor behind the Tories' 1987 election victory, the limited role of Parliament in toppling her was an undemocratic act, not a democratic one.

Looking Down our Noses

Certainly, there is plenty for MPs to worry about as regards their current condition. Year by year the signs of their slipping status become ever more embarrassingly obvious. Prime minister's question time has become almost entirely a backdrop for getting clips on the evening news programme. MPs seem not self-confident representatives of a free and alert people, but hopefuls auditioning for a speak-on part with the BBC. There is something pathetic about watching mostly intelligent, hard-working people holding up props like model aeroplanes or the mastheads of their evening paper, or making what they fancy to be shrewd 'sound-bite' assertions, desperate to be accorded the camera's blessing, a nod from the denimed youth with the video machine which tells the world they exist. MPs with small majorities cluster desperately on the second bench back, where the cameras will inevitably record their presence while focusing on a minister or shadow minister. Look, Mum, it's me; look, voter, it's me. And, yes, they are aware of the degradation involved. Some MPs, like obsolete functionaries insisting on their importance ever more strenuously as their real power dies, lash out at their tormentors, barring journalists from the Commons terrace, or from their offices. It is notable that those who are reported least are inclined to stamp their little feet the hardest.

The majority, though, adapt. Traditionally the place for a properly-accredited journalist to privately buttonhole passing MPs was the Members' Lobby of the Commons, a marbled and statued hall at the entrance to the Chamber. Useful conversations are certainly still had there, with journalists and MPs making eye contact and sidling together as if they were picking one another up at a nightclub. But, as we have seen, a journalist would do almost as well outside the Palace at the steps leading into a recently refurbished office-block where the BBC and ITN have their offices. The passing trade there is of a higher quality, and almost as numerous. The written press, perhaps in decline too, now scarcely bothers with what used to be considered the heart of the Parliamentary process, debates in the Commons chamber. The Labour MP Jack Straw commissioned a study of column inches of such coverage from a group of newspapers.[11] He found that 'Between 1933 and 1988, coverage of Parliamentary debates took between 400 and 800 lines in *The Times* and between 300 and 700 lines in the *Guardian*. By 1992 coverage had declined to fewer than 100 lines, in both papers.' The proportion of debates covered had halved. Instead, the press generally has turned to stories about internal divisions and arguments within parties and leaks from Whitehall. The Press Gallery, still packed for the twice-weekly asinine exchanges and animal noises of prime minister's questions, is often empty for hours at a time except for the compulsory attenders of *Hansard* and the occasional penitent from the Press

Gallery bar trying to sober up. (During hot summers it is also useful, because of the air conditioning.)

The trend shown up by Mr Straw's researcher is confirmed by the experience of journalists. In just a decade of covering Parliament, I have seen the job of gallery reporter – dashing out pages of shorthand notes, and staying at night until the final 'wind-up' speeches – move from being routine and expected, to being comparatively rare. Shortly after Straw's report caused a flurry of comment, the *Financial Times* dropped its respected political page. A year later, two of the last traditional gallery correspondents, people trained to transmit the views of politicians rather than their own views, or stories about party splits, were made redundant by their employers, the *Daily Telegraph* and *The Times*. This is not only of symbolic importance, the sign of a power-shift, but of practical importance too. How do you find out what your MP has said, and how he or she has voted? As the Straw report noted, interested voters used to be able to buy a copy of the full, official report, *Hansard*, for 12p in 1970 and 40p in 1979. It now costs £7.50, a tenfold rise in real terms in twenty years. How many of us can afford that each day? One way and another, the media is confirming the old half-joke from Enoch Powell that the best way of keeping something secret in Britain was to announce it on the floor of the House of Commons at 8 p.m. A tradition of verbatim reporting of Parliament, fought for by generations of journalists and publishers, is being wound up. Mr Straw, at least, is sure it matters. 'The only alternative to politics is violence,' he warned. Societies achieved peace by resolving conflicts over scarce resources through the political process. Argument was central to that: 'Nations only gradually acquire the ability to argue. Without it, effective democracy is impossible.' He believes that the lack of reporting of the arguments in the nation's debating chamber has undermined public confidence in democracy. He is surely right. But Parliament is under-reported for very strong (rather than good) cultural and political reasons. The media's attitude, boredom at the top end of the market and prurient contempt at the bottom, is not simply accidental.

This new order is cruel to the pretensions of those MPs who are less powerful than they pretend. MPs are lampooned in latex, butchered in blockbusters and squatted upon by the sitcom-writers; their sexual habits, as bizarre, no doubt, as those of the rest of the nation, are used as the disposable raw material for porno-journalism; their financial interests are scrutinized carefully; they are used as the dupes for 'sting' journalism; and their old sanctions, such as calling their critics to the bar of the House, have become useless. Some of the assaults on them are wholly justified: years of closer and closer links between companies, consultancies and some MPs produced a culture which justified the journalistic accusation of sleaze. Some backbenchers were taking payments of £1,000 a time to ask parliamentary questions on behalf of companies: in April 1995 two were suspended from the Commons after being trapped by the *Sunday Times* into accepting such an offer. Many more were taking a wide range of free trips, gifts and fees, not always declared in the Register of Interests. It has become rare to find a parliamentarian beginning a speech by telling the House that he is paid by such-and-such a company which has an interest in the issue, before spouting off. This led, not to curbs on the press, but to the 1995 Nolan Committee on standards, which will be discussed later, and its conclusion that MPs should be regulated by an outside Commissioner for Standards, and lose contacts with lobbyists.

In these circumstances, it is clear that the Press critics of the Commons have had a great store of material to pick from; it is not *all* a change in the broader 'culture', it is not merely 'the end of deference'. If we are vultures, there has been an abundance of rotten meat to feed on. Having said which, the individual examples of sleaze are not the full explanation for a shift in the attitude of reporters and commentators to the Mother of Parliaments. The thing goes wider. The period has seen, alongside the decline of straight reporting of Parliament, the rise of sketch-writers as the new stars of the trade. Some are exceedingly funny. Some are politically knowledgeable. Some are mere smirks in a sharp suit, sniggering at decline. They tend to be envied by humble backbenchers, as the ever-too-honest-for-his-own-good Julian Critchley acknowledged in 1988. When he retired, he said, he didn't want to go to the Lords, but to become a sketch-writer:

They live so high off the hog. They have an exquisite light lunch four days a week that is paid for by the proprietors of their newspapers; they arrive here at 2.30 and sit in the gallery; by 3.30 or 4 p.m. they adjourn for a cup of Lapsang Souchong tea; then they write their copy and go to bed. Any Honourable Member who speaks either on a Friday morning or after 4 p.m. on a weekday gets no mention whatsoever.

Think back to the glory days when early reporters fought a long guerrilla war to smuggle out accounts of the legislators' views, risking gaol, memorizing hours of speeches in the Public Gallery: who are the masters now?

Of course, the political journalists are polite, sometimes even deferential, to the politicians who provide their sources. But their corporate masters, the wielders of serious power, have no need to observe such niceties. One account of the rise of Murdoch's *Sun* has its foul-mouthed editor of the eighties, Kelvin MacKenzie, savaging the paper's then political editor, Walter Terry:

Forget all this crap about politicians – who's interested, eh? You only write this bollocks so you can look good with all your fucking mates in Westminster. You are not writing it for the readers – the readers don't give a fuck about politics. The readers, eh, Walter? Know who they are? Pay your fucking wages, eh? Why don't you get a story for them, eh? One with people they've heard of for a change?[12]

MacKenzie had been an ardent and effective champion of Margaret Thatcher, whose trade union policies (strong) and attitude to newspaper regulation (weak) proved so profitable for his employer. But the tirade is more eloquent about the true shifts of power than about MacKenzie's politics. Nor does the contempt for politicians generally among *Sun*-type journalists stop with the lesser-known names from the legislature. When John Major presided over sterling's ignominious exit from the European Exchange Rate Mechanism in 1992, he telephoned Mackenzie at the *Sun* to ask what the paper was going to 'do to me' the following day. 'Let me put it like this, Prime Minister,'

MacKenzie replied, 'I've got two buckets of shit sitting on my desk and tomorrow morning I'm going to empty both of them over your head.' Long pause. Then the Queen's First Minister replied in sickly tones: 'Oh, Kelvin, you *are* a joker.' As the next day's paper demonstrated, however, Kelvin wasn't joking. You can agree with MacKenzie that the ERM episode was disgraceful, but anyone with traditional notions of the British constitution must be a bit surprised about the relative status of the editor and the prime minister, expressed by such language.

Not surprisingly, given the falling status of politicians in the media, they are not regarded highly by the public, either. In Parliament's own journal, *The House Magazine*, the pollster Robert Worcester told MPs in 1994 that when voters were asked whether they generally trusted various professions to tell the truth or not, only 14 per cent trusted politicians, as against 18 per cent in 1983. The silver lining for backbenchers was that government ministers (11 per cent) and journalists (10 per cent) were trusted even less. But it must have been grim reading, nevertheless. Mr Worcester sternly told them: 'Surprisingly, there has been an overall *increase* across the board, by five per cent, of people's willingness to trust the whole range of occupations to tell the truth, so the decline in confidence in journalists and politicians is specific to them and not part of an overall pattern.'[13] MPs have long noticed and worried about the trends. Those in government are generally too submerged in policy and thinking too much about survival to break surface, though Douglas Hurd occasionally agonizes about the role of the media. But the Liberal Democrat leader, after touring the country for a book on the state of the British democracy, told fellow MPs: 'Everywhere I went I found disillusionment with the entire political class. I found a dangerous gap growing between government and the governed . . .'[14] He was roundly criticized by the other parties for this commonplace and obvious assertion. Other MPs have been even blunter. Tony Banks, the Labour left's leading stand-up comic, recently said in the chamber that, 'Many people would say that politicians rank only slightly above journalists and cockroaches in public esteem. I have always thought that this was a little unkind to cockroaches because they are perfectly evolved creatures, which is more than I can say for many Members of Parliament.'[15]

A Nervous Glance at the Library Shelf

These are, I hope, eloquent enough signs that something is wrong. But then, some weary voices will reply, something always has been. For the enthusiastic democrat, there never has been a golden parliamentary age. The era of the Commons' greatest lustre ran to the mid-Victorian period, when parties were looser combinations than today, were not legitimated by a full franchise, and still partly depended on a handful of grandees and grand families. Without the distractions of foreign travel, television studios, European summits and so on, the mid-Victorian ministers spent far more time in Parliament and paid attention to it more closely than do their modern successors. Robert Peel wrote to Gladstone complaining of the pains of the premiership, and noting that he spent 'seven or eight hours a day to listen in the House of Commons.'[16] Perhaps the best modern historian of Parliament has written of the time:

On less than 30 per cent of all issues did 90 per cent of either of the main parties vote together. Governments were sacked. Legislation was made and revised on the floor of the House. Individual ministers were hounded from office without the Government even daring to threaten a dissolution. The Commons controlled a very substantial part of its own timetable and it could be as tough with the bureaucracy as with the Cabinet. For example, it could compel the Foreign Office to divulge in Blue Books the details of negotiations with foreign powers, to allow the House to have meaningful debates on foreign policy.[17]

Oh, happy days! But they were hardly democratic days: at the beginning of the relevant period, after the Great Reform Bill of 1832, only 7 per cent of Britons over twenty-one had the vote and, by the end of it, the 1880s, when the party blocks of Liberals, Irish Home Rulers and Conservatives had become effective, and after decades of successful suffrage agitation, the figure was only 28 per cent.

The next phase of parliamentary government, from the 1880s to the First World War, was in many ways the most vivid and exciting: Westminster still controlled the world's greatest empire, while at home the new waves of dissent from suffragettes, working-class trade unionists and socialists were crashing at the doors of the Palace. But that era, ended by the triumph of the modern state, was brief, almost equally undemocratic, and profoundly unstable. Parliament was ceding more control over its business to the new class of professional politicians represented by Asquith and Lloyd George without having become a fully democratic body: the place was still stuffed with dim sprigs of landowning families. It had only been as recently as 1885 that the Commons lost its majority of landowning and aristocratic MPs. Britain's leading historian of the aristocracy reports that they were mostly glad to get out as the new professional age of politicians dawned. They weren't up to it and hated the dreary discipline involved. Lord Ernest Hamilton, MP for Tyrone, spoke for many future MPs when he complained that he was 'a mere brick in a buttress, whose sole purpose was to maintain a number of paid officials in their billets . . . Nobody wanted me except as a voter in divisions.' He, it seems, cheered himself up by engaging in bicycle races along the Commons terrace with his brother, on cycles borrowed from the dining-room attendants (a more innocent consolation than many frustrated backbenchers have turned to since).[18] More seriously, the period was marked by civil violence, the oppression of women suffrage campaigners, punch-ups on the floor of the Commons, and a pervasive atmosphere of constitutional crisis – a crisis so severe that it led Dicey, the most reactionary of constitutional writers, to call for referendums to solve those issues which seemed beyond the capability of Parliament. Aristocrats were contemplating rebellion over Ulster; landowners were engaged in gun-running. It has been convincingly argued that, had Britain not gone to war in 1914, the Irish crisis would have provoked a civil war that would have spread to England. Come closer into modern times and you find today's themes – the over-mighty state, the deadening hand of the party whips, the excessive power of rivals like the mass media – are already present in the 1930s and 1940s. All in all, this period does not make a convincing candidate for the Golden Age of Parliament.

And, indeed, it has been a permanent condition of its history that this institution is regarded by intelligent observers as being in a state of grave decline: the conviction that the Mother of Parliaments has become a senile old bat is a constant theme in British political writing. Back in the 1760s the Lord Mayor of London was warning that 'we now have only the name of a Parliament, without the substance' and the charge has echoed regularly since. In the modern era, the post-war Labour and Conservative Parliaments of the 1940s and 1950s are often seen as, at the very least, a silver age for parliamentary democracy. But critics of the time were churning out political apocalypses then, too. Many of the complaints were exactly the same as today – an arrogant executive, civil servants bypassing the Commons through 'semi-dictatorial techniques', the excessive power of the party whips. In 1949, the Conservative MP Christopher Hollis published a book entitled *Can Parliament Survive?*[19] in which he warned: 'If we go down now, we go down forever, and if we lose our freedom now, we lose it forever.' In 1953, which seems in retrospect such a gentle time, a conservative professor published another tome on the decline of Parliament, concluding that 'the threat is real, and the hour late. Our present predicament presents a challenge which it is impossible to ignore.'[20] Yet ignore it we all did. Few reforms followed. Parliamentary democracy survived, to allow others to fire off emergency flares at regular intervals. In 1971, the journalist Andrew Roth published *Can Parliament Decide?* which focused on the debates about British entry into the Common Market, criticized the secrecy and the commercial arm-twisting, and warned that, unless MPs were made more powerful to pursue the hopes and allay the fears of their followers, 'the danger mounts of bringing the whole system of parliamentary democracy increasingly into contempt.' During the Thatcher years, laments about the destruction of our ancient Parliament came regularly from pluralists and civil-rights campaigners on the left, anti-European Union partisans from the right, and parliamentary traditionalists across the political spectrum. A post-Thatcher history of Parliament, quoted above, was called *The Eclipse of Parliament*. Its conclusion was that it was in the nature of the British political system 'to trample on what an eighteenth-century Englishman would have regarded as his essential liberties. Despite the windy rhetoric of politicians with liberty on their lips and power in their hearts, the UK government by the second half of the twentieth century was neither a parliamentary regime nor a particularly democratic one.'[21] That conclusion would be assented to by many scores, perhaps hundreds, of MPs who believed themselves regularly hoodwinked, avoided, disregarded and even lied to by ministers during the past decade or two.

This true history of Parliament, so at odds with the lazy, hazy myth, can be used to calm those of us worried about the state of the British democracy. So the Commons is powerless and feeble and needs to be thoroughly reformed? 'My boy, it always has been. That is part of its magic.' Well, before alarming the reader further, something I hope to do, I must answer the charge. The first thing to point out is the obvious thing, which is that the warnings of the writers quoted above, and scores of others, have been at least partly justified in their analysis. The Cassandras have been vindicated. Granted, this sceptred isle hasn't been taken over by a gang of over-weight fascists in Ray-bans. But Parliament has indeed come into general contempt. No doubt electors have always been cynical about MPs, muttering rude commentaries at the breakfast table or in the pub. But the openness and near-universality of the contempt in which Parliament is now held is surely on a different level. When the European Court of Human Rights is used so regularly by British citizens to establish basic matters about their own security, and when it passes hostile judgement on an ancient parliamentary state, things have come to a pretty pass, and the fault is not with over-zealous Continental jurists, but with our own democracy.

The arguments may have been heard before, but they return

ever more strongly, and persuade ever more people, until their truth swamps us. It is futile to pretend that we can scientifically measure the depth of disillusion about our central democratic institution. Even modern pollsters are fallible. There is no way we can reach back into the private views of the past: memories are also fallible and the most compelling written witnesses may, in fact, have been minority voices in their own time. But the decline theme can be approached another way, by simply asserting that cynicism about the power and behaviour of Parliament is justified by its objective status in the system. If people don't take it seriously today, then it may be because they are right not to take it seriously. Rather touchingly MPs, including the Prime Minister, have the idea that popular hostility and indifference derive from the fact that Honourable Members work too long hours, and use some archaic rules in debate. If only it were that simple and easily-changed. We have seen that Parliament lacks status and popularity, that it is a mask for party power, and we have raised a few question-marks over its general ability to intervene in the administration of the country. But all that is a little too abstract and ephemeral to be wholly convincing. It is time to look more closely at how Parliament actually performs the other democratic functions it has – not in theory, but in practice.

Dull Government Re-examined

What are the basic functions? As we have seen, Parliament supports the government and supplies its small army of ministers. That latter function can be discharged as quickly as it takes to make a few dozen telephone calls once a year. More substantially, it is both the legislature – it approves the legal form of the political promises made to voters by the governing party – and it is the place where the actions and words of the executive are meant to be scrutinized. In both central roles it fails, and fails badly. The low esteem in which politicians are held derives, no doubt, from a clutch of popular perceptions: dirty newspaper stories, the real loss of power the state suffers from (of which more later), and a general feeling that Westminster's promises of national renewal have rarely produced anything much. But the prosecution case need go no further than the basic, humdrum job of getting laws made. If the Commons cannot do that, parliamentarians can hardly be surprised that they are not much listened or deferred to.

The failure of Parliament to produce effective and sensible legislation may seem a dry, 'dull government' thing, but it affects the lives of millions, year after year. Let us be conservative and acknowledge entirely the right of the government to propose and push through the legislation it wants, irrespective of whether the ministerial wheezes are brilliant or batty. Accept that and you are still left with the duty of Parliament to ensure that the laws MPs pore over and vote on are legally and practically effective. What else is a legislature for? If it cannot or will not achieve that minimal requirement, we would be as well building a replica of Westminster in balsa-wood, ceremonially stuffing legislation through a slot in the roof, pulling it out through another in the bottom, and declaring it passed. I repeat, this is irrespective of the sagacity or otherwise of the original idea of the new law. For instance, it is perfectly possible to have been either for or against the poll tax, and still to feel that basic flaws in the legislation were regrettable and a failure of Parliament. Its flaws, like those in the 1991 Child Support Act – again, pointed out by the relevant committee before the legislation was passed, and ignored – were taken seriously by ministers only after there had been riots in the streets and threats of violence against public servants. The fullest account of the poll tax has this to say about its passage through Parliament at committee stage, when flaws are supposed to be most seriously sought-after:

As with most controversial government Bills, the standing committee was a futile marathon. Between mid-January and mid-March 1988, the committee held 35 sessions, sitting for a total of 120 hours . . . The committee's proceedings went almost entirely unnoticed by the press. A colossal amount of committee time was spent on the first few clauses . . . after which the government resorted to a guillotine so that most of the later clauses went through with virtually no debate . . . it was scrutiny by slogan and soundbite.[22]

The results of this are well known. We have been brought up to think that one of the advantages of a parliamentary democracy, as opposed to an autocracy, is that bad laws are caught and prevented before bricks start whizzing and cars are overturned. It seems that in this matter, as in others, the British educational system has been deficient.

This is such a central question that we cannot leave it there. More examples: The Dangerous Dogs Act and the Football Spectators Act were two measures in the past few years which proved so badly flawed as to be, in part, unworkable. (They were both examples of Parliament acting quickly and responsively to national panics, which shows that a more responsive, fast-moving legislature wouldn't necessarily be a better one.) As the Liberal Democrat MP Paul Tyler told the Commons in June 1994:

On the Railways Bill, the government produced a huge number of amendments on the day that they were due to be debated. Once those amendments had been pulled apart, they were withdrawn, but further amendments were tabled at the eleventh hour. Therefore, once that Bill had received Royal Assent, a supplementary Bill had to be introduced to tidy up the mistakes. The Criminal Justice Bill of 1993 required about 100 government amendments and some parts of it were not even capable of being enacted.[23]

In his excellent account of Parliament John Garrett, a Labour MP and management consultant, devastatingly recorded his experience on the 1989 Companies Bill, an important and complex piece of legislation. It is a familiar but still shocking story, whose flavour is given by his summary of the state of the Bill after its committee stage:

The government's own amendments had reached the thousand mark and included no fewer than fifteen new clauses which were introduced on the last day of the committee's sittings. These new clauses, in effect a new Financial Services Act, introducing extensive measures to regulate the City and provide investor protection, were discussed for only four hours . . .

Most of the key criticisms were made, in temperate and careful language, by the cross-party and no-party Hansard Society

Commission on legislation which reported in February 1993. At its head it quoted a few lawyers and other public figures about the state of some of the three thousand Acts currently in force in Britain. James Goudie QC believed that 'legislation is becoming increasingly inaccessible ... and ... impossible to understand. Unintelligible legislation is the negation of the rule of law and of parliamentary democracy.' And Jane Hern of the Law Society was even blunter. Lawyers, she said, were constantly 'trying to find out what [statute law] is in force, when it came into force ... and when they have found out, what the hell it means.' Almost any lawyer working can come up with smaller examples of badly drafted legislation: when I recently moved house, I had to pay several hundred pounds of indemnity insurance because of a minor parliamentary mistake – literally, a piece of poor drafting. Our daily lives are affected more often than we know by Parliament's incompetence at performing its central role. Why does this happen, and how much does it matter? Although there are plenty of dramatic case-studies, it seems worth taking just one, and analysing it in some detail.

A Few Weeks one February

The sums involved ran into billions. The affair involved hundreds of thousands of people, by some estimates two million. The subject was both mundane and hugely important: pensions. If economics is the dismal science, demographics is the pessimistic one. Fear of a hugely ageing population, and the cost to the smaller working population of paying their pensions, started this particular tale of parliamentary failure. The state earnings-related pension scheme, or SERPS as it was known, could not go on as it had done in the past. Lloyd George in 1911 had introduced the idea of compulsory contributory state-administered pensions, and this had been extended as one of the fundamental planks of the Beveridge reforms following the Second World War. No longer would friendly societies and a host of small-time companies collect shillings street by street, often spending huge percentages on administering the savings.

There would be a simple, national scheme. All would pay in, all would be paid. But because of the simultaneous aspect of the system – today's payers-in are not saving for their own pensions, but are paying for today's pensioners – it has always been theoretically vulnerable to an ageing population. In fact, even among strong partisans of private pensions, there is now a strong feeling that the so-called 'demographic time-bomb' has been exaggerated. But there were other reasons for getting the state out of the pensions business, at least as far as possible. It is expensive yet, as these things go, ungenerous. Ministers shared the belief that it was old-fashioned and indeed unwise for people to transfer their wealth to the state for safekeeping. A nation of popular capitalism would be one in which each individual invested his or her savings as they saw fit. As for the eleven million or so adding to their state pension by paying into occupational schemes, benefiting from the employer's contribution, their system was also looked on with disfavour. Occupational schemes penalized their members for changing employer, and so the occupational system was bad for labour-market mobility and the economy generally.

These were among the arguments used by two of the crowd of clever thinkers at the right-wing Centre for Policy Studies. Nigel Vinson, now Lord Vinson, and Philip Chappell produced a paper entitled 'Personal and Portable Pensions for All' in April 1983 which advocated 'self-employed pensions for all' and enthused: 'it would give a new opportunity for 12 million people to have a real sense of involvement in the industrial success of this country.' It was an idea wholly in tune with the temper of the times and Vinson and Chappell, with the enthusiastic backing of John Redwood, later a cabinet minister, seem to have had no difficulty in selling it to the then Social Services Secretary, Norman Fowler. It was incorporated in his wide-ranging reform of social security. So far so good: an unexceptional story of the Thatcher revolution, featuring the obligatory egg-heads and can-do ministers. But pensions are special. For most people they are probably the biggest single financial decision of their lives. I say 'decision' but, because the subject of long-term investment can be pretty complicated, few of us are expert enough to make a fully-informed decision on our own. Whatever the drawbacks of the old system, it was safe and predictable. The state paid out. For those who wanted to live more than frugally and had been able to plan ahead, the company did. Private pensions were for the self-employed, or add-on schemes for the better-off. The importance of pensions to people's lives meant that the government had a particular responsibility, if they were changing the system, to ensure that the worse-off and the ignorant were fully protected.

This was particularly so in the late 1980s. The life-assurance industry had been hammered by Nigel Lawson's abolition of tax relief on life-assurance premiums in 1985 on the grounds that it unduly favoured institutional investment, rather than direct investment. Lawson followed it with an attack on the tax-free treatment of lump-sum payments from occupational pensions, which was initially rebuffed by what he called the awesome power of the pension-fund lobby – 'the most astonishing lobbying campaign of my entire political career'.[24] The insurance industry in general is massively powerful because of the sums its managers invest and its direct influence on government as the paymaster of the public sector borrowing requirement. Harold Wilson had famously asserted to the writer Anthony Sampson that, in his view, 'They could be more powerful than the cabinet.' At any rate, it ought not to have escaped anyone reasonably *au fait* with the financial community that here was a business which was both powerful and desperate for a lucrative new market. The personal-pensions revolution was going to provide it. But what about those who were about to be urged to change the arrangements for their old age, starting from a position of near-total ignorance and, in many cases, financial naïveté? If a democratic legislature exists to protect anyone, it existed to protect them.

That was the background for the meetings of standing committee B of the House of Commons between 4 February and 4 March 1986, when the legislation for these changes was discussed. Leading for the government was Norman Fowler, as Secretary of State. He was assisted by two of the Tory party's ablest technocrats of the day, Tony Newton and John Major, who had got his first leg-up on the ladder of government as Parliamentary Under-Secretary for Health and Social Security. The disturbing thing about re-reading the committee minutes afterwards is the accuracy with which MPs pointed to the key flaws in the legislation – the lack of proper protection against high-pressure salesmen, the opacity of the all-important information about how much of the pension-holder's money would be swallowed up by commissions and administrative costs, pocketed by the companies; the danger of innocent people (in both senses of the word) being bilked. All were preventable. What was predicted, then happened. In some cases, the very proposals which were laughed at by ministers were later adopted by the government to limit the damage that followed.

A constant theme of opposition and Tory backbench probing was the danger of hidden charges. This later proved to be an extremely serious problem. In the first year of some policies it was estimated that up to 90 per cent of the premiums were in some cases being swallowed up by greedy salesmen and companies in commission and other administrative costs. The expected loss of a fifth to a quarter of the investor's money on commission over the lifetime of a scheme was not uncommon. For the people worst-advised, those who opted out of the state scheme but paid in no extra to their private one, it was calculated that the charges and commission might result in no pension at all. This was hardly a new problem. The administrative cost of the old network of friendly societies and local insurance institutions was cited by Beveridge in 1942 as a reason for the national system. But one of the sceptical Conservatives on the committee in 1986 was able to tell the Commons four years later that: there had been 'a total inadequacy within the regulatory structure'. Had the Commons at the time had any inkling of the dangers ahead? It certainly had. Michael Meacher, leading for Labour, warned that a study by the Institute of Actuaries had shown that charges of 20 per cent were common. Mr Major said that 10 per cent would be too high, promised that 'increased competition from pension providers should greatly help to bring charges down' and anticipated Mr Meacher's 'discomfiture' on the issue. The same story is repeated through the legislation. The opposition and some Tory MPs were worried about misleadingly-sold pensions. Mr Major assured them that prospectuses for pensions would be 'expressed in real, realistic – and, I hope, understandable – terms.' The Financial Services Bill 'will safeguard people against unscrupulous over-selling of personal pensions.' It didn't. Again, despite clear expressions of worry on the committee, the assurances were broad-brush and bland.

To persuade people to change to new private pensions, the government introduced a 2 per cent inducement, described by Labour (and later, even by members of the industry) as a bribe, for anyone who opted out of SERPS. If they merely paid the same to their new private scheme, this would prove to be a bad move. If they were persuaded to leave a half-decent occupational scheme, it would be a terrible one. Labour's Margaret Beckett called for more safeguards for people who bought into private schemes, warning that some people would be 'putting at risk not only themselves but their families.' Mr Fowler retorted that it was 'illogical to believe that someone is going to leave a good occupational scheme for the benefit of a 2 per cent incentive.' As it turned out, tens of thousands – including 32,000 nurses, 58,000 miners and 27,000 teachers and 23,000 steelworkers – did just that. Back in 1986, the National Association of Pension Funds, which may have been parti pris, but was hardly a Marxist front, was even more withering than Labour about the policy:

It is as though the Government had come to prefer Everton to Liverpool and decided to make a cash payment out of public funds to every Liverpool supporter who switches his allegiance ... a gross misuse of taxpayers' money ... It is quite astonishing that any Government could risk proposing to hand over this huge sum of our money: and at the same time distorting the free market, to which it pays lip service.

(What huge sum, by the way? At the time, it was calculated

that the inducement, which would run for five years, would cost the National Insurance Fund £60 million. By the time the pay-outs finished, in April 1993, the total cost was £1.3 billion – and, no, the writer has not got his noughts muddled up.) And for what? In many cases, to persuade citizens to make a bad bargain about their retirement.

By April 1995, the pensions watchdog, the Personal Investment Authority, had estimated that up to £3 billion might be needed to compensate some of the 350,000 people involved. The Prudential, Britain's biggest insurance company, had set aside £20 million for possible claims.

The failure of those ministers, all of them thoughtful and intelligent men, during those few sittings, is also a failure of the parliamentary system. If legislation of such importance, which caused so much worry and misery to so many vulnerable citizens, can get through with so many holes in it, holes pointed out at the time, then the system has failed, not only the ministers. This failure to properly regulate the personal pensions revolution in 1986 is memorably summed up by a Labour backbencher, now retired, called Frank Haynes. He conformed to many Conservatives' nostalgic picture of what a Labour MP should be – a former miner with a foghorn voice, long on denunciation and, they felt, not too bright. When he rose in the Commons chamber, a collective ripple of pleasure ran through the government benches: it was a reminder that the class war in Britain is just a bit of fun, a pleasant show. In short, Reader, they patronized him. And here is what Mr Haynes, out of touch with eighties Britain, told the future Prime Minister, surrounded in 1986 by his civil servants and his helpful advice from the pensions industry:

It is crystal clear what is happening . . . I used to work down a pit. Often in the consultative set-up there were applications for collections at the pit from various organizations. One of the first things that the membership at the pit asked was, 'what sort of administration charges are there?' We wanted to know before considering who to contribute to. The same thing is happening here . . . The minister talks of consumer power. Who is he kidding? Consumers are said to have power in all sorts of ways, but what happens? The boys at the top get themselves together and fix things. They fix certain financial levels . . . Members of the government represent people outside, as we do. They deserve to be kicked hard for their proposals in this Bill.

I was not there that night, but I can imagine the chuckles all round. Mr Major dismissed his attack as vicious and unsurprising, and carried on giving assurances about private pensions for all. At one point Mr Newton chirruped: 'Everybody in his right mind should have one.' The government went ahead with a £1.2 million advertising campaign to persuade people to opt out of SERPS. Some 6.5 million people went for private pensions at the height of the boom. Many will have done all right. But an unknown number, possibly running into hundreds of thousands, were wrong to do so. They were too poorly paid, or too old, or in too good schemes already, to make it worth their while. These were not the people ministers met later at dinner parties. They were often recruited by friends or relatives whose brief and inglorious careers as commission-only pension salesmen lasted only as long as their address books. Salesmen bought up the internal directories of companies for large sums, to push their wares. Redundant miners were given jobs selling personal pensions to their redundant colleagues. According to an investigation carried out by the accountants KPMG Peat Marwick, some 83 per cent of transactions involving salesmen suggested that insufficient information was collected from the clients to ensure they got the right pension. The whole thing was a disaster. Later, to be sure, the life companies stored up sums for compensation, the regulators were given new powers and ministers moved to plug the gaps. But it was very late and not much comfort to those who lost. As Mr Dewar told the Commons later, it was 'a scandal that is no less serious because it was so long unrecognized and no less cruel because many of the victims were, and probably still are, unaware of their plight.'

This story could be repeated, with variations, in a vast range of cases, grave and trivial, narrow and broad. City regulation. The Broadcasting Act. The Child Support Agency. Similar mistakes are probably being made today, in some obscure and unreported committee. So who is to blame? The crucial point to grasp is that on that committee during those weeks in 1986 everyone involved was acting entirely rationally on the basis of their own self-interest. The civil servants, the grade-5 leader and his team on the Bill, had been instructed and chivvied by ministers with a strong ideological agenda. They had accepted the proposals put to them by their political masters and had them drawn as legislation by relatively poorly-paid lawyers hired by the state. As officials in the Home Office and the Department for Education discovered over the next few years, there was no promotion or future for bureaucrats who provided the 'wrong' advice to committed and impatient ministers. And by the time a team of civil servants which has been working on a Bill for perhaps a year or more is sitting in the officials' box in the Commons, they have become emotionally attached to their piece of work, and are instinctively likely to see attacks on it as attacks on them.

The ministers too, by refusing to listen and thus to improve a flawed piece of legislation, were acting wholly logically. These are people trying, as most of us are, to get on in life. How are they judged for promotion, and who judges them? Remember, the political culture sees the job of the minister, once a bill has arrived at Westminster, to get it through as quickly as possible and with as few U-turns or changes as possible. The minister who listens to opposition or backbench points, who publicly admits faults in legislation, is losing, both individually and on behalf of the government collectively. He's losing face. He's losing time. Who's watching? The power of preferment and of political exile rests with the party machines, and specifically, as we have seen, the whips. The parties are the real power-centres at Westminster. Each bill has its whip assigned to it and the whip is taking notes. Not only the whip, though, but the civil servants too. The minister who lets the opposition amendments through, however sensible, is letting down the department as well as the party. Word will get back to the permanent secretary and, through him, to the rest of the 'permanent government' of Whitehall.

But what about the minister who allows bad legislation to

progress because Parliament is not allowed to properly consider it: isn't he or she eventually caught out as the legislation fails out there, in the real world, in front of the rest of the country? Well, how often have *you* read the failures pinned on the ministers at the time, the ones who've moved on to new jobs, or been sacked, or promoted, well before the world catches up? The press generally fails to help the country hold ministers to account. They (we) are too busy trying to scurry after the current week's agenda to trawl back through debates which are five or six years old. No, for the rational minister the risks of being blamed for poor legislation in a few years' time are as nothing to the risk of 'Butterball in U-turn' stories if amendments are treated seriously. Did Mr Major's failure to listen to the flaws in his pensions legislation harm his career? Was he ever held to account for that failure? Does anyone now remember it? The opposition, knowing the game perfectly well, quite often give up the business of serious and constructive amendments to an entire piece of legislation.

And most of them, like most of the government backbenchers (and a few ministers) are wholly at sea in the dense legal language of legislation. The very idea that a bunch of former union officials, bankers, history teachers and estate agents should be expected to effectively and rigorously scrutinize legal phraseology is batty: as the Law Society put it,

Many legislative measures now considered by Parliament are mainly or partly of a highly technical nature . . . and few MPs or Peers have the necessary specialist knowledge or interest to contribute to a detailed debate on such issues. The traditional parliamentary forum in which the opposition opposes whatever the government proposes is not well suited to the process of legislation which is increasingly specialist and/or technical . . .[25]

Instead, opposition MPs try to wear the ministers down, forcing the government to timetable the bill, thus curtailing discussion; or they move largely by probing or wrecking amendments, intended to make strong, reportable points. Government backbenchers too often rely on lobbyists' briefing papers, or merely toe the ministerial line. Everyone is behaving rationally. It is just that the end result is barking mad.

Nor is it good enough to leave all the blame with individuals, as if the legislature itself could be exonerated. The culture has failed. If backbench MPs of all sides were a little more aware of the objective importance to Parliament of crafting workable legislation, and a little less ready to curry favour with whips, they might approach their amendments in a more constructive way. If standing committees were in the habit of inviting in outside interests affected by proposed legislation, and taking expert legal advice as to the likely effect of different clauses, they would become more serious legislative tools. If . . . if . . . if . . . Those reforms are in the hands of parliamentarians, individually and collectively. It is no good them whingeing about their poor status and subordinate role if they are also prepared to continue tolerating their own failure to pass competent legislation. Part of the problem is simply volume. More than 2,500 pages of primary legislation are examined by the Commons in a typical year, taking about a third of its time. The burden of legislation has grown absurdly, even under Lady Thatcher, who promised to reduce it. The great reforming Liberal administrations of the early part of the century managed with a few hundred pages of legislation a year. The post-war Labour government – which established the modern Welfare State, nationalized vast swathes of industry and generally engaged in frantic activity – passed a thousand pages or so a year. In 1985, under a 'small government' government, Parliament had to discuss and pass 3,233 pages of new rules – not counting the 6,518 pages of statutory instruments which it was unable to seriously look at. These statutory instruments contain many important instances of ministerial power that affect ordinary voters, benefits changes and social security levels among them. Ministers have steadily accumulated to themselves more and more power through indirect legislation, which avoids the tedious job of having to listen to elected Members before ignoring them. Parliament has scarcely bothered to complain, or claw back any of this lost influence. It cannot, quite literally, be bothered.

Yet perhaps there is little point in getting worked up about that when the big, mainstream, controversial, direct legislation is so slackly dealt with. You would expect to find the committees trying to scrutinize these torrents of paper engaged in sweatily frantic activity. Yet the average visitor, dropping in on such a committee, would find many of its members answering mail, writing Christmas cards, or hanging around making phone-calls in the corridor outside. If that visitor came across the same legislation during its passage in the chamber, it would probably be obvious that 'the full House' is a phrase which describes an awesome amount of empty green leather. Real people really suffer as a result of this complacency and mental sloth.

Heckling the Steamroller

The other great role of Parliament is scrutiny of the executive – finding out what 'they' are doing on our behalf, and telling us. The best known form of scrutiny, questions to ministers in the chamber, either during the early-afternoon sessions set aside for each department in turn, or during debates, is also the least effective. The deficiencies of Prime Minister's questions have already been discussed. It is not that they are not traumatic and difficult for the Prime Minister – they are, and require a huge amount of preparation. 'No one can have the faintest idea what it is like who hasn't done it,' one former victim told me. Often they produce press and television stories simply because the Prime Minister is publicly asked about something newsworthy. Sometimes he, or she, slips up, or cannot answer – as when John Major was unable, in February 1995, to support his Chancellor's view that joining a single currency did not threaten the nation-state – and light is publicly shed on a problem in government. Notwithstanding all that, though, the fifteen-minute exchanges have become widely regarded at Westminster as a puerile, uninformative turn-off which are doing the business of politics no good at all. Prime ministers and leaders of the opposition have privately worried about this for some time, yet seem unable to agree to change the format, for want of seeming weak in the eyes of the other. One opposition politician who has experienced the bouts first-hand in the past says: 'Sometimes I sat there, and I asked myself, just what the f★★★ am I doing?' – a question on the minds of many of those watching, too.

Yet on it goes, because no one wants to be the first to leave the ring to shouts of 'chicken'. Ministerial question-times can be more informative and are useful to campaigners, lobby groups and interested parties, but again rarely produce breakthroughs in public understanding. Ministers appear with full civil service briefings, and the civil service has developed a highly effective system of verbal camouflage and obfuscation. The ordering of questions and the habit of taking first a government back-bencher, then an opposition one, and so on, helps ensure that ministers are rarely pressed for too long on a single point, making evasion all too easy. In general, the thousands of written and oral questions pushed in by MPs provide only glimpses of light: to make progress takes patience and cunning, qualities many Members lack. The pursuit of Margaret Thatcher's authorization to sink the *Belgrano* took Tam Dalyell scores of frustrated questions and years of persistence. As with his other inquisitorial successes, he depended heavily on outside help and advice – in that case, from civil servants in the Ministry of Defence who wanted the truth to come out, and from friendly academics who pieced together and helped explain the shards of information. In earlier cases, Dalyell used congressmen and senators, senior scientists and even a contact with the White House during the Johnson presidency to help him as a seeker after Whitehall truth. But in that, as in so much else, Tam Dalyell of the Binns was a rarity. His secret weapon was his thick skin. Bluntly put, trying to get at the truth required him to become a House bore. He was undeterred. Most MPs are deterred.

When it comes to questions during ministerial statements on new policy, or during debates, ministers can usually rely on a supporters' club on their own benches to lob easy rhetorical points at them, and to drown out their less informative partisan answers with sycophantic laughter. It is rare for a minister to get in real trouble. One of the few candidly-recounted recent examples of a minister coming unstuck was Alan Clark's late-night embarrassment, featured in his famous *Diaries*. But, as he freely admitted, was muzzy after a fine-wine tasting and suffering from 'an odious over-confidence.' Mostly debates are exchanges of view, rather than occasions for effective probing. In an under-briefed House, the 'oohs' and 'aahs' are reserved for cheap party points rather than significant revelations about policy or ministerial thinking. Until a century ago, the most important old function of Parliament, close scrutiny of government expenditure, was still carried out in the chamber of the Commons, department by department, sometimes line by line. Individual items of spending were challenged and defended. There was real questioning of Whitehall's plans. But the state, arriving in the era of its greatness, could not allow this parliamentary impudence and, in 1896, the system was stopped. As John Garrett has said and demonstrated,[26] for the subsequent century, 'there has been very little detailed discussion of government spending and today billions of pounds are passed each year without debate.'

'Scrutiny' is not so very different from good journalism and, like journalism, is partly a matter of determination, and partly a matter of resources. The Commons, generally, has lacked both. The departmental select committees, which started to develop as early as the 1860s but which really only got going in 1979, are now the main system of scrutiny. Norman St John Stevas, then Leader of the Commons, said openly that the committee system was being extended because the British constitution was getting so tilted towards the executive that it was damaging parliamentary democracy (another example of the Tories' openness towards political reform after their spell in opposition). The select committees have huge advantages over backbench questions in the chamber: a regular, cross-party membership of MPs – around two hundred are involved at any one time – who become, if not experts, at least possessed with a nodding acquaintance with their subject. They have time, a small staff, and a little money (£3m or so a year, of which £2m goes on printing their reports and evidence). They can summon people and papers – though not MPs. They can, eventually and occasionally, get their reports debated in the Commons. Much more regularly, they win the power of publicity. A sub-branch of parliamentary journalism is now devoted to reading and reporting (preferably ahead of time, via a leak) the findings of select committees, whose chairmen, faintly irate about the leak, are then flattered to appear on television and discuss the report. They do undeniably useful work. Yet a great deal of self-congratulatory humbug surrounds this matter. The media frequently uses the formula 'the influential Commons committee today . . .' This suits the journalists or broadcasters because it implies that something will come of the report they are citing, making the story more important. It flatters the committee. But is it true?

The most serious and authoritative recent study of Parliament dryly pronounces: 'Select committees have not made a general impact on Government policies.'[27] True, the system has had its moments, most memorably during the Westland affair, when three committees homed in on the cabinet feud and skulduggery which nearly brought down Margaret Thatcher. Their hearings were riveting and got further to the heart of the affair than MPs would have been able to manage in the chamber. In the end, however, the ability of the civil service and ministers to block and avoid the most difficult questions meant that the investigations were neither fully satisfactory nor conclusive. Other occasions have included memorable clashes with Nigel Lawson and with Edwina Currie, following her resignation from the government over the salmonella in eggs controversy. So great was the press and public interest then that the agriculture committee had to sit in a large hall. Mrs Currie appeared in black velvet, like a Victorian depiction of Mary Queen of Scots facing her accusers, and her eyes flashed and the crumpled-looking men sitting in judgement looked most abashed. It was all very fine. More than that, we can credit the select committees generally with introducing television viewers to close questioning of ministers and civil servants. Occasional news clips result, and more substantial TV programmes; though these are hardly popular, televised select committees have, undoubtedly, extended the power of the 'media democracy'. Not all MPs have been much impressed. Austin Mitchell, the salt-tongued Labour tribune from Grimsby, who admits that the chamber of the Commons 'is merely an opportunity to heckle the steam roller', argues that the select committees have failed to live up to their promise as a serious alternative: 'Think of the great issues of the period: the insane deflation from 1979–82, the ERM disaster, the folly of the credit explosions and the folly of the Broadcasting Act, the repercussions of the Single Market and Maastricht, the end of full employment, Trident, the Falklands. Franks and the House of Lords have done better reports on some and committees have said nothing significant about any.' I think that's a touch harsh – the Trade and Industry Select Committee report on British competitiveness in manufacturing remains useful reading for anyone interested in the future of the economy. Nor can cross-party committees commit themselves repeatedly and unambiguously against the policies of the government of the day. But Mitchell's small, hard grain should itch and discomfort his colleagues: when he explains that 'the committees have been integrated into the patronage system of career politics by being viewed as a training ground for promotion or a parking place for loyalists'[28] the fellow speaketh truth.

Still, if 'scrutiny' is taken literally as looking, rather than influencing, then the committees have been a modest success. They are hampered by the need for cross-party consensus, and by stifling rules intended to keep civil servants from saying anything embarrassing when they are being questioned. They are badly under-resourced, and their impact lessens as elections draw closer. But hardly anyone would now wish them away. The most seriously-resourced and most serious of the committees is the oldest, the Public Accounts Committee, which scrutinizes aspects of public spending and is served by the National Audit Office, a two-thousand-strong organization of accountants and investigators whose origins go back to the days of Samuel Pepys and whose studies of value for money are the best public scrutiny of government of all. The Public Accounts Committee closely follows the investigations of the NAO in its own findings. It has produced excellent reports, rattled ministers badly and is one aspect of Parliament the executive would love to stamp on. Long may it flourish. But the NAO has a limited financial remit and reports, in obscurely technical prose, to only one committee which, in turn, guards its intellectual property pretty rigorously. This is not quite a rampantly independent Parliament at work.

For the rest, they do a reasonable job of looking, insofar as they are allowed to by the executive, armed with its prerogatives and little secrets. Yet if we agreed that the job of scrutinizing the executive was such an important role in a modern state that it conferred constitutional status, then the real British constitution would assign a larger position to a clutch of television news programmes – *Panorama, Newsnight* and *Dispatches*, among others – and the occasional newspaper investigation, than it would to select committees. All of these are better-resourced than the committees, are free from the threats of whips and party managers' bribes, are more single-minded when pursuing an issue of policy, and report directly and with some professional élan directly to the voters, rather than in expensive paper-covered obscurity to other MPs. And they carry fewer passengers. So far as the public is concerned, has *Panorama* or the Select Committee on Employment done more to scrutinize the executive over the past twenty years? *Question Time* or the education committee? You, sir, in the back row with the spotty bow-tie? Yes, quite right. Which, therefore, is more important to the real British constitution?

This is, I suppose, an impertinent point: select committees are still slowly evolving and their game is far from over. MPs' status gives them useful rights of questioning which journalists lack. The development of a more sturdily self-contained select committee culture would answer most of these criticisms. It is only when one turns to the matter of direct influence that the select-committee system really starts to look like a failure. As a reporter of it, I have sat through weeks of compelling evidence-taking, followed by the release of a pungent, factually-detailed and pointed report, only to see the whole thing dismissed by ministers months later in a couple of bland lines. In some cases a year's-worth of investigation by the NAO has been airily waved away by Whitehall. Or appears to have been. One can never be sure that the pointed remarks of select committees or the glare of the auditors don't produce hidden convulsions inside the departments concerned, which ministers are too embarrassed to admit to. But overall the record of direct influence is thin. You have to wonder: would the two hundred MPs have been more effective doing something else?

The plight of the British Parliament is a complicated, sad and fascinating story, and one could spend the rest of this book discussing the new developments in the European legislation committees (which are getting quite good at seriously roasting ministers) and the lamentable failure of Parliament to delve into the issues of the Royal Prerogative under which so much ministerial power is exercised without reference to the Commons. But if it is not proving truly effective at passing legislation that works, and if it is only a second-rate scrutineer of the executive, then it is failing at its central tasks and we need go little further. It lacks information about Brussels and Whitehall (and Whitehall has not been helpful in getting the Commons key pieces of information about Brussels). It is made a fool of by ministers and senior civil servants every other day. It is the butt of public abuse and media yobbery and it has little hold over either the actions of the executive or the affections of the public. As we have seen, it fails to legislate properly or scrutinize effectively. And yet, sitting surrounded by these failures and humiliations, it still insists that it is sovereign, a constitutionally and democratically special place. Here is the crucial conundrum for the British Parliament, which it alone can answer: if it is sovereign, indeed absolute, then why is it so weak? An absolute sovereign has no one else to blame. So why cannot the House of Commons – whingeing on about its lowly status, the contemptuous, bullying executive, the pushy lobbyists, the sneering hacks – reform itself? Physician, what's wrong?

And it could, if it had the will, wrest some practical power back from the European Union. It could wade in and start ordering the bosses of unelected quangos about. It could demand that ministers do this, and then change its mind and require them to do that, instead. In practice, in the real constitution, it has given away so much power to party managers and been so pusillanimous for so long about the executive, that its power has become the constitutional equivalent of the Loch Ness monster – asserted to be there by quirky researchers and occasionally claimed to have been seen by lonely men in beige anoraks, but never established to the satisfaction of the wider world. It is another bad business, this. It is about the failure of the parliamentary culture to survive in the modern world.

But even the story told here is not the end of the problem. For a strong, democratic parliament must have an effective state to operate on. If the state is weak compared to other forces which are beyond the control of the ballot-box, then even the most assertive and efficient parliament will be a weak democratic instrument itself. The lever must be connected to something. And there's not much point in ordering ministers about or asking them questions if they aren't powerful in the real world and don't know the answers. That really would relegate Westminster to being an empty relic of power – Charles Barry and Augustus Welby Pugin's beautiful but cold and empty casket. And everything we have so far discussed, from the problem of voters and quangos to the accountability of ministers at the dispatch box, is as nothing compared to the great issue of that melting volcano, that straw man with feet of clay, the British state.

CHAPTER FOUR

The Decline and Fall of the Free State

> I am the state's man. Stuffed
> Is my head with paper, clipped
> Is my tongue. Ask, Briton, for bread.
> I give you stone-coloured coupons. For love?
> Flags, electricity, a girl's silver face . . .'
>   – Philip Webster, 'For Wystan', 1949

In Bed with a Monster

The British state is a pretty odd beast. First, what is the state? It is the government of the country, the historical form of the nation, the accepted focus of political authority. It is not us, the people, but something which claims somehow to be over us and around us and to be in some legal way (though this is clearly nonsense) prior to us. It associates itself strongly with the Crown. We don't mean the headwear itself, of course: the days when we got worked up about fetish-objects such as the sceptre or the Great Seal are long gone. But we still associate the state with the person who occasionally wears and holds the fetish-objects, a shrewd and by all accounts sardonic woman in her sixties, of immigrant stock, and, by extension, with her rather curious family. More loosely still, the 'crown' refers to her less curious but also less amusing secretaries of state and ministers of state; her army, navy, air force, marines, judges, courts, police folk, tax-gatherers, lawyers, civil servants, incivil servants and so on and so forth – all the law-makers, law-enforcers, war-makers, peacekeepers and others whose jobs and titles descend from the heyday of the nation-state. They are the servants of the state which, alongside the Crown, appears to consist of a few lorryloads of case law, various Archbishops of advanced views and the Bank of England.

Because of the Civil War, the Commonwealth, the Restoration

and the Glorious Revolution of 1688, no constitutionalist would stop there, but would immediately go on to recite 'The-Queen-in-Parliament' as being the deep sovereign core of the British state, by which of course the constitutionalist would really mean the Queen-not-in-Parliament, except-on-the-very-rare-occasions-when-she-is-asked-along-to-read-somebody-else's-speech-like-a-very-grand-TV-newscaster. (Much insular merriment occurs whenever the English contemplate the difficulty of explaining the rules of cricket to a poor foreigner. Trying to explain the rules of the British constitution quickly falls into the same category, though this example of native eccentricity is less often glorified on tea-towels.) It is Parliament that is sovereign, then? We have just seen the trouble with that theory. For most practical purposes the fact of a Commons majority has conferred the right for a group of here-today politicians to behave as if their interests are identical with those of the state. They are under law but are also holders of quasi-monarchical powers. Are ministers, then, the true fountainhead of authority, the living expression of sovereignty?

The trouble with that is that fewer and fewer British people would accept it. We have become true democrats and, in our hearts, most of us now assume that it is 'we' collectively, the people, who are the truest and deepest source of legitimate national authority, a sovereignty we loan to our parliamentary and state institutions, and through them to ministers and the constitutional monarchy itself. No one much talks about this – it is an unspoken modern assumption. It is also, of course, a republican one which implies that the crown is not God-given authority but is merely a handy national emblem or badge representing the democratic system and people of Britain. This republicanism has already passed, like a computer virus, into the minds of even those Conservative traditionalists in government who are most respectful of monarchy. So when, in the search for peace in Ulster, John Major accepted that the future of the Province, whether as part of Britain or as part of a united Ireland, lay in the hands of the people of Northern Ireland themselves, rather than the British state or crown, he was talking like a good republican: the people are sovereign; they are the ultimate authority. Similarly, when the Scottish National Party leader Alex Salmond challenged Major and other ministers to confirm that if the people of Scotland voted for independence they would get it, and he agreed, he was accepting, whether wittingly or not, that the people of Scotland are sovereign. This is mere republican common sense but it poses questions about the real foundation for the authority and basis of British statehood which are bound to grow more insistent. If we are unsure as a country where the ultimate source of legitimacy lies, then much of what we call our great institutions are built on sandier ground than we thought.

At least we are not a nation of state-lovers, and that is a considerable national strength. Too often in its short global life the state has been belligerent, greedy and cold; it has preferred darkness to light, mistaken its own gloomy authority for patriotism, and seemed at times to think that bureaucracy can cure our human souls. Love the state and you will die unhappy. Love the state in Britain and people will think you are a foreigner. Occasionally, as when the Falklands armada set off, British patriotism erupts like a multi-coloured geyser. But for most of the time, these are not state-worshipping or politics-adoring countries. I use the plural advisedly; this remains a single-state union of different nations, in which the BBC is a bigger binder-together of the nation these days than the monarchy or the other trappings of old state power. Probe the soul of the nation and you'd be more likely to find Noel Edmonds on a sofa than Enoch Powell on a soapbox. The BBC is also subdivided. So there is Scottish patriotism, Welsh patriotism – and English patriotism. Yet even Englishness is less simple than it seems, and has little to do with the state. For the establishment, Englishness is white and rooted at the south of the country and in small towns or villages, not large ones: something that excludes rather a lot of people. If Surrey and Kent are Home Counties, what are Cheshire and Lancashire? The Neighbours' Counties? For the majority of the English, 'national' feeling is nothing of the sort, but is more associated with regional accents, which the state, because it lives in the metropolis, disdains; and sporting teams, which the state is too busy doing nothing well to notice; and with industrial cultures which the state has left to moulder silently like native Indian burial-grounds; and sometimes with soft green rural idylls, which the state drives thousands of miles of 'blacktop' through.[1] And for the smaller nations and peoples of the United Kingdom, patriotism is cultural and sporting – go to any Scotland-England rugby game – and intermittently political and certainly has nothing to do with the state.

And yet the potency and reality of the state is terribly important. A democracy without a state, which may one day come about, still seems hard to imagine. The tax-gathering, the law-making – the redistribution and the regulation aimed at making life a little more ordered and predictable – have depended on the state. It is well within living memory that we depended on the state to save us from the madnesses of other state-worshipping enemies. Thus, if it should be announced one morning on the Breakfast News that the state had passed away peacefully in the night, our first feelings might be of liberation, but most of us would quickly feel worried rather than relieved.

'Nanny state' or not, the British middle classes were brought up with the Bellocian rhyme about keeping hold of nurse for fear of finding something worse. Power does not just disappear. So where, we would wonder, might it have gone this time? Who had taken it? Would the new power-source give us a vote, or bother to pick up the phone, or be aware of us at all? Friedrich Nietzsche, the German philosopher, wrote that the state was 'the name of the coldest of all cold monsters. Coldly it tells lies too; and this lie crawls out of its mouth: "I, the state, am the people!"' Nietzsche, though in general a nasty piece of work, was right about that. Yet even as we approach the new millennium, the state remains the democratic monster. The state has not been a pleasant thing, but it has been a great thing, a necessary thing, a thing we learned about early on in life, were educated by, paid money to, obeyed. 'Britain' did this or that, and, in some part, we all did it. 'Britain' spoke at the United Nations, or invaded Egypt, or lost her car industry. And what the British state did, or was, affected us, however inappropriate the abstraction was, however far-away the events. So if we have never exactly *loved* the state, or identified ourselves fully with it, we have learned to live together.

But – and this is what matters – more and more of us are learning to live apart again. Increasing numbers of the British are opting out of state provision, in health, in housing, in crime-prevention, in transport. The long-term future for taxation has been clouded by international technologies and demography. At the same time, the state has been divesting itself of many of its old responsibilities, through privatization; cutting its direct workforce and spending taxpayers' money through private companies instead. And when it comes to the big things, including finance, pollution and defence, the state no longer stands nearly as freely independent as it used to. Everything about the state has been up for grabs. Even its territorial reach is today in question, as the old Conservative and Unionist Party involves itself in a peace process for Northern Ireland that makes it neutral on the Union, while in Scotland a formidable and popular Home Rule movement demands a parliament for Edinburgh. Our state is in a state of chronic instability

Imperialism to Welfare

What is its essential story through the democratic period? It can be summarized in a single, brutal sentence. It has declined. This decline has had three clear phases, though they are jumbled in time. First, it has lost world power. Second, it has compensated by attempting to become more powerful at home. Third, it has discovered that this, too, is a forlorn ambition. At its most simplistic, the story could be presented as the defeat of politics by economics. Twice in living memory the huge and complex organizational machine of the British imperial state, with its own propaganda-history, its island-terrain and its hold on many hundreds of millions throughout the world, mobilized the people and fought in titanic conflicts to protect itself. These were the great triumphs of the political state, from which it twice emerged apparently mightier than before. Though still within living memory, they were defining moments of modern Britishness, the heroic instants that the British look back to rather than the anti-French and imperial struggles which dominated the early years of Britain. The trenches and the Spitfire are key emblems of the British story. The English had earlier emblems – Runnymede, Agincourt; the Scots have Bannockburn; the Welsh have Owen Glendower; and the Protestant Ulstermen have King Billy. But, for Britishness, the big self-defining acts have been remarkably recent.

But they have been sandwiched by a grimmer story: relative economic decline throughout modern times. The historian Paul Kennedy has reminded us of the seemingly inevitable link between economic and other forms of power: the vast increase in the cost of armaments acts as a kind of brutal magnification of relatively modest industrial failures. As the *New York Times* pointed out in the mid-1980s, 'It is hard to imagine, but a country whose productivity growth lags 1 per cent behind other countries over one century can turn, as England [*sic*] did, from the world's undisputed industrial leader into the mediocre economy it is today.'[2] And in a world where bombers cost 200 times more than in the Second World War and aircraft carriers 20 times more, this mediocrity quickly brings its punishment in the big sticks department.

At home, the decline of the British state was not always as obvious as it was abroad because the state discovered an alternative form of mightiness, the Welfare State, hugging society ever more tightly to its clammy and caring bosom. It attempted to make itself into a giant equality machine, a guarantor of social decency and security. Nostalgic imperialists and right-wing observers like Philip Larkin, the Poet Laureate of Pessimism, were highly critical of the switch:

Next year we shall be living in a country
That brought its soldiers home for lack of money.
The statues will be standing in the same
Tree-muffled squares, and look nearly the same.
Our children will not know it's a different country.
All we can hope to leave them now is money.[3]

For at least some of the time, however, the majority of Britons were probably pleased that it was a different country, a state which had turned away from running other people's countries to trying to make this one happier and richer. For most post-war Britons, the state's existence as part of a world system was unimportant compared to its domestic agenda of national health, pensions, economic modernization and the rest of it.

Yet the rapid decline of the British state as a world player has been one of the Big Facts of modern life, with inescapable domestic results. In the post-war era, the international reminders of reality have come regularly and brutally. First, there was the exchange-rate crisis during the savage winter of 1947, reminding the world that military victory two years earlier had cost Britain about a quarter of her national wealth. There was the loss of an empire of some 800 million souls – one Union Jack after another hauled down, cracking in the windy dawn; the last post whimpering for the last time somewhere, it seemed, every year through the forties, fifties and sixties. There was the disappearance of the real Royal Navy, a mighty sunlit armada of steel, scrubbed planks and self-confident traditions that slipped silently into the Bermuda triangle of economic decline and was never seen again. There was diplomatic humiliation, bringing the swift end of the era when Churchill could suggest tripartite summits involving Britain, the United States and the Soviet Union as the 'Big Three'. There was the shame of Suez, reminding the country and the Conservative Party that not only was the United States the dominant economic superpower, but Washington was ready to use that muscle ruthlessly against the Old Country. Following that, there were all the demeaning kow-towings of British prime ministers to American presidents at summits, the attempts to borrow their lustre, the sentiment of the 'special relationship'. Much of this sentiment was perfumed hogwash, not returned by the Americans. As Dean Acheson, the US diplomat, noted:

Of course a unique relation existed between Britain and America – our common language and history ensured that. But unique did not mean affectionate. We had fought England as an enemy as often as we had fought by her side as an ally ... Before Pearl Harbor ... sentiment was reserved for our 'oldest ally', France.[4]

Then there was the destruction of the Sterling area, and de Gaulle's '*non*' and then, eventually, our belated entry into the Common Market. 'Going into Europe' was itself, after all those years of post-war huffing, another tacit admission of failure, masked by the optimistic rhetoric of an establishment which wrongly hoped Continental leadership might give Britain a new area of dominance. There was the Wilson devaluation and later falls of the pound against the dollar, as markets and governments made unsentimental judgements about British idleness and inefficiency and the dollar did that unpleasant thing to the pound that the yen has subsequently done to the dollar. There was the loss of almost every famous name in British manufacturing to foreign ownership or closure. There was Healey and the IMF. There was Major and the ERM.

These have been, as it were, unmistakable drumbeats of decline. Most thinking Britons are aware of some of them, at least, most of the time. But they have been partially disguised by the trumpets and flutes of the state's noisy attempts to find new roles for itself. Internal expansion was meant, consciously or otherwise, to compensate for external contraction. If Britain had lost an empire and failed to find a role, as Acheson also said, this wasn't true of the state itself. It might not be mighty in cavalry regiments or proconsuls, but by God, it became mighty in hospitals, insurance schemes and railways instead. From 1945, attended by Keynes and Beveridge, the born-again state dug deep into the country's industrial and social life. It has been well said that the state made war, and war made the state. Certainly, two world wars made the case for the ability of the British state to do extraordinary things, at home as well as abroad. Both saw public spending and the numbers of people employed directly by the state shoot up, not to mention the powers the state then took and never relinquished. Just as income tax had come from the Napoleonic wars, so giant bureaucracies, snoopers, forms and many more taxes came from the modern wars. Here was that Jerusalem of efficiency and order dreamed up by Sidney and Beatrice Webb, the Odd Couple of English socialism, the Britain caricatured by Sidney's wonderful (and apparently seriously-meant) remark to Virginia Woolf in 1918: 'My wife & I always say that a Railway Guard is the most enviable of men. He has authority, & he is responsible to a government. That should be the state of each one of us.'[5] Well, it wasn't quite like that, but the same administrative middle class which, a generation earlier, had been out ruling India, or running rubber plantations, or giving the orders on the bridge, eventually found itself ruling a complicated and bureaucratic domestic state, running schools and hospitals or giving the orders in the BBC: a class in authority, and responsible to a government.

And this state, completed by Labour under Attlee and by the Conservative administrations of Churchill, Eden and Macmillan, continued at a domestic level many of the characteristics of the old administration of the Victorian imperial era. On the plus side, lack of corruption, public-spiritedness and a genuine paternalist enthusiasm for improvement; on the minus side, red tape, inflexibility and a top-down 'we know what's best for you' culture. Loss of international standing did not lead to any loss of the state's standing at home. In some cases, it actually strengthened it. Britain's subordinate position to the US during the Cold War, particularly after the passage of the McMahon Act and the failure of the independent British nuclear project, led to a secretive Atlanticist state-within-the-state. The Prime Minister might be a small fellow in Washington, but his new shared secrets made him an even bigger cheese at home. Or, to give another example, the Foreign and Commonwealth Office might have lost an empire but it found a new source of authority in Whitehall once Britain had joined Europe – the Common Market gave it great new powers of involvement in most other Whitehall departments. Ministers, too, drawn into a web of private European meetings and negotiations, found a new and important status. In both cases ministers and civil servants have gained greater powers and hence prestige as against Parliament and the rest of society, *because* of Britain's lower global standing. Funny old world.

For the political system, Britain's changing place carried contradictory messages. On the one hand, real power was being exercised too far away from the British voter for 'democracy' to be applicable. Whichever way people voted, the basic facts of the post-war order – the Atlantic alliance, the American-run financial system of Bretton Woods, the steady spread of international treaties and organizations – were solidifying and becoming omnipotent. There were attempts to challenge the post-war Western order: right-wing nationalists like Enoch Powell fought ferociously to keep Britain outside the Common Market, which was strongly sponsored and desired by Washington. On the left, CND took on the military establishment, and the 'Alternative Economic Strategy' of import controls and a siege economy was developed in the 1970s as a way to escape the constraints of the capitalist system. But these were desperate political eddies, or back-currents rather, whose energy and intellectual sparkle merely confirmed the awesome power of the main flow of policy.

Yet the British political system was in other respects healthier than it had ever been. It was in control of a huge bureaucracy and wealth-churner which helped provide housing, health-care and security for the voters which sustained it. As we saw earlier, welfarist politics brought people into political parties in greater numbers than ever before. Equality was not only a theme for the Pathé newsreels but was a lived experience for millions of Britons who had felt excluded from the system before. State education, and then comprehensive education, was partly intended to produce a new Britain of equal and assertive, public-minded citizens. Interest in politics was high, for the first time virtually everyone was enfranchised, and the state was competed for by two big parties which attracted vast support. Keynesian economics, with its belief in demand management by experts at the centre, was the holy doctrine of the new order. At some elections, voters really did have a choice between competing political ideas, and the electoral outcome was of historical importance. Certainly 1945 was one such election, and 1979 another. It is possible to make a case for 1964 and 1966 too. If there ever was one, this has been the age of political democracy.

But this withdrawal from unsustainable empire to a statehood of prosperous independence wasn't the end of the story. Great rhythms of national power don't cease to flow when governments feel like it. The power of the global economy and the spread of supranational organizations have, in recent years, kept on coming, washing away most of the pretensions of the modestly-sized nation state, including this one. This means it has less power domestically, as well as abroad. If you compare what the state could do in its post-war heyday with what it can do now, the extent of the loss becomes clear. Then, it not only ruled an empire, but at home it ran heavy industries, the main forms of transport, the utilities, the telephone system. It was free to pollute the skies and oceans if it thought the economic benefits worth it. It rationed mortgages for homes and lending for other purposes too. The state could impose any rate of tax it liked, on who or what it liked, without facing quick economic consequences. It could refuse to let its citizens travel abroad, and, when it allowed them to, it could control how much of their money they took with them. It could hang them or flog them, without an eye on what foreigners thought. It could control the pay of vast swathes of the people and the prices of many of the goods they bought. It could control what they heard being broadcast, what books they read and the content of the plays they watched – and film censorship was no less real for being done at arm's length. Labour ministers in the post-1945 administration were against signing up to a strong European Convention on Human Rights because they believed it would curb the great powers they required to build a command economy.

In return for these huge powers, they offered hope – hope of endless and inclusive prosperity, security and even a measure of equality. Today the powers, like the hopes, have gone. Politicians and bureaucrats proved no good at running industries, and the industries died or were privatized. International trade agreements, membership of 'Europe' and the lifting of exchange controls stripped away more powers. The globalization of the economy, in particular the rise of the money markets from the 1960s, steadily cut away the ability of the state to carry out economic or fiscal policies which the liberal market-makers believed would not work. A state which taxed too highly started to lose its best people. New communications technologies made a nonsense of the old powers of censorship – *Radio Caroline* first of all, wallowing cheerfully offshore, then satellites and Europorn and the Internet. Even the ultimate power to annihilate, to hold lethal secrets and to wage global war, seems rather less relevant after the decline and fall of the Soviet empire. So the modern British state, which first compensated for its international decline by finding new powers at home, has more recently found many of them being challenged and often stripped away. The post-war 'settlement' settled, in the end, absolutely nothing. Keynes and Beveridge were no more timeless prophets of British state power than were Cecil Rhodes or Joseph Chamberlain.

The idea that the state has been losing powers may seem eccentric to many readers. This is because we are so used to hearing, from both left and right, powerful criticisms of the state for having too much power. They are so loud and so familiar that, before looking at what has been happening in more detail, they need to be dealt with. The right has warned us about the danger of a swollen state to private enterprise and private liberty. The left has focused on the oppressive nature of the state's attitude to minorities and groups challenging the existing order. Both criticisms stem from valuable political instincts, a libertarianism and a tradition of dissent firmly rooted

in British history; a democratic culture without its right-wing
and left-wing anti-statists would be weaker and duller. But, for
British politics today, their arguments are out of date and a bad
guide to the real world.

Two generations of thinking right-wing politicians and
opinion-formers were brought up on conservative philosophers
like Hayek and Michael Oakeshott who warned (in the latter's
phrase) against 'overwhelming concentrations of power',
whether or not it was power exercised for the benefit of the
majority. They argued that the rise in the share of GNP taken
by the state, and thus of taxation, removed economic freedom
from individuals and companies and crowded out their autonomous space, their room to act socially. This was a theme
which spread rapidly among conservative thinkers during the
late forties. By the sixties and seventies, the extremely high
marginal rates of income-tax and the corporatist culture had
convinced many mainstream writers and politicians that the
Hayek-Oakeshott analysis was being vindicated and that the
state had grown out of control. Margaret Thatcher, in many
senses Hayek's Revenge, was determined to cut it back. But for
her, as for most serious radicals on the right, the size and nature
of the state was essentially a moral question, not just a matter of
economic efficiency. David Green of the Institute of Economic
Affairs has put the argument as well as anybody:

Socialists have not seen the good person as someone who gave his
own time and energy in the service of others, but as the individual
who demanded action by the state at the expense of other taxpayers.
This politicized interpretation of moral responsibility, far from increasing consideration for others, tends to undermine the sense of personal
responsibility on which an ethos of service truly rests.[6]

There was no single 'Thatcherite' view of the state, but it is fair
to say that in general she and her followers agreed the large size
of the state was bad of itself, endangering what one Thatcherite
writer has called 'the vigorous virtues', but that a strong state –
one with power to confound pessimists and shirkers – was a
good thing. The state should do little, but should have real

authority. These points have been recently made with fiery polemical force by a Tory MP and a Conservative writer who see the democratic state as a despotism characterized by traffic wardens, foot-hygiene inspectors, social workers and, above all, Inland Revenue inspectors who are 'the moral equivalent of the Stasi, the Gestapo and the KGB.'[7] Yet, at the same time, they, and leading Thatcherite politicians, like Michael Portillo, want the state's political leaders to regain authority and to be heard more attentively by the rest of us. In Portillo's words, 'Our mission must be to rebuild national self-confidence and self-belief.'

Leaving aside the fact that, for many of us, traffic calming, the avoidance of motorway crashes and the ready availability of non-poisonous food don't amount to despotism, there is a fundamental contradiction in the small-state-but-strong-state argument.

The state's authority depends in part on what it does, the activities which citizens going about their everyday lives notice and, often, rely upon. The less the state does, the less reason to notice it. As it shuffles out of economic and social activities, it slowly edges itself off the mental radar of people who no longer regard themselves as 'its' citizens. Thus, a rhetoric and programme intended to remove the state from much of life through privatization and deregulation – getting 'off the backs of the people' – is likely, if it works, to make the state weaker, as well as smaller. From the end of the seventies, the Conservatives strove mightily to get the state out of numerous aspects of national life. At the same time, international economic and technological developments were pushing things in the same direction. High taxation in the nineties does not refute the general trend: it has been caused by unemployment as the state withdraws from the labour market and macro-economics: it has been a sign of a society struggling to retain its equilibrium as the state loses power – not evidence of a new despotism arising. People noted that the democratic institutions were unable to eradicate mass unemployment, or fix interest rates, or carry on running great enterprises. They became more orientated to the private, just as Conservatives wanted them to. But this meant that they were indeed less impressed by the old state institutions – and less likely to heed politicians who stand atop them. Margaret Thatcher's message that government was pretty hopeless hit home all too effectively; having been told that the old religion was no good, the people turned their backs on preacher and pulpit, too.

There is probably no going back to a bigger, self-certain state, speaking with bass authority. The Conservative critique is strongest whenever it homes in on the bureaucratic abuse of those powers still exercised by the state. Libertarians have been quick to notice that the shrinking of the state's central powers have not led to a new respect for the private citizen by the state. For the poor and unemployed, those most affected by the state today, the regulations and interference have grown greater, not less. Higher up the income scale, the rise in petty bureaucracy, destroying thousands of small businesses and interfering in the most mundane of matters, provides evidence of the continuing insolence of officials. In recent times, this has been largely caused by a flow of European directives, often interpreted with excessive zeal by British officials, and by an avalanche of home-grown legislation and directives about food hygiene, safety at work, the environment and other matters. The journalist Christopher Booker, whose devastating and often tragic-funny uncovering of the tyranny of health inspectors helped bring it to the notice of the Major government (causing vain promises of a new bonfire of regulations) has described it as 'a huge explosion of bureaucracy and bureaucratic modes of thought, extending its influence into almost every aspect of life – a monster out of control . . .'[8] There is a long tradition of writing on the political right about the oppression caused by regulations and bureaucracy – socialists were caricatured as faintly Prussian nosey-parkers from the early years of this century. This time, Booker and his colleague Richard North have been attacking measures taken under a Conservative administration and have uncovered a real national scandal, particularly for small business owners, fishermen, inventors, hoteliers and others whose interests are not represented by powerful centralized lobbies. But it is worth noting here that the bureaucratic offensive is also, in some sense, evidence of the weakness of the authority of the political state, not its strength. Bureaucrats, like anyone else, will grab more power when they can, finding and then enlarging a role for themselves. The core of the problem with rising modern bureaucracy is that weak politicians have passed power to unelected committees and individuals, while they themselves are becoming hopelessly ground down and entangled by pressure groups and media campaigns.

The left's worry about state oppression has derived from very different thinking and experiences to the above – it gets excited about the trampled-on rights of trade unionists, immigrants and gays, ravers and travellers, rather than income-tax payers, small businesses and farmers. The left has long believed that a conservative establishment, secretive and reactionary, comprising big business, the armed forces, the St James's Street clubs and the judiciary as well as the senior civil service and Tory politicians, was waiting to snatch back any rights that organized labour and minorities might have accumulated over time. Margaret Thatcher's attack on trade unionism and her illiberal attitude to any group she regarded as disloyal or outsiders – left-wingers, whistle-blowers, journalists, immigrants, nuclear disarmers, Irish republicans (even peaceful ones) – seemed to add up to that expropriation. The Thatcherites thought they were engaged in a genuine extension of individual freedom, through privatization, the destruction of the collective rights of trade unions and their political war against revolutionaries, but for the left this was irrelevant beside the simultaneous counter-attack on the rights of oppositional groups and the economic destruction of many working-class lives. Through this period both sides of the political argument were protesting about attacks on 'liberty' but neither was listening to the other, and each meant something wholly different by the word.

The left's fears were not merely a mulch of hysteria and sour grapes. Margaret Thatcher was determined to regain what she regarded as the tarnished authority of the state and she seemed unconcerned about the niceties. An 'us and them' politician, she stood astride a movement which was almost vengeful in its determination to defeat the enemies within. As her autobiography demonstrates, she herself always regarded the odds as long and her true allies as few. But once she survived her first few years in office, this was not the case. The Thatcherite army became steadily more formidable and determined, spreading through the press, industry and much of Middle England. It picked its targets one after another, sector by sector. Its greatest crises were caused by its own internal contradictions (notably over Europe), not by its enemies. The use made of civil servants and the security services to monitor and harass nuclear dissidents would have been excessive had Thatcherite Britain been in a state of virtual war; in a peaceful country, it was unforgivable. The attempted gagging of writers and journalists when it came to security matters was both incompetently heavy-handed and politically neurotic. There was a relish for the defeat of trade unionists, as well as trade unionism, which left a nasty taste in the mouth. There was, in practice, too little separation of powers within the state. Professor J.A.G. Griffiths, whose careful and descriptive work on the politics of judges caused a storm shortly before the beginning of the Thatcher era, concluded that the judiciary was

necessarily conservative and illiberal . . . [involving] judicial attitudes such as tenderness towards private property and dislike of trade unions, strong adherence to the maintenance of order, distaste for minority opinions, demonstrations and protests, the avoidance of conflict with Government policy even where it is manifestly oppressive of the most vulnerable, support of government secrecy, concern for the preservation of the moral and social behaviour to which it is accustomed . . .[9]

This was a perception shared by other academics and lawyers who specialized in liberty issues during the period:

Quite apart from the development of new police tactics and the emergence of new common-law public order powers, the open ended and vague nature of the traditional law has continued the erratic erosion of freedom for those whose views, attitudes or behaviour is out of the mainstream.[10]

But if the right-wing argument about the swollen powers of the state grossly underestimates the economic changes of the past fifteen years, the left-libertarian hysteria about state power argument is also out of date. It was easy enough to argue that the Thatcher years produced serious questions about state power. Illiberal aspects of legislation under the Major government – such as the Criminal Justice Act of 1994 – provoked a popular protest movement by young people, greens and travellers. But it has become harder and harder to argue that the state itself is oppressive. You just need to think about the political weakness of the Major administration; the rising importance of European law on human rights; the series of highly-significant legal battles won against government ministers by lobbies and individuals; the libertarian impact of the information-technology revolution; the fall in the status and budget of the security services after the end of the Cold War; the panicked resort to independent scrutiny of political wrongdoing, for instance in the Scott Inquiry and the Nolan Committee. The old ways are becoming ridiculous: the then Cabinet Secretary Lord Armstrong's inept defence of British censorship in an Australian court during the *Spycatcher* case, and the mouthing of the words of the Sinn Fein leader, Gerry Adams, by actors became defining examples of the retreat and weakness of this would-be strong state, not of its potency.

The right-wing vision of the swollen state and the left-wing vision of the oppressive state, different but powerfully represented in the media, are each in possession of a partial truth, but both have been given too much importance in our national political conversation. Vividly and passionately expressed by politicians and propagandists of great talent, they have hidden more important changes. And the lurid power of these distorted images has been intensified by one final phenomenon about which everyone agrees: the massive influence of Margaret Thatcher as a national leader. The political supremacy of that extraordinary politician and her agenda made it seem, to the short-sighted, that any talk of the decline of the British state was not only premature, but farcical. I'm not thinking of individual episodes like the Falklands War, but of the centralizing tendencies and frantic energies of her premiership. Here was someone whose determination to control the executive, whose contempt for vacillation and whose sense of purpose added up to a one-woman reinvention of politics. Thatcherism not only polarized the country, sharpening political choices and raising fundamental questions about our political economy, it also briefly raised the status of the state itself. Her interventions in foreign policy, whether at European Community summits or before the Gulf War, affected the international climate. For much of her reign, she retained the powers of a leading Western participant of the Cold War. She remains a living, snorting, fire-eating rebuke to political faint-hearts of any stripe. But in terms of the role of the state, the key to Lady Thatcher was that she was an asset-stripper. She was an economic anti-statist, who saw clearly where the state was failing, and, in her view, ought to get out. And, in many cases, she got it out. The getting-out was spectacular to watch. It was real politics. But we should not confuse demolition with architecture: where she dreamed of exercising strong state powers to re-moralize the country, turning us back to 'Victorian values', she remained just that, a dreamer.

At this stage, the key distinction is between the powers of the state overall (which have diminished, are diminishing and will diminish further) and the balance of powers within the state. It is perfectly possible to argue that some group has gained too much power — tax inspectors, Ministry of Agriculture officials, the prime minister's office, or whoever — but still to understand that the overall power of the state has been reduced. Both matter: the question of who exercises how much political power at any one given time, and how accountable they are, is central to democratic argument. But the wider and more difficult question of the power of politics generally should not be ignored as we concentrate on struggles within the system. Both the left and right have concentrated on the internal question – who has their hands on the levers of state power – rather than looking at the bigger question of whether the levers still worked. Both the left and the right were trying to defend a political vision of the state which was, in the real world, under terminal assault: the left's view of the big, redistributive, welfarist state was being rendered irrelevant by global economics and consumerism, while the right's hopes for a disciplinarian 'nightwatchman' state were being cancelled by technology, political change and liberalism.

There is one big question left to answer: how does one account for the state's greediness in gathering up local powers – a greediness that has already been identified as the key error of the Thatcher years? It is yet another symptom of the general changes, and can best be imagined visually. Think of all national debate as a pyramid. At the top are the more intellectual, abstract but highly important policy areas, such as monetary policy, international diplomacy, arms-reduction talks, trade policy. Then come more down-to-earth but still complex matters such as tax, education policy, regulatory functions, health care. Finally, when you get to the bottom of the pyramid, you find basic, relatively easily understood and fundamentally local policy choices – planning, roads, transport, the running of schools, local services. What has happened is that the policies at the top, which the state traditionally relied on for its authority and power, are being, or have been, sucked away from the level of the nation, either by the private sector or by various supranational institutions. As they go, billowing off into the political stratosphere, the state's standing in the eyes of its citizens diminishes and it digs further down the policy pyramid, desperately seeking things to do.

I have described the state in anthropomorphic terms, but in fact, in the real workings of the British constitution, this process can be seen working at an individual human level, as ministers of the crown search for relevance. The local council in Reekmarsh has introduced topless sunbathing outside the civic centre?

A matter for the minister! Especially so if that particular minister has just spent ten hours in a European meeting where he was outvoted eight times, won two important battles, and finds not a word reported about any of it in the newspapers. A lesbian teacher has said a rude word in front of eight-year-olds in Gobsmack Primary? Summon the parliamentary draftsmen! There is a row as to whether the new relief road should go left, through Dimbleby meadow, or right, through Paxman Farm. It must be, at all costs, a matter for the national roads policy team! I exaggerate barely at all. The phenomenon is a dangerous one: seeking to compensate for those things it once did adequately, but which are better done by the market or by new supranational organizations, the state tries to find a new role, in doing things it knows little about and which would be better left to the local level. The voter gets a bad deal all round: too far away to influence the macro-politics, and lumbered with an interfering, know-all national government when it comes to micro-politics.

At this stage in the argument we have, I hope, provided a short history of the state's fall in status and blown away some of the older and cloudier counter-claims. We have the broad picture. We now turn to the specific pressures on the British state: first, the great international and European assault on national sovereignty; then the commercial assault; and finally those attacks on the debilitated state which come from within its national culture.

The Age of the Death of the Nations?

Before the First World War there existed, across this planet, fewer than two-score multinational organizations. Now there are nearly four hundred and the number is still growing fast. Some of these bring little or no threat to the autonomy of nations, but most bring some, and some bring a lot. Britain has been an avid subscriber to the great clubs of the post-war era and it is worth reminding ourselves just how many there are. There was, first, the United Nations, born from the Second

World War and which has spawned a vast array of baby treaties, pacts and bodies, devoted to disarmament, development, aid, population control and a hundred other tasks. On the military side, there have been the Antarctic Treaty, the 1963 test-ban treaty, the 1968 nuclear non-proliferation treaty, the 1971 Treaty on the Prohibition of the Emplacement of Nuclear Weapons and Other Weapons of Mass Destruction on the Sea-Bed and the Ocean Floor and in the sub-soil Thereof, and the wonderfully-named 1979 Agreement Covering the Activities of States on the Moon and Other Celestial Bodies – and these are only some of the disarmament deals. No one would object to them but, as North Korea has discovered, even they can clash in practice with sovereignty. At the same time as Britain was committing itself to numerous peace-loving treaties, it was of course also signed up for the Cold War. This did not merely involve joining Nato in 1949, with its 'an attack upon one is an attack upon all' principle, removing from politics, for the purposes of split-second inter-ballistic duelling, the issue of whether or not Britain would go to war, but also required a host of subsidiary arrangements, including, for instance, SEATO (1954) and the Baghdad Pact of 1959. They may have been necessary and the least bad of various options. But they cumulatively helped transform the real freedom of the British state from global actor to one-voice-among-many.

The next group of post-war organizations which Britain helped form and joined were economic. Like the United Nations, which was born at San Francisco, this comprised an American-sponsored attempt to rebuild the post-war world in a liberal way which involved, among other things, destroying those vestiges of economic power that Britain still retained from her imperial era. The so-called Bretton Woods agreement was named after the Maine, New Hampshire setting for the meetings in 1944 which resulted in the formation of the International Monetary Fund and the World Bank. From Britain's point of view, Bretton Woods was a more direct diminution of national power than the military alliances because it (and the previous Lend-Lease deal) involved intense American pressure aimed at the eventual abandonment of the Sterling Area and the dismantling of the wall of imperial protectionism erected by London in the 1930s. British ideas, such as Keynes's for a new international currency called Bancor, were brushed aside by the Americans. Washington's blunt determination to impose a free-trading, multisided system which would benefit US industry caused shock and anger throughout the British establishment. It was a moment of national trauma, when the country confronted the penalties of its long history of economic weakness more clearly than ever before, and the expressions of outrage ran from City conservatives to intellectual socialists like Michael Foot. The Americans were proven right, however, and their success in creating a stable Western trading system made it as much a part of the British political furniture as Nato. This was the new world in which, on the biggest questions, British democracy was an awkward but ultimately reliable ward of American democracy – the African decolonization programme of Macmillan's government in the fifties and early sixties was, for instance, carried out under constant pressure of American criticism at the United Nations. It was significant that the Bretton Woods system was brought to an end in 1971 without consultation with London by John Connally, Nixon's Treasury Secretary (and the man who had sat with President Kennedy as he was shot in Dallas). Connally decided not to accept America's obligation to convert $3 billion into gold when London asked, so unwittingly helping usher in a new era of global financial liberalization and again transforming the British political landscape. The policy revolution then, as in 1944, was firmly and unambiguously, 'Made in America'.

Yet more than forty years of struggle between 'the free world' and the alliance of Marxist regimes gave this first generation of multinational organizations a basis of general assent in Britain which was rarely challenged. Liberty was more important than national power even though these institutions narrowed the field upon which the political game could be played. In theory, Britain could have revoked its membership of Nato, tried to retain its empire, and returned to protectionism. In practice, except among the leftist and rightist fringes, these options swiftly became unthinkable. Yet it is remarkable that so many learned and passionate discussions about British parliamentary democracy went on without reference to the wider facts which increasingly circumscribed it. Perhaps this was because these first-generation supranational bodies placed above the British state were reassuringly traditional in one key respect: that they were agreements between states about matters they were clearly in charge of – defence and economic policy. They removed some room for manoeuvre for democracies surviving on a weakened economic base, like Britain, but they were pretty conventional. We will come on to the great European question later, but it is worth noting that one of Britain's problems with partner-countries is that she has, against the evidence, persisted in regarding the European Union in similarly conventional terms, as an agreement between states which does not touch their nature or independence.

It is this familiar, first-generation multinational system which has been collapsing during the past decade. Its replacement looks far harder for nation-states to deal with. The great political issues at the end of this century – environmental degradation, pollution, overpopulation – make national borders seem even less relevant than in the age of military alliance and ideological confrontation. And when it comes to economics, power has passed from a big nation-state (America) to smaller nations and, more radically, to corporations and market-makers, seemingly outside the political system as even the most powerful countries understand it. The individual actions which hastened this along were often taken for traditional national-political reasons – Connally's refusal of the British dollar request in 1971, or the build-up of dollar reserves in London caused by US military spending and the actions of European governments, which led to the boom in the Eurodollar market in the 1960s. But the effect has been to savagely erode national political power. As the historian Paul Kennedy has put it, 'In an age of 24-hour-a-day currency trading or, for that matter, global warming, have national bodies such as cabinets or commerce departments much relevance?'[11] (The answer is: yes, but not as much as they think they have.)

Part of this generational shift can be seen by looking at the United Nations itself. For most of its life it was the Upper House of the Cold War, a place for rare petulant outbursts and endless fine words, signifying very little. It was the gentlemen's club of the superpowers, mitigated by Nordic idealism and disguised by the dignities of new nations – only on rare occasions, such as Suez, has it been used by one top-table member against others. But the end of the global confrontation between Marx and Adam Smith, and the confusion, tribalism and regional conflict that this has brought as its backwash, presents the leading members of the UN – and Britain is still one of them – with serious democratic questions to answer. In the mid-nineties, American Republican opinion has tilted ever more strongly against the UN and embarrassments such as the death of American soldiers in Somalia and French and British ones in Bosnia underlined the domestic difficulty of all democratic governments in allowing military deaths – sometimes witnessed on prime-time TV – for reasons which are less than critical to national survival. The same will become true for us. If British troops are to be sent to die for the UN, without Britain's own national interests being directly affected, there must at least be a political override. It may be objected that, in practice, there is: modern governments would not send British troops into danger without the prior assent of Parliament. But if the UN wants to get into a fire-fighting role, sending military force at short notice into civil wars which are far away and little understood by British MPs, will there be time for an effective and proper scrutiny of all the issues beforehand? These things happen in a mood of crisis and panic. And if British troops have been 'loaned' to the UN on a more permanent basis, as some suggest, the democratic override has even less chance of working.

Outside the military arena, multinational attempts to protect the environment (the Rio Earth Summit of 1992) and control population growth (the Cairo conference of 1994) point the way to a global politics that will be equally tough for Western nations hoping to retain maximum autonomy. So far the developed and powerful countries have been relatively successful in keeping control of the 'green' agenda, and focusing on the failures of poorer countries to save their forests or stop their people breeding so effectively. But this is bound to change, as the vast imbalances in consumption are attacked by the poor majority – it has been calculated that the average American baby will represent 13 times as much environmental damage during its life as a Brazilian baby, and 280 times as much as a Haitian. Even if these figures are excessive, the underlying truth they point to is one which poor countries will shout about ever more stridently. Will anyone listen? They will. In their vastly-increasing populations, the extra amount of heat they are likely to push into the atmosphere, and the destruction of their forests and topsoils, the poorest countries and the newly industrializing ones like China have a new human and ecological arsenal to aim at the West. When President Castro of Cuba stopped threatening the United States with Marxist rhetoric and started firing refugees and criminals at Florida instead, he was making early use of a kind of politics we will all see more of. If the West is concerned about global warming, the West will have to deal with India and China's development agenda. If the European Union fails to aid the countries of North Africa or parts of the former Soviet Union, the EU may face immigration and crime consequences that will rock its political stability. Our new 'one world' will demand trade-offs and financial subventions from nations which are unused to heeding foreign politicians. In future, our own energy consumption, our own agricultural policies, our own nuclear industry, may come under the spotlight of world opinion.

Globalization

The post-Bretton Woods global economy raises uncannily similar problems. The existence of a formidable system of international trade, challenging the culture, politics and economies of those drawn into it, is hardly a new thing. Indeed, it is the basis of the world's economic growth. The town where I grew up, Dundee, based its wealth on turning raw Indian hemp into jute for sacking; the money thus accumulated by a handful of families was then invested in a range of overseas projects, including the Canadian and North American railroads, so spawning some of the first investment trust companies, and a whole new financial service industry. That movement of goods and capital affected the lifestyles of Asian farmers, Scottish workers and bankers, American pioneers, Indian tribes, Californian fruit-growers ... This was the global market of a century ago, in some ways more savage in its impact than today's one, yet only a small part of the revolution which built our wealthier world. The British writer Vincent Cable has said that,

Arguably, the main achievement of the post-war international economic order has been to restore the degree of 'globalization' to a level close to that which existed in 1913. Many of today's global markets are ... not a creation of our contemporaries but existed in similar, if not identical, forms long ago. The 1980s boom in syndicated lending markets strongly resembles the 19th century cycles of lending, over-lending, default, rescheduling and fresh lending ... Many of today's big projects – like Eurotunnel or the Hong Kong airport – have a high degree of global complexity, but not significantly more than when the Panama and Suez canals were under construction.[12]

Today's globalization, though, has been strengthened in its impact on national governments by the speed and power which technological advance has given the market, by the sheer quantity of information available and the dazzling velocity of capital.

The Money

It's never a bad idea to start with the money. It has been estimated that the volume of trading on the foreign exchange markets in a day is fifty times the amount of world trade being carried on at the same time. This means that quicksilver judgements are being made continuously about national economic performance and policy. A government which behaves in a way the market-makers fear or dislike is swiftly punished. The most celebrated example is probably the Mitterrand socialist experiment in 1981–82, when the French government pursued a policy of vigorous reflation, involving a 28 per cent increase in government spending, a vast housebuilding programme, the nationalization of swathes of industry (specifically to defend the French national interest, as defined by the elected president), the creation of 54,000 new civil service jobs and big increases in welfare payments. There was a rapid decline in the franc, while monetarism and rationalization elsewhere made the French experiment seem hopelessly against the grain of economic trends. By 1982, a programme of cuts was being introduced and a year later, the Mitterrand government effectively U-turned. No such project was tried in Britain, though it was advocated strongly by the Bennite left at about the same period: had it been, there is no reason to think the consequences would have been different.

Since then, the power of the international market has been rammed home as the money-men grade national economies and political systems. The assault by the markets on the French franc and the European exchange-rate system generally in the summer of 1993 was greeted by the Parisian establishment as a direct attack on the French strategy of linking with Germany – economics savaging diplomacy. Briefly, hysteria reigned. 'The markets' or 'the speculators' were a good, anonymous enemy, certainly English-speaking, and probably, in the flesh, rather like Tom Wolfe's anti-hero in *Bonfire of the Vanities*, a New York 'master of the universe' high on power. But French politicians weren't the only ones to find 'Anglo-Saxon' markets difficult. In America the reformists of the Clinton administration found the markets no friendlier. James Carville, a senior adviser to President Clinton, put it this way: 'I used to think that, if there was a re-incarnation, I wanted to come back as the President, or the Pope, or a top baseball hitter. But now I want to come back as the bond market. You can intimidate everybody.'[13]

The days when governments could turn to an array of policies, including exchange controls, the control of the level of bank lending and even hire-purchase controls, have gone, probably forever. Politicians still pretend to take the rap when interest rates rise; and take the credit when they fall. But, by and large, 'pretend' is the word. The markets can penalize governments that seem either soft on inflation, or politically unstable – as they did during the rows over a single currency within the Major government in 1995 – but the politicians have relatively few powers of counter-attack. One chancellor of recent times told me he would wake sleeplessly at 5 a.m. and find his first thought was always the same – what were the markets doing to the pound? National governments and central bankers still have some control over short-term interest rates, admittedly. And they can, as the EU members did, operate policies designed to keep their exchange rates at certain levels, locking monetary policy to an anchor currency and policy – in this case run by the Bundesbank. But even this is limited, as the British government discovered on 'Black Wednesday', 16 September 1992, when Sterling was pushed out of the ERM. After that, Sterling floated freely and, cut off from the Bundesbank's anti-inflationary reputation, the Treasury was obliged to come up with a series of new measures to regain credibility with the markets.

These measures, it should be pointed out, were essentially about convincing the market-makers that the politicians weren't in control. Our constitution has been made by flurry and spasm, reacting to headlines and the short-term difficulties of governments, rather than by plan and foresight. This is what that attractive word 'organic' really means. The quite dramatic change in the way short-term interest-rates are set, which came about as a result of 'Black Wednesday', provides a pretty classic example. Before then this ticklish and high-profile business – for the timing, direction and size of rate-changes sharply affect millions of British home-owners and companies – was essentially a political affair. The Bank of England and the Treasury would haggle and argue endlessly in deep privacy but eventually the matter would rest for the Chancellor, who would rely for a final decision on the prime minister. A surprisingly high proportion of the one-to-one conversations between these two most important politicians concerned interest-rate movements which could be, and were, manipulated for short-term political effect – buying time, heading off a 'bad' party conference, responding to electoral pressures. As to their direction, the Bank would eventually get its way, but there was great bad feeling there about the 'bloody politicians'. The Bank's analysis and views would emerge through hidden messages in its *Quarterly Bulletin*, which private-sector economists then became expert in reading, like code-breakers or spooks poring through the Communist Party news in *Pravda*, circa 1950.

The Bank, resenting the relationship, could become almost gleeful when the politicians fouled things up – far from rushing to help when a political move on interest rates was under fire the Bank would, in the words of one Treasury man, 'simply slink away'. This system of setting rates also tended to set Chancellor against prime minister since the former, supposedly the nation's economic guardian, could be countermanded by the latter, the political guardian. Could be. And often was. As a result, almost all recent Chancellors of the Exchequer have left the job committed to the idea of giving the Bank of England full freedom over interest rates. There was one eminent exception. I'd better not give the game away, other than to note that he went on to become Prime Minister, which may explain it.

The system, at any rate, had to be re-thought after Black Wednesday. The triumphant markets had to be persuaded that economic judgements, not political ones, were determining British policy. Eventually, in 1994, Kenneth Clarke effectively destroyed the Prime Minister's role by authorizing, six weeks afterwards, the publication of the minutes of the monthly meetings between himself as Chancellor and the Bank governor, Eddie George. This means that the markets know what the Bank and the Treasury both think about inflation and the strength of the economy. Any 'political' tinkering, or any failure then to move rates appropriately, becomes immediately apparent and must be openly justified unless the markets are to sell sterling and force higher-than-otherwise interest rates. Treasury insiders, ministers and Bank people have all privately used the phrase 'de facto independence' for the Bank, though it isn't quite that. During May–June 1995, Clarke, who sympathises with independence for the Bank, refused to accept its arguments for higher interest rates. He reckoned he had a better instinct for the condition of the real economy, and the markets, more interested in the dollar–yen drama, gave him the benefit of the doubt. But in the medium-term, there has been an irreversible shift of power to the Bank and this considerable constitutional move has arrived with barely any debate, a reminder that quite a lot of the 'traditional British way' was scribbled down on the backs of envelopes by men in a hurry.

If that is the story of short-term interest-rate policy then when it comes to what is called 'the long end' (interest-rates on money borrowed for periods of a few years to a few decades, the money used by companies and indeed governments themselves to invest and modernize) the power shift is even more dramatic. Voters may not notice when it comes to modest changes in their mortgage costs: they may still think politicians decide. But at the long end, there is no room for illusion. International markets are making constant judgements about the credit-worthiness and economic health of all the relevant nations, regions, cities and projects. They are moving in and out of government bonds and currencies daily as these judgements shift, and the effect is to set the price of long-term borrowing in ways that the politicians cannot affect. Within the markets the leaders, the biggest speculators, have real personal power. One of the best-known, George Soros, who was rumoured to have made $2 billion in the assault on the pound, later said that 'I could actually influence the behaviour of the markets, and it would be dishonest of me to pretend otherwise.' He could have pushed the franc out, he said, in 1993, but 'I did not want to be responsible for the French franc being pushed out of the Exchange Rate Mechanism. I abstained from speculating . . .'[14] Soros later compared currency markets to stampedes – his influence came from his fame: he was, in effect, the animal that the herd was likeliest to follow.

The demise of the (historically brief) period when politics

had some claim to power over the cost of money is now obvious to most people; there have been enough big crises, like that expulsion of sterling from the European Exchange Rate Mechanism in 1992, to strip away the veil. One of the best polemical accounts of the change came in the House of Lords in May 1994 from Denis Healey, who mocked the Foreign Secretary Douglas Hurd for promising that the European Union could no more aspire to abolish the nation state than to end history. Lord Healey said Mr Hurd was missing the point:

The plain fact is that the nation state as it has existed for nearly two centuries is being undermined by many factors – mainly technological – of an international nature. The ability of national governments to decide their exchange rate, interest rate, trade flows, investment and output has been savagely crippled by market forces . . . The globalization of finance, under which Mafia-gilded young lemmings can move 1,000 billion dollars a day in micro-seconds across exchanges, pushed us out of the [European] exchange rate mechanism. So this government had to jettison within 24 hours something that they had called the 'sheet anchor' of their economic policies. What I cannot understand is why members of the Government worry so much about what Jacques Delors might do when they have seen what George Soros has done, and may do again.[15]

But Soros and Delors are connected in this squeezing of the nations. The speculation against ERM currencies had been made possible by a political contradiction built into the European Exchange Rate Mechanism. As Soros later pointed out himself, German unification meant that the Bundesbank had to act fast to stop inflation getting a grip inside Germany, as it was legally obliged to do. But the rest of Europe was in recession and required the opposite policy; and the Bundesbank was also acting as the anchor of the ERM. The German central bank was caught between its two functions: its national constitutional function and its *de facto* European function. The 'motor' had moved into reverse, just when most of the train needed to go forwards. So there was intense pressure inside the system, particularly on the weaker currencies, and the speculators, seeing their moment, struck. The event of 'Black Wednesday', which resulted in a fall in British interest rates was caused by a half-formed inconsistent supranational system. It could not have happened had the pound either been free-floating, or locked into a single European monetary system – and of course could not have occurred had there been a single European currency.

So, although it was a dramatic reminder of the force of market opportunism, its message could be taken two ways. Norman Lamont, the chancellor at the time, later argued strongly that Britain should be ready to consider leaving the EU and should certainly not join a single currency: instead the power must go to the markets, and the pound must float. What of George Soros? Far from being the demonic Anglo-Saxon plotter portrayed by some Continental politicians, Soros was in fact a keen supporter of the European Union and drew the more 'political' conclusion – one of life's little ironies. A Hungarian Jew who had escaped Nazism and Communism, he saw the EU as a bulwark of the open society. He may have humiliated national politicians and been 'the man who broke the Bank of England' but Soros argued for the creation of a single currency as soon as possible, this being the only way the politicians could reassert their European agenda against the anarchic forces represented by – well, by people like himself. Both Soros and Lamont would agree, however, that there was a serious, perhaps terminal, threat to one of the central functions of the traditional state in all this: the implication is that governments can choose whether to surrender power over their currency to a larger political union or to the markets; but must make that choice.

The Trade

If we turn from money to things, and so to trade, we find a passing-over of power from national politics which is scarcely less remarkable. As became clear in the final stages of the interminable round of trade talks known as the Uruguay round of the GATT (General Agreement on Tariffs and Trade) which ended in 1993, the free-trade issue is an intensely political one. It always has been, at any rate whenever world trade is expanding and so breaching protected markets. Thus it was a century ago when the Conservative Party went to war with itself over the anti-free trade idea of 'imperial protection'. Thus it was when the Scottish Parliament voted to unite with the English one and found that the Scots' textile industry and ports were quickly bankrupted by southern competition. The arguments about allowing others to trade their skills and lifestyles openly against our own have not really changed. But, again, the difference today is about scale and speed. The adjustment Western countries in particular are likely to have to make in the era of the rise of Asia will be dramatic. It won't be made any easier by the fact that the internationally traded sector now includes things once regarded as safely national – like services and culture. Vincent Cable reminds us that 'Hollywood and CNN are arguably now more important in trade than General Motors or United States Steel. The British music industry "exports" more than the aerospace industry. These are . . . traded services which . . . cut to the heart of nations' sense of identity.'

Here is one of the great developing political arguments of our times: it has been well said that trade negotiations are the arms control talks of today. The questions raised for the existence of national political cultures are serious ones. If nations have evolved 'inefficient' service or agricultural sectors because they like the social cohesion and employment that goes with them, or if they choose, like the French political establishment, to try and protect their film industry against the power of Hollywood; and their voters are then told that they must abandon these things because unelected global institutions require them to, then voters may rightly ask why they bother to register a vote. Despite the doom-laden rhetoric of the new protectionists, Western countries have by and large been powerful enough to negotiate trade-offs (literally) which are acceptable to their electorates. To that extent, democracy still works. So long as voters see greater choice and greater wealth coming from open trade, they will be hard to sway. But the protectionist argument is growing. In essence, protectionists attribute all the human economic virtues to whatever group of foreigners are currently feared; but none of the vices. The protectionists of the West talk today as if Asians will not spend their money on Western products, but bury it sneakily in paddy fields; as if Asians never tire, never fail to pass on the work ethic intact to the more pampered third and fourth generations; as if, in short, Asians are not really human, but a species of humanoid worker-ant. The gap between this sort of awed economic racism, and the political racism that seeks to stamp on the ants, or rats, or whatever odious term is fashionable, is perilously narrow: it is the gap between the eye-contact being made, and the first fist being swung. When it comes to the Americans, the European protectionists talk as if the American film industry was pumping a form of cultural heroin into the minds of little Europeans who would otherwise choose to spend their time leafing through Racine and watching the films of Fassbinder. They talk, in short, a mighty load of manure.

But they are unlikely to go away or even to stop talking, and the politics of free trade will dominate the 2000s. For poorer countries, the tests set by the West on environmental protection, human rights and other 'fair trade' hurdles seem like a new form of imperialism. (And there is some truth in the charge: it is vital to stop the destruction of the rain forests; but the lesson might come better from the West were the United States not so grotesquely environmentally destructive an economy, and were the Europeans not at present happily and innocently engaged in wiping out their own fish stocks.) For the richer countries, the world of free trade means a continual exertion to think faster and work better, a world in which growth is no one's birthright. As Paddy Ashdown, the Liberal Democrat leader, has noted, political leaders can no longer say: 'Vote for me, and the good things in life will be yours.' He argues rightly that the contract under which rulers were able to get on with their business, unmolested by voters, in return for providing eternal growth, or at least the promise of it, has been broken. Other political leaders have been too timid to acknowledge this quite so openly; but the time is coming when they are going to have to.

The Companies

The increasing velocity and openness of world trade connects closely to the democratic nightmares some see in the encroaching power of private corporations. The World Trade Organization is at least distantly connected to ballot boxes via its signatory-states; transnational corporations and market-makers are not. There have been similar institutions for centuries, of course, including the East India companies of Holland and Britain but the trend today is stronger and faster. It is of a different magnitude entirely. With the denationalization of capital in a world of low trade barriers, the denationalization of ownership and eventually of management follows. It isn't simply a case of takeovers across borders. It's about the mixing of people, ideas and capital from so many national sources that the company becomes somehow 'above' national identity. A good example is given by the journalist and commentator Hamish McRae who cited the case of Glaxo, the largest British pharmaceut-ical company in 1993 by market capitalization. McRae went on: 'But how British is it? Its chairman and chief executive were both UK nationals, as were nine of its board of direc-tors but seven other members of its board were non-British; 33,000 of its 45,000 employees were located outside the UK; and only 11 per cent of its sales were in Britain.'[16] Go to City firms in London and you will meet Greeks, Germans, Americans, Australians and South Africans among the native British.

Such companies, and there are thousands of examples, pose serious questions for anyone who still thinks that national political systems control economic destiny, or who think of 'national economies' as clear entities. Imagine the subsidiaries of one company, owned in numerous different economies, man-aged somewhere else, selling components produced in a third group of countries, to a sister company somewhere else again. What does that mean for 'national' trade figures? It means that they are at least partly bogus. When British ministers laud the revival of the 'British' car industry, they are referring to the use of global capital, Japanese management, German technology and in many cases Continental salesmen. Yes, the operatives are Geordies, or Welsh, and the soil on which the factories sit is good old British loam. But these are not great national enterprises – far from it. It is increasingly the same across Europe. Travelling by plane to Holland recently, I found myself surrounded by businessmen and women talking English. They were workers for Philips, in theory a Dutch company. In supermarkets in the part of West London where I live, the babble of voices at the checkout includes Americans, French, Swiss, Germans and Swedes, some working for overseas branches of companies from 'back home', others working for 'British industry'.

These developments are remorselessly tilting the odds against any politicians who might be tempted to tinker with Mitterrand-style programmes. But they also affect a huge range of other policies, including of course trade policy. As McRae has put it: 'From a company's point of view an international spread of shareholders provides a defence against protectionism: it has a local lobby of share owners [and, one might add, workers too] whose interests would be damaged by trade barriers.'[17] Since the very notion of companies being comparable in power to countries is such a curious one, it is worth recalling the scale of the world's biggest business empires. General Motors, for instance, has annual sales of around $133.6 billion, more than the gross domestic product of Austria ($130 billion) and not far short of that of super-rich Switzerland ($149 billion).[18] On the same cash basis, Ford is roughly similar to Hong Kong, while the Royal Dutch/Shell group (turnover of $95 billion) beats Denmark (GDP of $94 billion); Toyota ($85 billion) beats Finland and Norway ($83 billion and $75 billion respectively). The sales of Volkswagen ($46 billion) and Toshiba ($42.9 billion) beat Ireland's GDP ($42.7 billion); South Korea's Samsung ($51 billion) and Britain's Unilever ($41.8 billion) beat New Zealand ($41.1 billion). These are only a few of the big companies – I haven't mentioned IBM, General Electric, Exxon, Matsushita or Daimler-Benz, all ranked in the top ten for 1993.

And I have confined the countries to relatively prosperous developed states – the comparisons become vastly more disproportionate if African countries (Malawi, $1.9 billion) are included. (Britain, since you ask, has a GDP of around $911 billion, thus being seven times larger than the biggest multinational company.)

Now clearly, the nature of the power held by companies and the power held by countries is very different. Companies have economic leverage, countries have people and land. Companies have power, but they do not have sovereignty. And even then, by the most brutal and final definition of power, which is force, companies do not count. Except for the drug cartels, some of whom probably ought to appear in the lists of top companies, commercial power is unarmed, while even bankrupt Third World states still boast tanks and missiles. The mightiest global companies have workforces which are tiny in comparison to most nations – Shell may have sales which compare to Denmark's entire GDP, but the company 'owns' a workforce of only 117,000 compared to a population of five million Danes. And companies, of course, possess negligible amounts of territory – the Republic of Kiribati in the Pacific, which boasts the trappings of full statehood (a rather fine flag with a golden frigate-bird in flight above a rising sun, a president, and so forth) would not rate in the balance against a medium-sized commercial outfit but it still owns more of the earth's surface than the biggest company. Companies rely upon countries for almost everything outside the narrow ambit of their decision-taking and their corporate culture – law, regulations, healthy and educated people, clean water, roads, raw materials. They, in turn, possess technologies, a small clutch of bright and aggressive people, ideas, know-how, a corporate memory and a corporate culture. They are rather like wandering craftsmen upon whom the medieval baronies and villages depended for much that makes life more colourful and exciting. The power is not one-way but symbiotic.

Corporate power is also rather a narrow thing; it is in general power directed at the survival and expansion of the business.

rather than wider ends. Business leaders may occasionally pose as quasi-politicians, professing to be deeply concerned about the condition of Europe or the need for 'green growth'. But by and large, they are successful, when they are, because they stick, with remarkable single-mindedness, to the business in hand, which is complex enough. They are interested in one variety of human transaction, and in increasing the number and value of such transactions. Their wider interests in the human condition are subordinate, and must be; often they are mere posturing or camouflage to disguise the embarrassingly narrow nature of the business leader's ambition.

This is even so when you look at a global tycoon as controversial and feared as, say, Rupert Murdoch. In some senses, he is an extraordinarily powerful man, standing astride a business empire that is both unusually close to politics, because it is a media empire, and unusually far-flung. He has power, for instance, to threaten rivals with extinction by using his business muscle, and to threaten elected politicians with the withdrawal of support of his newspapers: the *Sun* claimed (wrongly I suspect) to have won the 1992 election for John Major. Murdoch can dangle the carrots of support to opposition contenders, as he did to Labour's Tony Blair. Focused narrowly, he uses that power ruthlessly in support of the growth of his companies, Fox and News International. He smashes unions. He squares politicians. He keeps in with national leaders, offering them news-space and book contracts (Thatcher and the Speaker of the House of Representatives Newt Gingrich, to name but two). Everywhere, he lobbies. He attacks regulations that threaten him, or tries to sidestep them. He is, in return, regularly described as a menace to democracy. And he is indeed, as one of his American critics has said, a man with 'a bias for incumbency and the old boy network ... someone for whom citizenship is a matter of business convenience.'[19] The world stands gaping; national leaders feel a little smaller in his presence. His power is intense.

But how wide is it? Not quite as wide as it seems. Take his alleged making and breaking of national leaders. This assumes that, without Murdoch, there wouldn't be a rightward-tilting populist press of the same magnitude. I'm afraid this is nonsense. Had Murdoch never been born, and had no similar tycoon changed the newspaper scene in Britain, then John Major would still have been fighting the 1992 election with the help of a similar range of Tory papers, playing to their proprietors' prejudices and to a populist suspicion of Neil Kinnock's Labour Party. There would have been a group of mini-Murdochs with public-school accents, and much the same effect. As we have seen, if it was really true that Murdoch helped get Major back, then he and his editors must have been sorely disappointed with the result. We can go further. Though his most decisive moment for Britain was his teaming up with Larry Lamb to produce the tabloid breakthrough at the *Sun*, the coarsening of pop journalism associated with Murdoch would have happened sooner or later without him: it is a cultural development, with its roots in old British traditions of scandal-mongering, abuse of leaders and scurrilous sexual tittle-tattle – hardly the sole invention of one leathery antipodean. And the alleged 'republican plot' of Murdoch's British papers would probably have been seen in other papers too. Do we think royal deference was demolished single-handed by Andrew Neil? Do we believe that editors working for other proprietors than Murdoch would have turned down the royal kiss-and-tell bonkbusters? We do not. Without Murdoch, the range of ownership might have been wider, but it is harder to argue that its political and cultural effect would have been greatly different. Media owners are trend-spotters not seducers, followers not leaders. Their own vanity and the petulance of excuse-seeking politicians conspire to hide this truth, but it is a fairly obvious one.

After all, if Murdoch really was a political titan then he would have spread his own views and instincts wherever he went. He hasn't. Here is a man who is said to be deeply religious, yet whose papers and broadcasting stations churn out filth and bigotry where those commodities are profitable: he cannot, one suspects, be a fan of either the pinheaded soaps his channels spew forth, or the youth-cult series such as *Beavis and*

Butthead. Here is a man who may have had a bust of Lenin on his fireplace as a student, but who is now fiercely conservative in politics and liberal in economics – yet whose papers have backed socialist and nationalist positions when business conditions dictate (for instance, the anti-West German Berlin tabloid *Super!* and the Scottish edition of the *Sun*, which backs the leftish Scottish National Party). Here is a man who postures as an outsider and bringer of diversity but who is, in reality, a monopolist dependent upon supine establishment politicians, whose 'diversity' is generally the same global-culture pap. Here is a man who says he hates tyranny but who will deal with Marxist censors to gain access to the 800-million-strong market in China. In terms of all human creativity beyond corporate growth, in terms of the making of ideas, of technologies, of designs, of visions, Murdoch is a zero. Has he said one memorable thing? Transmitted one new thought? He has helped spread the crude social gospel of the American sociologist Charles 'Underclass' Murray, but that's about the lot. Has Murdoch produced *anything* that nobody else would have produced? In the end, like most businessmen, Murdoch possesses power directed with unblinking single-mindedness at the growth of his organization. He is a business monomaniac. His power is in the service of his inclination, which is, as it were, to grow a very big vegetable. Nothing matters except the vegetable – surround it with ordure, water it, shoo away anyone who threatens it.

And this is the case, even more so, for most global executives and corporate barons, and is useful as a corrective to our wilder fantasies about them. The trend, according to some business gurus, will be increasingly towards the radical devolution of power in the biggest companies and the death of the vast corporate machine. But this would merely make more anonymous that which is now so neatly personified by Murdoch and his like. It would further disperse narrow power; it would not diminish it; and it would not turn it into broader, political power. Certain businesses are more directly dependent on governments than others – oil companies have to negotiate drilling licences, airlines have to haggle about landing slots and flight restrictions, banks have to thread their way through complex national laws, food companies must conform to local hygiene regulations. Those running such businesses rarely feel powerful in the old sense – they are struggling daily with rivals, with governments, continually being judged from inside and out, and working always under the critical gaze of market-makers in their shares and corporate stakeholders. They are as harassed as the cabinet ministers.

But this is not the whole picture. Even if we reject the demonization of the business leaders, the globalization of business does have serious democratic implications. It affects a multitude of things over which politics once asserted unquestioned authority – labour law, consumer regulation, tax rates, even the quality of education. Many manufacturing and service companies are able to adopt an almost high-handed approach to the elected representatives of the states when it comes to the conditions which govern their operation. When they come to consider siting a new plant they arrive like eastern potentates (and come to think of it, a lot of them are eastern potentates, or at least Japanese and East Asian ones). Western ministers and officials from the relevant government departments do not actually kow-tow at the airport, but there is no doubt which side is the more powerful in the negotiation that follows. Increasingly this means that what the successful international companies want, they get. When one talks to senior executives with the clout to make big investment decisions about the way they regard politicians, one is left in little doubt that many do see themselves as fickle, powerful buyers of labour, land and regulation, and the politicians as sellers of those things. The companies can decide not to invest, and can often whip away their cadre of brainy senior people to enrich another town under another jurisdiction. They can leave the store and go down the street. Among big companies, one of the continuing discussions is how to balance a nation's tax rates against other factors – how much should a good quality of lifestyle for executives, the nearness of airports and the local laws on trade-unionism weigh against a corporation tax rate of X?

Again, it is important not to get hysterical about this power-shift: successful companies are often the ones which acknowledge their debt to the local environment and people, build up long-term links and loyalties, and willingly fund national administration. But where the power is shifting most dramatically to the multinational companies, the losers are not only those countries which fail to acknowledge the change but also smaller national companies who may suffer from a tax or regulatory system biased against them, and workers who find their wages, maternity or pension rights eroded. The influence of global corporate culture on nation-state politicians moves parallel to, and reinforces, the influence of the liberal trade environment and the twenty-four-hour-a-day financial markets: it rewards states which follow orthodox liberal economics, with deregulated labour markets, moderate to low levels of direct taxation, relatively small central bureaucracies and low-inflationary cultures; and it penalizes states which don't. Just as most countries, for the reasons described above, cannot determine their own interest-rate levels or run independent defence strategies, so they also have less practical freedom over tax and investment levels than we often suppose. Countries which slash taxes and spending will start to find that they cannot offer a workforce sufficiently well-educated, or a modern-enough transport system, to attract the capital they need. But countries which push up tax rates, either corporate or personal, well beyond the levels of their neighbours will also fail to attract the investment on which their future prosperity will depend. Everyone is increasingly working within the same quite narrow bands of realistic taxation.

One thoughtful and experienced figure from a transnational company compared the dilemma for countries with the eternal balancing-act faced by businesses themselves. For a successful company, everything goes right: banks queue up to lend at favourable rates; as the share price soars, shareholders are content to take relatively low dividends, leaving more for investment; the good reputation of the brand or name makes further advertising that much more effective, and so on. But if the company tips over the line into perceived failure, it becomes hard to borrow money, the shareholders get difficult, there is less for investment, managers are struggling too hard trying to keep the ship afloat to think ahead, and a spiral of decline sets in. So for countries selling themselves in the global market. The countries with good reputations attract companies, which can then be taxed, providing more money for education, better roads, cleaner air, so attracting more companies, who can be taxed and so on. But countries which are not on this upward spiral find capital leaving and therefore find the struggle to educate, build and attract that much harder. True, they can offer cheap labour. But then so can everyone else. (Of course, this ruthless grading also affects individuals; the accentuation and acceleration of success and failure is a characteristic of all strong markets, affecting whatever they come into contact with. The instinct to buy success and mark down failure provides their forward drive – both the reason why they are necessary and the reason why they are not enough for human organization.)

The Culture

The diminution of national relevance and diversity implied by the new globalism can be seen in popular culture which, disseminated by satellite, cable and now by the computer Internet, is also beyond the control of any government. This was seen as a clear political good when, in the final stages of Soviet imperial rule, Western images, films and ideas helped fuel popular dissatisfaction and rebellion. But the thing cuts two ways. Britain has an open culture, since our historic language has become the dominant world language. But this is an ambiguous thing for us in the global market. We are already being recolonized, as it were, by the language our forebears invented. Neologisms, images and values disseminated by the big American, Japanese and Australian entertainment machines quickly saturate Britain. The same Conservative politicians who applauded when videos and satellites carried messages from the Coke culture into East Germany, now find that similar technology has removed their power to prevent people at home watching things they disapprove of – at the soft end, the curious mixture of violence and sentimentality that characterizes Hollywood culture; at the worst, paedophilia and sado-masochistic porn. In the United States in 1992, the writer Michael Medved published a ferocious attack on the values of the American entertainment industry. His *Hollywood Vs. America* lambasted film and television executives for feeding his country a diet of violence, irreligion, foul language, hostility to the family and much more. Whether you applaud Medved for standing up to what he called 'poison factory', or find him an illiberal publicity-seeker, it is worth pointing out that such an attack from a British perspective would be politically pointless. Such matters are far beyond the control of our state and of our political culture. On a rather less dramatic level, we have become used to seeing our classics, including children's classics, taken up, given the Disney treatment, and then sold back as something rather different – something more easily swallowed, but also sweeter, schmalzier and less sophisticated. Thus Kipling's hard and knowing *Jungle Book* returns for a new generation of British children as a politically-correct Hollywood assault on British imperialism. It may seem a long way from the bond market and George Soros to Shere Khan the tiger (all right, not so far) but there are parallels – the same technology-driven globalization is reducing the level of national competence. And it is idle to pretend that this is somehow not about politics.

But there is no easy road back. We have seen how a great part of the role of the state as a vast equality-machine is over and how, as it goes, part of the justified self-importance and potency of the nation-state goes too. Already many citizens are better trained in the new skills of the information age by their multinational companies than by the state. They rely on company pensions before state ones. Their jobs cannot be conjured up by some Keynesian bureaucrat in an office overlooking St James's Park, but depend on decisions taken by managers and shareholding institutions located, perhaps, thousands of miles away. They are company men and women, almost as much as citizens. The cost of their housing is not determined by elected politicians but by the international money market. Their entertainment, and the values therein, is mostly manufactured abroad. If allegiance is based partly on self-interest, then their allegiances are shifting too. They belong, potentially, to a post-democratic order, networks of interest beyond even the theoretical control of ballot-boxes.

The Backlash

For national politicians, including ours, who are accustomed to thinking of themselves as relatively free and important agents, with agendas which are not those of global business, this new world may prove an unforgiving one. Globalism is certainly harsh in some of its effects and is uncaring of its local impact. Is there any escape? Only if you are also prepared to accept the lower growth and lack of economic development implied by abstention from the globalized economy, as a price worth paying in return for keeping your traditional culture stronger. The great example of this is of course the Islamic revolution which opposes a theocratic and reactionary world-view to the West's liberalism and growth-obsession. In this, Islam is even more alien to liberalism than the Marxist world, which at least shared the materialism of the West. But for those who reject the Hobson's choice of theocracy or neoliberalism, is there any hope?

There is a great and growing movement which rejects the whole global economic package – the movement against free trade links together many trade unionists, socialists, environmentalists, economic nationalists and right-wing traditionalists. They tend to share the idea that 'thinking global' implies a level of abstraction and economic theorizing which mindlessly discounts the costs in sundered communities, polluted local environments, unemployed workers, migrations and so on. How do we measure the loss of a species of tree, they ask, or the loneliness of the old people left behind in a village which has lost its young to economic migration, or the spread of Aids in a shanty-town serving one of the new industrial mega-cities, or the disappearance of a French rural landscape painted by Pissarro? These things don't register in GNP or output figures and what we might call the World Opposition Movement is possessed of a single and priceless truth: there is, in our times, a terrible danger of slipping into an arid economic determinism that becomes contemptuous of anything it can't measure, and tots up the consequences of environmental or social catastrophe as if they were growth and prosperity. Wendell Berry, the great ecological writer and farmer, says: 'Abstraction is the enemy *wherever* it is found.'[20] Indeed, any economic or political system that sets itself too narrow an aim, whether it be square miles conquered or factories opened, is doomed to collapse. So the fact that the anti-globalization coalition has been defeated at every stage thus far should not make the supporters of free trade triumphalist or blind to their enemies' arguments. I have already explained why I believe free trade liberates people, as we in the West have been liberated. But all politics is a dynamic — action and reaction, thesis and antithesis — and if globalisation is not answered and educated by the assertion of local and regional priorities it may do more harm than good.

Although this may seem (literally) many thousand miles re-moved from the discussions of local politics and local government that came earlier in the book, I would argue that globalization is bound to cause agonizing side-effects, perhaps side-effects so bad that they become the main problem, unless it is balanced by strong and democratic local communities, as well as functioning nations and regional groups. The multinational company whose senior management are paid on profit-share and who consider themselves world citizens, beyond the constraints of national identity, may not care whether placing a plant here or there will kill off a river or destabilize a company town. But if, everywhere they go, they find a local politics which is strongly rooted, self-confident and possessed of powers to make decisions, they will be forced to think harder. There is a competition for capital and know-how, but companies and markets also require stable com-munities and environments, so the power is not all one-way. Globalization, in short, doesn't mean that politics has become futile; it means that democracies face challenges which are more difficult than before, and therefore that the reform of political structures to make them both more effective and more democratic is urgent.

The Rebel Colony of the Belgian Empire

These economic and cultural changes to the standing of the British state are the essential, and usually missing, background to a proper discussion of this democracy's relations with the rest of the European Union. Mainstream British politicians rarely make clear the extent to which the small size of our economy and the globalization of finance have reduced their power. Nor do they go on to ask whether or not such changes require greater exercise of political power by cities, regions, smaller nations, communities, and so on, perhaps at the expense of the old big nations. No one likes to wallow in their own weakness. But it is hard to avoid the impression that the exceptionally bitter argument about Europe is to some extent an act of emotional displacement. The erosion of national independence is a marginal subject, it seems, when we are talking about Nato, the bond market, real freedom to set corporate tax rates, or environmental standards. But it arouses hysterical passions when the European Union is at issue.

The great theoretical and – it may turn out – political difference between the impact of the EU and of these other matters is the difference between national sovereignty and national power. Sovereignty is the claim of ultimate political authority both internally and externally. It is constitutional independence, and has been described by one of the most lucid writers on the subject, Noel Malcolm, as 'a matter of enjoying full authority internally and not being subordinated to the authority of another state.'[21] Powers can be lost, while sovereignty is retained, so long as the nation involved has the constitutional right to act on its own, without being subordinate to another state – however far-off such a reassertion of independence might be. Put like that, the threat of the EU to sovereignty is obvious. It binds the nation-states which compose it ever more closely into a new constitution which is superior to, in the sense of taking precedence over, their own. The treaties, of Rome and of Maastricht in particular, form the basis for a rival constitution: ultimate authority resides, it seems, not in the peoples or parliaments, but in permanent deals drawn up by transient political leaders, and the supranational bureaucracy they have spawned. In that sense, certainly, the creation of the EU is a matter not merely of a power-shift but of a threat to sovereignty which, being the ultimate authority, cannot be divided.

It is clear that the idea of an irreversible and locked-in European Union is what most frightens its opponents – the sense that there is to be no going back to national sovereignty. They are right to be concerned. A nation which signs away its own final authority has indeed committed an act of legal self-liquidation. One may consider this to be a good act, carrying mankind towards the end of a bloody era of competing nationalisms. But it clearly carries a serious democratic risk. If the supra-nation follows policies that the ex-nation's citizens find intolerable, then there is no alternative but revolt, and probably violent revolt. So long as people feel themselves to be the citizens of sovereign nations, and those nations have the right to say no, the citizens have a certain self-confidence about their ultimate status, their standing-on-the-groundness, which is an important matter, whether or not it comes to be exercised. To that extent, an interest in sovereignty is not archaic flag-waving, but mere democratic prudence.

The difficult question as regards the EU, though, is at what point the constituent nation-states have passed beyond merely having a strong treaty-relation with one another, to having merged and handed over their sovereignty to a new European state. We are now pretty close to this point. If control over internal borders and economic policy, including the currency, has passed to a new authority with its own flag, executive, bureaucracy, parliament, anthem and founding fathers, then the sovereign nations are surely gently subsiding into, say, the same relationship that the Kingdom of Mercia has to the United

Kingdom. So it seems. It is this perception that has ripped the Tory party apart and led to some of the most passionate political argument in post-war Britain. But I have bad news. There is no clear solution to this argument. Why? Because the distinction between sharing power for practical purposes and surrendering sovereignty is ultimately a matter of political will. So long as the power of decision is passed to a joint, supra-national body by a sovereign nation which is willing under some foreseeable circumstances to take that power back, then sovereignty need not have been lost. But if, for whatever reason, it is inconceivable that the relevant authority would ever again be reclaimed and used by the national government, then the shift has happened, and sovereignty lost.

Putting it like that explains why there can be no clear answer, even when something as apparently clear as the idea of a common currency is under discussion. You don't need a metal-detector and a knowledge of Roman emperors to know that the right to make money is, along with the right to wage war, among the oldest definitions of sovereign authority. But it is hard to disagree with the proposition that the right of defence comes prior even to the right to mint or print. And the surrender of British national authority on that issue during the Cold War, binding the country into a Nato command structure under the control of the US President, rather than the British Parliament, was an act which, for most politicians and citizens, seemed irreversible. It was an act of carefully meditated national policy, certainly, but the majority did not contemplate with-drawing from Nato while the Cold War continued. We had locked ourselves in and buried the key. Let us apply the same logic to the single currency. German ministers occasionally talk of joining a single currency as being an 'irreversible' act. Such talk, understandably, puts the wind up British ministers. But were a single currency to produce unacceptable economic reper-cussions for the British people, or one day require the creation of a single European Chancellor to set pan-European rates of taxation, borrowing and so forth, then is it conceivable that a future British government would withdraw from it and re-establish Sterling? Given that, after nearly three hundred years, a sizeable proportion of the Scottish people are ready to contemplate a much more dramatic withdrawal from the internal British political and monetary union, and that British Conservative ministers have not attempted to deny that they have the right so to do, the answer is clearly 'yes'. Would Britain be 'allowed' to pull out of the single currency? There might be economic costs, but the thought of an invasion force of Belgian and Italian paratroopers landing to seal off the Royal Mint is a pretty implausible one. Those who argue, therefore, that membership of the single currency *must* be a question of sovereignty are exaggerating. Such an act would pass over powers which would further limit the authority and practical power of elected politicians to decide things, notably to debauch the national currency or borrow excessively. Well, that is true, but it is only the passing-over of a power, which, as we've seen, otherwise passes to market-makers. To mark this one out as crossing the line is to confuse sovereignty and power.

No British parliament or government can bind its successor and it seems to me, therefore, that the right of the British people to vote in a government which can withdraw from a single currency, a defence pact, or the European Union itself, remains a guarantor of ultimate, legal sovereignty which overrides even the single currency. It comes down to the authority and will to say no; neither of which seem to me to be in any serious doubt. The writer Nico Colchester has produced a further possible objection to this relativist, messy attitude to sovereignty. He has argued that since 'going to war is the ultimate exercise of sovereignty', during which the right of a government to issue and debase its own legal tender is an important weapon, then the lack of this ability affects sovereignty: 'When and if European countries link currencies and throw away the key, they will, for good or ill, be greatly reducing their individual ability to wage total war. Few things are, at the ragged edge, more sovereignty-sapping than that.'[22] Yes, but not sovereignty-destroying. In the horrific and for most people unthinkable case of another big European war, then the withdrawal from a single currency and the establishment of emergency national currencies ('the Bulldog'?) would be the least of it.

To state that even the decision to join a single currency need not mean the end of national sovereignty is not to dismiss its huge importance for identity, for democracy or for prosperity. It isn't a way of defusing the argument, which is an emotional one about belonging and a practical one about the management of different economies. But it goes right to the heart of whether the EU is or ever can be a super-state, a federation of subordinate territories that were once known as the nations of France, Germany and so on. This seems to me inconceivable, a spectre to frighten the children. This doesn't mean that it is right to push more and more powers to the centre. Quite the reverse. The best guarantor of stability and democracy in Europe is for all levels of authority to be secure in that authority and clearly under democratic control. Democratically-run towns and regions, as well as nations, are the best check on bullying centralizers. And whatever one's doubts about the bureaucratic nature of the EU, it is surely obvious that it remains fundamentally a political organization, subject to the political pressures faced by democratically-elected national politicians. The endless fudges and compromises for which it is notorious are caused by the absolute necessity for national ministers to go no further in promoting the common good than the voters 'back home' will tolerate. This doesn't mean that there have not been decisions taken which have been extremely painful for different groups, whether British fishermen or French farmers. But politics marks the limits, and I can see no reason for that to change. Furthermore, the bigger nations have more clout than the small ones, and that isn't going to change either. If the German voters are really determined not to give up the Mark, their politicians will not allow the single currency to happen. If the British ministers say that the removal of border checks is something that their people will not tolerate, then, whatever the legal formalities of the Union, in the end no one can force them to give such checks up. The argument over Europe is bedevilled by what we could call the fallacy of small clauses, which implies that the EU is a legal juggernaut which overrides political realities; it isn't and cannot be. Where the laws meet popular and national resistance, they will be changed or ditched, and if they are not, the Union itself will fall.

A whole section of British politicians and opinion-formers have, though, become convinced that they need to oppose any further European integration as a last-ditch stand against the final overwhelming of democratic British politics. Given that the same European project is seen on the Continent as partly being about the protection of political life and European power against the encroachments of global economics and culture, this is almost amusing. Almost, because the British perspective is at least partly a dangerous illusion: it implies that a political withdrawal from 'Europe' (there can be no such trading, economic, strategic or cultural withdrawal) can re-establish a successfully autonomous national politics here. That sentimental view is contradicted by the great movements in economic power.

'Europe' has been an issue of sentiment despite being almost always an élite issue in Britain. Most things arouse stronger, rawer passions as one moves down from mandarins and business leaders to the mass of voters: the world is viewed by hurried non-experts in simpler and cruder terms. But Europe often seems to work in reverse: the more elevated in the political system you are, the more you are likely to be self-interested in it and the cruder your image of political union is likely to be. This is not the place to rehearse the long and complex history of British attitudes to what has moved from being the Common Market to the European Union (snort of relief from reader). But the point worth hanging on to is that it has been something that worried and obsessed the Foreign Office, rather than the works canteen. It has been about national status rather than daily life, though some of the pettifogging directives on food safety and other matters have started to alter the balance. In the early days those members of the establishment who favoured some form of post-war European union, such as Churchill, did so because they wanted to bolster British standing in the world as against the other victors, Russia and America. A famous memorandum from Orme Sargent, who later became head of the Foreign Office, spoke in 1945 of the need for British leadership of Western Europe 'to compel our two big partners to treat us as an equal.'[23] Similarly, those who were chary about the early stages to federalism were so because they feared the diminution of British world power that it would bring – Ernest Bevin's famous and glorious assessment being, 'When you open that Pandora's Box, you'll find it full of Trojan horses.'

In the political parties and the think-tanks, there was a strain of British Euro-idealism which strongly affected young Tory politicians like Chris Patten and Kenneth Clarke, and Labour ones like Roy Jenkins and John Smith. But outside the ranks of the politically committed, there was little parallel to the widespread Continental yearning for a fresh start to political life, for a new Europe to replace the devastated and discredited Continent of nation-state rivalries. For Germany and to a lesser extent Italy, Europeanism was a way of coping with the grotesque perversions of nationalism those countries had indulged in. For France it was a way of overcoming the occupation and the political disasters of the Third Republic, and finding a new leadership role in a world dominated by America and the Soviet Union. For Spain and Portugal, it was an escape from the history of dictatorship and obscurantism; a ticket to the late twentieth century. For the smaller countries it was a way of binding themselves to the bigger ones in a system which would ensure that their borders were not regularly overwhelmed by the larger tribes. All these perceptions about a new Europe were simple and important enough to command attention and assent outside the political classes, or what remained of them. But with us, it has been different: most people thought our system had 'won'; Europeanism has been the preoccupation of the smallish political and business élite who knew that it hadn't.

It is significant that the biggest exception to the élitism surrounding the European issue, the 1975 referendum, was caused by a split in the ruling Labour government that could not be resolved in any other way than by the expedient of the last resort – asking the people. Despite the similarly grave division of opinion in the Conservative Party after the Maastricht Treaty was negotiated (a division that did not, however, divide the cabinet, as it had in Harold Wilson's day), the Tory Prime Minister John Major first rejected calls for another referendum. But then, just like in the seventies, a split in the ruling group vivified the European question, as Tory newspapers, factional leaders and business supporters took their arguments to the party in the country. And the Prime Minister started to buckle. One way or another, it would be surprising if Britain joined a single currency without there being a further referendum.

This élite nature of European politics in Britain has slowly but surely provided a fertile ground for the growth of popular suspicion of the whole project. The voters have been drawn in not through the original vision, nor through an honest national discussion about Britain's place in the world, but through the most bizarre and painful consequences of integration – all the stuff about straight bananas, fishing wars and the survival of the Briton's historic right to consume inedible sausages. As the élite project for Union has run on too quickly and too undemocratically, it has begun to hit a rising and novel mood of popular resentment. There is an element of hypocrisy about Tory politicians' criticisms of the EU for being out of touch with the people, given the way they themselves have happily run things behind closed doors for so long – it has been striking to hear the arraignment of Brussels on charges of centralism, bureaucracy and regulation made by British Conservatives who regard all of the above as natural and virtuous elements of political order back home. Nevertheless, however mixed and dubious the motives, the charges are fair. The EU has not yet laid down even the basis for a popular European democracy. Only around a third of British voters bother to take part in European elections, despite a barrage of publicity and party propaganda. The situation is better elsewhere, but uninterest and disillusion are quite widespread on the Continent, too.

National rivalries and prejudices, which have scarred, impoverished and depopulated the Continent for centuries, have survived a few decades of political idealism all too easily. The MEP Louise Weiss noted in 1980 that 'European Community institutions have produced European beets, butter, cheese, wine, veal and even pigs. But they have not produced Europeans.' It's still true today. The EU flag is suitable for car-bumpers but has never produced the crowds that turned out for German unification under the gold, black and red banner; or even the crowds that rally to the Scottish saltire. And the EU's Parliament has proved too far away and too abstract to provide a political focus. The protectionist tycoon and French MEP, Sir James Goldsmith, has noted of the Strasbourg Parliament: 'There are some German MEPs here with 800,000 constituents. *Eight Hundred Thousand!* Democracy only works when it is local and there is direct contact between the voter and the person he votes for. No one ever knows the name of their Euro MP, let alone what they do or what they stand for.' One is deservedly drummed out of the Brownies for agreeing with Goldsmith about anything, but the fellow is right about that.

This is, to be fair, a criticism echoed by some of the most Euro-adoring MEPs themselves. The problems of distance and language and the lack of a direct connection between taxation and spending are serious enough. Many Italian and French MEPs seem to solve the problem by not treating the place seriously either. But the British, engagingly earnest and hardworking, tend to be almost guilt-ridden about the Parliament's failure to connect with voters. When one remembers that, across most of Britain, the local press is far too impoverished and understaffed to seriously attempt to scrutinize what their MEPs do (even supposing they had the inclination), then the democratic deficit between European Parliament and national electors becomes grotesque. British national newspapers are little better: the reporter who arrives by plane from London is almost mobbed by relieved Euro-politicians who are pink and nearly expiring for want of the oxygen of publicity. One strongly pro-European Labour member told me wryly that he simply sent off faxes recounting his latest successes and sayings at Strasbourg and found them repeated verbatim in his local newspapers. This was highly convenient for him, he admitted, but it was hardly accountability. Like most other British MEPs, this man was hardworking, genuinely committed to making Strasbourg work – and dealing with large issues and huge sums of public money.

Strasbourg, however, is the most democratically-connected of the three main bodies of European Union. Of the other two, it is a nice point to determine which has been the more impenetrable: the European Commission, particularly during its supercharged era under Jacques Delors; or the secretive ministerial councils, admittedly representing governments, but working behind closed doors and virtually impermeable to parliamentary scrutiny. Anti-European Union propaganda has focused on the Commission, for obvious reasons: it is unelected, it is ambitious and it is in Belgium. But there are signs that its glory days are over. Further European integration will succeed or fail by the political will of the big member states, not because of the unity and determination of the Commissioners. The Council of Ministers, which because it is dominated by national leaders is a somewhat harder target, is less talked about but is almost as democratically offensive. And because the European Parliament wants to extend its powers at the expense of the Council of Ministers, the issue of the democratic legitimacy of the latter conclave is unlikely to disappear.

It works by secretive haggles, not open government. One only needs to attend a European Council summit, usually held twice-yearly, to appreciate the nature of this form of politics. In a central room, there are the heads of governments and the Commission president, plus a small gathering of officials and translators. Outside that room, but still part of the inner clique, are groups of other ministers, and platoons of roving ambassadors, civil servants, and other riff-raff. Excluded from this inner circle, but within the summit perimeter, are several thousand journalists and cameramen, attending briefings, being fed and watered (wined, rather) at the taxpayers' expense, smoking vast quantities of foul tobacco, talking loudly, and sending obscure bulletins to the outside world. Round them are thousands more policemen, security guards, gun-toting special soldiers and only beyond that is there a glimpse of whatever part of open, democratic Europe this particular summit is happening to. Of course, the vast majority of ministerial meetings are far more mundane and unceremonious than the summits, but the basic message of remoteness holds.

Much of the rolling agenda for the endless cycle of meetings between ministers from the member countries is processed and haggled over by their various ambassadors to the EU. They meet each Wednesday, assembled as 'Coreper', or *Comité des Représentants Permanents*, and cut deals, leaving only the most important and difficult decisions to be made during ministerial negotiations. At one level, this is merely a sensible screening process, without which the national ministers would never get home from Brussels to report to colleagues and parliaments at all. But of course, this perpetual multinational negotiation is itself an important power-centre, making the ambassadors who spend their lives engaged in it politically potent but mostly anonymous people. Britain's ambassador in recent years has been a wiry, chainsmoking, cynical and very highly-regarded Scotsman, Sir John Kerr, who is in conversation dismissive of his powers but is not known for nothing as Machiavelli. One journalist who spent years in Brussels concluded that Sir John and his colleagues were

taking an increasing share in the running of Britain . . . They make fiscal policy, trade policy, environmental policy, for Europe's 340 million citizens; they cut deals on everything from culture to telecommunications, from the amount of magnesium that may be imported from China to the amount of cheap booze you and I may bring from Calais.[24]

Foreign Office people agree with that, though they point out that the ambassadors are working within a broader political framework set by the national politicians and affected, however hazily, by the wider national moods.

This is just the criticism commonly made of powerful civil servants at home, however, and it is true that any deal they cut which offends large numbers of citizens will have to be answered for by the ministers. Nevertheless, the private world of inter-governmental muttering that constitutes the workings and surroundings of the Council of Ministers is not an attractive democratic alternative to the remoteness of the Strasbourg Parliament. Ministers will often speak privately in tones of disgust about the bullying and crude haggling that goes on at such meetings out of earshot of their national democracies. As we have seen, the British Parliament is not an effective backstop scrutineer of this private world. It has moved slowly, unenthusiastically and tepidly towards the intellectual challenges of European directives and legislation. It has, admittedly, created a new committee-hearing system to grill ministers on European issues, but this is very little, very late. In turn, ministers have developed as members of the European ruling class, establishing closer working relationships with their opposite numbers in the executives of other nations than with their own parliamentary colleagues in London. They have ascended and, in their upward-mobility, they have left behind the cobbled streets of Westminster Town. And the rest of us, too.

But perhaps there is no need to further labour the undemocratic nature of the European Union, for hardly anyone tries to defend it on democratic grounds, and there has been a long history of democratic objection to this particular form of supranationalism. In Britain, long before the Tory 'Eurosceptics' had achieved fame, left-wing politicians like Michael Foot and Tony Benn, and right-wingers like Enoch Powell, had been united by their fervent, almost pious, anti-Brussels parliamentarianism. For both sets of dissidents, Europe directly threatened the Settlement of 1688, the foundation of British liberties. As Michael Foot put it in the Commons in 1971:

This House and the British people will have less power to protest against VAT than John Hampden had to protest against ship-money ... The instinct of the British people in these matters, particularly when it is sustained in the teeth of persistent opposition and propaganda from the main organizations and newspapers in the country, is not to be despised.

For Enoch Powell, speaking in the same year, it was also about the instinct of the people, only to be expressed through their historic parliament:

There is something almost uncanny, something which makes the pulse beat a little quicker, in watching a whole nation instinctively cut through and thrust aside details, pretences, trivialities, and go to the heart of the matter. Untutored, uninvited, and indeed unwelcomed, they have insisted upon discerning the one simple, overwhelmingly important question: to be or not to be, to be ourselves, or not to be ourselves.

Except that they haven't, so far, so insisted: both men were wrong in their political prognostications, for the British stuck with European integration, and have continued to, so far. Both men extended their analysis, rightly, to the role of the United States as an arch-sceptic about post-war British autonomy. And it is worth noting that the great parliamentary performers, of which Foot, Benn and Powell are certainly three, have often tended to be in the anti-Brussels camp: the same political personality which prizes eloquence and passion is loath to see the echo-chamber's power surrendered. It is the lean men with forelocks, wit and stabbing fingers who are against Brussels. And, in general, it has been our sleeker, rather overweight politicians who are not natural orators (Roy Jenkins, Leon Brittan), who have prospered in Belgium.

Indeed, to a great extent, the argument between British anti-Europeans (I use the shorthand term, knowing it to be a slur, for convenience) and pro-Europeans has been conducted as the argument between politics and economics, or between democracy and wealth, or even between thin and fat. Neither side would want it put like that: the anti-Europeans argue that a free-trading Britain, unshackled from the bureaucratic burdens of Brussels, would be richer, while pro-Europeans argue that they are the real democrats since the European Union is so powerful, the choice is to be democratically involved or undemocratically acted upon from outside. Nevertheless, the antis have tended to speak most enthusiastically about Parliament, the voice of the people, the iniquity of lobbyists and big business, the democratic tradition; while the pros have sounded most sure of themselves talking about markets, exports and the standard of living. This is in marked contrast to the debate on the Continent, where pro-EU leaders have been so for political reasons, seeing 'Europe' as a bulwark not only against Communism but against American influence and, today, the power of the global economy. Economics was the method: politics one motive. The first manifestation of the Union, the post-war Schuman Plan for the unification of the French, German and Benelux coal and steel industries, was a perfect example of this; and with its Common Agricultural Policy and enthusiasm for quasi-corporatism, the EU has been in some ways an anti-economic organization. It has been intended to defend political democracy, not to subvert it. In Britain, however, this perception has rarely penetrated the national argument which remains one between thin men and fat men.

There is an awkward question for parliamentary romantics, and indeed democrats generally, here: could it be that the nature of the choice, politics *versus* economics, conditioned the outcome? That it was precisely because the British thought that more freedom was involved in staying out, and more wealth in staying in, that they chose to stay in? Powell, at least, has had his moments of doubt:

A suspicion lurks that will not be repressed. There is a doubt not far below the surface. Perhaps after all the people do not care? Perhaps it does not matter to them who will inhabit and control their country a generation hence? Perhaps it does not matter to them if they are a pawn in the power game of others?[25]

Or perhaps the phlegmatic, materialistic Britons merely look idly at some of the advocates of heroic independence and mutter, 'No thanks, chum.' For the antis, however, low rates of

European growth may soon give them their chance to beat the drum for prosperity and withdrawal. That would heavily shift the argument.

The European Union certainly offers fundamental challenges for any democracy. The introduction of a new supreme law, standing above Parliament, will be discussed in more detail later. More generally, though: is it possible to have workable democratic structures which are not based on the shared allegiances, history and language of a nation-state – which are new and the result of compromise and, being so, are almost impossibly complicated? Was it democratically right to agree a binding political settlement at Maastricht so long and involved that no ordinary, and few specialist, voters could understand it? This is a problem which concerns people at both ends of the political spectrum. The Scottish socialist writer and poet Tom Leonard made the key point, though without relating it directly to Europe, when he cited Tom Paine, the great English radical: 'The enemy of democracy, Paine argued, was the mystification of government because it made equality of dialogue impossible. With mystification, one might add, comes the caste that can be called the Keepers of the Mystery.'[26] Just as abstraction is the economic enemy, so mystification is the political one.

And there's no doubt that the European Union is for far too many people merely a mystery today. One Conservative minister believed he had worked out that it was well beyond the known capacity of the human brain to recall all the significant aspects of the Maastricht treaty ramifications and balances at one time. It was a problem which John Major's Home Secretary, and later Chancellor, Kenneth Clarke, famously solved by not bothering to read it. But he was not alone in finding the Euro-constitution mind-numbing: Lord Cockfield, the senior British Commissioner at Brussels in 1985–89, records a conversation with Margaret Thatcher about whether or not value added tax was included in the Treaty of Rome: 'Myself: "It was in the Treaty of Rome." The PM: "It was not." Myself: "It was." The PM: "It was not." Myself: "It was."' The argument was ended only when a private secretary was sent to find a copy and read out article 99, which confirmed that it was in the treaty – 'This was greeted in complete silence.'[27] How, if someone of the mental power and personal involvement of Margaret Thatcher can get something so basic so wrong, are the rest of us supposed to understand the system under which we are ruled? Even in the United States, which has a common language and history, and a comparatively simple constitution – one written in English, in the days when English was at its purest and most classical – the federal government has never enjoyed the unalloyed support or enthusiasm of Middle America.

Can there be a meaningful European democracy? There are only two ways of trying to build one and both are fraught with difficulty. The first is the federal way, steadily increasing the power of the European Parliament and making the European Council of ministers more open. That way the Strasbourg assembly might start to feel like a real parliament, and the Council would seem less like a private treaty and more like a senate. The advantages would be those of true political union, binding in states and peoples which were recently the warring tribes of the north into structures which – perhaps – slowly won common assent. This could only happen if the central political structures had their power tightly circumscribed, and if the local, regional and national power-centres were allowed their measure of power. As a Scot, it would make far more sense to me to have an Edinburgh Parliament looking after education, the local environment, training etc., and a European Parliament negotiating with other world powers about trade deals, security and the big stuff. Westminster often seems too far away to do the former well, and now too peripheral to be convincing when it comes to the latter. (The State Department in Washington says, for instance, that it prefers to speak first to Paris about important commercial or military matters, rather than London, 'because although the French are difficult, if we can get them onside, the French deliver the Germans and the Germans deliver Europe. The Brits are friendly and helpful but they don't deliver anyone.'[28]) A federal Europe makes sense to all those parts of the Continent with geographically-small loyalties – regions like Catalonia and Bavaria, small countries like the Netherlands and Portugal, dissolving countries like Belgium.

But it also needs convinced leadership from the big countries if it is to have a chance of happening. It had it for as long as post-war Germany was determined to bind itself into a common political structure, with the assistance of the French, who aspired to be the political leaders of the German-dominated economic superpower. But these post-war perspectives are a declining force in Europe today. The biggest problem has been with British voters, whose apathy about European elections, despite being chivvied and hectored by the establishment, is so resolute as to be almost admirable. It suggests that they do not see the Strasbourg Parliament as mattering (about which they are wrong) or as being an organic part of their democracy (about which they are, thus far, right).

There could be no more dangerous federalism than one which was simply imposed on unwilling or ignorant peoples. But the big states will fight it in their own interest. These 'big' countries are small enough to see that their national economic sovereignty has been lost, and they need a wider home market than their own populations can give them. Yet the nation-state has the same instinct for self-preservation as any organization. Making a distinction between the fate of the nation as symbolized by its economy, and the nation as symbolized through the state, can be tricky. A good example came in 1994, when John Major's government not only did nothing to prevent the sale of Rover, Britain's last volume car-producer, to Germany's BMW but, with sound economic logic, lauded it. A little later, Mr Major indulged in brinkmanship and courted humiliation by fighting and then losing an obscure battle about proposed changes to the qualified majority voting system in the European Council. His relaxed attitude to the former contrasted sharply with his mood of near-hysteria about the latter. The Rover sale was business. The qualified majority voting row touched the political potency of the state. Yet for most voters, surely, Rover was a far more emotive symbol of Britishness than QMV. Increasingly, governments will find it hard to explain to their electorates why, if the loss of state economic power is to be welcomed, the loss of other state powers are such a terrible danger. This is the great conundrum for the free-market right, which has not yet been convincingly solved by politicians such as Michael Portillo or indeed Mr Powell. People do not compartmentalize their minds into 'political' and 'economic'; nor should they, for those compartments don't exist in the world, either.

The only other plausible route to creating a European democracy is the one test-flown by the Major government, building on Margaret Thatcher's speech at Bruges in 1988 and on the Maastricht treaty. The 'Europe of nation-states' would extend the complexity of the web of inter-governmental deals and cut back the quasi-federal bureaucracy of Brussels Commission. Such a multi-track or 'flexible' Europe would allow nation-states to pick and choose what things they did, with which partners. There are obvious advantages. It allows more countries to join, at different levels of wealth and development. It would unpick some of the more controversial aspects of post-war Union, such as the agricultural system of subsidies – some countries would try to opt out of the CAP, while others opted out of military alliances. Meanwhile, the nation-states would not only retain power and prestige with their own peoples, they would possibly gain more than that. The trouble is, the complicated nature of this idea of Europe, betrayed by the terminology – 'the pillared approach', the 'Schengen group', even 'variable geometry' – would inevitably make the true source of power even more obscure than it is today. Only specialists would be able to understand why this particular minister was meeting with six, and not eight, other European colleagues, to discuss this matter, but not that one. The Keepers of the Mysteries, in every Whitehall department, would rise a little further over the heads of the puzzled and confused Members of Parliament, never mind their constituents. Lobbyists and political consultants would thrive on the confusion. There are anti-European Conservatives who are in favour of 'flexible Europe', dreamed up to help close deep divisions in the party, because they think it marks the beginning of the unravelling of the European Union itself. But why pro-European Tories should think this necessarily brings greater democratic involvement, or brings 'Europe' nearer 'the people' is a puzzle. An absolute precondition of democracy is that the location of power should be clear. Multi-speed Europe would be based on byzantine deals between chancelleries, a reversion to earlier, pre-democratic centuries.

In France, Germany and Italy, as well as Britain and Denmark, there is a mood of rising impatience with the heavy-handed bureaucracy built by the first and second generation of 'good Europeans'. The great challenge of monetary union remains, like a dark question-mark hanging over the Continent, and will prove the making or breaking of federal Europe. If it is the making, and Britain stays out, then the problem for British democracy will be intensified, not diminished. British anti-Europeans and German and French federalists will make common cause, excluding this country from the core and, in practice, more and more of our trading, diplomatic and monetary decisions will be made by others at private meetings from which we are self-excluded. But if monetary union is the idea too far, the thing that breaks the progress to ever-closer union, British Euro-sceptic relief may soon be tempered by the new difficulties of coming to terms with a more nationalistic Europe, in which Germany will loom no less large, and France will be no less single-mindedly French. Either way, we would quickly re-learn the truth that global interdependency does not mix well with national sovereignty. Pretending that the decline and fall of the free British state is the result of a Continental plot, rather than the biggest forces operating in the world today, is a gross fraud.

What, the reader has a right to ask, is my answer? There have been so many thick books written on the subject that I feel as dazed and cautious as anyone – this has become a subject on which to be strident is to be stupid. But we must start by thinking of the EU not as a sovereignty problem but as a democracy problem. Then things start to become a little clearer. Imagine a form of minimalist federalism, in which there was a

European constitution, written in relatively simple terms, and superseding all the various treaties and amendments, but which allocated only modest powers to the centre. The centre would be in charge of supervising the internal market, conducting external trade policy and, if it eventually happened, running a single currency. This currency would be introduced slowly, and would not be considered irreversible, and would circulate alongside national currencies wherever the people preferred that to happen (as John Major suggested before Maastricht). Nor would it be introduced for economies that were significantly behind the others, requiring either agonizing transitional pain or huge subventions of money which would, almost certainly, be resented by the richer countries, ripped off by criminal middlemen and often wasted by politicians in the recipient countries. The European centre would not be responsible for defence – after Bosnia, the EU should avoid making any new pan-European claims on this subject out of sheer shame. Nato and the Western European Union are adequate – or at least, less inadequate than an EU army would be. The centre's powers would be firmly fixed and considered immovable, and balanced by strong 'nation-states' rights' clauses in its constitution, making it illegal to push for ever-greater federal control. Further changes would be sanctioned only after referendums showing an absolute majority in every single EU member. The centre itself would be run by the current Council of Ministers, but transformed into a semi-permanent senate, meeting in public; plus the European Parliament, directly elected, as now. The ministerial upper house would function as the executive and would require parliamentary assent for all measures. The court structure would remain largely unaltered and the Commission would become the subordinate civil service for the European government.

The above is a thumbnail sketch of a thought experiment, which has its own drawbacks – it would satisfy neither the true federalists who want a superstate, nor nationalists who would see any federal constitution, however limited, as a destruction of national autonomy. It has the further drawback of being like nothing else in the modern world. But some such model for a minimalist federalism has, it seems to me, huge advantages. So much of the worry about the EU is because of its endless movement and obscure destination. There is no European constitution because a constitution implies something settled, generally agreed and understood: this is not the case today, and that is the trouble today. A real constitution seems the only serious alternative to the loosening and eventual disintegration of the Union, yet the democratic arguments against a do-much, heavily bureaucratic centre are also persuasive. A federal solution dependent upon a small and limited centre would end the confusion and stop the movement; would keep in maximum democratic accountability both at the level of nations (and in enlightened countries, regions) and at the centre; and would place at the centre only those powers that absolutely have to be there. At this point those readers who have not slowly sunk sideways and started to gently snore may be bubbling with questions, objections and alternative notions. I hope so: I am no constitution writer, and this is one of the great issues of our time which requires something more serious than the Punch-and-Judy knockabout between 'Europhobes' and 'Euromaniacs' we have endured thus far. There should really be a few blank pages appended here for scribbling on. But Michael Joseph is probably too mean.

CHAPTER FIVE

In a Bit of a State

> 'Yince on a time there wes a king, wha sat
> screivan this edict in his palace – haa
> til aa his fowk: "Vassals, I tell ye flat
> that I am I, and you are bugger-aa." '
> – Giuseppe Belli, 'Lisoprani der monno vecchio',
> trans. Robert Carioch

The Magical State

We turn now from looking at the British state from the outside in, to its daily domestic reality. The outside rivals to British state power described in the previous chapter are the context, the surrounding seascape, which we need to be always aware of. But state power inside the islands is also a fluid and controversial subject and, here too, authority and everyday competence have moved from the elected heads of the traditional state to others. This shift is complicated because the politicians themselves have willed some of it. There has been a shuffle of authority between the centre, unelected bodies and the bureaucracy. There are trends here which we are starting to become familiar with – the fuzzing of lines of accountability; the curdling of the culture of public service with that of the narrower culture of the market; and the rise of new pretenders (pressure groups, corporations, journalists, judges) who chip away at political authority, but are not by themselves a good substitute for it.

Let us start by looking again, because everybody always does look again, at the monarchy, symbol of the continuity and centralism of the British political system. In the previous chapter, I discussed the function of the monarchy as a theoretical fountainhead of legitimacy and authority; here I want to look at it as a functioning part of the state. And even today, no one has written more engagingly about this survival of archaism in modern times than Walter Bagehot – yes, him again, that thickly-whiskered Victorian super-pundit whose flashes of insight some 130 years ago have stayed scorched on the country's retina ever since. Most students of British politics have heard of his phrase about the Victorian Monarchy, at the beginning of the period of mass politics, when he warned of the danger of letting 'daylight in upon magic'. He meant that the mob needed its suspension of belief in the charade. But even then the mob wasn't quite so sure. It is less often remembered that Bagehot was writing at a time when there was in fact a lively and vociferous republican movement in British politics: in the 1860s, Queen Victoria was not popular. The sentences he dashed out remain vividly relevant to our times, when the monarchy is again on a descending curve:

Above all things, our royalty is to be reverenced, and if you begin to poke about it you cannot reverence it. When there is a select committee on the Queen, the charm of royalty will be gone. Its mystery is its life. We must not let daylight in upon magic.[1]

To get his message aright, you need to read those words with a faint, worldly-wise sneer in your voice. Bagehot was a robustly cynical writer, who did not revere the monarchy himself. He had begun his account of the institution by suggesting that, without the Queen, the government of his day would fail and pass away. But he quickly went on to admit that the attention paid to Victoria at Windsor, or the Prince of Wales going to the Derby, was faintly silly: 'it is nice to trace how the actions of a retired widow and an unemployed youth become of such importance.' This is hardly the hallowed BBC Richard Dimbleby tone. Yet after Bagehot wrote, the monarchy became more popular, reverenced and un-thought-about, so that his dictum about secrecy and magic came quickly to seem like an approving description of the British monarchy's dignity, rather than a cynical one-liner. This obscurity held until comparatively recently. In the first edition of his ground-breaking *Anatomy of Britain*, published in 1962, the writer Anthony Sampson was still able to say:

The palace has succeeded in maintaining not only wealth and dignity but also secrecy ... this inaccessibility is the essence of the royal magic: in spite of the hundreds of journalists who have hunted for royal stories, no one yet knows how life is led in the royal palaces ...

Wull, they ken noo.[2] We live in a different world: here is not the place to recount in full or even full summary the sordid and self-destructive exhibitionism of the younger air-headed Windsors, the sexual secrets spilled out, the marital misery publicized, the open acknowledgement of betrayal and bed-hopping. But it is worth noting that this has not been a simple tale of a great institution assaulted by journalists and eventually surrendering, but of the willing involvement of silly people with famous names in a circulation-boosting newspaper game which could only end in their personal and constitutional humiliation. The Waleses fought out their incompatibilities through biographers and journalists, heedless of the pain it would cause to their children or the damage it would do to their special status. The toe-curling stuff that came out ensured that no one could ever pretend, as they once had done, that these were in any sense special people. It wasn't just daylight that was let in upon the magic, and destroyed it, but volleys of revolutionary flashlight. It hasn't been Kalashnikovs or Mausers which accomplished the assassination of monarchy here, but Leicas and Nikons.

Now, it may be that in the less deferential climate of modern Britain, the willing suspension of disbelief was bound, eventually, to collapse. A world of mobile phones and telephoto lenses, of global entertainment and a highly satirical public culture is not an easy one in which to maintain the mystique of bloodline. (Unless we are talking about horses.) The Queen, widely held to be no fan of Margaret Thatcher, perhaps recognized some threat to her own status in the raw, abrasive meritocracy that her rival's decade so happily celebrated. If so, she was right: in the eighties the search for national renewal involved an impatient audit of many of the institutional bastions of post-war Britain, including the judiciary, the BBC, the universities, the civil service and the welfare state. This aggressive

British cultural revolution with red-braced accountants playing the role of Red Guards. Lady Thatcher may have hoped and assumed that it would stop well before the institution of the monarchy was threatened, but she had no control over the logic of what she had unleashed. When issues arose such as the amount of tax the Queen paid, the future of the Royal Yacht *Britannia*, and how much of the repairs for the Windsor Castle fire should be funded by the state, the debate was conducted in the same unemotional value-for-money terms that Thatcherism had made fashionable, indeed dominant, in almost every other walk of life.

The result has been exactly as Bagehot predicted. If we do not yet have a select committee on the Queen, we do have the beginnings of parliamentary auditing, and a generally sceptical, businesslike tone when it comes to the Civil List and royal wealth generally. Things are changing fast. The acid dissection of Royal wealth published in 1975 by the republican Labour MP Willie Hamilton made him a hate-figure: today similar points are made on the Tory benches, while a play and a novel about the eviction of the Royal Family to a council estate have become mainstream, uncontroversial mass entertainment. Where will this process end? In a republic? The idea is slowly gaining ground today, as it was in the 1860s, and the pace of changing attitudes makes it dangerous for even the most dogmatic royalist to sound wholly robust. A visceral dislike of the whole monarchical business is widespread among younger voters. But this is still a conservative and nervous country. A less decisive outcome is still much likelier – a further shaving-away of the wealth of the less central royals, and perhaps the main ones too, and an assault on the final political powers of the monarchy. Thus it may come that we achieve what Bagehot wrongly thought the Victorians had done, and find that 'a republic has insinuated itself within the folds of a monarchy.'

The possibility of a further move to a disguised republic suggests, of course, that the monarchy retains some genuine role in the real British constitution today, that it is something voters should bother to think about. This is so, but the practical aspects of

Royal power have become tightly circumscribed. The Queen's powers to make war or peace, conclude treaties, appoint officials and achieve numerous other things, have largely been passed to the Prime Minister, who combines the title of the Queen's First Minister with many of the practical powers of a republican president. From there is suspended a giant mobile of committees and quangos, appointments for professional busybodies and snobbish bureaucracies which depend ultimately upon the authority of monarchy. For the Prime Minister, the monarchy acts as a kind of grand PR agency. The famous (and inevitably Bagehotian) dictum about the Queen's right to advise, encourage and warn is not substantially different from what such an agency would do for a client: the monarch can be a kind of candid friend to the Prime Minister, but the daily struggle of government makes this friendship of limited practical importance. She is less, much less, than the Chief Whip. The real muscle of the monarch only comes into play in the highly unusual circumstances of there being no president-mimicking figure resident at Downing Street when illness, parliamentary putsch or an indecisive election result give Buckingham Palace an umpiring role. The historian Peter Hennessy, giving a lecture in 1994, found only five 'real or near real contingencies' since 1949 where the Queen's reserve powers were relevant.[3] (Though a further example occurred within days of his lecture, when John Major threatened his European rebels with a general election should they defeat his government over a finance measure – presumably with the acquiescence of the monarch, who would have had to sanction the dissolution of Parliament.) Of these examples, only two actually involved a choice between rival candidates for the premiership – in 1957, when Macmillan became Prime Minister, beating R.A. Butler, and in 1963, when Alec Douglas-Home was chosen to succeed Macmillan, again beating Butler. In the most recent example, Tory Euro-rebels complained that the Prime Minister was dragging the monarchy into political controversy at a time when it was already badly weakened by scandal. In fact, though, the Queen's position never became an issue of serious public debate.

To the extent that there is real monarchical power still left in the system, it is increasingly under threat. Take the evening of the 1992 general election. Three keen sportsmen, Sir Robert Fellowes, the Queen's Private Secretary; Andrew Turnbull, then the Prime Minister's Private Secretary; and Sir Robin Butler, the Cabinet Secretary, sat together watching the results coming in on television. They had been preparing their collective advice to Herself about what to do if neither of the big parties won enough seats for an overall majority – whom should the Queen ask first to form a new government? If neither of the bigger parties came to a deal with another one, should she agree to a further election? How much time should she require be spent on trying to get a deal first? Etcetera. These might be, one day, not only real questions but questions of intense political controversy. Here is where the Queen matters, according to doctrine, where she has a rare unchallenged power. Yet, unknown to those three state servants waiting to advise her, the Opposition leader had already been to see senior lawyers for advice of his own. Although, before 1992, the Liberal Democrat and Labour leaders had been involved in discussions about what might happen, Neil Kinnock was mistrustful enough to have taken separate legal opinion: even here, the unchallenged right of the head of the state to act politically might have been challenged in practice. The Queen is said to be a knowing lady. Even so, it is a fairly safe assertion to say that her real powers are even more modest than she assumes them to be.

The Conservative State

This raises the second big question about the image of the centralized British state, which is the extent to which it is the possession of all of us, whatever our views or income. To what extent does 'the state' exist above and beyond the party which happens to be in power? Generations of British students were brought up on the vital distinction between state and party – it was only in totalitarian regimes like the old Soviet Union that the interests of the ruling party and the state became intertwined and indistinguishable. The great democratic scandals of modern times, whether Watergate, or the Italian octopus, or the bribery cases in France and Japan, have been about policing the boundary between the interests of the ruling party and the wider interests of the state. For a representative democracy to retain public faith, the distinction between party and state comes early and prominently in the rulebook. So the question which has come to be asked more frequently after such a long period of one-party rule – is the state now a Conservative state? – is a pretty serious one.

How would one distinguish between a Conservative state and a neutral state which happened to be run by Conservatives? It turns out to be a subtle distinction. They would, after all, do much the same things; the policies would be the same; the people identical. But Kinnock's suspicion about whether the state would play fair after an inconclusive election result was widely shared: opposition politicians during the Thatcher and Major years felt increasingly cut off from the state as it changed quite drastically, shedding nationalized industries, creating new quangos and, as we shall see, altering the civil service too. This was partly a matter of their lack of involvement in high-profile public appointments, the paucity of appointments of left-wingers to the Queen's Privy Council and the Lords, and similar trivial-seeming matters. But these reflected a wider belief that the identity of the state was changing to reflect the business culture favoured by Thatcherite Conservatives. The dividing line between a state which is neutral and one which is ceasing to be so comes down to the behaviour and culture of those senior members of the state machine who must be the guardians of its integrity – the permanent secretaries and the inhabitants of the private offices. But there is a problem. These people are themselves the appointees of the party politicians, albeit on civil service advice; and the longer a party is in power, the more of them come to have been appointed by its political leaders and the more they all depend for the top jobs on those party leaders. In our case, eventually and inevitably, all senior civil servants became Conservative appointees. And I believe that the

closeness to Tory politicians caused by custom, for even mandarins are human, was exacerbated by the lack of any social
contact with the excluded leaders of the left. In another era,
opposition leaders would have been, like the mandarins, members of the Reform Club, ex-Oxbridge men, and generally
people who moved in intersecting social circles.[4] But one of the
electoral consequences of the Thatcher years was that Labour
and the Liberal Democrats became ever more clearly regional
parties, based in the Celtic fringe and the North of England.
Their leaders tended to have been educated in Glasgow, Cardiff,
Edinburgh or provincial English colleges and universities. They
were out of London by Friday morning. They were emphatically not club-joiners. And so a social silence divided the people
running the bureaucracy from those who were in theory the
alternative government.

Unease became most manifest when civil servants seemed to
the opposition to be acting rather too closely on behalf of their
political masters. The role of civil service information officers
during the Westland affair; Sir Bernard Ingham's robustly partisan use of the Number Ten Press Office throughout the
Thatcher era; the readiness of the Treasury to pay legal fees in
an embarrassing personal affair involving the then Chancellor,
Norman Lamont; the alleged involvement of Home Office
officials in digging up details on Bill Clinton when he was
running for the White House; the opportunities for wealth-
making and higher salaries offered by agencies and privatizations
to former civil servants . . . all these have been the stuff of
genuine resentment outside the system. Inside the system, there
has been some real anxiety too and by the spring of 1995, the
Head of the Civil Service, Sir Robin Butler, had agreed that
senior mandarins could start talking to Labour front-benchers as
early as January 1996 about how the system worked and what
their requirements might be in order to prepare for an eventual
changeover of government. The civil servants weren't only
keen to talk to the opposition in order to help prepare for its
policies – though the lack of new ideas in the Major government was boring some of them. More basically, though, the

mandarins wanted to disengage themselves from their image as functionaries of the Conservative state.

We shall look at the condition of the civil service in more detail later. But here it is only necessary to note that, too often for comfort, questions emerged about who was the eventual and final guardian of the system – who spoke for the democratic state, not the ruling party? For instance, the use of more and more private companies to work on contract meant that MPs found their questions to government departments were being met with refusals on the grounds that the information was 'commercially confidential'. This clearly raised a conflict of interest between the commercial rights of contracting companies and the right of a supposedly sovereign Parliament to information. Yet there was no one who was able to adjudicate. A similar problem recurred over the duty of civil servants to tell the whole truth to committees of MPs, versus their duty of loyalty to their minister. Rules were set and published but, again, the question of the ultimate arbiter hung unresolved.

A fascinating example of the problem of ultimate authority emerged during the winter of 1994. There were a spate of newspaper attacks on the probity of individual ministers and MPs, following controversial but powerful stories in the *Sunday Times* and the *Guardian*. These stories led to the resignations of two ministers, Neil Hamilton and Tim Smith, and a week or two of severe pressure on a third, the Chief Secretary to the Treasury, Jonathan Aitken. More important, they persuaded the Prime Minister that some independent authority needed to be called upon to look at the condition of public life. He had been worrying about this for some nine months, but had been persuaded by civil servants not to act. Now, he felt he had to. But Mr Major found that the state itself was unable to provide a level of usable authority higher than party politicians to judge the matter, and decided he needed to set up a new body, a standing committee under a judge, Lord Nolan.

At the time, Major told the Commons that the Cabinet Secretary had already investigated the particular allegations but that 'there is public disquiet about standards in public life and I have concluded that action is imperative.' (Acknowledging, implicitly but most significantly, that the Cabinet Secretary's investigation would not be enough to dispel the disquiet.) He said he had considered various bodies such as a Royal Commission, a committee of Privy Councillors [senior MPs], a Speaker's Conference [lots of MPs] and a Board of Inquiry, but none had been right. Rumour at the time said that Sir Robin Butler had advised Major not to be so open about the inadequacy of the alternatives. The Prime Minister's solution was a constitutional innovation of some significance: it brought an *ad hoc* group of parliamentarians, academics and others into being to sit in judgement over the behaviour of elected MPs. After a couple of afternoons of informal discussion in Downing Street, he created a scrutinizing body which, in another country, would have surely figured in its written constitution, grandly titled, carefully described in about the tenth paragraph, and considered of special importance. I was struck by this because I had been enjoying a convivial and relaxed lunch with one of those asked to participate. We had been discussing the condition of the British political system: shortly after we had finished coffee and parted, the call came through and my lunching-partner had suddenly been transformed into part of the constitution. The parallel with the shift in power as between the Prime Minister, the Treasury and the Bank of England is obvious: at this rate, Downing Street will be running out of spare envelopes.

Many MPs and ministers quickly let it be known that they hoped and believed that the Nolan committee would be merely a passing inquiry, which would propose little fundamental change to parliamentary self-regulation. Lord Nolan, though, after only a couple of days of blistering evidence, made it clear that he thought there was a case for a permanent outside element in the oversight of MPs' conduct. His committee quickly seemed to understand that, in the hysterical sleaze-hunting mood of 1994–95, it had been handed real power by John Major, since he needed its energy to dispel the stink. It certainly grabbed its chance, brushing aside ministerial anger when it turned its attention to the need for a 'cooling-off' period between ministers leaving office and them taking private-sector jobs in areas relevant to their former responsibilities. For all the reassuring words about general aspects of British political culture, the Nolan Committee pressed home its opportunity to confront the Major administration with a package of tough recommendations about the conduct of public life which it knew full well the government was in little position to resist – assaulting MP's deals with lobbyists and company consultancies; suggesting a new code for ministers; reforming the appointment system for quangos, and so on. After much delay and controversy, a radical package of measures was finally voted through the Commons in November 1995. These included a blanket ban on paid advocacy and, most controversially, the public disclosure, from April 1996, of MPs' earnings from all consultancy work connected to their parliamentary status. The advocacy ban was agreed by all main parties and may be of limited use; it is very hard to legislate against private conversations or hinting half-sentences at the club. The disclosure of earnings was highly controversial and bitterly opposed by many Conservative MPs as an infringement of their privacy and a disincentive to talent which might otherwise have gone into politics. According to the Nolan Committee, in 1995 twenty-six MPs had consultancy arrangements with lobbying or PR companies (the so-called taxi-rank phenomenon of 'MPs for hire' to any bidder). This has now been forbidden. But 142 MPs had consultancies with companies or trade associations 'which might reasonably be thought to influence their parliamentary conduct'. They are the ones who now have to choose between giving up the deals or seeing them published in their local newspaper; hence the roars of real anger at Major for allowing this issue to reach the floor of the Commons, and at the phalanx of Tories who reckoned that public distrust of politicians was so dangerous that this measure, however unpalatable, was a necessary medicine. It is too early to tell whether these reformist changes will end the sleazy reputation of politics in the mid-1990s and stop talented people who could earn higher salaries from entering politics. But it can no longer be argued that the Commons has failed to confront the issue of sleaze with determination. The Nolan Committee had said in its first report that 'a degree of austerity, of respect for the traditions of upright behaviour in British public life' was essential to restore public confidence. For once, politicians heard the message and acted decisively. Optimists will see Nolan as the self-correcting mechanism of flexible constitution. William Waldegrave, the Conservative politician and writer, has spoken of the British constitution as an old country house: 'The shadow of a Norman arch here; a medieval foundation on solid rock down below; a Tudor hall there; some fine Georgian rooms and a somewhat overdone Victorian wing; some twentieth-century moderniza-tion, still looked at with suspicion but undeniably useful. The result can be seen in a hundred villages up and down the land . . . the most desirable places to live in the world.'[5] On that architectural reading, though, the creation of the Nolan Committee is more like the hurried erection of a steel radio-mast straight through the ancient library roof − the sort of act guaranteed to have a snatch squad from English Heritage banging on the door within days. Waldegrave's country house has been being sadly disfigured by modernists for some time − and one of the amateur and maverick architects involved is a certain Waldegrave, W.

Politics and the Business Culture

Has it mattered? Is it important that we increasingly have to question the state's neutrality from the political party which has governed Britain for most of modern times? Is this any more than a constitutional philosopher's worry? The answer is that there is plenty for the rest of us to worry about, whoever wins the next election in Britain. But to examine why the idea of a 'Conservative state' is dangerous, we have to move beyond the narrow definition of political power and look at a separate world of influence-brokers and private links which burst through the covers of the constitutional textbooks. The spread of this 'auxiliary state' is neither alien nor unnatural. It is what happens whenever the political, constitutional state fails to guard its autonomy with sufficient rigour. Then, the auxiliary state begins to wrap itself around the other, like a glossy vegetable parasite. It is a neat point to determine when the state is corrupted by this: as with a vine round a pillar, at some point the vine becomes stronger and no longer depends on the stone-work, but surrounds and overwhelms it.

Yet, even now, some senior politicians say that issues of private influence and deal-making are not of general political importance. The Old Constitution is not violated because, in the end, 'ministers decide' and they are, in the end, responsible to the House of Commons which is, in the end, responsible to the electorate. Enough in-the-endings, already: in the four-dimensional world where most of us live, there is no clear distinction between influence and power, or between suggestion and decision. Ministerial decision-making is not a sterile, autonomous activity. If a minister has lunch with a man whose company spends huge sums supporting his party, and who regularly invites the minister to sporting events, and who later provides to the department's permanent secretary detailed and exhaustive briefings about why the environmentalist group opposing such-and-such a thing is wrong, then the minister may 'decide', but his decision will have been three-quarters taken by the time he sits above the relevant folder with his pen poised. How pressure and advice is applied to the guardians of the state is just as much a matter for constitutional research as is the role of the Lord Chancellor or the voting system in local authority elections.

In modern times there has always been a certain amount of auxiliary foliage, composed of the party machines, the networks of contacts and favours owed and the activities of the rising class of opinion-shapers, think-tanks and journalists, pollsters and lobbyists. Informal pressures on ministerial and civil-service decision-making have always existed. It is just that the forms change, and also the degree. It is degree we are concerned with today. So let us start with some perspective. Once, professional politicians and bureaucrats had to worry constantly about the auxiliary politics of court faction and aristocratic clique. But these are now of interest only to Nigel Dempster, a turgid social gossip. Rather more significantly, the era has also passed of a quasi-official system of economic decision-making which brought trade union leaders into the business of the state, and even into the government itself. Both, so different, are united in being seen to be subversive of proper parliamentary politics: the bawdy and violent street-literature attacking the Prince Regent's faction in the early nineteenth century was a symptom of public unease analogous to the satire boom of corporate Britain in the sixties and seventies when again the feeling spread that Britain had been taken over by an incompetent clique of trade union fixers which somehow existed above politics. (Though the first clique gave us the Brighton Pavilion and the second only managed the Brighton conference.)

More generally, though, the eruptions of public anger about clique-politics are merely punctuation marks in a system which has depended upon small inner groups deciding things amongst themselves. One historian of the Conservative Party cites the diary of the deputy cabinet secretary before the General Strike of 1926: 'It is impossible not to feel the contrast between the reception which ministers give to a body of owners and a body of miners. Ministers are at ease at once with the former, they are friends jointly exploring a situation. There is hardly any indication of opposition or censure. It is rather a joint discussion.'[6] When the same historian comments of the 1920s that 'Retiring politicians continued to slip quietly into the boardrooms of friendly companies or banks,' it is impossible for a politically-conscious modern Briton not to grin. As we turn to the current state of auxiliary politics, we should remember that it is nothing new.

Today's story really begins with the sweeping-away of the Labourite corporatism referred to above by Margaret Thatcher. For the first five or six years of her rule she and her supporters really did seem to be outsiders who had seized control of the system. But as the eighties progressed, the outsiders and mavericks hardened and solidified into a new establishment clique. The radical businessmen who had chafed at Wilsonian Britain became the Downing Street trusties of Thatcherite Britain. There were the advisers, informal and sometimes formal: Sir

John Hoskyns of the Burton Group, Number Ten Policy Unit and the Institute of Directors; Lord (Jeffrey) Sterling of P&O and the Department of Trade and Industry; Lord (Derek) Rayner of Marks & Spencer and the Prime Minister's Efficiency Unit. Below them, the pamphleteers and ideologues of the Centre for Policy Studies, the Adam Smith Institute and the Institute of Economic Affairs found themselves enjoying unparalleled access to ministers, including the Prime Minister. Revealingly, in the 1993 Hansard Society study of legislation, while consumer groups, local authorities and professional bodies expressed concern about the extent of ministerial consultation, the right-wing Institute of Directors found the British government 'very open' and chirruped happily that 'its approach to pre-legislative consultation [ie the most important kind] with interested organizations is a model.' And the IoD can indeed get top ministers to its briefings at its Pall Mall headquarters easily; even if, in the influence-bazaar, it is inclined to overstate its importance, its staff have long enjoyed a frequency of access to Downing Street which would be envied by many bigger outfits. Some of the outsiders of old are outsiders still – no one was ever able to tame the extraordinary, rough-tongued and multilingual Sir Alfred Sherman, who started as a leftist member of the International Brigade in the Spanish Civil War and turned steadily rightwards, helping found the CPS. But others entered and became the new establishment. There were the pamphleteers who became ministers, such as John Redwood, Peter Lilley and Michael Forsyth. There were the policy-wonks who arrived at Number Ten, such as Ferdinand Mount and David Willetts, and then spun off again, as novelists, writers, MPs. There were the rudeboy journalists who became valued advisers, such as Lord Wyatt of Weeford.

In Margaret Thatcher's famous phrase, they were all 'one of us': but what started as a guerrilla raiding-party against the corporate state eventually aged and spread into an auxiliary state, an influence-network run exclusively through Downing Street and barely connected to the official civil service or the Commons. Enoch Powell, one of the early prophets of what later became known as monetarism, derided the abstraction of the state as 'a little group of fallible men in Whitehall, making guesses about the future, influenced by political pressures and partisan prejudices and working on projections drawn from the past by a group of economists.' He said that in 1965, attacking the Wilson government, but it could stand as a restrained description of Powell-influenced Thatcherism in office twenty years later. There was much muttering against the gurus, some of them odd-ball, some batty, some brilliant, some all of these, who had special access to Downing Street, and who seemed to be far closer to the heart of state power than mere secretaries of state and privy councillors. But these boys had captured the heart of the Prime Minister during her time in opposition. It has been estimated by one of those responsible that the shift in thinking away from Keynesianism in the seventies and eighties was accomplished by no more than 'about 50 people'.[7] They had worked long and hard for their place in the sun – the right-wing Mont Pelerin Society had been spreading 'Thatcherite' ideas from the late 1940s and the Institute of Economic Affairs had been doing so from the fifties. The split between neo-liberals on economics and the corporatists can be dated right back to Peter Thorneycroft's resignation as chancellor in 1958. So the 'new right', despite its glossy American image and brassy self-promotion, was not really very new at all. And its role had been in essence no different from the long trek of the Fabians, who also took about thirty years to get their ideas into Downing Street.

The arrival of policy outsiders at the heart of the Thatcherite state was only part of the story. The Conservative Party, establishing its unquestioned right to be considered Britain's natural party of government, became itself so closely interlinked with the state and with its corporate supporters that the three seemed at times indistinguishable. The party was the key to promotion or exile for the politicians. It was the gateway to ministers for the big company donors who had policy axes to grind. Both Lady Thatcher and John Major hosted regular gatherings at Number Ten which were clearly party occasions, for corporate supporters. Ministers travelling abroad solicited money for the party as well as drumming up business for the country. Civil servants strove to keep the work of the state as separate as possible from the work of the party. In my experience, the vast majority were punctilious. But increasingly, the fact that speeches made by ministers to Tory associations were not distributed by departmental civil servants seemed like a minor institutional hypocrisy. Bernard Ingham was fighting day in, day out for Margaret Thatcher. The interests of industrialists in what government did was interwoven with their interest as effective shareholders of the Tory Party. United Biscuits contributed £130,000 to Conservative election expenses in 1992 and a year-and-a-half later helped persuade transport ministers to scrap a London lorry ban. The government's deregulation task force included Duncan Bluck, a director of John Swire and Sons, which pays around £25,000 a year to the party. It included also Graham Miller, operations director of Youngers plc, which had donated £413,000 to the party. The task force's job was to get rid of regulations which interfered with business, including these businesses. Another example was the involvement of Sir Philip Harris, the carpets king and a Tory treasurer, in lobbying Downing Street on behalf of Guy's Hospital, threatened by partial closure and a recipient of his personal generosity. Or the covert attacks on the anti-smoking campaigner and highly effective junior minister Sir George Young by tobacco companies whose support Lady Thatcher valued and who were blamed by his friends for his sacking and period out of office.

By the Major era, this interpenetration of government and business had become complex. There was a long list of ministers and civil servants who left government to take jobs with companies they had helped privatize or otherwise dealt with – Lord Tebbit at British Telecom; Sir Norman Fowler at National Freight; Lord Young at Cable and Wireless; Lord Wakeham at N.M. Rothschild; the former industry minister Sir Giles Shaw at British Steel; Duncan Nichol, ex of the NHS, at Bupa; Sir Archie Hamilton, former Armed Forces minister, at Saladin Holdings, the arms-dealing company; and many more. Some then lobbied their ex-colleagues on their new colleagues' behalf. (Do you think, Reader, that they were treated by the colleagues exactly as if they were strangers?) Big firms of Tory-supporting merchant bankers, management consultants and advertising agents were earning regular and substantial fees from government. Privatization fees rose and fell year by year but amounted to £1,512,000,000 from 1979 to 1994. It was hardly surprising that City firms developed special units devoted solely to winning such business, or that they recruited and struggled to get the ear of senior Tories – some of these firms were also training grounds for young Conservative politicians. Much lesser sums were also relevant – management consultancy money paid to the private sector from central government rose, for instance, from £18 million in 1985 to £93 million in 1993; government spending on advertising rose from £24 million in 1979–80 to £154 million in 1991–92 (election year). Governments have to advertise, but when one party is spending so much of the taxpayers' money on contracts for firms with which that party's members are also connected, the divisions between state, party and private interest become too tangled for even the least suspicious eye.

Meanwhile, senior executives in public utilities had become, in effect, spokesmen for Conservative policies of privatization and deregulation. They knew perfectly well that getting their organizations into the private sector would mean huge rewards for them personally, even when the privatized company remained a monopoly, without the real risks of the private sector. When Cedric Brown, chief executive of the privatized British Gas, which had then virtually 100 per cent of the domestic market, and whose pricing policy was controversial with the public, got his salary increased to £475,000, one of the 'remuneration committee' responsible was Lord Walker, who had earlier carried through the privatization as a near-monopoly. At about the same time, in the autumn of 1994, Cedric Brown's equivalents in the Post Office were eloquently pleading the case on radio for the government's planned privatization of the Royal Mail. They too would have done very nicely out of this, though no doubt their thoughts were entirely focused on the best way of serving the public. In the event, that privatization had to be withdrawn because of the government's parliamentary weakness.

My unease about this was reinforced by talking to a senior executive of a public-sector company who was pleased that the 'campaign' to get her organization into the private sector had failed. Who had been campaigning? Ministers? Not exactly: she and her colleagues had been wined and dined by merchant banks keen for the fees that privatization would involve. Various arguments had been used to persuade her of the value of privatizing the company. But, by the end of the lunch, the temptation was being clearly dangled: 'Think of what it would mean for you personally' – the share options, the bonus schemes, the salary boost. She discovered later that the same merchant bankers were simultaneously lobbying civil servants at the Treasury and, no doubt, ministers. Here again was a corporate, insiders' auxiliary state in action.

At times, the corporate/state interface is useful to ministers and hugely influential on policy. The Thatcher government's suggested alternative to the single European currency was called the 'hard ecu' and was intended to be an anti-inflationary currency moving alongside national ones. This idea in fact emerged from the City traders and provides a neat example of the daisy-chain of influence. It was licked into shape by a banker from Samuel Montagu who passed it to Sir Michael Butler, an ex-ambassador who had moved to another bank, Hambros. Butler lunched with Sir Charles Powell, also of the Foreign Office but then working for Margaret Thatcher, who then passed the idea to John Major, then Chancellor; to Douglas Hurd, the Foreign Secretary; and to the Prime Minister herself. Within a few months, it was official policy.[8] Similarly, though without the easy consensus of that, the battle about whether Britain should or should not join the single currency is conducted by merchant bankers and City types who furiously lunch, brief and lobby sympathetic pro or anti ministers. If Britain eventually joins a single currency, then the merchant bank Salomon Brothers will be able to give itself a pat on the back; if it doesn't, the senior players at the IoD will be cheering.

Those are important but wholly conventional and legitimate examples of corporate lobbying. A rather more dubious example was that of the Pergau dam affair. The pro-Third World lobby, the World Development Movement, had been a fierce critic of British government aid priorities and successfully took the government to the High Court over the use of aid money to build the Pergau dam in Malaysia, which it believed was a useless, environmentally damaging white elephant, for which British 'aid' was merely a quid-pro-quo for a jet plane contract. This, the protestors felt, was a general trend: more taxpayers' money had gone to rich Oman, with its military links to Britain, than to starving Ethiopia, and the £56 million which the National Audit Office agreed had been wasted on the Malaysian dam project was as much as Britain gave to Somalia, Ethiopia and Tanzania combined in the same year. Officials inside the Overseas Development Agency were worried about the Pergau payments' legality even within the blurred boundaries covering such matters but Douglas Hurd, arguing that Margaret Thatcher as Prime Minister had given her word to the Malaysian government on the matter, felt he had a duty to support her and decided that there was no alternative but to pay out. He was badly shaken by the court's decision against him and was obliged to change the way the aid policy worked. The Pergau affair, he later told friends, had been one of the two worst incidents of his tenure at the Foreign Office (the other being the qualified majority voting row referred to in the previous chapter).

Again, it is perfectly possible to argue that this was a sound, patriotic policy: Britain's competitor countries link aid to trade deals and so, perhaps, must we. But when one looks at the way aid and trade policy (ATP, in the jargon) actually works, directly using taxpayer subsidies to buy trade openings, the new corporatism is again unmistakable. The ATP is intended, according to the department responsible, 'to help British companies win sound investment projects in developing countries where there is a reasonable prospect of follow-up business on commercial terms.' The money – some £1.37 billion from 1978 to 1992 – was doled out by British Overseas Trade Board, advised by its subsidiary committee, the Overseas Projects Board. Who got it? Nearly 43 per cent went to just five companies, of which the two biggest gainers were Balfour Beatty, which netted 21 per cent, or £287 million, and GEC. Balfour Beatty's parent company, BICC, had been a generous donor over the decade to a variety of Conservative causes, including the front-company British United Industrialists, and the campaigning organizations, the Economic League and Aims of Industry. The chairman of BICC was also involved in the British Overseas Trade Board and the three other companies which mainly benefited from the taxpayers' largesse, Amec, Davy and Biwater, all had representatives on the Overseas Project Board.[9] This board's official objectives include giving 'industry a voice in the formulation of government policy in relation to major overseas projects . . .' It has to be said that it seems to have performed that arduous function remarkably efficiently. Again, all this may be in the interests of Britain generally, providing the right companies with the right help to generate jobs in the right places. But it was also naked corporatism in action, and a classic example of how auxiliary power has been winding round and at times almost obliterating the Old Constitution.

The culture is most clearly tainted when it comes to money passing not through the state itself, but from the corporate beneficiaries of the state to the party which has been running the state. The Conservative Party has not been terribly lucky in its admirers. Octav Botnar, the Nissan UK chief who was a generous funder of the party, fled the country to Switzerland following allegations that he was involved in a £97 million tax fraud. Asil Nadir, the disgraced boss of Polly Peck, paid over nine donations to the party between 1985 and 1990 before fleeing to Cyprus. Mohammed Hashemi, an Iranian arms dealer whose brothers were arrested in the United States on eighteen counts of supplying arms to Iran, was a Tory donor in 1989–90. Kamlesh Pattni, wanted by the Kenyan police for fraud, was a donor and a guest at the Conservative Winter Ball at the Grosvenor Hotel, London, in February 1992, at which the hosts were the Prime Minister and the Foreign Secretary. Nazmu Virani, jailed in May 1994 after being convicted on seven charges of false accounting and providing false information in the BCCI (Bank of Credit and Commerce International) affair, paid sums to the Conservatives over many years, including £4,500 worth of office equipment to the constituency association of the Putney MP, David Mellor – who as a Treasury minister later met members of the BCCI creditors' groups and assured them of government help. These are a few names picked out by the press from a system which is mostly confidential and successful in hiding its secrets. But they combine in the public mind with lesser events, such as the willingness of Tory backbenchers to take money to put down parliamentary questions and the resignation of a Tory party treasurer accused in America of 'bucketing, wash sales, illegal cross-trades and fictitious sales' in the cocoa futures market. They produce an impression of a closed world of deals and favours which appeals to voters no more than the corporate Wilsonian system which the Thatcherites busted.

And that impression is right. Britain is a small country where the top people in power, whether commercial power or political power, tend to become acquainted and lobby one another in a personal, private way that entirely bypasses the formal constitution. It is impossible to draw neat lines. N.M. Rothschild, the City merchant bank, is one of the training-grounds for Tories and maintained close links during the privatization years. It became, for a while, quite close to the state. It took on former cabinet ministers and picked up contracts for organizing the sale of a range of public bodies, including Railtrack. Saatchi and Saatchi in its heyday was not simply an advertising agency the Conservative Party happened to use: it was deeply intertwined, and in summer 1994 the two new deputy chairmen appointed to Conservative Central Office were both Saatchi men as well as Tory men. In the words of one alarmed Labour observer then, 'Saatchis are moving out of Berkeley Square and into Smith Square.' The Royal Bank of Scotland, whose chairman, Lord Younger, served in the Thatcher cabinet as Scottish Secretary and Defence Secretary, has been most understanding in its treatment of the Conservative Party's huge overdraft. And so on. If you wanted to see the most involved and important Tory businessmen chewing the fat, you'd find them chewing it at some sporting or operatic entertainment where, in the words of one cabinet minister, 'You are lobbying and being lobbied, but so effectively that you never have to finish your sentences.'

This recalls, unmistakably, the 1920s world described above. But there are important differences to note, too. Then, the common enemy of business, finance and the Tory party was socialism, revolutionary abroad and militant at home. Today, the links are more to do with specific deals than ideological struggle. They are about the conjunction of interests of a fiercely pro-business Conservative administration, operating in a globalizing economy; and a wide range of companies for whom deregulation, privatization and the unbundling of the state offer rare opportunities. Because economic power has been eroding political power, the influence of business is, if anything, more important, not less. By 1995, as John Major's administration seemed to be doing hopelessly badly in the polls, so its corporate backers started to back away, announcing their conversion to the idea of political independence – even United Biscuits did so, once one of the staunchest. But this was merely a pause. If the polls turned, the companies would be back, and the auxiliary state would try to wrap itself round the other even more tightly than before. Nothing is surer. Similarly, however welcome the creation and attitude of the 'sleaze-busting' Nolan Committee, it was, as we have seen, the product of Government weakness. It was warned off launching a pre-election inquiry into party funding and, were the Conservatives to win again, it is not self-evident that this Committee of Public Propriety would be able to keep the auxiliary state at bay. In the meantime, any account of the British constitution today which omits to mention the refreshment tent at the Stella Artois tennis tournament, as well as prime minister's question time; or the good seats at Covent Garden as well as the good seats on the government benches, is a little naïve.

The Disintegrating State

While this dealmaking at the top of government and business has grown more intense, other aspects of the post-war identity of the state have been crumbling away. The rise of the business-man's state has been matched by the fall of the bureaucrat's state, and the two changes are intimately related. A major theme of the past decade has been the unbundling of the state apparatus and the pushing of what was done by the public sector into the private sector. This was done first, and most famously, through straightforward privatization of state industry. Then came the hiving off of swathes of the bureaucracy and civil service as self-managed agencies, the so-called 'Next Steps' programme, which may or may not lead to their eventual privatization. Then came 'market-testing', which means that large swathes of the civil service must try to discover whether private companies could perform the same functions for less money, and to hand the work over to them on contract if they can. It could as well be called 'auto-privatization'. And there has been, alongside these central initiatives, the spread of local quangos, which has already been described.

This change has been big and extraordinarily fast. The great privatizations of the Thatcher years were often pushed through Parliament with excessive speed and lack of preparation – resulting, in some cases, in flawed private monopolies. Similarly, the 'Next Steps' initiative was launched by Margaret Thatcher's Efficiency Unit in 1988 and, by April 1993, eighty-nine agencies had been established, and more than 260,000 civil servants, 45 per cent of the total, were working for them. By the following summer, the proportion had jumped to 64 per cent. These agencies remain part of the civil service but they have contracts with government and a measure of self-management and the aim is to have 90 per cent of the civil service under their aegis by the mid-1990s. Market testing, which was launched in November 1991, has been rather less dramatic. By the summer of 1994, £1.3 billion of public activities had been tested but, in the vast majority of cases, the civil servants stayed in charge. Savings of £150 million had resulted and 12,200 jobs had been lost to private-sector contractors. A 1994 White Paper on the civil service proposed giving the managers of agencies and departments greater freedom in finding savings – they wouldn't be forced to market-test in the same way. But the same package of changes created a small senior civil service of 3,500 top and generally protected jobs and gave it the task of putting pressure on the rest of the service, leaving little doubt that more and more work would be pushed outside the state bureaucracy to lower-paying and more aggressive private companies.

Taken together, these changes merit the over-used term of 'revolution'; they help return Britain to an era where state servants will do less. Sir Peter Kemp, one of the most energetic mandarin architects of agencies, who later fell out with his political bosses, and left the civil service, described his dream of 'moving away from the model of a single service monolith to one where a loose federation of many smaller agencies, units and cores predominates.' The core civil service, which had grown to a peak of some 500,000 people serving twenty cabinet ministers by the late seventies, was being dramatically shrunk: Sir Peter wrote in 1993 that 'If present Next Steps agencies and agency candidates are taken into account, we can see that the remaining core service is returning to nearer the 50,000 employees we had in 1900.'[10] This revolution has been energetically sold by ministers as an extension of good business principles into government, and a sloughing-off of the old post-Victorian attitudes. The language of 'reinventing government' came from the United States and much of the practical inspiration came from New Zealand. But in many respects Britain herself has been a world leader in this new attitude to the state. The theory is appealing: just as businesses are no longer run on the rigid, bureaucratic and hierarchical lines established during the Industrial Revolution, so governments should ditch the stultifying and rigid administrative machines they have inherited from nineteenth-century statesmen. Managers should be free to manage without the constraints of being part of a vast, almost military-style machine. The efficiency savings brought about since 1988 at local government level, forcing councils to offer contracts to private companies rather than try to do everything incompetently themselves, should be extended to the state itself.

Yes, yes; and the unbundling of the state *will* produce real benefits for the citizen. This is a worldwide movement, pursued by governments of the centre-left, as well as of the right. The old ways of measuring public services by their inputs – the amount of taxpayers' money swallowed up by 'successful' departments after each public-expenditure round, and the number of jobs involved – seem increasingly absurd. Government became a conspiracy of unthinking spending-machines which simply grew a little each year as the departments haggled and measured what they produced only in the crudest terms. The new measurements are still crude. Listing the performance of schools, of hospitals, of train services all produced spasms of anger from the professionals involved. But it was an advance from simply measuring the number of schools, or of hospital beds, or of miles of railway track. The consumer power of measurement has arrived, has given individuals a new weapon and cannot easily be abolished by the state. That has been a Conservative achievement, relentlessly opposed by Labour in opposition. Similarly, the unbundling of the state has confirmed what privatization suggested, that the same jobs can be done for the citizen or consumer at lower cost and by fewer people. But the result for the interpenetration of business and politics, described above, is dramatic. It was well put by Labour's Jack Straw, in a submission to the Nolan Committee in 1995:

The policy of 'rolling back the frontiers of the state' has led to a paradox. While the numbers directly employed in the public sector have indeed shrunk, by nearly 50 per cent since 1979, the amount spent by the state has not. Public spending as a proportion of national income (GDP) was 44.1 per cent in 1979, and is 44.3 per cent today. The reduction in the numbers employed directly by the state has not therefore led to a corresponding reduction in the functions of the state. Instead, these functions, previously provided by the state, are now provided by government contractors, through the process of privatization, compulsory competitive tendering, and market testing. This has led to a great increase in the number of private firms and individuals wholly or largely dependent upon the state for their profit and their livelihood.[11]

Is there any alternative to this process? There have been several lines of attempted counter-attack. The Labour Deputy Leader, John Prescott, has argued an economic case for what appears to be public-sector inefficiency. He argues that other successful societies, including Japan, differentiate between an aggressive trading sector, which earns national wealth, and a less aggressive domestic service sector, which supplies jobs, social cohesion and continuity: he asserts that the economic and social impact of mass, long-term unemployment, exacerbated by the unbundling of the state, outweighs any immediate benefits. Unsurprisingly, the public sector unions agree, but add their own criticism, which is that the private companies are simply less good at the job, driven by profit, not public service, and relatively inexperienced. The Council of Civil Service Unions compiled a list of blunders, including the tale of botched repairs to Tornado aircraft, which cost some £60 million of damage in 1993. There was the story of Astra, a private company formed to run the Skills Training Agency in 1990, which received £11 million from the government, plus headquarters and training centres, but which, after closures and job cuts, went bankrupt in July 1993, with 950 staff placed in the hands of the receivers. Group 4's privatized prison at Wolds in Lincolnshire was heavily criticized for a high level of violence and drugs culture by the Prison Reform Trust, and the company became national news when it lost prisoners from its privatized prison escort service. Then there was the story of the contracting out of the Inland Revenue service providing employers with personal tax details of their staff. This went wrong and, in the words of the unions, 'many of the 84,000 packs [of mail] were sent to the wrong companies while other firms received junk mail including frocks, tights, a spare-part calendar, advertisements for pregnancy testing and time-share villa details. More than 400,000 new envelopes had to be re-posted by the Inland Revenue.' Failures in publicly-run prisons and bureaucracies are not, however, blamed by the unions on their ownership, but on lack of taxpayers' money. And not all the left is convinced that private means bad. Labour needs to be able to claim it too can run the public services efficiently and, as one leftish critic of the party's attitude wrote,

Labour retains a faith in the ability of top-down administration to make public services efficient in the absence of competition. It opposes the use of rewards for good performance, either through performance-related pay or profit for entrepreneurs in public services. Stakhanovite exhortation can raise the productivity of Labour in the short term, but the consequences in the longer term of the planned economy are evident in Eastern Europe.[12]

These controversies are likely to be as central to the political debate towards the end of the millennium as straightforward privatization was during the Thatcher era. For our purposes, however, the economics and efficiency or otherwise of this huge change in our national life can be put to one side: the questions for students of the real constitution are to what extent power, as well as functions, have been privatized; and whether democratic accountability to the voters has been sacrificed?

The first obvious, but important point to make here is that there is no absolute division between the carrying out of a function and power over it; and that the fuzziness between the two gets more pronounced the more complicated the function is. If the function is to lay paving-stones in a straight line between two given points, according to a contract, the paving-stone-layer has virtually no power: he can fulfil the contract correctly or not. But if the function is to run a modern prison, then, however detailed the contract with the Home Office, the company has a real degree of leeway in thousands of small details of everyday life which, so far as the prisoner is concerned, represent real power. (Alternatively, if the contract is fantastically detailed, and this power circumscribed, the private company will be unable to perform the job any differently from the state, and the whole exercise becomes futile.)

This is a serious dilemma for politicians, and possibly irreconcilable. In the case of the privatization of utilities, the government has largely passed over the interests of consumers to a series of new regulatory bodies – Oftel, Ofwat, Ofgas and the rest Ofthem – who fix 'acceptable' profit levels, scrutinize investment and report on competition or the lack of it. The regulators themselves, who head these bodies, have wide discretionary powers and are starting to become visible and, in some cases, controversial, figures. People like John Swift, the rail regulator, and Professor Stephen Littlechild, the electricity regulator, have moved beyond being mere whistle-blowers to become policy-makers: whether the question is the ability of travellers to buy through-tickets covering different train services, or the availability of subsidies for energy insulation, or the balance between gas and coal, such people are making profoundly political decisions which affect the national interest and the consumer. Ministers pretend that, somehow, all these concerns have become matters for 'the market' – the very word 'regula-tion' implies that the job is merely about ensuring fair play, rather than about making political choices. But ministers' own propensity to interfere and criticize shows that they know this to be hooey. They know it's political.

So how are the regulators to balance public goods – for instance, the conflict between the lowest possible price for the user and the need for longer-term investment, or between the privatized company's job as a service-provider in Britain and its desire to spend time and publicly-accumulated capital becoming a player overseas? These are genuinely difficult problems and there are often few 'objective' criteria to steer by. In the end, left to themselves, the regulators are only human and will behave like other politicians, letting their own prejudices deter-mine their decisions. If all the utilities were operating in real markets, with real competition, their job would be far easier. But, as Peter Riddell has put it, 'regulators have been unable to escape the dilemma that caused these industries to be nationalized in the 1940s. They provide essential services, in which consumers have no real choice . . . Wider social and environmental regula-tions cannot be ignored. It has been impossible just to issue licences and let regulators monitor them.'[13] If the citizen is to retain even a weak and indirect say over the behaviour of these virtual monopolies then ministers have to ensure that the regula-tor is tough on profits and keeps a close eye on wider social requirements. But the tougher the regulator, the less profit the privatized companies can make and the less room the new

managements have to take decisions. So which is more important – the residual rights of the democracy, now expressed at
fourth-hand (voter to Parliament to minister to regulator) – or
commercial freedom? Where power has been ceded by the state,
particularly to a monopoly, doesn't the state have special
responsibilities, long after privatization? And if these are the state's
responsibilities, can ministers really slough them off on to
'independent' regulators, washing their hands of the decisions that
result? These may seem abstract problems but any MP, with a
postbag of letters about supplies being cut off, or soaring bills, will
confirm that they are anything but. In the end, where there is a
monopoly, publicly-owned or privately-owned, on which the
citizen depends, then it is impossible to exclude politics. In the end,
therefore, the regulators are going to have to come under stronger
political control than they are today, probably through Parliament.

When it comes to the next form of unbundling, the creation
of agencies and market-testing, the democratic problems are
different, but parallel. Like the privatized utilities, the new
Whitehall agencies are intended to give their bosses greater
freedom to manage – to set wages, contract out work – than
under the old civil service order. Yet, in theory at least, ministers
are still responsible for these agencies, just as under the old
system. As with the regulators, this poses an unresolved question.
If an agency manager cuts pay in a Birmingham office and
provokes a strike, is the minister responsible for the strike, or
the manager? One of the most serious thinkers on the subject
has been William Waldegrave, whose architectural simile for
the British constitution featured earlier. From 1992–94 he was
the Conservative cabinet minister responsible for much of this
unbundling. He has argued that the changes improve accountability, and his argument is worth following:

The old myth of personal ministerial responsibility for every action
undertaken by each government department was, in Herbert Morrison's words, 'The minister is responsible for every stamp stuck on an
envelope' or, as Nye Bevan more colourfully had it, 'If a bedpan is
dropped the minister will hear of it.' As Sir Robin Butler (Head of
the Home Civil Service) has said, this was not only a myth – it was a

dangerous myth. In reality, no minister can check the stamps and the bedpans ... What we have done is to make clear the distinction between *responsibility*, which can be delegated, and *accountability*, which remains firmly with the minister. The minister is properly accountable for the policies he settles, and the service his department purchases or for which it contracts; those who have agreed to provide services are quite properly responsible for their provision. Thus, far from impairing accountability, I believe that the purchaser/provider separation, executive agencies and management by contract have helped to make a reality of it. [My italics.]

Taking Waldegrave's point about the absurdity of the old system, particularly in a complex modern state, let's linger a little on his distinction, apparently essential to the argument, between responsibility and accountability. What, really, is the difference? It seems to be an important one. But the Collins *Concise English Dictionary* on my tabletop defines accountability as 'responsible to someone or for some action'; and responsible as meaning both 'having control or authority over' and 'being accountable . . .' It treats the two as virtual synonyms: if anything, responsibility, which Waldegrave makes the role of the lower agency or company, is placed higher than accountability, the role of the minister. This seems a worryingly thin distinction, if it is one at all, which the minister and the cabinet secretary have happily used to re-write part of the real constitution (yes, envelopes again). It is remarkable that the change has been so little commented-upon, though academic observers have been worried by it. One complained to MPs in 1994 that, 'Nobody is sacked for making mistakes, the deal being that ministers are to protect chief executives [of agencies], they for their part must shield ministers . . . a compact of sorts has been struck between ministers and chief executives which ensures that neither of them assumes the ultimate risk.' Others warned of buck-passing by ministers and a 'bureaucratic Bermuda triangle' in which accountability disappeared.[14] The academic Vernon Bogdanor and the former mandarin Sir Peter Kemp have separately come up with one plausible answer, which is that Parliament should become directly involved in the performance of agencies, with select committees acting as annual 'shareholders' meetings', scruti-nizing the achievements and failures of the agency managers. The Treasury and Civil Service Select Committee agreed, sug-gesting that agency chief executives 'should be directly and personally accountable'[15] to select committees of MPs for their performance, while ministers remained responsible for the con-tracts they worked to. This would mean stripping the people running the agencies of the traditional defence of being able to hide behind ministerial responsibility. It implies that they could be sacked, or at least forced out of their jobs, by the Commons.

This seems a minimal requirement if accountability is to be restored, for if we toss to one side the polysyllables and ask in plain English, who is to blame, the Waldegrave distinction seems to collapse. A classic and highly embarrassing example of the problem came in December 1994 when Michael Howard, as Home Secretary, was obliged to come to the House of Com-mons and report the conclusions of Sir John Woodcock, the former Chief Inspector of Constabulary, into a breakout at the special secure unit of Whitemoor prison some fourteen weeks earlier, which had involved IRA prisoners and led to the discovery of a stockpile of the terrorists' explosive of choice, Semtex, inside the prison. As Howard himself admitted, the report conveyed 'a devastating picture of the regime' and was spattered with comments such as: 'everything which could have gone wrong has in fact done so'. The inquiry had found that there existed, at all levels in the prison service (which is an agency) 'some confusion as to the respective roles of ministers, the agency headquarters and individual prison governors. In particular, the Inquiry has identified the difficulty of determining what is an operational matter and what is policy, leading to confusion as to where responsibility lies.' (Over to you, Mr Waldegrave.) Sir John declined to give his view, stating enigmati-cally that it was beyond his remit to inquire further.

A cynic might have expected that nobody would take the blame – that the Home Secretary would regard it as an opera-tional matter, not for him, while the director-general of the prison service would decline to resign either. A cynic would be right. Despite a snowstorm of recommendations accepted, and the setting up of a 'new unit ... in accordance with the framework document', nobody just stood up and said: I am responsible. Nobody said sorry. Derek Lewis, the head of the prison service, had in fact just been awarded a bonus of £35,000 for his first year's work and the most Mr Howard was able to tell MPs following the Whitemoor incident was that he had spoken with Mr Lewis, who was 'responsible for the day-to-day management of the prison service' and he 'has agreed that there is no question of a bonus during the current year.' At which point, the Official Report blandly records 'laughter'. Damn right there was – an incredulous, angry torrent of laughter and protest spluttered and foamed across both government and opposition benches. It is hardly as if prison problems are so rare that the accountability problem had not occurred to anyone before. In the next such episode, involving the escape of three prisoners from Parkhurst prison on the Isle of Wight, Howard quickly removed the governor from his duties, along with six other officers; but there then appeared to be a split between him and Lewis about the governor's conduct. Following a withering report about the Parkhurst escape in October 1995, Michael Howard first asked Derek Lewis to resign and then, when he refused to go quietly, sacked him. Lewis was furious and accused the Home Secretary of scapegoating and failing to be fair about the relative blame that should be taken by the politician and by the executive underling. The row spilled into the Commons again and, in a performance of brutal power, Michael Howard easily survived an Opposition attack on him for misusing his power. Even so, the underlying problems of accountability were not resolved. They are going to return, as surely as night follows day, and become more complex, particularly since private companies, including Nashville's Correction Corporation of America and the Wackenhut Corporation of Florida, are already running British prisons.

Buck-passing and fading lines of responsibility destroy faith in the system and rot public trust. In most cases, it takes little imagination to guess the likely result: the minister will blame the company or the agency managers and they will blame the Home Office and, perhaps, the Treasury. MPs will conduct an investigation and retire, puzzled and calling for 'stronger guidelines to prevent such a thing happening again': they will have been struggling in a new and disorientating part of the constitution where cultures are clashing and where there are no excuse-free zones. Labour's public service spokesman when the agency reforms were being implemented, Michael Meacher, put the problem like this:

How can the replacement of a simple hierarchical system by a wholly disintegrated system be managed by ministers or be controlled by the Treasury or Cabinet Office, or be accountable to Parliament? . . . The ethos of the private sector is, where demand rises, to increase supply. In many cases that is not an appropriate model for the public sector, which is often about rationing and arbitration between competing rights. The Government cannot see, or will not acknowledge, that the professional ethic, the source of the highest standards of conduct in the civil service, cannot be replicated by the narrow obligation written into a private contract.

Vernon Bogdanor agrees:

The root of the trouble is that the analogy so often drawn between management in the public service and management in the private sector is deeply flawed . . . If we consider such matters as the compulsory purchase of land, planning appeals or immigration control, we can see this difference very clearly. For those who take decisions on these matters must, under our system of democracy, be accountable to the electorate through Parliament . . . there is no equivalent in the private sector . . . nor is there any equivalent in the private sector to the ethical code which civil servants are required to adopt.[16]

His example of compulsory purchase orders is particularly important, since the proposed extension of private capital into public-sector infrastructure projects implies that people will have their land and houses compulsorily purchased by the state in order to build something which will be partly for the profit of other private individuals. Where in that bizarre use of power could one possibly define the line separating the public interest from the rights of individuals?

The use of private companies to perform functions on behalf of a self-managed agency further complicates the problem: in the case of a serious cock-up, Parliament (should it wish, on behalf of the democracy, to investigate) could be faced by at least three parties – the private contractor, the agency which contracted-out the work, and the minister standing above the agency. Nor will Parliament be left with the one investigatory agent of its own which, as we saw in the previous chapter, really works: Sir John Bourn, head of the National Audit Office which reports to Parliament's Public Accounts Committee, complained in 1993 that his organization had no right to go in and examine the private contractors' books to see whether taxpayers' money was being spent efficiently. These are changes which alter the balance of power further against the voter and the democratic system, in favour of the executive and its friends.

The final aspect of the unbundling of the state and the turn to private-sector thinking by the Major government, the Citizen's Charter, was launched in 1991. It is meant to give the recipient of state action, whether in benefit offices, or slowed down on a motorway by roadworks, rights of redress and complaint. This is a narrow definition of citizenship: ministers have subsequently admitted that it would have been more accurately called the Consumers' Charter. Performance targets and charters have been published for schools, hospitals, benefit agencies – almost every aspect of government. These charters have been much mocked and parodied – there have been calls for a politicians' charter, a spooks' charter, even a beggar's charter. Attention focused on the shallow changes in language which accompanied individual initiatives – the transformation of British Rail 'passengers' into 'customers' and the way 'claimants' became 'clients', as if they were attending their stockbroker rather than a benefit office. Language is never trivial, and the mockery echoed a certain unease about the move from one culture into another. But the underlying aim of the charters, to give the citizen consumer rights over public services, is entirely serious and likely to become more popular. If the individual cannot, as a voter, play a role in the way a hospital is run, then perhaps he or she can do it as a consumer, through quality controls and lists of rights? Democracy is not currently part of the deal in the old way; rather, the individual has power through information and (in some areas) choice. John Major has been pilloried for his 'big idea'; yet it may eventually stand as his biggest domestic monument. This leads back to the biggest philosophical question for our democracy now: can individual choice through the market be an effective alternative to individual choice through the ballot-box? Is the traditional nineteenth-century machinery of voting any longer central to the modern market economies? Or, to put it again, can we make do with shopping, not voting?

The Fellers at the Top

The normal way of discussing the constitution of the British state is to begin with the prime minister, the cabinet and so forth. This account has started with a series of problems, or challenges, to that familiar picture of power. It has drawn an alternative picture of a hemmed-in nation, whose ancient sources of authority have been polluted, whose political culture has been eroded and whose centralizing state reforms have thrown up new questions about the reality of democratic control. Combined with the accounts in earlier chapters of the voting system in this country, the weakness of local government, and the failure of Parliament, the cumulative effect may be just a little depressing. But we have not yet turned to the traditional centres of British power, Downing Street and the Whitehall ministries. Now we finally do; here is where many of these state problems are meant to be resolved and explained. Ministerial authority connects the magic of monarchy to the political process, the world of business to Whitehall, the civil service to Parliament. A small number of individuals, offices and phone-lines clustered in Westminster comprise, as it were, the essential software of British political life. If there are easy answers to the problems so far described, they will be found here.

Let us start with the idea of 'cabinet government'. After more than a decade of reporting politics, eating innumerable lunches with politicians, drinking drinks, visiting them in their homes, reading their speeches, talking with their civil servants and tracking the vicissitudes of their careers, this writer is convinced that no theoretical blueprint of the balance of powers at the very top of government can be relied on. Some of the crude generalizations are generally true enough: the prime minister has become vastly more than a first among equals; the Treasury is the most important domestic department, and always seeks to extend its power; the network of permanent secretaries does exercise huge influence, independent of ministerial volition. But when one is discussing a power centre of fewer than 100 individuals, most general rules are at some stage broken or overturned by the personalities of those involved. It was evident that the prime minister had an unhealthy amount of power during the zenith of Margaret Thatcher's time in Number Ten, and other thoughtful ministers, like Douglas Hurd, made it clear they were worried. But this proposition seemed much more dubious once John Major had his feet under the desk. Similarly, it is futile to try to establish what is the 'real' amount of power exercised by the cabinet minister of any one department. That depends upon the drive and competence of the minister concerned, and the priorities facing the government: during the later stages of the preparation of the Northern Ireland peace plan, Michael Ancram, the relatively junior Northern Ireland Office minister in charge of political development was a more important figure in the government than most members of the cabinet itself. Whatever the paper pecking-order, the real ranking shifts almost daily. At different times, groups of senior ministers form powerful alliances which can inhibit a prime minister – the European monetary alliance of Sir Geoffrey Howe and Nigel Lawson is an obvious example towards the end of the Thatcher era. But these alliances are unstable and often end in recrimination or even resignation.

Cabinet committees are where most decisions are taken towards the apex of the state machine and, here again, the only rule is that no rules are adequate. A prime minister can give a colleague who has relatively little departmental power a huge leg-up by asking him or her to chair a range of important committees – on economic policy, foreign affairs, Northern Ireland, or whatever. At times, it becomes clear that there is a cabal of ministers who form a semi-collective government at the heart of the formal government. When John Major and Kenneth Clarke, the Chancellor, decided to threaten Conservative rebels with the dissolution of the government and a general election, the Prime Minister convened an informal supper at Number Ten for six senior ministers. The rest of the cabinet was merely consulted afterwards, by telephone, making it clear that the administration was divided, like British Rail, into First Class and Standard Class carriages. (Hot suppers only in First.) Similarly, Major's decision to resign and re-fight the Tory leadership in July 1995 was taken with only a few key ministers. The friendships and habits of prime ministers can make committees more or less important as compared to meetings of the full cabinet. Informal ad hoc committees are used to second-guess and then capture full cabinet committees. Nigel Lawson, the former Tory Chancellor, said with his customary brutal candour that he found the actual Thursday meetings of full cabinet unimportant: 'When I was a minister I always looked forward to the cabinet meeting immensely because it was, apart from the summer holidays, the only period of real rest that I got in what was a very heavy job.'[17] Most committees can be fixed to achieve the desired outcome, and this is one of the most powerful tools of a prime minister.

So we have a disparate collection of individuals, of varying degrees of personal and group authority, at the top of the administration. What gives them their real constitutional status, though, is a sort of grand and once necessary silliness called 'collective responsibility'. When constitutional experts and politicians say that Britain has a system of cabinet government, they mean that the senior ministers hang together as a kind of composite ruler. When one speaks, then, in effect, all speak. Ask any one of them a question (so the theory goes) and any other cabinet minister would give the same answer. This is said to be necessary to the system, because if each minister pursued his or her personal departmental policy, independent of the rest, then the notion of a single government would crumble. There would be 'Her Majesty's Ministers' but not 'Her Majesty's Government'. There would be no central direction. Instead of a team of horses galloping at the same pace and (allegedly) pulling the nation creaking and rumbling behind them, we would have a paddock of happy mares and stallions, cavorting aimlessly about. It is also necessary (doctrine says) because ministers must be able to have real, frank, open discussions about different policy options amongst themselves, and with their senior officials, safe in the knowledge that, once they have decided to do something, every other minister will rally round. No rival minister will go on the telly, or to the Commons and say, 'well, so-and-so is introducing this new bill to the Commons, but I reckon he's barmy. It's fundamentally flawed and politically incredible.' (The latter five words being, as it happens, Chris Patten's post-collective responsibility assessment of the poll tax.)

Were there to be no such doctrine, it is clear that government would be more confusing. Party discipline would fray. Laws could still be made, however, and departments could still be led by politicians. Individual ministers would still go to the House of Commons to ask for support for their measures, but they would be genuinely asking, without a collective disciplinary machine behind them. The heads of departments would rise or fall depending on their personal following in the Commons. It would all be rather closer to the condition of the early Victorian Parliament described earlier. However heady this prospect, it describes a way of doing politics that has not been ours for 150 years or so. A moment's reflection shows that collective responsibility, the 'glue of government', is less a functional matter than a matter of authority and 'face'. It is about the elected administration holding together strongly enough to convince the voters that it has a single view, that it can be respected, that it should be obeyed. There are enough outside sources of criticism, ministers will say, without us adding to them.

Yet collective responsibility is a silly doctrine to the extent that its assumption of unanimity is clearly and demonstrably false. This falsity is becoming ever more apparent, partly because of splits in a party that has been in government for so long, but partly also because of changes in the media. The country doesn't think that ministers agree, or even that they respect one another very much. With an active and resourceful network of lobby journalists, and given the natural competition among cabinet ministers, the differences between them become well-known. At the same time, the speed of the communication of news, and the quantity of it, mean that ministers are being asked to comment on a wide range of things so frequently that it is impossible for them to be properly briefed on the right 'collective' answer all the time. During party conferences, the BBC circulates hundreds of transcripts of ministerial interviews carried out on dozens of programmes. Inevitably, differences of emphasis and sometimes of view are exposed and commented upon. Because most ministers think that it is good for their careers and image to be heard and seen as often as possible, it is impossible for government as a whole to control what we might call the transcript trap. But it is making a monkey of collective responsibility.

For the problem is deeper than the vanity of individuals. Each departmental cabinet minister is already heavily loaded with his or her 'own' responsibilities. Cabinet committees allow them to chat about their mutual problems. But ministers are necessarily ignorant of the detailed work and decisions of others, which they must, however, publicly endorse and defend. From time to time they have serious but honest disagreements about major matters of policy which, again, they are obliged by convention to pretend that they all see identically. Sometimes their differences are so fundamental that the authority of the government is indeed damaged. It has been happening to the post-1992 Major government, in which the European visions of the rival groups of ministers are so far apart and their animosities are so well-known that they might as well be in different parties. Serious public breaches in collective responsibility happened, to a lesser degree, to the Thatcher government over the Howe budgets of the early eighties, during the Westland crisis, during the furious wrangle about British membership of the European

Exchange Rate Mechanism, and over her own leadership.

In the media age, the doctrine of collective responsibility not only suppresses public thinking by the government, it can make a sensible and thoughtful minister sound like an unthinking automaton, with no unpredictable, arresting or vivid views on anything of public importance. He or she can't think out loud, or say 'what if?' or admit there is one grain of truth in any alternative view. If, on the BBC *Today* programme, it is the minister who often sounds the dullest and most narrow-minded interviewee, then the doctrine of 'collective cabinet responsibility' is partly to blame. Future governments may, or may not, be as divided as the Conservative ones over Europe. But the coalition nature of governments is unlikely to change, while neither the avidity nor the number of media outlets is likely to lessen. Our varied, undeferential and inquisitive society is not going to become easier to hoodwink. It follows that, if governments wish to retain respect and authority, they are going to have to loosen the bonds of collectivity and allow in some fresh air. It also means that the rest of us are going to have to become rather more grown-up about the fact that serious politicians are bound to differ and stop reacting to the mere fact of disagreement with the exaggerated horror of Victorian matrons chancing upon a labourers' outdoor orgy.

The ministeriate also face rational doubt about their ability to decide wisely and to control the system they oversee. As already noted, they are generally overloaded with work, lacking the necessary time to ponder and weigh evidence. The problem is worst for the prime minister, who has always had a ridiculously large personal burden – many incumbents have complained bitterly afterwards. Professor Peter Hennessy has compiled a list of thirty-three different political duties of a premier, ranging from ones which require a few minutes – giving ministers permission to be out of the country – to the stress of prime minister's questions and the lengthy obligations of the European Union. He concluded that anyone

would be hard pressed to meet the modern job specification, exhausting week upon punishing year . . . To have a fighting chance it would require a kind of grotesque composite freak – someone with the dedication to duty of a Peel, the physical energy of a Gladstone, the detachment of a Salisbury, the brains of an Asquith, the balls of a Lloyd George, the word-power of a Churchill, the administrative gifts of an Attlee, the style of a Macmillan, the managerialism of a Heath and the sleep requirements of a Thatcher. Human beings do not come like that.[18]

The obvious retort is that all these have managed the job, without the offices of Dr Hennessy-Frankenstein stitching on pieces of predecessors and successors. But the equally obvious re-retort is: what do you mean by 'managed'? I would add that the physical overload is partly due to the grotesque inadequacy of the Number Ten machine, which is understaffed, poorly organized, and badly resourced for the job it has to do. The prime minister can receive as many as three separate sources of paper advice on any one decision. His, or her, Policy Unit is meant to be a source of forward-thinking strategic advice and pitfall-avoidance suggestions. In fact, it spends most of its time struggling vainly with the daily and weekly agenda. Prime ministers never admit that Downing Street is anything other than marvellous. This is presumably because they owe such a strong personal debt to the people who do work there, and wish to cast no aspersions on them; and because they believe it would be seen as weak to complain. But the combination of roles requires an office that measures up to the French president's, if not the American one. From time to time John Major suffered mock-sympathetic and somewhat jeering criticism to the effect that he seemed 'tired', 'ill' or even 'drained'. Anyone with access to his real schedule would confirm that the remarkable thing was that he was still able to stand. Here again, British amateurism is not helping good government; and poor control at the centre undermines the democracy in theory as well as practice.

But the problem of overload isn't confined to Downing Street. The ministers with robust constitutions, very robust minds and great energy – recently, Kenneth Clarke, Nigel Lawson and Douglas Hurd would all be in this category – manage.

Cecil Parkinson had no doubt that on a whole range of key decisions, from the fossil-fuel levy in electricity pricing, to the expansion of the London Underground, he had enjoyed real, personal power as a minister working for Margaret Thatcher. But plenty of ministers, including people in top jobs, don't feel like this. The Whitehall stories abound. Some civil servants attempt to tame their ministers by overwhelming them with paperwork: piles of red boxes accumulate towards the end of the working day. One minister responded by curtly informing his permanent secretary that he was in the habit of drinking heavily after 8 p.m. and believed it would be wrong to carry out the Queen's business while drunk; he therefore required that all departmental business for his attention should be completed by the early evening. He won but, no doubt, at some cost to his reputation in Whitehall. Another minister in the Thatcher government simply used to pile difficult decisions into his red boxes and leave them for weeks in the boot of his ministerial Rover: he reasoned, rightly, that if the paperwork was withheld from the system, it would be impossible for the bureaucracy to press him into making his mind up. By hiding the paper, he bought himself the time he thought he needed to come to a considered judgement.

Even if the minister is robust enough and determined enough to press his or her agenda firmly forward, our system does not guarantee this individual any assurance that the decisions will materialize in the form of legislation or changed policy. One minister who had been in business before entering Parliament has developed the habit of tracking his decisions and trying to establish which had actually been carried out. Many were not, and for perfectly good reasons. Perhaps his original decision had been wrong, and had been caught by an alert colleague, or had concerned something that was out of date by the time action was mooted. Perhaps the order was simply impossible to carry out. Perhaps sloth, incompetence or bad timing were to blame. At any rate, as a businessman, he reckoned a 70 per cent success rate was good, and 90 per cent was excellent. Once he became a minister of state, halfway up the government hierarchy, he tried the same decision-tracking game. He reckoned 20 per cent of his decisions were eventually implemented. *Yes, Minister* was rooted in reality. But much civil service obstruction is designed to stop inexperienced ministers making fools of themselves and the department: in general, civil servants much prefer a decisive and effective minister to an incompetent or shilly-shallying one. The bitchiest Whitehall stories are about the decision-averse ministers, not the masterful ones.

The final reason for being suspicious of the ability of the ministeriate to control the state as well as they claim to is that so many of them are in their jobs for such a short time. Two years or so is a not-untypical stint. During that time, the politician is expected to become an expert decision-maker in a field of policy which he or she may know little about; and to achieve major changes in the form of legislation; and to oversee a bureaucracy involving many thousands of people – as well, these days, as undertaking several monthly negotiating visits to other EU countries, and elsewhere, and fulfilling the parliamentary duties of attending debates, answering questions and meeting MPs. Again, the political culture inhibits any complaint or much discussion about the absurdity of this. Ministers are supposed to achieve and then move on, up or out in brisk time. Ritual demands that they always express obsessive interest in whatever department fate has given them (even though the work may be dull as sin) and yet colour with pleasure when asked to move up. For a prime minister, the ability to appoint and sack is one of the key powers, enabling the politics of the party to be balanced in government, snubbing X, rewarding Y, satisfying regional groupings of MPs, and so on. It often seems that the requirements of efficient administration and clear thinking come a poor second to the grand political game. It is the inoffensive middle-ranking ministers, who no one expects to make it to cabinet, who are sometimes left uninterfered with for long enough to become competent at their departmental specialities. The high-fliers are moved so quickly that they are condemned to a kind of rational ignorance. Ministers like Kenneth Baker (under Thatcher) and Kenneth Clarke (under Thatcher and Major) flung themselves into huge social reforms and were then whisked briskly onwards, leaving the legislation and the after-effects to be coped with by others. The system rewards movement and defines achievement narrowly by cabinet rank and volume of legislation. This is not a recipe for effective ministerial power. When he became Prime Minister, John Major decided that it would be saner to try to keep people in place for most of the lifetime of a Parliament – four or five years. He tried. But it didn't prove as easy as he had thought: press campaigns, incompetence, and party management dictated first one then another reshuffle. The result was that, for instance, in the four years covering the biggest shake-up in English schools for a generation, the Education Department had four secretaries of state.

Some will say that the ability of ministers to do their jobs properly, and the exact demarcation of civil service influence, are matters to do with the efficiency of government, not the condition of our democracy. Yet under our system the democratic machine is meant to conclude, after various pulleys, cranks and handles have moved, with a decision by a minister. The less able ministers are to properly take such decisions the less the significance of the original vote that put them there. Further, the more time and energy the bureaucracy sucks out of them, the less they have to keep in touch with the elected chamber, to which they are supposedly responsive. Hidden or bureaucratic checks on ministerial function are checks on democracy, too. There is an absurd populism that sees all ministerial power as somehow inherently oppressive. In a parliamentary democracy, it is wholly essential. The proper way to look at it is to distinguish benign, democratic checks on ministerial power (which need to be sustained and expanded) from malign checks or blockages – exhaustion, bad job-specification, outdated doctrines, the passing of powers improperly to others – which ought to be extirpated. The sad thing is it wouldn't be very difficult to greatly reform the position of the ministers. It is largely their own collective pride that prevents it happening. Like macho executives, they are likelier to work themselves to a breakdown or into terminal incompetence than stand back, evaluate their own condition and call for help.

The exhausting ministerial whirligig has been a prime piece of evidence cited by those who believe that Britain is 'really' run by the top civil service and that politicians are merely the masks behind which the permanent state hides. Do ministers have the time and ability to think about the wider public good, and keep their officials in check? The arms-to-Iraq scandal investigated by the Scott Inquiry posed serious questions about the way government servants became heavily entangled in defending the web of ministerial and bureaucratic interests, as opposed to the wider interests of the democracy. What the Scott Inquiry stumbled upon and became interested in was the almost neurotically secretive and defensive departmentalism that afflicts Whitehall. Information is hoarded. There is, as one ex-minister puts it, good vertical integration, but hardly any horizontal integration. Civil servants act to protect themselves and their political masters. Sir Richard Scott, appointed by John Major to investigate the arms-selling affair which resulted in the humiliating collapse of a trial of businessmen accused of illegally exporting gun parts to Iraq, used the powers given to him to thoroughly investigate this wider problem of secrecy, silence and protectiveness. Whitehall, which saw the South African-born judge as an alien and an unsympathetic intruder, hated the baring of its soul that the Inquiry demanded. Ministers were aghast at his single-mindedness and 'naïveté'. As I write, the conclusions of the Inquiry have still not been published. But it looks possible, even likely, that Scott's marathon journey through the recesses of the hidden places of Whitehall will eventually provoke heart-searching and reform. If so, it will be further evidence of the importance of flurried, short-term political responses to passing crises as a key force behind constitutional change.

The judge's journey has already taken him past the promotion by government lawyers of so-called 'public interest immunity' certificates to prevent a court from knowing the full truth about the arms trade, and thus, potentially, sending innocent men to prison. When the system feels threatened, as during this case or in the earlier Westland crisis, law officers, senior mandarins and ministers have tended to close ranks as tightly as a British square at Waterloo. In such cases, defensive precedent is used to repel all outsiders. In the Matrix Churchill 'arms-to-Iraq' case, Anthony Sampson described his shock at discovering the 'secret garden' of bureaucratic power, guarded by the government lawyers (of whom there are about a thousand). He felt that 'smug arrogance has lain behind the assumptions of . . . government lawyers: that ministers, even on a critical issue, should not follow their personal instincts and beliefs, but should rely on lawyers who know all the precedents and can provide the necessary safeguards.' This 'crucial frontier . . . reveals a serious flaw in the democratic system.'[19] Lord Justice Scott seemed to agree. But ministers were not without power over the officials even in that overgrown legal minefield: as one particular minister, Michael Heseltine, demonstrated by refusing to immediately sign the relevant certificates. The former Lord Chancellor Lord Hailsham had advised him that 'he shouldn't have bothered his little heart about it', but he did, and rightly, and emerged smelling more sweetly as a result. That said, the involvement of senior civil servants in such defensive manoeuvres by what we can still call the Establishment has raised widespread worry about the crucial frontier between ministers and mandarins. The civil service select committee of MPs went on patrol along that frontier in 1994 and concluded that it was necessary to make the duties of civil servants rather clearer. They dismissed the idea that the current bundle of memoranda and advisory documentation was enough of a guide. And they described the situation like this:

In the last century Mr William Gladstone remarked that the British Constitution 'presumes more boldly than any other the good faith of those who work it'. This remains true today and it need be no reflection upon the good faith of the current generation of ministers and senior civil servants to suggest that public trust in such a system is diminishing and is likely to diminish further.[20]

The committee went on to propose its own version of a code for the mandarins, which read in part:

Civil servants should conduct themselves with fairness, integrity and honesty in their dealings with Ministers, Parliament and the public. They should make all information and advice relevant to a decision available to Ministers. They should not deceive or mislead Ministers, Parliament or the public.[21]

The Cabinet Secretary, Sir Robin Butler, whose enthusiasm for the agency reforms has already been noted, denied that any change was necessary. But as the political flak whizzed round the Major government's head, he was overruled and, in January 1995, it announced that a new single code of conduct for all civil servants was being introduced after all – one which, in binding them not to act in a way that was 'illegal, improper, unethical or in breach of constitutional function . . .' strongly followed the MPs' version. That was a real advance which showed that public criticism of the 'Tory constitution' was hitting home. More cynically it was seen as a defensive and reluctant manoeuvre – part of the political preparation for the criticisms of the Scott Inquiry which had started to leak round Whitehall at about the same time.

For most civil servants for most of the time, however, the problem has not been their own prominence as political actors, but rather the reverse – the impact of the politicians on the traditions and ethos of the civil service. Aside from crises and the deepest recesses of the state's subconscious, the mandarins' culture makes them happier as advisers and managers than as decision-takers. The incompetence of the political system, both in scrutinizing the executive properly, and in providing long-term and well-resourced ministers to run it, has inevitably left the permanent secretaries and their senior officials with large reserve and administrative powers. Someone has to control access to the ministerial diary, help divert impractical ideas, ensure that the decisions that cannot be put off are not. In addition, there are departments whose particular culture has had an impact on policy: the Home Office has a strong corporate view on prison regimes, which conflicts with the instincts of the Tory right wing. The Department for Education gave traditionalist Conservative ministers a hard time – or so they complained. But in general the evidence is that civil servants prefer to be given a task, and to demonstrate their intellect and ingenuity in solving problems set by a minister – the team which worked on the poll tax included at least one member who was personally opposed to it, and that would be normal. In acting this way, civil servants rely on a universal perception that they are outside politics, working as policy technicians and service deliverers; the servants of the state, not of one party or its ideology.

Yet the relationship between ministers and the three thousand or so senior civil servants cannot be easily disentangled from the huge changes in the service – the agencies and the market testing – described earlier on. The reason that the two are connected can be summed up in the single word: culture. The mandarins have traditionally derived their self-assurance and moral geography from a view of themselves as part of a single, homogenous and public-spirited system. As that is broken down into numerous agencies, private companies and contractual arrangements, so the self-assurance and ethical culture come under threat too, buffeted by private-sector criticism. That culture may have been pompous and self-important and a bit stuffy. But if you are dealing, day in, day out, with assertive and ambitious politicians, perhaps you need some of those qualities as a defence. And, today, many senior civil servants are worried that market thinking is corrupting and blurring that vital independence, eroding the spirit of the service itself. The Nolan Committee cited decentralisation, contracting out, scepticism about traditional institutions and short-term contracts as reasons for not assuming that 'everyone in the public service will assimilate a public service culture unless they are told what is expected of them and the message is systematically reinforced.' Elizabeth Symons, General Secretary of the mandarins' trade union, the First Division Association, told MPs that many of her members felt 'relationships between civil servants and government ministers are not as clear-cut and straightforward as they maybe used to be and certainly not as straightforward and clear-cut as they should be.'[22] More starkly still, the Labour MP and constitutional writer John Garrett argued that

The British civil service is faced with no less than a threat to its existence . . . In nearly thirty years of working in, working for, and studying the civil service, I have never known morale in the service to be so universally damaged by government action, not only because of the uncertainty about the future of its staff, but because ministers treat them as expendable.[23]

Garrett's conclusion that the entire system is being dismembered may be going it a bit, but he is describing the world in which civil servants increasingly operate. 'I want you to explain to these people a little bit about the real world,' a businessman was told recently in front of embarrassed civil servants. The danger is not just that some London bureaucrats are unhappy. It is that, by undermining the self-confidence of the state machine, ministers reduce it to a pliant and nervous class of administrative helots, lacking any focus on the longer-term and any independent belief in the public good. It is that the civil service ceases to see itself as the ultimate public service and becomes merely the ministers' service.

The Pretender-Politicians; Journos and Judges

Earlier on in this section, we reviewed the formidable limitations on state power at the international level – the markets, the transnational companies, the organs of European and world government. We have already noted that Parliament has failed to be an effective check to much state activity. But there are two kinds of checks on British politicians and their servants which are still exercised in London and other cities, and are so formidable and dynamic that they merit separate consideration. They are the judges, operating judicial review, and the journalists, whose elevation as a fourth estate of the political system long since passed from whimsy to hard reality.

The traditional position of judges is straightforward enough: despite their wigs, formidable jowls and huge personal powers within a court room, in the wider world of public policy, they are merely the servants of Parliament. As Lord Lester, an eminent QC and Liberal Democrat has put it, doctrine states that:

British judges remain lions firmly beneath the throne of the Crown in Parliament ... The traditional constitutional theory upon which we were reared ... tells us that the task of law-making should be the exclusive province of the Queen's ministers and of the elected representatives of the people in Parliament. According to this conventional wisdom, it is undemocratic for the non-elected judiciary to act as law makers. It is also inappropriate, because judges are ill-equipped by their narrow origins, training and professional experience, and by the very nature of the judicial process itself, to make laws.[24]

This is indeed the position as anyone studying the British constitution in our schools would have been taught it.

Yet, as Lord Lester went on to argue, it is clearly nonsense. Barely a day seems to go by without the Home Secretary being chastised for some decision or other by the judges. Immigration policy has been affected particularly by judicial law-makers, as has government policy on the rights of defendants. Faced by legal challenge after legal challenge during his tenure at the Home Office, Michael Howard developed more form than an unlucky local cat-burglar. A dramatic example came in April 1995 when the Law Lords attacked a scheme by Howard to cut the cost of criminal-injuries compensation, declaring it unlawful and accusing the Home Secretary of flouting the will of Parliament and abusing his powers. Lord Browne-Wilkinson, backing various trade unions, said Howard's argument about his right as a minister to bring in a fixed rate of compensation for people who had been attacked or raped – a move widely attacked as 'mean, arbitrary and unjust' – was 'not only constitutionally dangerous but flies in the face of common sense.' But the dissenting Law Lords showed they understood also the perils of judges taking on ministers. One, Lord Keith, said the Home Secretary was answerable to Parliament, not the courts – the other, Lord Mustill, said the attack on Howard's powers 'push to the very boundaries of the distinction between court and Parliament established in ... 1688.' At least everyone understood the significance of this attack on the mightiness of ministers. Yet the case, though unusual in its political edge and the sharpness of the language, was part of a far bigger trend. Secretaries of State for Social Security and for the Environment have also been metaphorically hauled before the bench. Ministers as eminent as the Foreign Secretary have to go to the Commons and announce substantial changes in the budgeting and policy on overseas aid, not because they have been defeated in a parliamentary vote, but because they have been ordered to by judges. The oddity of these cases is neatly summed up by their legal form: they are 'R versus The Secretary of State for . . .' – Regina, the Queen, against the Queen's Minister: the crown against the government. In each case, of course, the real challenge comes from some group or individual using the courts to take on the government. Groups as diverse as the Fire Brigades Union, the World Development Forum, the Child Poverty Action Group, parents' groups, Friends of the Earth, Spanish fishermen's lawyers, architectural conservationists and London residents angered by aircraft noise are seen celebrating political victories not outside Parliament but the High Court in the Strand.

At Whitehall, sandwiched between those two piles of Victorian Gothic, civil servants are now expected to brief themselves about the danger of court actions against their departments: a tellingly-titled pamphlet prepared for them by the Cabinet Office and the Treasury Solicitor's Department was called *The Judge Over Your Shoulder* and warned of 'an increasing willingness on the part of the judiciary to intervene in the day-to-day business of government.' Law Lords intervene to probe and extend the law in such highly-sensitive areas as rape in marriage (1991) and a doctor's duty to keep a patient in irreversible coma alive by artificial means (1993). Nor is the rise of the political judiciary confined to central government – far from it. Judges have been called on to arbitrate about homelessness policy, the anti-racist politics of local authorities and the internal finances of London boroughs. And it is steadily becoming evident to everyone involved even vaguely in the world of politics that Britain now has, in effect, a supreme law, imported from the European matters. It amounts to a quiet revolution. What has happened?

As with most revolutions, various barely-related events have suddenly combined with explosive force. First, there has been a steady generational change in the attitudes of British judges to challenging the government. The forties, fifties and early sixties were the heyday of what we could call judicial passivism, when the generation of wartime judges rarely tried to extend their political role, and interpreted their own constitutional powers modestly and bookishly. They didn't read the records of parliamentary debates to try to discover the wider policy thinking behind laws, nor did they bother with the too 'political' world of Royal Commission documents or ministerial speeches. They stuck doggedly and sometimes pig-headedly to the text of the legislation. This timidity was wholly understandable: these judges had been educated in the Victorian doctrines of Dicey and parliamentary absolutism; they had come through the Second World War, when the state had taken huge powers to itself, and seemed vindicated in doing so; and they were working in the post-war heyday of big state politics, the era of the man from Whitehall. At its worst, the resulting timidity produced obvious injustices, as when a landowner was unable, in 1956, to involve the courts in reviewing a compulsory purchase order even though there was evidence of fraud by bureaucrats.[25] There were always dissidents seeking more power for the judiciary, such as Lord Denning who was arguing as early as the late 1940s that judges should 'iron out the creases' and 'fill in the gaps' where the law was evidently deficient. But he and his kind were famously slapped down by one of the dominant legal figures of the period for recommending 'a naked usurpation of the legislative function.'[26] And the consensus in those days was firmly with the slapper-downers, not the gap-fillers.

Slowly, though, attitudes have changed. This is hardly surprising: judges-to-be were also alive in the sixties and were almost as liable to be affected by the growing anti-statism and suspicion of traditional power as anyone else. They too saw miscarriages of justice and politicians behaving, at times, like arrogant asses.

The older generation of post-war judges, brought up in an era when the government was assumed to be brimming with rectitude, are retiring. Younger barristers are being appointed as judges, including some whose views would have excluded them before. Stephen Sedley was said to have been unable to become a high-earning and prestigious Queen's Counsel for eight years because the Tory Lord Chancellor, Lord Hailsham, objected to his Communist past. But Hailsham's successor, Lord Mackay, made him a judge – the first judge, one guesses, who has listed 'changing the world' among his hobbies in *Who's Who*. The appointment of people like Lords Nolan, Woolf, Browne-Wilkinson, Goff and Slynn has changed the mood in the Lords too. It was a sign of the times that it proved difficult in 1994 to get the requisite five (out of ten) Law Lords to sit on the criminal injuries case already mentioned because so many judges had already spoken out against the Home Secretary during Lords debates. The readiness of judges to extend the law to bring it into line with changing social trends, and to speak out on issues of public controversy is something that still divides and worries them. Recent cases have seen a stepping-back from lawmaking, particularly over issues of privacy, as they too agonize and argue about how far they can go. Nevertheless, the broad trend is inescapably clear.

But judges with attitude need tools, and the second reason for their political potency today is the formidable tool called judicial review. This is explained by the government itself as the means by which courts 'supervise the exercise of powers conferred by public law on ministers, departments, agencies, local authorities . . .' In similar terms, the *Judicial Review Handbook* states that it 'allows the High Court to supervise the activities of public bodies . . . judicial review casts itself as the central feature of administrative law, in which the judiciary seizes the responsibility to curb abuse of executive power.'[27] If so, this seizure is a dramatic and novel event. Although the principles of judicial review go back a long time, originating in the desire of senior courts to regulate lower ones, and spread slowly during the sixties and seventies, the thing only really took off after the procedure was simplified by the Supreme Court in 1977 and 1981. And then . . . Whoosh!

The figures are eloquent about what happened next: the number of applications has risen from 160 in England and Wales in 1974, to 1,230 in 1987, to 2,886 in 1993. The new and easier rules and the more sympathetic judges were coming into play, it is worth noting, at a time when many more single-issue pressure groups were also joining the political game, and during a long period of one-party rule. The new politics of high-profile, extra-parliamentary campaigning, and the arrogance that inevitably goes with long periods in office, combined to give judicial review the final push it needed to take off. Immigration and housing cases are the two largest categories, but as judicial review can cover anything where there is cause to believe a minister or public body might have acted illegally, irrationally or improperly with regard to a particular procedure, the scope is wide, and being tested all the time. The survival of old buildings, the rights of mentally ill patients, sex discrimination, educational policy, welfare benefits, planning and environmental issues . . . the list is huge. It covers great stretches of public policy which the constitution naively teaches is the prerogative of Parliament. Barristers such as Lord Lester, David Pannick and Helena Kennedy are among those who have carved formidable national reputations because of their activities in judicial review cases; the number of senior judges involved in hearing them has risen from two to a dozen in just a decade. If there is a market for power, here is where some of the political winnings are accumulating.

The final reason for the rising power and influence of the judges is Europe. Here the issues are often of great political sensitivity, erupting vividly on to the front pages. Whether the issue is Spanish trawlers' rights in British waters or the ability of the Home Secretary to determine the length of time the child killers of the toddler James Bulger should serve before release, or the rights of part-time workers to the same legal protection as full-timers, British ministers have regularly been worsted by European law in cases which are innately political and which provoke intense emotion at home. Increasingly, British citizens who want to challenge the actions of ministers or civil servants 'go to Europe' to do so. At times, this trend provokes outbursts of constitutional anger from British politicians. Confronted by a ruling which questioned his powers to determine how long young criminals stayed in jail, Michael Howard said that: 'In these matters I actually think it is right that the Parliament of this country should be sovereign . . . I think it raises very serious questions indeed.'[28] In most of these cases, though, it is British lawyers and British judges who make the running, either at the House of Lords, or the High Court or the Court of Session in Edinburgh, and their target is more often the executive power of ministers, either through delegated legislation or Prerogative powers, than Acts of Parliament. Clearly, though, because European law frequently requires all domestic legal avenues to be exhausted first, the scope for British legal power to be extended over the executive is great. Even when powers have originated in treaties signed by ministers at the European level, they are in practice often exercised in British courts – and directed back at those same ministers.

Though populist politicians are prone to blame the European Union for subverting British law, in fact the issue long predates British membership. It goes back to the European Convention on Human Rights, formally ratified by the UK in March 1951, and in force since September 1953. It contains a series of basic rights, including the right not to be tortured or subjected to inhuman or degrading punishment, the right to be considered innocent until proven guilty and to a fair trial, the right to freedom of thought and expression, the right of respect for private life, home and correspondence, and the right to join a trade union. The Convention has had a powerful impact on British law but not nearly as powerful as it might have had. It was based on a draft from the Council of Europe which had included legally-enforceable guarantees and rights for the citizens of all the countries which signed up to it – a visionary attempt to ensure that Western Europe saw no return to the totalitarian statehood from which she had been recently rescued. But, as

Anthony Lester has related, 'What is less well-known is that the Convention had a painful beginning, barely surviving the strenuous efforts of the Attlee Government to stifle or cripple it at birth, and that, because of those efforts, the Convention is weaker than its begetters had intended.'[29] The Labour government's objections then mirror the fears of many mainly Conservative politicians now about the business of allowing a supreme level of law to overrule Parliament. The Lord Chancellor of the day, Lord Jowett, told a cabinet colleague he was not 'prepared to encourage our European friends to jeopardize our whole system of law, which we have laboriously built up over the centuries, in favour of some half-baked scheme to be administered by some unknown court.' More shortly, the Attorney-General Sir Hartley Shawcross, said that 'Any student of our legal institutions . . . must recoil from this document with a feeling of horror.'[30]

Still, the Convention was ratified and, since then, British ministers have suffered their series of reverses at the hands of the European Court of Human Rights. These have included issues like the use of the tawse, or leather belt, as a punishment in Scottish schools; the criminality of homosexuality in Northern Ireland; discrimination against British–Asian passport holders; the detention of suspected terrorists (a judgement the British government refused to accept); and the rights of free speech in the Thalidomide and *Spycatcher* cases. The Convention has never been incorporated as such in British law. Though the European Convention predated the EU, it stands alongside the Treaties of Rome and Maastricht and the various directives and regulations from EU institutions, as a kind of congealing upper layer of law, beyond the direct control of Parliament, and to which ministers are subject. When Britain joined the European Economic Community, or Common Market, ministers assured Parliament that there would be no erosion of essential national sovereignty and that, as the 1971 White Paper put it, 'our courts will continue to operate as they do at present', though 'in certain cases they would need to refer points of Community law to the European Court of Justice.' Some provisions would be 'included in our law'. But, as Lester puts it, 'The phrase, "included in our law" obscured the vital piece of information that, where the European Community law reigns, it is "included in our law" not as ordinary law, but as the paramount and supreme law, taking precedence over all inconsistent national measures.'[31] Or, as we experts in constitutional matters would put it, the government was lying.

This was dramatically underlined in the controversial (but wholly unsurprising) 'Factortame' judgement of 1990, which supported a group of Spanish fishermen who claimed that the 1988 Merchant Shipping Act was contrary to EC legislation and should therefore be suspended. But the supremacy of European law, deriving from international treaties, should not have been a shock to the Conservative ministers who had signed up to all the relevant bits of paper. This point was noted quickly by Lord Denning, who, within two years of the 1972 Act giving expression to British membership, noted that, 'The Treaty is like an incoming tide. It flows into the estuaries and up the rivers. It cannot be held back.'[32] Anyone who had any doubt as to the truth of this was brutally disabused by the former president of the European Commission, Jacques Delors, who said in 1988 that he believed that, within a few years, 80 per cent of economic legislation would originate in the Community. Tides, of course, are bound to roll back again; otherwise they would not be tides. There were signs throughout post-Maastricht Europe of a turning back from the full federalist flood but, so far as the British system of government is concerned, the importing of Continental notions of justiciable rights has already changed our political landscape, perhaps forever.

The odd thing is that the British system has not tried to grapple and bind in the new reality, but has let it continue, as it were, at the elbow of our politicians and judges, hugely powerful and yet politically unacknowledged. As Ferdinand Mount, one of the wisest recent writers on constitutional matters, has put it, 'The European Community has, in effect, endowed us with a written constitution and a Bill of Human Rights. The question is not whether we wish to have such newfangled things – we already have them – but whether we wish to *patriate* them . . .'[33] But we are straying back to mainstream politics: in the context of the rise of judicial power, the vital point to note is that the European dimension, unincorporated and probed piecemeal, is the third aspect of judges' new power. It is, in particular, intimately connected to judicial review, for reasons explained by the Major government: 'European Community law has provided new rights and expectations, some of which may only be vindicated within the context of judicial review . . . [and] in order to petition the European Commission of Human Rights it is necessary first to have exhausted domestic remedies.'[34]

Having analysed the judicial uprising into politics, it is necessary finally to ask what it means for the democracy. It is hard to give a definitive answer since the whole area is so fast-moving and blurred. If one asks what is the clear division between the proper prerogative of the politicians and that of the judges in social policy, there is no easy response. Lord Goff, one of those involved, has candidly admitted that 'although I am well aware of the existence of the boundary, I am never quite sure where to find it.' The government describes the position with fine understatement as 'flexible and dynamic'. And Lord Diplock, though once cautious about judicial activism, now simply calls it 'the greatest achievement of the English courts' in his lifetime in the law. Lawyers concerned with human rights, and those generally on the left, have seen the European context as wholly beneficial, importing rights and practices that the British ought to have thought up for themselves years ago, and sweeping some of the more cobwebbed and secretive aspects of traditional state power away. But there are grounds for worry. It was very recently that the accepted progressive wisdom about judges was that they were not only interfering, but reactionary too. Much of the current enthusiasm about the rise of unelected judicial power at the expense of the executive may turn out to be mere displaced anger about the activities of Tories in office. As the journalist Sir Alan Watkins wrote, referring to recent cases of judicial review,

Progressive persons approve the courts' judgements because they disapprove of the two ministers' actions and of the government generally. But what would Mr Robin Cook say if the courts prevented him, as Foreign Secretary, from donating money to what a Labour cabinet considered a worthy cause? ... When and if the Bill of Rights promised by Mr Tony Blair becomes part of our law, the judges will inevitably possess more power than they have already taken to themselves over the past thirty years through the expansion of judicial review. This may be a good or a bad thing. It will certainly be a different thing.[35]

The citizen, in practice, is unlikely to bother much about where powers come from, and will be more interested in their effect. The idea of a European court telling a British minister when the killers of a toddler must be released is popularly felt to be outrageous. But if the minister is trying to stop British citizens enjoying rights, for instance at work, which European law states they should have, then people will be more inclined to support the court. Wherever 'Europe' is thought to be offering rights and benefits, then the judicial system is likely to prove more popular than ministers attempting to prevent those rights being exercised. But this brings the judiciary, inescapably, into the political arena which it has historically tried to avoid. Where judges are confirming and implementing European law, or are lawmaking in a domestic context, they will themselves be judged by the people on the sense, humanity and rationality of their judgements. Senior judges have enjoyed the popularity and power which judicial review and the rise of European law has given them; talking privately, one senses that they are fully aware of their upward mobility in the British system. But it is not so long since the judiciary's name was mud after the Guildford Four and Birmingham Six miscarriages of justice. In future, where they seem out of touch, or silly, they will find themselves pilloried and criticized, by politicians as well as the media, more openly and harshly than they are accustomed to. In the fluid, ever-changing 'marketplace of authority', where the judiciary is hawking its judgements so happily, no authority is sacrosanct or forever; it has to be earned, and earned again, day after day, instance after instance. The more that judges overturn or challenge the deeds of elected politicians, the more they themselves will come to be judged in a similar way.

In that, and in one other way, they resemble the other source of daily checks on executive power – journalists. The Fourth Estate has cropped up regularly enough in this book already, but it would be wrong to complete a description of the checks and balances on state power without a closer and more critical look at the effect of journalism on the democracy. We saw earlier how parliamentary journalism has been changing its nature, shifting from being a report of the views and sayings of politicians to being an opinionated running commentary on them. The manipulation is two-way, for astute ministers and others have become adept at fashioning and selling 'stories' which get the reporter a plaudit from the newsdesk, while at the same time promoting the views of the minister, under-mining a rival, or whatever. Nietzsche, the excessively German philosopher mentioned before, said that politicians were people who divided mankind into two classes – tools and enemies. When it comes to journalists, they are more sophisticated, however: the journalist-tool can suddenly become an enemy, while the journalistic enemy can still be used as a tool. The implicit negotiation between the politician wanting a particular thing said, and the journalist wanting to maintain a reputation for impartiality while relying on such sources, is one of the most delicate and subtle transactions outside sex.

But if journalism is still a 'platform' for the political classes, then it has become a swaying, unsteady and perilous one. Coping with a daily torrent of press and broadcast stories and comment has become essential to political survival. Reflecting this, one of the few growth areas in a civil service being cut back has been in 'information officers' or press-handlers. Addi-tionally, and more influentially, every self-respecting senior minister has a political adviser or two whose job includes having confidential and revealing conversations with journalists. These advisers, a rather underestimated and little-known group, act as roving political ambassadors and agents for their ministers, picking up what rival ministers are saying, spreading the 'line' and meeting lobbyists. They also provide a source of deniable but authoritative briefing for journalists. The Secretary of State for Hot-Air Balloons might not wish himself to point out that the Political Secretary to the Treasury is an incompetent liar whose views on European Union have changed five times in as many years, and who is losing the trust of the prime minister . . . but his political adviser, over a plate of rabbit and polenta at some Tuscan eatery round Covent Garden, may well admit, privately and on a never-to-be-repeated (until Wednesday) basis that such is the case. The information that 'senior colleagues' so regard the Political Secretary may be enough to make the great man break cover, or to persuade *his* adviser that the time is ripe for a young grouse at Rules in Maiden Lane, and a few home truths about the inefficiencies and cowardice discernible at the Department of Hot-Air Balloons. And so it goes, merrily enough, with everyone thoroughly enjoying themselves, and profits accruing to newspapers and restaurateurs and the people who run Mastercard, and no harm being done to anyone at all, except possibly to fastidious ministers and the reputation of Her Majesty's Government.

And so it has been, more or less, for a very long time. The power of the press over politics is one of those constants in almost any modern political system. Throughout this century, the relationships between senior politicians and Press barons have been the stuff of gossip and suspicion – Lloyd George and Northcliffe, Churchill and Camrose, Thatcher and Murdoch, Everyone and Beaverbrook. Politicians have always leaked and newspapers have always provided the lead piping; the same restaurants patronized by ministers and Press people in the nineties saw very similar gatherings in the forties, fifties and beyond. Today, leading editors and proprietors are visited and visit at Tory politicians' country homes, and so it was before, though the homes were once rather grander and more heavily turreted than they are now. Generally, such relationships have caused more suspicion on the left than the right. When in 1945 the war leader warned that the election of a Labour government would involve the setting up of 'some form of Gestapo', Attlee replied that 'The voice we heard last night was the voice of Mr Churchill but the mind was that of Lord Beaverbrook'; and Ernest Bevin summarized a thousand later Labour complaints when he observed that he had no quarrel with the Prime Minister but 'I object to this country being ruled from Fleet Street.'[36]

What has changed in our time in press–politician relations is a matter of degree, not kind. First, the ferocity of the attacks on out-of-favour or failing politicians has increased, largely due to the social changes and the disappearance of social deference: no leader in modern times, not even Harold Wilson, has had to cope with the personally abusive attacks that John Major has faced. But, and this leads on to the second change, the worst attacks came from the right. In our days, the war in the Conservative party over Europe has divided the press, and indeed divided the staff of some newspapers (such as the *Daily Telegraph*). Some ninety years ago, the free trade versus imperial protection argument similarly divided the press, with fifteen big dailies ranged on the protectionist side, seven of them controlled by two proprietors, while just six were on the free-trading side. As between 'Eurosceptical' newspapers and pro-European ones today, the balance is similar. But it takes an internal party war of this gravity to produce the deadly and relentless abuse that has been evident in the modern Conservative press.

The third change is in the steady rise of 'star' journalists, with bylines and pictures, and regular access to the radio and television studios. Once politicians dealt largely with the proprietors, who would then direct the newspaper line. But 'editorials', the unsigned leading articles, carry less weight these days than front–page scoops, commentaries and other innovations. (Though a blast in the *Daily Mail* or *Telegraph* leader can still wreck a Tory ministerial career.) More and more, therefore, the relations are between politicians and writing journalists. This was starting to be so by the fifties, when senior lobby men were courted with whiskies by politicians of the eminence of Iain Macleod and R.A. Butler. Given the need of the journalists for access, balanced by the need to be tough on politicians; and the politicians' need for coverage, balanced by their suspicions about the intentions of the journalist, this makes for a particularly mobile relationship. Some journalists solve this by simply joining up with one party, faction, or whatever. Others weave endlessly between the groups, passing on information and gossip and picking it up, like sparrows eating and voiding seeds, and so keeping the secret garden growing greenly. A third group find that writing tough 'knocking copy' about the sins and idiocies of the elected decision-makers comes more easily if one simply doesn't bother to meet or talk with them at all. This mixture of verbal aggression and rising status can be seen in most Western democracies. The American writer Adam Gopnik could have been describing the British scene when he said that 'the media have in the past twenty years claimed what amounts to prosecutorial and judicial powers . . . The reporter used to gain status by dining with his subjects; now he gains status by dining on them.'[37]

Where does the status come from, though, and what does it mean for the political system? Partly, the press (and the broadcasters, of whom more shortly) are the beneficiaries of the dispersal, or democratization, of information. In the old days, a part of the government's authority came from its special knowledge, its private and important sources of information, which may be hinted at, and used to subdue scepticism. Today, a serious newspaper often knows almost as much about the world from its correspondents and wire services, its academic contributors and its friends in the think-tanks, as the Foreign Office does. The knowledge communicated by the Secret Service from its gleaming post-modern palace overlooking the Thames at Vauxhall remains private to ministers. But in the post-Cold War world, it also seems somehow less immediate and it grips the imagination of the public rather less than before. The scientific and research resources available to central government are rivalled and often surpassed by outsiders, including lobby groups and private companies. It was television's *The Cook Report* which carried out its own research into the causes of cot deaths and directly challenged the Department of Health with failing to do the necessary tests on babies' mattresses. The government's Chief Medical Officer criticized the programme and the research for being inadequate, but judging by the reaction in the shops, the public listened to the television journalist and his scientific adviser, not the government.

On pollution levels, radiation problems, projections for inflation, predictions about foreign relations, health advice, we no longer turn automatically to the ministeriate. What does this afternoon's Budget really mean? Millions turn to the BBC's Peter Jay, rather than to the chancellor's, or shadow-chancellor's, broadcast for an answer. Do the Labour Party's figures add up? Politicians are not trusted for fair replies, so the country turns to people like Andrew Dilnot, of the Institute for Fiscal Studies. When it comes to the things the ministers really should be expert in, constitutional matters, who do we turn to for authoritative advice? Professor Peter Hennessy assiduously searches for the answers in obscure prime ministerial notes and dusty box-files stored at the Public Records Office at Kew; but all the time it is Mr Hennessy himself, author, broadcaster, lecturer, who has become the voice of such authority, the loose-leaf folder for which he is hunting. Sometimes, it is figures appointed by the government itself who become rivals for the public trust – on prisons, Judge Stephen Tumim, Her Majesty's Chief Inspector, won such a position of authority that the Home Secretary decided not to renew his contract. His outspokenness received its petty ministerial punishment: most unusually for such a distinguished public servant, he was given no honour or official recognition. In 1996, as Whitehall received the Scott Report, ministers launched a savage counter-attack on Lord Justice Scott's status as an independent and knowing searcher after truth: fundamentally, they suggested he should not be trusted. This was a struggle which typified the new politics, in which there is a free market in trust and public standing. If everyone is working from roughly the same pool of information then, by definition, judgements based upon that information become more susceptible to challenge and refutation. Knowledge is power, and power of that kind is leaving the political system, whatever party label the ministers wear. One of the places it has been going to is the press, aided and assisted by the numerous lobby-groups and appointed experts who try to prove daily that the government knows less about the world than they do.[38]

Is this a good thing? It is undoubtedly good that freer access to information is enabling millions more voters to form their own opinions. Ministers and civil servants can no longer say to the rest of us that such-and-such a thing is so and requires a certain action, without challenge and cross-examination. We are liberated by knowing more. But it is far less obvious that the press, which is a sort of semi-organized movement on behalf of mayhem, provides a sufficient or effective democratic check on political power. It is no fit substitute for a proper Parliament. For one thing, as with the judiciary, the Press generally gets excited about a policy only when it is too late and something has already gone wrong: the coverage of the poll tax fiasco once there were riots and resignations to report contrasted sharply with the virtual silence about it when the relevant legislation was proceeding in Parliament, and during the general election campaign which preceded the bill. The historians of the poll tax saga note that during that 1987 campaign 'the community charge was barely discussed' and that the 'futile marathon' of its passage through the Commons committee stage 'went virtually unnoticed in the press.'[39] This is a phenomenon which is not only general but is inevitable given the nature of daily journalism. We are far better at pursuing a 'hard' story than seeing where things may be going wrong during the abstract and often complex process of policy-formation. Papers have always been better terriers than bloodhounds. Today, the constant pressure on costs caused by the concentration of ownership makes this truer than ever: investigative journalism is a particularly expensive business, since it can tie up expensive writers for months without producing guaranteed material.

Newspapers are also competing with one another in the entertainment business as well as the information business. This also means that they suffer from a very short concentration-span and memory. Each day brings its crop of fresh and sharp-smelling stories which are rooted out and dropped into the public consciousness, only to be replaced by another crop the next day.

Competition produces a kind of collective mania for particular stories – one week the entire country is full of slavering killer dogs; the next, they have mysteriously disappeared, to be replaced by giant bees or mysterious flesh-eating viruses. Yesterday's stories, no longer so tasty, are discarded to rot away in the collective public mind, an evil-smelling tip of neurosis. Few papers ever go back later and ask, what happened? Were we right to get worried? Are there still those killer dogs about? Policy coverage is less lurid, but suffers from the same problem. The press goes galloping off after a particular kind of story – the rise of the Tory rebels, say, or consultancy payments to MPs – and a huge swathe of other policy stories are left untouched. If one really wants to understand what is happening in Whitehall then, generally, there is too little continuity, too little comparison, too little reference-back: the reader is confronted by headlines about new policy announcements or splits, but is rarely able to gauge their importance compared with last month's announcement, or the similar 'cabinet split' story a few weeks earlier. Newspapers are bad at comparing large sums of money: after a few noughts in large type, any figure – £400,000 or £4 billion – looks equally huge.

The press has huge influence on the political game and is clearly far more than the medium through which politicians contact the public. But it is far easier to find examples of newspaper power working destructively than constructively. When a draft of the British and Irish governments' framework document for the Northern Irish peace talks was leaked by a pro-Unionist journalist in *The Times* in February 1995, this was a genuinely powerful political act. It prevented the Prime Minister from taking the Ulster Unionist leaders into his confidence before the document was published, giving them his spin on it and trying to charm them into giving it serious consideration. Instead, the leak meant that the Unionists were confronted with the most hostile-possible spin on the most sensitive parts of the document, and provoked into saying things which were hard to take back. Certainly, Downing Street believed that, by stealing the initiative, the leak damaged that part of the peace process. This is a particularly vivid and important example of the press's methods but it isn't untypical in its impact on the administration. Journalists can, at their most effective, force resignations, expose humbug, destroy carefully laid plans and generally make life harder for the politicians. It is rarer for us to formulate policy, sharpen choices, support decent MPs in difficulty and communicate the complexities of government decisions which may hurt two people to help three. None of this is meant as a call for the reform of the press to make it more effective as a part of the political system: it would be absurd to expect newspapers to be policy journals, or daily select committee reports. But these truths about the press are necessary to restate given its huge importance in the British system. It is a check and an entertainment, but it is no more a substitute for properly working democratic systems than a court of law is.

Similar cautions need to be applied to the rise of the broadcast media, which have their own strengths and weaknesses as channels for political conversation. In many respects, they are better than either Parliament or the press at holding politicians and senior officials to account. The morning interviews on BBC Radio Four's *Today* programme are as established a part of the political week as question time in the Commons and, often, more important. Everyone who is part of the political class tunes in. Even in an era of proliferating media outlets, *Today*, like the main television news bulletins and *Newsnight*, is an essential element of a national conversation about how we run our lives, without which our democracy would be the poorer. On radio or television, a good interviewer can give a minister just as rigorous and effective a cross-examination as he or she will face in Parliament; there are fewer potential questioners but there is no loyal audience of backbenchers to appeal to, and less room for histrionics. One example must stand for tens of thousands. On the day when the Home Secretary had to announce the devastating assessment of an inquiry into the Whitemoor prison escape, discussed above, Michael Howard had a hard time in the House of Commons, facing pointed and serious questioning from his Labour and Liberal Democrat shadows and from backbenchers. But he had numerous helpful interventions from Conservative loyalists to help him. He had a much harder time that night when BBC's *Newsnight* programme decided to home in on whether or not he had been warned beforehand about security at the prison – a matter directly affecting whether or not he ought to resign. The presenter Peter Snow opened with a stern series of questions to camera about whether the minister should take responsibility and this was followed by a short and critical film on the prison. Then three key witnesses were interviewed about what they believed Howard had known – Paddy Seligman, the former chair of the board of visitors at Whitemoor, who had sent him warning reports; Lady Olga Maitland, the local Tory MP, who had had a private meeting with him about the prison; and John Bartell of the Prison Officers' Association. Only then was a grim-faced Home Secretary questioned. He survived the ordeal, but no viewer would have finished the programme with a better view of him than they would have had at the start. This was in effect a political and public trial of the Home Secretary's competence, barely diminished in its impact by the fact that Snow was unable to pass sentence at the end[40] – the judgement and punishment being a matter for the million or so viewers.

Television is very good at telling the voter certain things about a politician or other interviewee. One can read the facial tics and expressions that suggest tension, lying, anger and so forth. One can make a personal judgement about an individual minister or leader in a way that earlier generations never could, unless they were part of the privileged political élite. If before, one could read X's speech given verbatim in *The Times*, and treat X solely on the basis of his language and arguments, now one can conclude that X's grandson, the new minister, is a sanctimonious creep. And in the real world, the fact that 'X is a creep' is a valid personal assessment and matters to most of us just as much as his speechifying. It is a useful thing to know. There is, in the political world, plenty of nostalgia for the great days of public oratory and packed meetings. But the orators of forty years ago relied on tricks which have changed little since

Ancient Greece, tricks like repetition, the use of alliteration, exaggeration, pathos, mocking humour, and so on. These tricks provide great entertainment, but they are as effective in disguising bad arguments as developing good ones – a savage joke or sibilant ripple of poetic words can deflect the listener's attention from a ropey argument underlying them. If we want to have a serious discussion about some important matter of public policy, then a television or radio studio, too small a place for histrionics, too informal for the deceits of oratory, is a better format than any public meeting. It is far closer to what would happen if an ordinarily intelligent and reasonably well-informed voter was able to question the political leaders directly. Evasions glare. Cheap points sound as cheap as they are.

This is all pretty familiar to us now, after a couple of generations of such programming, but they have greatly improved the quality of the democracy, and we should not allow familiarity to blind us to that. Similarly, it may be banal to note that the undeferential and satirical tone of much broadcasting coverage is a powerful bulwark against demagoguery. But it's true, too. It is rather hard to imagine the rise of a genuinely threatening fascist leader in a country with as varied and ill-disciplined a media as Britain's. By the time he had been given the treatment by *Spitting Image* and *Have I Got News for You*, never mind Jeremy Paxman, it is hard to imagine a modern Mosley retaining much dignity or authority. Laughter is the secret weapon of democrats. Again, though this may be an obvious point, it is not an inconsiderable one.

As with the press, though, the power of the broadcast media in the political process is not an unqualified good. Despite the famous 'mission to explain' proclaimed by John Birt of the BBC, television and radio are bad at conveying facts. Lists of policies, or figures, however beautifully arranged on the screen, vanish from the mind almost as quickly as they do from the retina. By the time the sixth point has been reached, the first is forgotten; no sentence of more than a few words remains with the viewer. One vivid image will blot out the strongest argument, and television, in the end, is a succession of images. Long sentences and argument suffer. American research suggests that the typical 'soundbite' comment by a politician on television in the 1966 election lasted for 42 seconds and that it shrank steadily until it was down to just 9 seconds by 1988 and then 6.5 seconds in 1992.[41] Hardly good news for the deliberative democracy. As compared to newspapers or books, television allows no reflection, no re-reading, no comparison of one thought against another. Similarly, television has no sense of hierarchy or history. It flattens and equates those seen on it, so that a rebel backbencher can seem as important as the Foreign Secretary. If one relied on television as a guide to which politicians mattered, one would be badly informed, because the 'rentaquote' MPs who are always willing to 'do a turn' and work up a vivid sentence or two are often those who have failed to make their mark in the formal political hierarchy and who, in an earlier age, would be unknowns. Television is selective, but its selection is a politically quirky and unreliable business. Its flattening effect is a democratic thing, but it can damage one's understanding of what is going on. These flaws are inherent in the medium, as the flaws of the press are inherent in the newspaper market. There is nothing to be done about them, except to be aware of them and, being so, to realize that neither medium is an adequate check or balance to political power.

There is one final and serious flaw in the idea that the mass media, on paper, amplifier or screen, are a sufficient system of political scrutiny. It is that they – we – have been too naïve and unquestioning about the rise of the pressure groups and single-interest groups which manufacture and manipulate so much 'news'. It is remarkable how often their spokespeople are treated as unpolluted sources of information and light. Their funding is rarely questioned, their 'surveys' are faithfully reported, their leading figures rarely subjected to hostile and critical questioning. Most weeks show a high proportion of press stories and broadcast news which originates from pressure groups, either through the release of reports, or opinion polls commissioned by them, or because they have achieved some high-profile publicity coup. The mindset of a journalist and of a successful campaigner is quite similar; the latter requires a nose for the unexpected, the salient fact and a sense of timing, too.

As a result many pressure groups have benefited from a style of reporting which political parties would die for: their data and beliefs are reported as news in its own right, rather than as claims or as part of a campaign. In some cases, the para-politicians have successfully 'captured' the specialist journalists who rely on them for tip-offs, stories and thus, ultimately, for promotion and pay. You don't bite the hand that feeds you, particularly if you are being fed predigested 'exclusives'. This is a familiar form of corruption for political reporters, who endlessly have to balance the need to get stories against the need to keep some senior politicians, at least, 'sweet'. But at least in traditional politics there are plenty of sources to choose from: it is hard to alienate everybody.[42] If the Labour Party launches a survey of poverty and proposes to change the benefits system, the event is analysed in terms of its internal party politics, its campaigning programme and the cost of the proposals. This is considered routine. But if pressure groups launch survey findings or propose new spending they often get an easier ride. A Social Market Foundation study of BBC Radio's Today programme over one week – 10 to 25 February 1995 – claimed that, if all the calls for extra public spending were added up, they would cost £15 billion, equivalent to another 10p on the standard rate of income tax. The programme's editor strongly contested that pressure groups or opposition politicians had been given an easy ride. Today does not deserve to be singled out. But in general plaintive calls for extra spending fail to get aggressive questioning about where the money will come from. Ministers, who are after all meant to be there to represent the public good, to balance the interests of the pressure group against those of other groups, including taxpayers, are treated as suspicious, faintly sleazy characters by comparison with campaigners who are less hardened. Yet pressure groups raise money too, and are influenced by commercial considerations; their internal politics has an effect on the body politic; their rivalries and different strategies are becoming as important to much policy-making as the internal rivalries of, say, the opposition parties. There are signs that this may be changing – scandals in some campaigning organizations have hardened attitudes, and there is a more general understanding of the power of the lobbies spreading through the system. If so, not before time.

Thus far we have moved through the situation of the state, and how it affects our politics, in a sequence, taking in the generally-accepted route-marks of Brussels, the monarchy, civil servants, journalists, and so forth. But even a list as long as this one cannot hope to convey the feel of how our changed political system is operating in practice. So, finally, let us look at one example of how politics here actually happens, an example which doesn't take in everything mentioned before, but which does show the interconnectedness of what I have been trying to describe.

New Politics in Action: the Middle English in Revolt

Here's a picture of politics happening in England. Huge nets are spread between trees and houses. Men nail themselves into the rooms of tottering houses. Women rope themselves to one another or lock themselves into basements. Roadblocks made of supermarket trolleys, concrete, bricks, wire and rubbish are thrown across suburban roads. Young and angry, old and angry, strange collections of people, dressed in a mixture of styles, glimpses of Cyberpunk and druid-warrior, whiskery urban preachers, solemn-faced people dressed as for mountaineering, all gather to confront ranks of embarrassed policemen, themselves dressed up as for a low-budget remake of the Battle of Hastings. Or it can happen out in the country, where tribes gather in the Home Counties, urban rejects dreaming romantic visions of Olde England, politically sophisticated young anarchists linked by computer lines, finding themselves at times in curious alliance with tweedy and forthright Tory ladies, local schoolteachers, or whoever. And again, mustered for confrontation, sometimes in local meeting-halls where officials sit for public inquiries, but more often and more telegenically across bleak, scarred landscapes – valleys of mud, hills with the turf torn off. Confronting them again are lines of dirty police Range Rovers and, alongside their JCBs and tipper trucks, the orange-vested men from the construction companies. For we are, of course, talking about roads.

The battle over the future of the roadbuilding programme ranks with the Victorian struggle between industrialists and the landed interests over free trade. It involves Britain's ability to compete as a successful member of the single European market. It has international implications, and its planning controversies draw in the new law makers and law-enforcers from Brussels. It mobilizes large numbers of disaffected and angry voters from wildly different social backgrounds. It pits large semi-political organizations in great coalitions against one another – the AA versus Friends of the Earth, the Royal Automobile Club against the National Trust. It has drawn the ragged networks of green activists and anarchist youngsters into conflict with the successful players in Margaret Thatcher's 'great car economy'. But it has also divided Conservative associations and brought Whitehall departments into confrontation, pushing rival groups of experts, economists, environmentalists, scientists, into the centre of controversy. It presents MPs with difficult choices, sometimes obliging them to choose between their party and philosophy, and their constituents' interests. It provokes questions about the influence of big businesses on government, and the relative powers of central and local government. It throws up serious philosophical problems, as between the preservation of the country we have inherited, and the need for our children to inherit a country which is economically successful. And, at times, it has provoked scenes of mayhem and physical confrontation. Yet the impact of the great roads battle on the Commons has been minimal and it has been our 'supreme institution' carried out between unknown leaders using little-understood weapons.

The history of the modern British roadbuilding programme can be fairly accurately dated to 1 April 1937, when the Ministry of Transport took over control of around 4,500 miles of the country's most important highways. In the early years of the century, roads had been under the control of some two thousand local authorities but, from early on, a motoring lobby had developed which demanded central control, most forcefully during the 1935 general election. The relevant bill was passed remarkably quickly and without much comment, though buried in it were new powers which have caused deep controversy and done the cause of democracy in Britain real harm ever since.[43] In particular, it created a system under which the minister was both the promoter of new roads, and the final arbiter at public inquiries about them. This system is responsible for much subsequent popular anger about the high-handedness of roadbuilding – and, indeed, a whole genre of literature which sees the driving of motorways through rural idylls as a powerful metaphor for the destruction of Old England by modernizing bureaucrats. It all derives from schedules in the 1936 Act, deliberately hidden there in obscure language to avoid alerting Members of Parliament. The parliamentary draftsman who drew up the act was one Sir Harold Kent who wrote later that, 'the prospect of driving these big roads through the close-knit countryside of England was rather horrifying ... (but) the Permanent Secretary knew exactly what he wanted in the Trunk Roads Bill. The most awkward feature of the bill, politically speaking, was that ... the minister ... would be "judge in his own cause". Then, as now, there was a powerful backbench lobby against ministerial powers and bureaucratic tyranny and much talk of natural justice and its denial ...' But, by hiding the relevant powers, 'even the backbench lobby passed them by in bemused silence.'[44] So we start the story in familiar constitutional territory, with ministers, eagerly aided by civil servants, hoodwinking a rather lazy and generalizing bunch of parliamentarians. The explosive results of this were not seen until decades later, because the Second World War brought most roadbuilding to a halt, and post-war governments took time to restart it. But it helped create the bureaucratic machine which has shaped long stretches of modern Britain.

From the first, that machine was heavily influenced by the commercial road lobby. Again, right at the start of the story, we have to recognize that the commercial and business pressures on government are nothing new. Today, the main pro-road organization is the British Road Federation, whose members include the AA, the RAC, the big construction companies (Balfour Beatty, Mowlem, John Laing, Trafalgar House, Tarmac, Amec), cement and gravel companies, roadside caterers like Forte, the Road Haulage Association, the car dealers' Retail Motor Industry federation, oil companies like Shell and BP, and a host of other organizations and companies – TNT Express, National Car Parks, Volvo Trucks. It is an immensely powerful and important lobby, led in the mid-1990s by Richard Diment, a former Conservative Party official. But it has been influential and active since well before motorways were built in Britain. In September 1937, the BRF took 225 MPs, surveyors and county roads committee chairmen to Nazi Germany to see the autobahn system. In the pre-war atmosphere, the ministry itself was unimpressed, producing an absolute classic of Whitehall put-down-manship: 'among the personal attributes of the rulers of Germany . . . is a mania for speed, which has found one of its expressions in motor roads. There seems no reason why this country, with its different traditions, should blindly copy [this] at the behest of a delegation led by the chairman of the Cement Manufacturers' Association.'[45] Yet the County Surveyors' Society went on to publish a plan in 1938 for a thousand-mile motorway network which eventually took shape in Britain after the 1950s. Lobbying, if carried out with panache, pays off.

What happened was that the Transport Department became essentially a roads department and, more than that, a road-building robot which operated almost outside the rest of government. After the war, the growth area was in car and lorry traffic, while the nationalized railway system, operated at arm's length from the politicians, made a series of dreadful errors of judgement about the likely nature and volume of traffic. Transport ministers were working on roads programmes from the 1950s onwards backed by pseudo-scientific assertions about the national economic benefits of roadbuilding. The only area where the roads lobby failed in the sixties was in its campaign for urban motorways. Although governments were warned about the problems of increasing congestion in cities, ministers were not ready either to limit car traffic or to demolish and rebuild great swathes of inner-city Britain to make way for it (two options suggested by the 1963 Buchanan Report).

Otherwise, the Department of Transport was backed throughout by the BRF; it developed regional staffs called Road Construction Units, or RCUs, with a quasi-military terminology ('Unit HQs' and the like) which operated outside local democratic control; and it had the powers from the 1936 Act to make a farce of public inquiries, rendering protest seemingly hopeless. Added to which, over time the department was able to retreat, when attacked, behind a thicket of economic projections and extrapolations which proved utterly impenetrable to most outsiders until well into the 1980s. In the words of one Whitehall insider, the projections, which should have been a decision-making tool, became a decision-making procedure: X road was 'revealed' to produce Y economic benefit, so the minister simply said yes. One oddity about the statistics used by the department in modern times was that they rejected the common-sense argument that more roads actually produced more traffic. This allowed the road-planners to respond to any projection of higher traffic levels with the uncomplicated answer that more roads would therefore be required; the roads were seen simply as the solution, and never part of the problem.

The Treasury was as in thrall to the promised economic returns as everyone else. Within the department, the Highways Directorate was a law unto itself, described by a civil servant from a rival department as 'a roads machine cut off from the rest of Whitehall – unaccountable, unmonitored, unchecked.' Even when the department was merged into the Department of the Environment from 1970–76, the Highways Directorate managed to stay aloof. It was, and is, a formidable machine which undoubtedly did a lot of good in getting the British road system modernized after the war, but whose power made the old dream of an integrated transport system (which the department had been founded in 1919 to achieve) an entirely vain one. The example of the Highways Directorate in its heyday should offer serious food for thought for all those who trumpet enthusiastically for agencies operating entirely outside the more political culture of Whitehall and Westminster. The dividing line between making the policy, and merely carrying out the policy – which includes, of course, providing the figures and expertise to explain and defend the policy, is a dangerously narrow one. The job of politics is to balance and resolve competing claims – rail versus road, nuclear power versus coal. Whenever a function of government is cut off, as an agency, or quango, or whatever, from the rest of the general political balancing-act, it is by definition unable to judge its own value to taxpayers and citizens. This is, in fact, another consequence of the obsessive, secretive Whitehall departmentalism which the 1993–95 Scott Inquiry struggled to understand in the case of export guidelines. Had the Highways Directorate been more a part of the general department, and the department more connected to a wider public-spending debate, Britain might have had a better-balanced transport system today. And the directorate's impact on Britain went wider than transport policy. As the Council for the Protection of Rural England (CPRE) has put it: 'Its motorway and Trunk Road schemes, built outside any planning authority's control, have been facilitating the pattern of faster and longer journeys on which the new lifestyle depends. In effect, the department has been acting as a prime agent in the social and physical restructuring of large parts of the country . . .'

Before we get to the present, and what happened to the Highways Directorate, we need to look at the history of the other counterposing force in the great roads war of the 1990s. The anti-roads case was originally left to landowners, local amenity societies and the occasional national charity, like the CPRE itself, which was founded in 1926, campaigned against ribbon development in the thirties, and was influential in the Town and Country Planning Act of 1947. The big change came with the rise of environmentalism in the seventies, combined with juggernaut lorries which damaged villages and infuriated many towndwellers, too (the limit went up from 24 tons to 32 tons in 1964, and to 38 in 1982). The ideological opposition of green groups to roadbuilding began to combine with local opposition to particular schemes, often in Conservative heartland territory and among Tory voters and workers, in a way which seriously threatened the old industrial–Whitehall lobby. Having looked in some detail at the power and tactics of the roads lobby, it is worth looking in similar detail at the way the green anti-roads one works, too. It is fighting across the same bureaucratic battlefield but the sources of its political power are very different.

There are now around 215 environmental lobby groups listed in Britain.[46] They range from the most moderate, even genteel, organizations, such as CPRE and the Royal Society for the Protection of Birds, to extreme groups, notably the Earth First! cells which originated in America in the eighties. The familiarity of some parts of the anti-roads coalition and the obscurity of other parts has tended to disguise the scale of what is happening. Collectively, however, they comprise a new force in British politics: it is wrong to think of them simply as pressure groups, for they are really a movement. The distinction is that a movement is broad, both socially and politically and has staying power, whereas a pressure group is a more modest set-up aimed at achieving specific changes, and often lacks staying power. The women's movement, which has had huge political influence, was not a pressure group. The gay rights movement is not a pressure group. Similarly, green campaigning can be seen as a new politics. On the roadbuilding issue, as on others, the rise of green politics can be compared to the rise of socialist politics in the early part of this century, at least in the range and variety of its operation. You have the parliamentary road to greenery, which has thus far proved totally unsuccessful, though the Green Party did win 2.3 million votes at its high point so far, the 1989 European election. (The early Labour Party did almost as badly.) You have 'ginger group' influence on established parties: as Fabianism and trade unionism influenced the Liberals in the 1900s, so greenery has influenced the Liberal Democrats, and the others, now. You have the driven individual campaigners seeking to win influence in Whitehall by striking alliances, providing unanswerable evidence and using the power of the media. These are no longer social reformers like the Webbs or Rowntrees but environmental campaigners like Jonathan Porritt and Tom Burke.

Environmental politics, though, reaches groups which are virtually part of the establishment themselves. The National Trust is Britain's third-largest landowner, boasts a membership of some two million (four times that of any political party) and was affected by forty roadbuilding schemes in the mid-1990s. But because it was set up by Parliament in 1907 under an Act giving it 'inalienable' rights over its land it can summon both Houses of Parliament to debate these schemes if it so desires – a dangerously great power, since its regular use might persuade Parliament to change the law – but a great power nevertheless. Nearer the centre of the huge green spectrum there are groups like Friends of the Earth, founded in America in 1969 and in Britain in 1971, and Greenpeace, with 4.5 million members worldwide and 400,000 in Britain, which are clearly radical in mood and intent. Then, finally, at the opposite end to the gentlefolk of the National Trust, there are the direct-action protesters, sitting in trees, blocking bulldozers, sabotaging construction vehicles ('monkeywrenching') and threatening worse. These include young hippies and well-organized protesters in groups such as Green Man Earth First! which was involved in the campaign against the M11 link road. These could be compared to the syndicalists and revolutionary socialists of the early century, and in April 1995 some set up as latter-day 'diggers' on St George's Hill in Surrey, where the seventeenth-century revolutionary and democrat Gerard Winstanley – who believed that 'the poorest hath as true a title and just right to the land as the richest man' – led his band of radicals 'to dig up, manure and sow corn', in defiance of property rights. Although there are plenty of Conservatives and right-wingers of all sorts involved in the anti-roads movement, it is fair to say that that movement is heavily anti-establishment in its politics, and that the anti-roads movement is only one aspect of a form of politics which is spreading and subdividing almost as fast as left-wing politics a century ago. There are internationalists who focus their attention on global issues and who believe that this struggle cannot be won except at a world level. There are the localists who admit this, but concentrate on regional and community issues, rather like the early socialists who went into local government. There are moderates, Fabians and those who thirst for the destruction of the wasteful, corrupt civilization of today – just as left-wing anarchists did a century ago. And there is a vast literature, with its gurus, satirists, theorists and ideological splits, which keeps the intellectual life of the movement in ferment.

In this case, the mirror-image of the British Road Federation is the umbrella group Transport 2000, founded by environmentalists and railway unions in 1973. Under that umbrella a variety of tactics, from FoE protests to discreet CPRE lobbying, are used to push the case against more roadbuilding. One Whitehall mandarin reckoned that the environmentalists were working cleverly at several levels: first the 'nice cops' like the RSPB and the CPRE, speaking in polite, well-modulated tones, were trying to persuade ministers and policy-making officials, using detailed arguments and the unspoken electoral threat of their big memberships. They were extremely well-informed about the latest scientific data, sometimes more so than Whitehall itself. This is not so surprising, given the singlemindedness of the environmentalists and the wide range of political concerns the civil service attempts to keep an eye on. Whitehall gossip said that before the Rio Earth Summit, of six scientists available to the Department of the Environment, five had been diverted to deal with the latest popular outcry on dangerous dogs! This was a gross exaggeration. This is the Met Office's Hadley Centre is one of the world authorities on climate change – but beneath it lies the uncomfortable truth for government that scientific expertise is almost as freely available to the lobbyists as the ministers. Then there were the direct-action 'nasty cops' and the organizers of demonstrations, pickets and letter-writing campaigns.

It was the 'nice cops' of CPRE who were among the first to spot a weakness in the Department of Transport traffic projections in the late 1980s. These projections finally seemed to go wildly over the top in 1988–89, when the then Transport Secretary Paul Channon used them to justify a doubling of the roads programme. His White Paper, 'Roads to Prosperity' was gushing in its joyous enthusiasm for concrete and tarmac, promising £2 billion a year for expansion of the very roads network that was starting to cause the Conservative Party such problems locally. It was, in retrospect, a turning point, because it seemed to imply a nightmarish view of the future in which, unless motorways were plastered across most of the country, the nation was doomed to seize up. More traffic demanded more roads. That produced more traffic, which in turn automatically spurred the government into providing more roads. Eventually such simple logic starts to seem mad. If this was success in transport policy, what would failure feel like?

Something seemed badly wrong. The Treasury started to look rather more aggressively at the department's mathematics and assumptions. It helped the environmentalists' case that at the same time a series of huge costs overruns on roads were being highlighted by the government watchdog, the National Audit Office, and that evidence came to light in Whitehall suggesting that the department was being soft on construction companies which failed to meet their time targets. At around the same time, the DoE was finding that on almost every issue of public environmental concern – global warming, air pollution, out-of-town planning – it was running into opposition from the Department of Transport. Relations between the two departments (which still shared a hideous office complex at Marsham Street, a few minutes' walk from the Palace of Westminster) started to become strained. If the roads programme was wound down, then the DoT would lose much of its reason for existing, and would probably be closed or merge back again.

But the DoE was also fighting for status. Almost regardless of who was in charge – for Chris Patten, John Gummer and Michael Howard were very different politicians – it took stronger pro-environmentalist positions during those years. Part of the reason was to do with key officials; Tom Burke, the green campaigner, had joined as special adviser. Part was to do with corporate muscle. The doctrine of 'sustainable development', however vague, had been adopted by the government and gave the DoE licence to range more freely over other departmental business. In its struggle with Transport, the DoE, which had been behind the establishment of a Royal Commission on Pollution back in 1974, was well aware that it was working on a politically explosive report on traffic and air quality which would, in time, provide invaluable propaganda against the roads programme.

Then, the victories started: the tide of bureaucratic war turned. John Gummer announced tough new laws on out-of-town shopping centres – one of the first reversals of the reshaping of Britain hitherto carried out by the Highways Directorate. Inside Whitehall, an obscure judgement by the Chancellor of the Exchequer in the 1994 Budget about grants for landfill sites was hailed as signalling the conversion of the Treasury to environmental arguments. Finally, a group of transport experts working for the government, the Sactra committee, blew apart the argument that had underpinned the roads expansion by stating that roadbuilding actually increased traffic, rather than merely coping with it. One member of the committee, Phil Goodwin of Oxford University, later reflected on the mystery of the statistics. The old orthodoxy, from the 1930s, had admitted that roads did create traffic. Then, as the modern roadbuilding era arrived, that changed. Dr Goodwin said that 'I have not been able to track down a single piece of empirical evidence between 1965 and 1975 which could explain the transition from one orthodoxy to its opposite.' He concluded that 'a procedure of convenience developed in which, first, such extra traffic was ignored. Over the years, this ignoring became an assumption and the assumption became a "tried and tested" practice, the practice became a "known scientific fact" ... and, finally, pantalooned, sans eyes but not unfortunately sans teeth, the scientific fact became a legally enforceable axiom, unchallengeable at road inquiries.'[47] This can stand as a pretty convincing sketch of how civil servants often behave when they're cut off from political or democratic control. It is a sketch worth remembering whenever one is told that the experts have long since justified anything.

As all this started to dawn on the outside world, some environmental groups began to regard the DoE as 'their' department and promote its interests. Ministers, in turn, began to find that the more 'establishment' lobbyists in the green movement were people that they could do business with: one minister told me he believed there were the 'pros' and 'antis'. Pros realized that the minister was representing the rest of society. They realized also that their pressure group could not replace the government and accepted that, in a sense, it would be a bad thing if it could: their job was to push, the minister's to resist a little. A compromise would then be struck and sold to the rest of the government machine. The 'antis', by contrast, saw the minister not as a potentially sympathetic holder of the public ring, but as the enemy. For this minister, it was a psychological thing. His officials suggested quietly that he simply found some campaigners more socially acceptable and agreeable to work with than others.

Although this struggle, fought out on the fringes of London and across rural England by protesters and police, and in Whitehall by ministers, industrialists and lobbyists, was remarkably unconnected to the Westminster agenda, the role of Tory MPs became increasingly important. Many of the direct-action protesters were supported by local residents and by Conservative voters. MPs spoke of worrying evidence that anti-motorway campaigns were attracting large numbers of previously loyal Tory supporters and activists. This may have been because of successful propaganda by green lobbyists over air pollution and other issues. It may have been more evidence of the less deferential attitudes within all parties. But Conservatives in counties like Surrey, Buckinghamshire, Hampshire and Manchester began to revolt. MPs from Outer London and the Home Counties whose constituencies were threatened by the department's plans, and who were already worried about the future of their commuting services after rail privatization, warned ministers of electoral disaster. Until now, as one Tory knight put it, news of a road in one's constituency was treated like a 'death in the family' — something not to be talked about outside, however difficult it was to cope with. Now, the controversy started to break into the open. Ministers remained sceptical — some of them had vociferous pro-roads lobbies in their rural constituencies. But even the British Roads Federation recognized that the climate was changing and withdrew its support for the controversial Oxleas Wood road scheme in South-east London. Ministers then followed the BRF, as they had so often before, and withdrew too. A year later, a £66 million, six-lane bypass slicing through an area of exceptional natural beauty near Newbury was abandoned, and the new Transport Secretary Brian Mawhinney announced that, in effect, Britain had enough roads and that future spending would concentrate more on improving and repairing current ones, rather than building more. Something momentous had happened in British politics.

This story is instructive for anyone looking at how British politics really works because it brings together so many relevant themes. The green organizations involved in the anti-roads campaign muster far more active members than all the political parties sitting in the House of Commons, and the disproportion is particularly large among younger voters. The main parties were all split on the roads question and rarely led the argument. The anti-roads movement used a wider variety of political protest, ranging from sabotage and mass civil disobedience on the one hand, to a subtle understanding of the Whitehall power-play and the use of research to sway opinion, which left most opposition politicians wallowing far behind. They threatened, as so many other pressure groups have done, to 'go to Europe' and try to find judicial checks on ministerial power. The pro-roads lobby had their success, too: the potentially fissile coalition between road hauliers and private motorists, big companies and small-town supporters of bypasses, never broke up, and the BRF was able to stage tactical retreats and to regroup effectively. But, on both sides, the competing political power of the car-dealers, the cement industry, local Tory associations and green lobbyists seemed at least as decisive as the actions of Parliament, civil servants or even ministers. The action went on away from Westminster, or behind closed doors in Whitehall where it had little of the colour and easily-described drama of the Commons chamber, but rather more importance. The bureaucratic battle between rival departments was a key part of the policy switch. Ministers rarely spoke publicly about the issues involved, and political leaders found themselves unable to make capital from them. The players, including senior officials, lobbyists and scientists, were unknown to the general public and stayed that way. Here is a new politics, confronting an Old Constitution.

Conclusion: the Fall of the Free State?

In earlier parts of this book, we saw how the British have become more cynical about their political system, and how their historic Parliament fails them. This sketch of the real condition of the British state towards the end of the century has, I hope, explained why that cynicism is soundly based. Power has not only moved from the traditional system, both outside Britain and inside Britain; the authority that remains has not been wisely deployed or sustained. Though some of what I have described can be blamed firmly on the failure of individual politicians, much more of it is simply part of the new world in which we live, and has the capacity to undermine any elected government. At the moment, failure and disillusion is built into the conventional political system. Recognizing that has led many people to turn their backs on politics altogether, and has led some thinkers to propose that we are entering a world in which politics no longer matters. This political fatalism is terribly wrong: real, practical reforms are both necessary and – what is more – within our ability to achieve. Whatever the limits on a free state in the modern world, there is plenty of room for an effective democracy and a free people.

CHAPTER SIX

Culture and Anarchy

'The circumstances of the world are continually changing, and
the opinions of men change also; and as government is for the
living, and not for the dead, it is the living only that has any
right in it. That which may be thought right and found convenient in one age, may be thought wrong and found inconven-
ient in another.'

– Thomas Paine, *The Rights of Man*

'Denounce the government and embrace
The flag. Hope to live in that free
Republic for which it stands.'
– Wendell Berry, *Manifesto: The Mad Farmer Liberation Front*

The dominant Western thinkers today are a gloomy lot. There
is a huddling round the campfire going on, a closing of mental
doors, a creeping ungenerosity of spirit, a pessimism about the
wider world. Serious voices from the right suggest that we are
condemned to increasing economic insecurity and deeper social
division, a harsh era in which the international economic élite
thrive behind the barriers their money builds for them, while the
losers fester hopelessly and violently in the ghetto. The time has
come, they seem to say, to recognize that the post-war welfare
societies are unsustainable. Rejecting that as unbearably harsh,
others warn that we cannot compete at all with the rising
Asian nations and must, to save our societies, partly cut off from
world markets – as Sir James Goldsmith suggests. Some propose
that, either way, the societies of the West are stuck with an
unemployable underclass and mutter ominously about the
utter failure of the state. In France, the writer Alain Minc stirred
up that nation into a brief frenzy of modish pessimism when he
suggested Europe was entering '*Le Nouveau Moyen Age*' or,
rather, a New Dark Age, characterized by plagues, beggars and

collapsing cities, the revival of superstition and the return of outside threats from the East – from Asia and from Islam.

On the one hand, decaying Western systems. On the other, the anarchy of the unleashed market. Our home-grown thinkers are generally less apocalyptic, but only a bit. David Selbourne, the Jewish moralist, suggests that for many the existence of a functioning civic order has become 'a lost hope' and inveighs in Old Testament style against 'the civic deserts of the modern nation'.[1] If one took some of our social philosophers seriously, one would conclude that the democratic impulse, the essential spirit of fraternity, is dwindling as the majority become increasingly scared about their futures, their tax bills and a babbling host of demons beyond the front door, from drug-addicted (subhuman) criminals round the corner to (superhuman) competitors abroad. Some of the despair is moral and religious in tone, some is environmental, but most of the gloom derives from that same system of political economy which had so recently delighted itself by winning the Cold War.

Has there ever been a time when societies so rich, so relatively secure and so peaceful were so close to losing their collective nerve? At its moment of political triumph, there has been an anguished rethinking of the limits and consequences of the global market – in particular the consequences for the social cohesion and future prosperity of the West as other competitors move in and the Old World asks itself whether the insecurity and accelerating change is worth any material gain. Increasing competition means increasing division between success and failure, not only among companies and nations, but among neighbours too and even within individuals who no longer look forward to an orderly working life but now find themselves succeeding one year and failing the next in a dramatic and unpredictable way. The rising wealth of the best-educated, best-connected and most determined people in work has been matched by falling real incomes for many of the old working class. Unemployment is no longer an experience confined to the shadowy margins but has become so widespread that it has now affected two-fifths of the workforce in Britain at some stage in their lives. Nor is it an experience confined to one class. In the nineties, the middle classes are being convulsed by the stripping out of layers of management in the big corporations and professions as organizations struggle to raise productivity – just as their working-class neighbours were hit by the same experiences for the same reasons in the eighties. So, the questions continue: are we locked into an impossible choice between economic advance and our basic social values, the building-blocks of our civilization?

The constitution has been part of the old world under challenge and in decay, and the political class has signed up to the idea of a serious malaise – except for those who happen to be at the top of the political tree and who are obliged by the rituals of office to pretend an idiot optimism on all occasions. John Gray, a champion of market Conservatism in the eighties, dramatically recanted to proclaim that, 'In Britain, the desolation of communities by unchannelled market forces and the resultant pervasive sense of economic insecurity have . . . been crucial factors in an epidemic of crime that probably has no parallel in national life since the early nineteenth century.'[2] (Though readers will recall the vision of criminal horror in 1909 quoted in the opening pages of this book.) David Green, of the ferociously free-market Institute of Economic Affairs, wrote that 'in drawing attention to the merits of markets, some advocates of freedom lost sight of the historic ideal which in reality made Western civilization superior to communism . . . Markets generate more prosperity, but "more goods" do not make a good society . . .'[3] David Willetts, a Tory MP who had worked closely with Margaret Thatcher, noted a feeling in his party that 'contract culture appears to have triumphed and the accountants rule. That leaves many traditional Conservatives uneasy.'[4] Chris Patten, one of the cleverest and nicest of those traditional Conservatives and party chairman during the 1992 election, said later that,

I am increasingly obsessed with . . . the problem of the underclass, which I believe we cannot ignore. In the past it has usually been true that when a community gets better off, everyone gets better off. But that has stopped happening. People with skills get better off, people with no skills get left behind. We have a bigger and bigger underclass because the jobs they used to do are now being done in Guangdong province and in East Asia generally ... I find myself in complete agreement with somebody like Tony Blair and his stress on social cohesion and community values.[5]

Not only Tony Blair, but most opposition politicians have, at some stage, professed serious worry about the divisive and unpredictable consequences of the new global market. That is hardly surprising. There is a vast library of left and left-liberal writing about this which we can, for the purposes of this argument, take as read. What is more intriguing is that the leftish politicians are in step with the business gurus themselves. Charles Handy, for instance, perhaps the most admired of Britain's management prophets, produced a chirpy bestseller in 1989 called *The Age of Unreason* in which he celebrated 'an era of new discoveries, new enlightenments and new freedoms'. Its tone is conveyed by a couple of sentences: 'Change, after all, is only another word for growth, another synonym for learning. We can all do it, and enjoy it, if we want to.' But five years later, he returned to the theme in *The Empty Raincoat*, finding darker messages in the casualization of the economy and the increased speed of change. Bleakly, he announced:

It hasn't worked. Management and control are breaking down everywhere. The new world order looks very likely to end in disorder. We can't make things happen in the way we want them to at home, at work, or in government ... We thought that capitalism was the answer, but some of the hungry and homeless are not so sure.[6]

Having been a writer who directed his lessons on self-improvement at individuals and corporations, Handy was driven to think and write more politically than before. Another thinker from the business world, Oliver Sparrow, who worked for Shell, recently wrote that great competition was making firms more like one another 'in a marketplace suddenly bereft of profit but churning in ceaseless change.' The result was that 'The situation of those of modest ability ... has become uncertain ... Those whom change most threatens are the less able in the rich countries; and those who are not inalienably lodged at the core of a profitable business.'[7]

If the moral anguish was merely a philosophical problem, we could nod, and pass on, and turn to more concrete things. But, as we have seen, it has risen from the lived experience of millions, the insecurities of workers expelled by the big corporations, from the crime-ridden ghettos, from the more frenetic, short-termist life of contract workers and part-timers; from the endless struggle for those in work to upgrade their skills and learn the latest tricks in the uneasy knowledge that these too will soon be useless. The gloominess of the 'thinkers' has reflected the experiences of the rest of us. We have become the harried society. And the political question that flows from this is a simple one: is it possible for the harried society, fighting to stay afloat, to maintain a generous, decent political culture? There was, after all, something like a hunger to believe that state provision is bound to be unsuccessful (this was perhaps the strongest single message that Margaret Thatcher lodged in the collective consciousness of her compatriots), even though the most careful study of the costs and likely developments of the welfare state suggests that doom-laden predictions of a crisis are grossly exaggerated.[8] More logically, some argue that the very business of competitive individualism, in which we value goods more for the status they give us compared to others, than in themselves, is incompatible with the common culture of the past.[9] On this reading, politics, as expressed through that equality machine, the welfare state, mass parties and representative institutions, is in hopeless competition with sophisticated market economics at a global level, continuously producing new goods, new goals, new standards of success and failure, and hence new economic divisions – a giant inequality and insecurity machine. The British sociologist and moralist Zygmunt Bauman speaks for many when he says that

the new spirit is sceptical about the possible uses and benefits of acting together and joining forces, and is resigned to the idea that whatever you want to achieve, you had better look to your own cunning and ingenuity as the principal resources . . . A privatized existence has its many joys . . . But it has its sorrows as well – loneliness and incurable uncertainty.[10]

Good doomsters are proved wrong because they have alerted their fellow citizens in time. What too few of today's prophets have included in their calculations is that humans are an adaptable lot; we are slime, no doubt, but we are pretty shrewd slime. Just as the chorus of predictions of individualistic mayhem rises to a crescendo, another counter-line of more affirmative song has been swelling up. It has consisted of a single word, 'community'. Everyone, it seems, is in favour of community, or nearly everyone. Community has become the intellectually respectable form of nostalgia, but also the propaganda of optimists everywhere. It is the watchword of penitent free-market Conservatives, and impenitent ones too; of the Labour and Liberal Democrat parties, of Greens, of church leaders, of moralistic journalists. There are, no doubt, eighteen-stone, shaven-headed neo-Nazis who start to blub quietly whenever community is mentioned; and, at the other end of the spectrum, extreme greens like Rudolf Bahro call for a return to Benedictine-like communities as a way of spiritual and economic renewal. (Strange but true.) At a more cerebral level, there has been a distinct revival of interest in the socially richer *Theory of Moral Sentiments* by Adam Smith, at the expense of his eighties blockbuster, *The Wealth of Nations*.

From America has come 'communitarianism', something like an intellectuals' political movement dedicated to spreading attitudes and policies for community feeling and social cohesion. Its guru, an Israeli-born academic called Amitai Etzioni, hopes that it will become a large-scale movement like the women's movement, or the green movement (political ecology, again) which will have more sustained impact than mere pressure-groups or even a political party. He explains it thus: 'We suggest that free individuals require a community, which backs them up against encroachment by the state and sustains morality by drawing on the gentle prodding of kin, friends, neighbours and other community members, rather than building on government controls or fear of authorities.'[11] This movement has spread, in a so far small and semi-organized way, to Britain too. Etzioni rightly notes that British politicians, including Blair, have shown interest in these ideas, but there are the beginnings of a separate British communitarian movement. In May 1995, a group of academics, community leaders and business managers launched what they called *The Citizens' Agenda: for Building Democratic Communities*[12] which contained the same mix of moralism and community politics as the American version, though the British communitarians were distinctive, placing far more emphasis on democratic structures.

More significantly, perhaps, there are many examples, some of them given earlier in this book, of spontaneous 'communitarian' developments, from Camden to Glasgow, where local groups take charge of schools, housing schemes, or whatever, and try to develop stronger local control: if there is a yearning for 'community' in some vague way, then there are still plenty of concrete, mundane examples of communities in action. There are of course the tens of thousands of councillors who, for all their lack of power, remain by far the most popular stopping-off-point for people with problems, and the Citizens Advice Bureaux and thousands of self-help organizations, charities and campaigning groups. Some of the latter, like the National Childbirth Trust, operate almost like local parties used to, though on a far narrower range, organizing meetings, publishing newsletters, raising money, conducting arguments about relevant policies. Across the country, civic groups still propose local reforms – sometimes these can lead to unlikely alliances, such as the joint campaign for the regeneration of the Devon town of Exmouth by the local civic society, the Chamber of Commerce and Friends of the Earth. And there are a vast range of other activities, from collecting books for Russia and parcels for Bosnia, to supporting charities (a rising trend), credit unions, housing cooperatives, anti-crime initiatives and 'friends' of hospitals. Some of these – for instance, the involvement of parents in schools – have been fostered by Conservative governments, others (the local environmental campaigns) are seen as hostile to the political establishment. In most cases, any connection with the formal, inherited democratic system is haphazard or coincidental at best. Yet it looks as if, wherever people feel they can make a difference, or affect real things, they are as prepared to be political as ever they were.

Even if the word community is in danger of becoming so over-used that it is subsiding into bland nothingness, the instinctive turn to it by so many is itself an important sign; a feeling in the herd that something has gone wrong and requires corrective (not to say collective) action. Critics of the trend remind us that communities were not always liberating. Bauman puts it vividly:

modernity spent most of its time and a lot of its energy on fighting communities – those larger-than-life groupings into which people are born, only to be held inside them for the rest of their lives by the dead hand of tradition strengthened by collective surveillance and blackmail.[13]

It is also true that the interconnectedness and technological richness of modern life make the traditional village or small-town community difficult to recover – even if we wanted to do so. The rising level of violence in many Western societies, or at least the rising fear of violence, puts many people off the idea that they should go about poking their noses into other people's business. Whether it be Michael Howard's much-mocked enthusiasm as Home Secretary for people 'walking with a purpose' or Etzioni's 'gentle prodding', many are too frightened of a biff on the poking nose, or worse, to be interested in a revival of neighbourliness. And, on the other side of the street, many of us value the freedom from twitching curtains and pointing fingers, the ability to be different, to be unconventional and to live our lives unscrutinized by others who may have a more censorious, or simply different, moral code. Geographic 'communities' can be hard on, or savage to, other sorts of 'community', be they Asian, or gay or simply eccentric. Local communities too can be coldly selfish about keeping out the less attractive things that cities and countries require – mental homes, prisons, new housing developments, even sewage works and local dumps.

Yet it would be wrong to brush aside this contemporary fascination with community as illiberal or irrelevant. It may be vague, even woolly. It may not be a new idea. It may be open to abuse. But it is also, quite simply, a return to the values that have sustained human societies for a very long time, and which seem pertinent today precisely because of the opposite pressure of globalization. Wendell Berry, the American writer, has put his finger on the pulse of this truth:

Can a university, or a nation, *afford* this exclusive rule of competition, this purely economic economy? The great fault of this approach to things is that it is so drastically reductive; it does not permit us to live and work as human beings, as the best of our inheritance defines us. Rats and roaches live by competition under the law of supply and demand; it is the privilege of human beings to live under the laws of justice and mercy. It is impossible not to notice how little the proponents of competition have to say about honesty, which is the fundamental economic virtue, and how *very* little they have to say about community, compassion and mutual help.[14]

It may then be objected that 'all this community stuff' is 'mere words' and lacks a firm programme, a leader, a manifesto. I think this is to misunderstand how political change happens. The ideas always come first, and are disseminated, and take root if they accord with the daily experience and instincts of enough people. As we have seen, some of this instinct is being put into practice, more commonly than the national political conversation has yet noticed. But even for the majority of citizens who are not involved in schools, churches or whatever, the emotional charge of 'community' matters. Dreams of past Edens have always been one of the chief spurs to political change, an emotional resource which overwhelms the fact of whether that past Eden actually existed or not. Contemporary reformers' feelings for a lost community, which they would like to regain, can be compared to the ancient idea of liberty, the belief that 'once upon a time' we were all free. For the English, it was the distant and confused folk memory of 'Cockaigne', the land of milk and honey commonly supposed to have been in decline since the Norman conquest. That, at any rate, was how generations of English reformers and radicals saw the matter − a political paradise lost, or at least always decayed in their own time, yet always retrievable, too. The radicals on the winning side in the English Civil War believed that 'the land is now to be set free from the slavery of the Norman conquest.' That inspired and rough-tongued rogue John Wilkes, scribbling furiously to the electors of Middlesex from the King's Bench prison in London, on 5 May 1768, reminded them of 'the generous plans of freedom, which were the boast of our ancestors, and I think will remain the noblest inheritance of our posterity, the only genuine characteristic of Englishmen.' Without that belief, however historically suspect, British radicalism would have lost one of its chief motors. Today, few mourn the arrival of the Conqueror or the decline of Anglo-Saxon freedoms but, in a small way, our memory of a kinder, gentler, more community-minded country, located variously in the thirties, forties or fifties, is a political memory of some significance too. In Britain, of all countries, the revolutionary power of nostalgia and bad history should never be underestimated.

Community is code for the countervailing force to economic globalism, the democratic instinct, the essential missing element to the faster-moving, rougher and world-sized economy whose effects have inspired and haunted these pages. Those who make it more than words will come from all political backgrounds, and none. There is, for instance, the wasting moral energy that has been dammed and frustrated by the failure of the socialist project − a great impulse to answer the first political question of all, which is 'how should we live together?' Socialism, as a programme dependent upon high taxes, specific statist levers and solutions, is dead. But is it therefore the case that all the energy which powered the socialist dream has simply evaporated into the far blue yonder, doing its bit for global warming? After all, the earlier socialists worked through communities, whether industrial ones or through local councils, or by doing social work and organization in the poorest areas − as Attlee did. In a book on civil society the British thinker Ernest Gellner describes how the political failure of the seventeenth-century English puritan revolution helped kick-start the greater revolution of capitalism:

obliged to renounce their ambition of imposing righteousness on earth if necessary by military and political force, [the once-extremist puritans] turn instead to pacifism and tolerance. Their efforts to impose righteousness on earth are defeated, but they are not so crushed as to be prevented from practising righteousness within their own moral ghetto ... Unable to ensure that the will of God be done on earth as it is in heaven, they turn inward, impose it on themselves, and in the outer world turn towards productive activity as much as to religious zeal. Or rather, they turn to economic activity, practising it with religious zeal and disinterestedness. Only such Platonic, pure, disinterested acquisitiveness could engender that work ethic and sustained accumulation which produces a modern economy.[15]

Perhaps the failure of the project to impose socialist righteousness on earth by military and political force may have, over time, a similarly dramatic and unexpected coda. Is it impossible that tens of thousands of people will quietly and slowly regather their energetic altruism, and take it back into the world around them – that is, their communities – and achieve a raggeder, grander change, as the Puritans did, though, of course, with rather different results?

A few Bad Ideas

My final suggestion, though, is a simpler and less controversial one. It is merely that we cannot propose and carry through a successful reform of our politics without relating it to the economic and mental background described above. These changes are the reality, the moral and intellectual environment in which we have to test and fashion our political system. A democracy is not simply a mechanism, but the spirit in the machine too, something that exists to express the human purposes and fears of the times in which it operates. So how does this surrounding mood connect to the power-system described in the book?

We can agree, first, that there is something approaching a consensus about the problems of social division, increasingly fast change and insecurity thrown up by globalization; hardly anybody, from the right, left or centre, politician or writer, business executive or philosopher, thinks it can simply be switched off. Similarly, the critics of what has been happening to us are almost all united in the view that, like patriotism, the market is not enough – not enough morally, but not enough economically, either. Unprotected by a wider system of human and social values, the global market is inclined to eat away at the foundations of its own success. Its inbuilt acceleration and frenetic apportionment of success and failure are, left alone, incompatible with a long-term economic community. They are not enough to nourish secure, forward-looking and confident people who will defer gratification, educate themselves, think about longer-term choices, and invest. To do these things, people need to feel that the future may be benign; and to feel mutual trust and belonging. And if market mechanisms are not enough, then the only other mechanisms are political ones. It takes us straight back to the condition of the democracy.

Were we to stop there, this climate of opinion might amount to an uncomplicated call for a return to the leftish consensual and paternalist politics of the pre-Thatcher era. This would be a disaster to try and impossible to do. That political model, already in crisis by the mid-seventies, has been killed by the global economy and by the communications revolution. And it looks as if the big shifts of power from the nation-state discussed in earlier chapters are mostly irreversible; the levers in the Treasury and other parts of Whitehall have finally been disconnected from real life. The man in Whitehall hasn't a clue, or any more of a clue than any of the rest of us, and this is now obvious. High-tax, high-spending policies from a Labour administration would bring swift and brutal punishment, meted out on the economy, that is the people, as a whole. The old state bureaucracies no longer answer to the impatient needs and standards of a people tutored in consumerism and choice; in business, the state models of ownership have failed everywhere, and have been rightly described by Hamish McRae as 'one of the most unsuccessful forms of corporate ownership ever developed, lasting less than fifty years, in contrast to partnerships, co-operatives and joint-stock companies, all of which have stood the test of several centuries.'[16] In short, social cohesion and 'community' cannot be bought or imposed according to methods developed by socialist and liberal intellectuals in the first half of the century. That world has died; kneeling by the bedside and lisping 'community' twenty times won't bring it back.

But the Conservatives have had no coherent solution to offer, either. As they see themselves, or those quoted earlier do, there is an inherent contradiction between traditionalist Toryism, with its emphasis on hierarchy, order, continuity, duty; and the effects of market liberalization, which flatten old hierarchies, produce and require a world of dynamic disorder, and are the antithesis of continuity. This is a philosophical contradiction. It's a moral dilemma too, clearly, and a political one for Conservatives struggling to maintain respect for 'the institutions' alongside the economic dynamism that brushes them aside. The new economics is not easily compatible with a conservative social order because it demands questioning, discontinuity, change. Some conservative orders have adapted to it, notably the Japanese one, but ours has not and there are no signs of a reversion to a country in which people 'know their place' – even the most malign model which presupposes a sort of economic apartheid, in which the failures are excluded and the rich majority continue to vote for lower taxes and less politics. That model was lambasted by the liberal economist J.K. Galbraith as the 'culture of contentment', in which two-thirds did well and let the other third go to hell. It was savaged too by the American intellectual Christopher Lasch as 'the revolt of the élites' who had bought themselves a privatized and privileged existence and 'removed themselves from common life.'[17] It was also described with more relish by the American sociologist Charles Murray, who argued that Britain was in the process of dividing into a middle class of 'New Victorians' who were virtuous, hard-working and lived away from state institutions; and a 'new rabble' pullulating in housing estates and living off welfare.

It wasn't so long ago that this seemed a plausible future for us, in which the state, incompetent, disliked and unable to command assent for its taxation, would wither. The middle classes would shop in huge, protected malls, live in private estates guarded by private security firms, run their children to private schooling, and rely solely on private health care. The privatization of life, with the sharp division it brings between those who can afford to exercise choice as shoppers, not voters, and the ostracized minority of failures, would continue, even accelerate. Just as the rich of Beverly Hills know nothing of the gang-world of South-central Los Angeles so close to them, so Britain and France and other European countries too would arrange themselves into an ever more distinct system of economic division. This may not have been a pleasant prospect. But, with the spread of private security firms, private prisons, and the promotion of private health and education, it seemed a possible one.

It doesn't now. There aren't enough secure successes in middle Britain to sustain a stable system of economic apartheid. The impact of change on the middle classes has not produced a comfortable or smug voting majority who can afford to turn their backs and live well in mental ghettos. In the words of the writer Matthew Symonds, that 'culture of contentment' described by Galbraith has proved to be at best 'a fragile commodity mixed with trepidation and foreboding' – middle-class complacency has given way 'to an unprecedented (for the middle classes) culture of anxiety.'[18] Politically, that suggests an erosion of the Conservative vote, as fundamental economic change and decades of underinvestment dampen the effect of the recovery on middle-class incomes and prospects. Sitting at the controls of the traditional nation-state, the right can try to produce a wealth-friendly and competitive culture, but is no more able to promise good times for the majority than the left was in the seventies. It has the further handicap of basing its appeal and authority on an established Church, Parliament and Monarchy which seem in their impotence and confusion less relevant to the harassed electorate than ever. Some may stay with the Tories and tax cuts, though feeling deeply cynical about the promises of security made by them. Others may turn to Labour or the Liberal Democrats, hankering after another form of security which, as we have seen, is not honestly on offer either.

Either way, to carry on with the traditional remedies looks like a recipe for more disillusion and ever sourer cynicism. Where does that lead? There are plenty of bad political solutions on offer, plenty of paperback nightmares – a revival of the nationalisms, whipped up perhaps by right-wingers desperate to exploit fear of European Union and Scottish Home Rule. There is the protectionist answer, which is very close to xenophobia and whose last outing, in the thirties, hardly produced a safer or happier future. There is the possibility of a left-of-centre administration trying to rule as if this were the sixties, failing badly because of that and producing a further period of political drift and government ineffectiveness, ending perhaps in some unforeseeable political convulsion and an attempted return to authoritarian-style politics.

Back in the Real World

Are any of these scenarios likely? No, frankly, not very. A country which largely avoided the excesses of xenophobia and authoritarianism in the extraordinary conditions of the Second World War seems unlikely to be driven to them by Chinese imports and redundancies at Barclays Bank. For, on the 'plus' side, we still retain a strong political culture, in the widest sense; good civic traditions; and a certain store of native wit. As Professor Anthony King has noted, hardly anyone thinks that there is any defensible alternative to democracy as a political system. Although liberalism may have triumphed over politics across much of life, democracy remains the key Western creed. If we are outraged by something done by those in power, we are far likelier to say 'that's not very democratic' than 'that's

not very liberal'. If democracy is partly about understanding
that everyone else has a valid point of view and the right to be
heard, then our culture is saturated with the spirit of democracy.
The multi-viewpoint was invented by nineteenth-century novelists and has been diffused into popular fiction and film narrative
ever since. We instinctively feel that, in the words of the
irritating British Telecom advert, 'it's good to talk'. We are a
tolerant culture whose TV soaps and dramas pump out the
virtues of tolerance night after night. We have racists and bigots
of all kinds, but the common culture seems to be becoming
more liberal, not less.

And although party-political activity has declined, for very
sound reasons, this is not true of political activity at its widest.
The agitations against the poll tax or the Criminal Justice Act,
or the M11 roadbuilders, or the export of live animals by boat,
or the Child Support Agency, are examples of a contemporary
protest politics that involves huge numbers of citizens, focusing
their attention narrowly perhaps, but more effectively for all
that. It is limited; pressure-group politics cannot, by definition,
balance one social good against a complex array of others,
which is what politicians are elected to do. In the nineteenth
century it was said that the Russian political system amounted
to despotism tempered by assassination; sometimes it seems as
if ours now amounts to centralism tempered by the *Today*
programme. But it shows that, wherever politics touches them,
people are still easily roused and formidably active. This is not
the land of passive, doped consumerists that some have painted.

This ought to make the professionals all the more embarrassed
about the inadequacies and failures of the Old Constitution in
their trust. Cynicism about national politics doesn't derive from
an innate failure among voters, but from their experiences of it:
it is, I repeat, rational. Nor is it the case that it is too difficult to
reconnect voters and the political process. On the contrary, it
has never been easier. There is a literate, well-informed, opinionated public, connected as never before by a range of media. The
inadequacies of the press and broadcasting as constitutional
checks on executive power have already been described; but

they remain political channels of great power. New systems of sampling opinion and discussing issues have already been mentioned – the ways in which technology could make local and national referendums easier, the possibilities of citizens' juries and 'deliberative polling'. Where direct democracy has been offered, as in local referendums on the ownership of the water industry and nuclear waste dumping in Scotland, they have been popular. No doubt there are many difficulties with all this. But it is perhaps time for politicians to start thinking more about how to rebuild the democracy than whingeing perpetually about the difficulties of doing so. Ignoring change has never been an effective way of preventing it. There is, in short, no reason to be depressive about our basic political culture or the possibility of reasonably effective reform of its institutions. This is not a hopeless case.

What is to be done?

There are numerous sophisticated and carefully thought out plans for political reform in Britain, and many specific ideas have been referred to throughout this book. It would be tedious and otiose to produce now, another, mostly familiar list: there will be enough manifestos shortly. Much more to the point is to try to clear our minds about what powers are fit to be held where and by whom, and so to find a way in which those manifestos may be fairly judged.

The highest function of the state is to protect our political culture. Globalization is shifting the economic culture, and is producing an opposite, though not yet equal, impulse towards the local. But between them stands the nation-state, challenged radically by both impulses, yet replaceable by neither. Its history and hold on the imagination, as well as its institutions, will remain important to our democracy for the foreseeable future. The state's responsibility for the sustenance of that democracy involves, naturally, responsibility for the physical defence of these islands, and the need to ensure that its people do not fall under the political authority of another power. But it also involves the need to maintain the democratic culture and mechanisms so that they remain potent, even against the global forces. This is not a forlorn hope: the apportionment of power, for instance, between multinational companies, which have capital and know-how, and national governments, which have territory and markets, is not all one-way. But it does mean that national politicians will have to rethink the business they're in.

It means that the continuous negotiations between supranational forces, whether they be Honda or Nato, and the national democracy must be more visible, and the choices faced by the democracy in each case be made plainer. Increasingly, the prime job of national leaders will be not to conclude the deal, or sign the treaty (though they will have to do those things, obviously) but to explain the consequences and options to Parliament and the voters. The biggest recent example has been European Union. Though I am a pro-European, I don't think it would be a catastrophe if we left the Union. On balance, it would represent a loss of power because we would remain, for the purposes of trading with the Continent, subject to regulations about trade, technical standards, and many other things. But instead of being decided in a system in which we were a minority player, they would be decided by our competitors in meetings we had excluded ourselves from. For instance, the fact that we got more out of the world trade negotiations from being part of a bloc than we would have won as a single-nation participant must be balanced against the frustrations and disbenefits of lost national autonomy over a whole range of other things, from fishing rights to environmental standards. The current trend in our political culture, which is for one lot of people to complain ever more angrily about the loss of power to the European Union, while the other lot connive in the bureaucratic and undemocratic haggling that constitutes its everyday reality, denying all the time that anything has changed, is surely a recipe for political failure. It pushes us either towards leaving, or towards a publicly-denied and endless series of compromises by a Europhile establishment which has lost the faith of its voters. Instead we need a European agenda which focuses first on the real benefits and penalties of membership, unclouded by economic determinism or nationalistic posturing; and which then turns to how Europeanism can be made compatible with the democracy we have inherited.

That means structural change, like opening up the council of ministers and perhaps the minimalist federalism I discussed earlier on. But it also means the culture has to adapt, so that ministers are able to say openly that they lost that argument, or gave that concession, in return for X or Y. If we carry on pretending that every encounter in the EU is a defeat or a victory, the humiliating failure of some 'Brussels poodle' or, alternatively, 'game, set and match' to Britain, rather than a set of trade-offs, compromises and deals, then we might as well leave now. If we want to retain a simplistic, nationalistic rhetoric then we cannot function successfully in the European Union and the only question is when, not if, the rupture occurs. More generally, we desperately need to get away from 'government' as a private series of meetings between ministers or officials, and others, which are then presented for outside consumption as heroic political successes. This is not peripheral to political reform. It is essential if we are to mesh our democracy into the wider world. The dream of some on the right, which is to restore the old, free nation-state as before, repelling all the multitudinous hustlers in the market for power and influence – the lobbyists, the international corporations, the global organizations, the unpredictable market-makers, the European bureaucrats, the journalists, the judges, the pressure-groupies, the environmentalists – seems to me mere romanticism, a game doomed to failure because it cuts against the grain of almost every modern economic and social development. The world's political economy is growing more complex, loud and interconnected. It is speeding up. And it doesn't look as if it is about to become simpler and slower again. For national politicians, including ours, shouting down this babble is impossible, and pretending not to hear it is plain ridiculous. But the cacophony of modern life does summon up another, older model of leadership.

It cries out be interpreted. If 'leadership' is to mean anything useful now, it must surely be about plain-speaking – explaining the world to busy and distracted citizens, giving advance warning of new problems and dangers, teasing out the choices that need to be made and, ideally, giving a sense of forward movement and purpose. Charles Handy has put the argument very well, though he is referring more to company executives than MPs:

Only those in the centre can have a view of the whole. They cannot run it, and should be too few in number to be tempted, but they can nudge, influence and, if they have to, interfere. The centre's principal task is to be the trustee of the future, but it needs to ensure that the present does not run out before the future arrives.[19]

That seems to me to be about as good a description of right national leadership under our new conditions as I can think of. But it is not, of course, a good description of how our leaders actually behave. To be trustees and describers, they need to learn to speak more freely than the conventions of party competition and collective responsibility have allowed them to. In professional mode they seem, so often, to automatically switch off that part of themselves which is best and most thoughtful, and switch on a pre-recorded message. As a result the nation, which does not like recorded messages, tends to hang up. When a politician, either by accident or through an involuntary eruption of human feeling, speaks normally, we tend to sit up, suddenly alert again. (I think of Tony Blair talking about his children's schooling, or Kenneth Clarke talking about Tory rebels, or John Major's quirkily personal defence of the boringness of government at the 1994 party conference.)

These are, however, exceptions to the glum rule. Where we have badly needed frank and serious discussions about the pros and cons of a floating exchange rate, of sustainable development, of the British interest in Bosnia, we have had instead low-grade party badinage or defensive whuffle. Most of us have been growing increasingly worried about the curious weather changes and have been wondering whether, and how much, we will have to change our lifestyles if there is a serious threat from global warming. Many people are already changing their behaviour and are ready to change it more. But the political leaders have not led this most intensely political of national conversations. There has been the odd flurry of interest, as when Margaret Thatcher was said to have 'gone green'. But, given the importance of the subject, you might have expected it to be something they regularly and publicly talked about. Far from it. Or think, turning from the supranational to the national, of the outpouring of grief and depression caused by the killing in Liverpool of Jamie Bulger by two children. Again, one might have hoped for a serious debate about whether something had gone wrong with our attitude to children. But politicians, by and large, left all that to the newspaper writers and engaged instead in the familiar, tedious and party-ridden dogfight about whether there are links between crime and unemployment. The issues that set arguments going among ordinary Britons – animal rights, the legalization of drugs, the effectiveness of prison – are things that elected politicians tend to flinch from as being too difficult, too awkwardly outside the old left-right language. No wonder people turn away.

Political authority is not God-given, or even Queen-given. Once it depended upon the military prowess and success of the state; and then, later, on the size and importance of the institutions the politicians ran, and the contract offered by them through the welfare state. Increasingly now, political authority is going to have to be earned and won through the persuasiveness of the arguments, the clarity of the vision and the honesty of the words. This has led some to ask, who needs professional politicians in a world where power is dispersing so fast, where old national structures are disintegrating, and where citizens are so well-informed already? This is too neat. If politicians make sense, they will regain authority. If their words seem to be true, and their perceptions mesh with the world the rest of us live in, they will add to that authority. They will have more chance of becoming trusted and powerful negotiators at supranational level. No programme of political reforms is going to restore the nation-state to its earlier prominence, or prevent the winds of economic change sweeping across Europe. No one has yet found life's reverse button. But politicians who try relentlessly to focus on the essentials and speak vividly about them, rather than continuing as the evasive and competing administrators of decrepit institutions, may find that, after all, there is a golden age ahead.

Honesty about the political culture and relevance from its leaders, then: maybe we should go for free supplies of Ben & Jerry's ice-cream and the abolition of unemployment while we're about it? All I am sure of is that, when it comes to political reform, it would be a bad blunder to start with the mechanics. We have to start with the political spirit and language. If the House of Commons was redesigned and the language of current politics remained unaltered, then we would have no reform. Plain speaking about the condition of our political culture is the first essential. Without it, no serious conversation can happen, nor can a sense of proportion be developed, nor can the priorities and the relationship between different reforms be considered.

With it, though, we have only begun. I would like to start not with the now familiar remedies of bills of rights or a freedom of information act, valuable though they be. I would propose sorting out the constitutional mess over sovereignty, and who has it, with a one-clause, one-sentence act of Parliament declaring simply that the British people were sovereign, the ultimate masters and mistresses of their own political destiny. This would have two virtues. First, it would be true. Second, it would be a clarifying, liberating and cheering-up act, which is more than can be said for most acts. That said, however, any reform programme must quickly turn to the condition of Parliament itself. This remains at the heart of the democratic system we have inherited, and which we have failed to properly maintain in this generation. One of the most important things to remember about our democracy is that it is more recent and fragile than we tend to think. The suggestion that British democracy is threatened by the dislocation of power from electoral machinery looks a lot less wild when we remember how short a time that democracy has been in business. Politically, we are only the second or third generation of democratic frontier-families and a bewilderingly few human lifespans take us back to a country where the very idea of democracy was regarded as ludicrous. British democracy is younger than most pensioners alive today – it was only in 1928, after the final victory of the suffragettes, that some 97 per cent of adults over twenty-one were included. Yet we have tended to assume that a working knowledge of democratic machinery, rather than its spirit, is somehow innate in these islands, passed on like a stamp on the birth certificate. One very modest reform, which would cost little, would be to ensure that every British child left school well-educated in citizenship and the basics of the democratic system, knowing their political rights and how to use them, and educated in their political duties too, having met the local MP, councillors, opposition party representatives, and so on. Specialism has become our great educational disease; it sometimes seems as if we have forgotten that we must educate our children to be good people and good citizens first – and good doctors, or lawyers or engineers second.

When it comes to the workplace of the MPs themselves, many of the necessary measures are obvious. I hope they have virtually suggested themselves in earlier passages of this book. But, again, it is right to look at the reforms from a simple perspective: what should Parliament be for in a modern state? It is there to sustain a government and to pass legislation, of course. But if it fails to be the centre of democratic legitimacy the heart of its function has been lost. The sprawling and insufficiently-accountable domestic state is therefore a matter for parliamentarians themselves. They must, above all else, reassert their authority over the patronage state based at Downing Street. This is their high task which, if refused or evaded, makes the further decline of Parliament inevitable. If, as the theorists assert, Parliament really is sovereign, then there can be no reason why MPs should not agree that the heads of executive agencies, and of the big quangos, and of many other public bodies with real power over our lives, should be confirmed in their jobs by parliamentary committees, and hold them subject to parliamentary approval. Most of the executive powers held by ministers subject to 'Royal Prerogative' could, and should, be similarly brought under the control of the Commons, as should the appointment of judges, since they now operate what is in effect a supreme court system. For better scrutiny of the activities of the executive, Parliament should insist that the main value-for-money watchdogs, the National Audit Office and the Audit Commission, are merged and are allowed to report directly to select committees. And if one wanted to be really radical about a revival of parliamentary power, there is a case for making the appointment of all members of the government subject to a vote of the Commons. In most cases, assuming a majority administration, this would be a formality, but it would give individual ministers more weight in the system than they have as the temporary appointees, sackable by whim, of the Prime Minister.

Similarly, if we are concerned to rebuild the democratic power of the Commons, it is hard to defend the retention of a hereditary second chamber; there is a strong case for outright abolition of the Lords, but there are also various sensible and less drastic alternatives. The removal of speaking and voting rights from hereditary peers, as suggested by Labour, is a reasonable though modest first step. In the Commons, the processing of legislation is an absurdity and could be greatly improved if MPs took evidence from the interested parties and the public before considering the bill in detail – as has been proposed for the Scottish Parliament by the cross-party Scottish Constitutional Convention. Then again, is it sensible to have a bill committee, a collection of former teachers, garage-owners, trade union officials and so on, struggling (or not) with the legal language in which bills finally appear? There are various possible solutions. A plain-English explanation of the bill could be appended, produced in sufficient detail to be amended and debated. It would then be available for the courts thereafter if controversies arose about what Parliament had intended – though the courts can now consult parliamentary debates for this purpose, following the 1992 Pepper v. Hart case. Better, perhaps, for Parliament to provide expert legal advice to backbenchers and opposition front-benchers, thus balancing the playing field and making up for the decline in the numbers of lawyers in Parliament. Either change would greatly help committees make sense of the laws-to-be that confront them.

These are only a few of the many ideas available for making the Parliament of these islands matter again; they would vastly increase its effectiveness. Today, they may seem a dream. But we come back to the need for politicians to reconsider their own language and status before they sink completely from the intellectual radar of their fellow citizens. Either Members of Parliament are significant people or they are not. If they want to be taken seriously, then the restoration of their Parliament is entirely in their own hands and could be achieved in a matter of months. And if they are not inclined to bother, then they can hardly complain when the rest of the country continues to ignore them or sneer at their pretensions.

Since I have proposed a prolonged and hungry raiding-party upon ministerial powers by the Parliament, it may seem odd to go on to propose further measures to strengthen the ministers. But restoring the proper powers of Parliament (I think in particular of its mid-nineteenth century heyday) is entirely compatible with clearing more space for senior ministers to think and act. Today, they are overburdened with sordid administrative tasks and excessive demands from a multiplying number of media outlets for instant comment and policy-making on the hoof (or the buttocks, rather, as they shift uneasily from government Rover to radio studio and back again). They don't have to do this. Nor is it vital that the prime minister continues to try and fail to run the nation from a rambling and ad-hoc mini-bureaucracy that is itself overwhelmed by the day-to-day and the inessential. Number Ten is not the miraculous machine that its inhabitants sometimes pretend it is; there is a case for having a proper Prime Minister's Department, with a cabinet minister whose full-time job would be to progress-chase the premier's initiatives through Whitehall and, where necessary, to speak for him, or her. This wouldn't stop weak or foolish prime ministers from making mistakes. Its lack won't prevent good ones from succeeding, at least some of the time. But such reforms would improve the odds in both cases. And that would not be a bad thing.

Take, next, the civil service. There was a case for introducing more people from the private sector into Whitehall. The creation of agencies has produced a more efficient despatch of business. But no one, it seems, bothered to sit down and ask what this meant for the ethics of public service upon which all modern politics rests, even though there were numerous instances of problems. The original constitution of our civil service, the Northcote-Trevelyan report of 1854, was intended to clearly map out a space for public service, outside the reach of political patronage. The fulfilled ambition was to create 'an efficient body of permanent officers ... possessing sufficient independence, character, ability and experience ...' and to eradicate the old, sleaze-tainted culture which Edmund Burke had described as 'a sort of temperate bed of influence; a sort of gently ripening hot-house.'[20] Producing a clean, clear area for public administration was a great and lasting achievement. One would have thought that any tampering with it, however necessary, would have produced a serious debate first and a cautious response afterwards. But no; all we had was a sudden coup followed by bland assertions that nothing had changed, even when it was clear to everyone involved that something fundamental had changed. Civil servants need a new kind of contract, and a new kind of training, if the essence of Northcote-Trevelyan is to be saved.

Or take the growth of judicial review and the arrival of what is in effect a Bill of Rights from Europe; a supreme law. This is a matter of some importance. You would have expected politicians to draw it to the country's attention and provoke a national debate about these changes. Has any senior minister tried to do so – issued speeches, tabled parliamentary motions? No. To get a frank acknowledgement of the issue you have to go to lawyers and judges, or an obscure piece of evidence to a Select Committee.

There was no move to go the obvious further step and patriate those rights in British law. It has been more convenient for the executive to keep mum, exploit the fact that the European journey for British people seeking justice takes longer and deny the scale of what has happened. And this despite the fact that modest moves to repatriate a Bill of Rights by Lord Lester was backed by some of the most eminent legal minds in the country. And if we look at the piecemeal and reactive lurches towards the greater independence of the Bank of England in 1992–94, or the creation in different bills in 1988 of a huge new network of locally-planted patronage for schools, hospitals, training and the like. We find the same trend, of real changes to the constitution, reacting to changes in the world outside, yet rarely frankly acknowledged and discussed for what they are. This is not sturdy pragmatism; it is the decadence of a political system utterly lacking in self-confidence.

The biggest test for a revived political culture comes, however, when the centre contemplates the threat from below – from local government and community politics. A beleaguered, retreating political culture will be inclined, as ours has been, to try to stamp down on regionalism and localism. But this would be disastrous. It would be to deny the ability of the British to respond to the pressures of global power by shoring up those parts of the democracy which are, or could be, nearest to them. It would be to reject those structures which may be most effective in giving a sense of rootedness and belonging, and offering some ownership of our immediate environment. It would be, for those reasons, a profoundly outdated nationalist attitude. Much of the anti-European rhetoric about unaccountable bureaucracy, centralization, lack of understanding of local conditions applies just as forcibly to British government. Is it really sensible that Whitehall should in effect dictate the planning policies of towns across England, or the details of what is taught in every school, or that the Scots must be denied the measures of control over their own affairs they have wanted for so long? It may be sensible that local schools, hospitals and training organizations are not owned or managed directly through the elected councils; but is it reasonable that the elected councils have no voice at all, on behalf of the local residents, parents and patients, in how they are run? At root, the proposal that local services should best be overseen by secretive and unelected boards of ministerial appointees is a deeply insulting one. It implies that, in a hierarchy of political values, the convenience of the central state comes higher than a sturdy, responsive democracy. It suggests that the voters are not in general capable of running their own affairs, as if (like the Scots) they cannot be trusted by grown-up politicians in London.

As with the Scottish Parliament, there are numerous questions to be raised and answered about a new settlement for the local governance of Britain. Labour toyed with the idea of English regional assemblies, then backed away a bit. As we saw earlier, there is a tier of regional government through the civil service, and there are jobs for the regional level – particularly in negotiating with Brussels, considering transport planning and so on. These do not need a directly elected assembly, at least not yet, but some form of indirectly elected regional chamber or body would be useful and may come to seem essential. For local authorities themselves, some of the answers have been bandied for years – annual elections for a third of the councillors, elected mayors, paid chairmanships, referendums wherever increased spending beyond a certain limit is proposed. It certainly must not be centralized, bureaucratic local government in the old way. As Michael Howard has pointed out, opponents of the Tory changes 'mistakenly equate local communities with local authorities'.[21] (Though centrally-controlled, party-politicized quangos don't equate with local communities, either, minister.) Instead, one can imagine a system of local councils with regulatory powers, which worked through contracts and devolved more power to neighbourhood councils, community schools and the like. Councillors would cease to be largely administrators, burdened with endless Westminster-mimicking committees and could become more obviously the leaders of their communities, with freedom to encourage local experiments, put groups in touch with one another, and so on. Such authorities, and such councillors, would be powerful agents for reviving the sense of local pride and identity which is latent and living everywhere in Britain.

The opposition parties, and some Tories, have already done serious thinking about how to rebuild local and community government in Britain; but on their past record they cannot be trusted by themselves. They have screwed this up too often before. We need the leaders of local authorities, local community groups and others to lead a much wider debate about what the well-run neighbourhood of 2010 might look like, and the parliamentarians to hang back until there is something approaching a consensus about what reforms are needed. The ideal would be for the main parties to eventually agree a set of principles for local government which could then give it a chance of surviving unscathed and unfiddled-about-with for more than a few years. For that to happen, the party politicians have to consider the matter not merely as something that touches their own political organizations, friends and interests, but as a question of good governance generally. A lot to ask? Yes, but this is the flip-side of the agenda which starts with Parliament reasserting its authority over the patronage state. Once it has refound the proper national democratic task for itself, it can afford to disburse and pass down those more local jobs for which it is not suited and never was suited.

This might be Utopian, were it not that such a transfer of political power would be moving with the grain of economic and social change, not against it. There are simply far more adults at home these days, either because of the casualization of work, or unemployment, or technological changes. The 'home working' revolution has been long trumpeted but has now actually started to arrive; one estimate is that 15 per cent of the salaried workforce is now using home computer technology, and that 45 per cent of the British workforce is involved in some way in the processing of information. Among the British employers running 'teleworking' schemes now are the National Westminster Bank, Sainsburys, Shell, Allied Dunbar, Trusthouse

Forte, BP, British Gas, ICL, Mercury Communications, Rank Xerox, British Telecom and Grand Metropolitan.[22] Many more people are also said to be working from home than most employers acknowledge. Include the growth of freelance, 'contract culture' work, plus early retirement and stagnant house prices, and it adds up to a social change of some political significance. It suggests the growth of a more local, informed political base than at any time during the era of mass industrialization and state bureaucracy. These will be people for whom the immediate environment – its criminality, its parks, its transport, its level of pollution, the behaviour of its children, the quality of the skills training on offer – will be more important than ever. These are presumably some of the people responsible for the rebirth of community politics, campaigning and 'civil society' described earlier. Nor is it the case that local democracy need be impotent beside the big social and economic changes that have caused such problems for the Old Constitution. American states' experiments with direct democracy have affected company taxation and environmental standards, while the Swiss referendum system discussed earlier allowed one small canton to block the EU's road network plans. If there is to be any hope of democratizing the EU from the inside, then local initiatives have surely to be part of the counterbalance to Brussels bureaucracy. When communities have the mechanisms and ability to speak for themselves, it is far harder for centralists based in Belgium, as well as in London, to override them.

Some people shiver at the thought of stronger local democracy, on the grounds that it is bound to turn illiberal, to divide up the nation between rich areas and poor ones, to produce little local xenophobias and reinforce village bigotries. These are dangers, though it seems to me that our political culture is liberal enough and strong enough for this not to be a threat across most of the country. But this is another area where an effective national politics could regain its authority and popularity, acting as the guardian of our rights and individual liberties – in Handy's words, nudging, influencing and sometimes interfering. There is no inevitable conflict between national political power and local power. It is only the decadence of our political system that makes us suppose one can only survive by grinding down the other. There will always be tensions. But, across the world, constitutions exist to define the relationship and, after all, the country is a sort of bigger local community too, albeit offering another sense of belonging, and bound together by history, language, cliffs and government, rather than by streets and families.

All that amounts to a brief pencil sketch of what a reformed political system might look like and feel like. I have tried to avoid theory and abstract constitutional analysis about rights and principles. Instead, I hope to have convinced the reader by now that a political reformation is necessary – not a convulsion, necessarily, but rather more than the sort of Glorious Evolution which some of our Conservative writers believe is the inevitable British way. The question is whether we choose to reform our political machinery so that it fits with the new conditions; or whether we complacently burble on ('our ancient institutions . . . stood the test of time . . . Queen in Parliament . . . sovereignty of the British people . . .') while the great forces of our time silently strip away their power and meaning. We are, let's face it, quite capable of making the wrong choice. We have been stroppy and disputatious as a people, and shown collective bravery and, more rarely, some wisdom too. But we have also inclined to various democratic sins – such as sloth and complacency. In each generation there is a contest between reform and reaction, which is never predictable. Political history, like any other, is the tale of forks in the road, and paths untaken. We start afresh each generation or so, a single road behind us, but many new choices ahead. That being so, it is possible for us to wander down paths that lead to the toppling of real democratic control, particularly if the undemocratic path seems comfortable and prosperous.

Will reform happen? That depends on the British people. In the end, of course, it will be carried, or dropped, by the small class of professional politicians themselves. A further Conservative victory would presumably mean the spread of quangos and a further squeeze on local government – or, if it would not, it would be interesting to hear what they do suggest. But the politicians' actions will depend on the rest of us. Tories need to press their leaders about what they really think of Parliament's effectiveness, of the dangers of the interpenetration of business culture and public-service culture, of the slow arrival of a supranational layer of law and rights. Reform is, pretty obviously, likelier to happen under Labour, and likelier still under a Lib-Lab coalition. My guess is that there would be no grand blueprint and that Labour would charge at a few selected changes, including Scottish Home Rule, the incorporation of a European bill of rights into British law, a referendum on voting reform, and reform of the Lords, and that these would prove bitterly contested. But, if a few large stones are removed from the current edifice, the whole may start to slide and crumble. For instance, the existence of a Scottish Parliament would raise a whole series of questions about the relationship of the rest of Britain to London; and about the way Westminster works, and possibly about the voting system too. Yet if reform is to happen that way, then here too the country needs to have thought harder about what the priorities are and about which parts of the current arrangements it values and which it doesn't.

The great problem for British reformers has been that one party, the Conservatives, are so long and so regularly in office that they are unable to look at the big picture – that, as ministers and MPs, they have utterly lost the gift of seeing themselves as others see them. The treadmill and crisis-management of modern government seems to repress the ability of office-holders to imagine a different way of doing things. It makes them instinctive apologists for the furniture around them. So the same Tories who were so vociferous about the menace of quangos before reaching power, turned themselves to quangos when in power. So Malcolm Rifkind and Michael Ancram were keen devolutionists, until they became ministers and decided that somehow change was a bad idea after all. Thus even as impeccably conservative a Conservative as Douglas Hurd was arguing a Tory case for electoral reform before the Conserva-

tives went into government in 1979.[23] But the very weakness of
the opposition parties could lead to a similar effect. They are so
rarely in office that they feel obliged to seize their brief spell in
the sun and rummage frenetically through a basket of favourite
economic remedies before being expelled again: the power of
Labour centralizers and conservatives should never be
underestimated.

So, one way or another, merely electing a different government and then sitting back is unlikely to give John and Jean
Bull a nice, shiny new constitution. The country, it seems, is fed
up to the back teeth with politicians and the system: you hear
the same gripes from business executives, from the opinion
polls, from the drinkers at the next table in the pub and the
people sitting opposite in the train. We all whinge. We all seem
to agree about this. If only a small fraction of this national
clucking was diverted into pressure for reform – just as it needs
only a small proportion of the sou'wester to run a wind-turbine
– what power would be unleashed. Individual politicians are
sensitive to their postbags, to the people they meet on doorsteps,
to phone-in programmes, to the audiences of television shows,
to their local parties. The biggest changes in the political mood
have been wrought by movements – the green movement, the
women's movement, even the growing movement against European federalism. The Communitarians aspire to be such a movement, too, and today we could do with a big, informal movement
for political reform. In a sense, there already is one; its leading
organization is called Charter 88, and has itself helped change
the terms of the debate. The Liberal Democrats are in essence a
political reform party and so too, though in a more dilute way,
are Labour. Many Conservative councillors are also reformers
in that they are bitterly hostile to quango-ization of local life.
But, unless the case for reform billows through the general
national conversation about politics, and affects the next election
campaign itself, then we cannot be sure that anything will
happen.

And something must. It is in the nature of things that no
grand programme of reform will be accomplished quickly or

easily or in one piece. But if we are to prepare ourselves well for the next century, and to repair the mistakes of the past few decades, some such programme of modernization and mending is needed. We don't have a corrupt system, but we do have a system in decay, in which you find vigour everywhere but in the traditional centres of political power. As metaphors, 'corruption' and 'decay' are not so far apart. It is only a few more years until the end of the millennium focuses our minds on where, as a country, we are going. Grand committees are conferring about whether this should be marked by a ferris wheel on the banks of the Thames, or some new piece of architecture, or perhaps by the replanting of a forest. None of these are disreputable ideas. But how much better to design ourselves a strengthened and trusted political system. Getting from where we are, our current grumpiness and pessimism, to a more secure and optimistic identity, is the great political challenge of our times.

If we don't rise to it, it is not clear that anything terrible will happen, at least in the immediate future. But we will become less. We will feel less secure, less confident about our country. We will become shabbier and grumpier and these islands will slowly become a less pleasant place to live in. As against that, the changes required now are no big deal. They need effort, determination and just a little vision too. But no heroes are required to die, few profits need to be forgone. Compared to the achievements and perils of the past, reforming our country today is an easy, almost a minor thing. Unless we fail to do it.

AFTERWORD

Second Thoughts

Dr Johnson, Books and the Spirit of the Time

Do these books matter? *Ruling Britannia* came out in its first edition in a year when what one might call the 'condition of Britain question' was spreading through the newspapers, airwaves and bookshops. Will Hutton of the *Guardian* had published his polemic *The State We're In*, which showed that economic books could sell; it was one of the great success stories of 1995. Simon Jenkins of *The Times* produced an astringent, fact-packed assault on Conservative centralization, *Accountable to None*. At the pleasantly bibulous launch party for that book, held appropriately enough in London's Reform Club, I was speaking to one of the brightest right-wing Conservative ministers, who confessed that he thought these criticisms of his party in power were serious and desperately needed to be answered. Among the academics, Peter Hennessy, referred to earlier in this book, published his own detailed analysis of the core of the old constitution, including in it proposed reforms of Number Ten, the Commons and Whitehall. The rising tide of interest was not only an elite preoccupation. The traumatic break-up of the Waleses' marriage set the whole country talking about the future of the monarchy, and even provoked one leading newspaper to declare for a republic. When the Scott Report followed, a matter of weeks later, it seemed that the constitutional argument had finally tumbled into the political mainstream. Certainly, the serious media produced a stream of articles, programmes and interviews grappling with the theme of political decadence.

We may never get there. But for the first time in my memory, there is now a mood of determined interest in political reform. I don't pretend that it spreads through the whole electorate, but it seems to be moving out from the smallest coterie of reformers to a wider audience. I have been showered by letters from organizations, private individuals and politicians explaining their ideas for reform, telling me about small-scale or local civic organizations I hadn't heard of, pleading for a higher-quality argument about these matters. This may be political romanticism; but the impression is of a hunger for seriousness, of dissatisfaction with trivial abuse and soundbite answers. In one of his first conversations with the young Boswell, Dr Johnson proposed that: 'Mankind have a great aversion to intellectual labour; but even supposing knowledge to be easily attainable, more people would be content to be ignorant than would take even a little trouble to acquire it.' By getting this far, the reader is already in Dr Johnson's minority; I believe this minority is now larger with regard to reform than conventional wisdom supposes.

How have the politicians reacted? John Major's resignation as Tory leader in the summer of 1995 and re-election shortly afterwards highlighted the desperation he felt about the flaking of party loyalty in the Commons, described earlier. Like other senior Tories, he takes seriously the complaint that the Commons has become a degraded cock-fighting ring, is worried about politics being thought sleazy and is frustrated at the difficulty of conveying any but the simplest argument through the blizzard of soundbites and blaring pop-paper headlines. Nor can one say that Conservatives have failed to grapple at all with the reform of politics. It was interesting that the tough proposals of the Commons committee that responded to the Nolan Report on standards in public life were passed through the Commons thanks to a considerable minority of Tory MPs who voted with the Opposition in favour of the compulsory declaration of their earnings from consultancies. At a minor, personal level I was surprised and interested that so many of the most thoughtful and serious reactions to the first edition of this book came from Tories, whether in reviews from politicians and right-wing commentators, or in letters and conversations with

MPs. Most Tories oppose reform of the Lords, the establishment of a Scottish Parliament, the returning of authority over quangos to local government, and so on. Collectively, they would fight many of the ideas advocated here to the last late-night division. But individually and sometimes privately, they are more open-minded and more worried than their reputation suggests.

Through Admiralty Arch to the Wider World

Yet whenever politicians have confronted hard decisions in office where political reform conflicts with the conveniences of power, they tend to flinch. The Major administration's unseemly effort to wriggle out of taking responsibility when the Scott Report on exports to Iraq was published – no apologies, no resignations, despite the judge's finding that Parliament had been deliberately misled – was a dramatic example of how words like 'accountability' shrivel into empty pieties. The pressure put on a once-proud political system by the desire to strike trade deals with ruthless foreign regimes has been a recurring feature of the Thatcher–Major years. Since this book was first published it has continued to be a source of periodic embarrassment. When, for instance, at the beginning of 1996, a Saudi dissident, Muhammad al-Mas'ari, learned that the British Government intended to deport him to the small Caribbean island of Dominica because the Saudi Royal Family, the autocratic House of Saud, were irritated by his presence in the UK. They were raising doubts over the future of the £20 billion oil-for-arms al-Yamamah deal, signed between Britain and Saudi Arabia in 1985 and the biggest arms deal ever done. Dominica was allegedly paid off with British aid for its banana industry. At the heart of the campaign against Mr al-Mas'ari were a cluster of Ministry of Defence civil servants and ex-MoD people now working for big private defence contractors – particularly Vickers, who make the Challenger II tank. The interconnection of business and politics was, it seemed, closer and more intense than earlier examples given in this book. In these cases, liberal outrage isn't quite enough; there was a genuine dilemma for the Government in trying to balance this country's reputation for standing up to bullies and preserving a generous attitude to dissidents – its self-respect – against the desperate need for jobs and contracts.

This wasn't uncharacteristic of what faces our politics and indeed our self-respect. At about the same time, official Chinese fury was being expressed about a British television programme on the murder of children in Chinese orphanages; again, a tremor ran through corporate Britain and Whitehall about the possible effect on British trade to fast-growing China. An absolute refusal to count the economic consequences of shunning authoritarian regimes means that the punishment falls on workers and families far from well-heeled London suburbs. But the opposite worldly wiseman response, that everything is justified that brings work, leads us down a degrading slippery slope. Eventually, it would take us to a country in which every non-economic value became negotiable – what we said publicly, what we watched, which frightened refugees we chose to help. That country wouldn't be Britain. There is no golden mean I can define, and each case is different. But we need a tilt back to a more aggressive liberalism. If we do not respect ourselves, then no one will respect us either and our decline will be assured. At the moment we are selling ourselves in more senses than one. Philip Larkin's lines, quoted earlier, about bequeathing our children a different country – 'All we can hope to leave them now is money' – seem bleakly appropriate.

At the very least, this confirms a central message of *Ruling Britannia*, that there is no dividing wall, Chinese or otherwise, between economics and politics; and that British political autonomy is losing out to world commerce and supranational bodies. Somewhat to my surprise, the book's argument that the state had lost power to markets, global institutions and transnational companies provoked the most serious attacks on it, notably from the *Economist* magazine and William Waldegrave, the Conservative Cabinet minister. They argued that all that had happened was that the post-1945 'delusion of omnipotence' of socialistic states, who thought they could control more than they could, was coming to an end, and that most of the powers allegedly lost to global markets had never been possessed by governments in the first place. In the words of the *Economist*, 'global integration has left governments with about as many economic powers as they ever had'. Yet the magazine's own survey of the world economy concluded almost the opposite. It noted that on fiscal policy, 'globalization has restricted governments' ability to increase taxes, particularly on business. Multinationals with global investment strategies can quickly shift production to countries with more attractive tax regimes.' Similar points were made about the effect of the global capital market in setting interest and exchange rates. Similarly rightly.

That state power has been affected by globalization still seems to me to be obvious, and an essential backdrop to any serious discussion of British politics. The traditional state weapons of military force, the minting of currency, territorial control, secret diplomacy and censorship have less practical or daily meaning in the mid-nineties than perhaps ever before in human history. They have not disappeared and may return, for good or evil, but they are currently retreating. In economic policy, globalization has increased the severity and speed of punishments meted out on governments which fail to follow orthodox macro-economic policies. Is this the end of old illusion or is it a new constraint? The best answer I eventually heard came from Nico Colchester, the writer cited earlier in the book, who compared the condition of the modern government to that of a driver in a car moving through heavy traffic. The driver had as much authority – as much sovereignty – over the car's controls, including the accelerator and steering-wheel, as before. But if the driver actually used it to accelerate or change direction, the car would immediately crash, horrifying the passengers. We can pretend that we are autocrats of the Saab or Ford; looked at from outside, we are governed and constrained by traffic regulations and the state of the roads.

Tony Blair and his Big Idea

This doesn't mean, though, that the state has no power, or that politics is futile, or that we should all give up. In *Ruling Britannia* I tried to describe the effect of global free-market economics on people's sense of belonging and security, suggesting that what was needed to counterbalance strong market forces was a greater sense of political gravity or 'standing-on-the-ground-ness'. We needed a trustworthy public life and a sense of community, of social inclusiveness, to stop us becoming mere thistledown people. Tony Blair has now proposed his version of the 'stakeholder economy' as Labour's big idea in response to globalization. Since stakeholding is mooted as the answer to some of the problems raised earlier in this book, and others, and since it has caused some confusion as to whather it is a big idea, a little idea, or no idea at all, it may be useful to dwell here on what a 'stakeholder economy' might be.

In origin, stakeholding is a piece of business jargon to describe a company which isn't obsessed by its shareholders' interests, but which also concentrates on and invests in its employees, subsidiary suppliers and industrial partners, its customers, and its community. This model of the good company, so different from the typical product of British takeover-mania and short-term share-price performance, has become fashionable and is advocated by business gurus such as Charles Handy and John Kay. Handy, in *The Empty Raincoat*, rejects as un-British the notion of a corporation as a community or a family, then makes a nice point: 'There is a word, however, an old Anglo-Saxon word with all the right history, until recently: it is "company", meaning a fellowship, a group of companions. Somewhere along the line it acquired its technical legal definition and lost its connotations. There was a time, maybe, when we had got the concept right.'[1] Blair has, in essence, picked up this business idea and used it as his central metaphor for good politics. Speaking to Japanese businessmen in 1996, he told them: 'The successful firm today works through partnership. Class distinctions are unhelpful and divisive. The good company invests in its people and takes them seriously. This is not kindness. This is good business. A country is not that different.'[2] There has been a long history of government borrowing the latest ideas current in business for itself; the centralized bureaucracies with tiers of managers built by the mid-century governments mirrored the great corporations of the time. Margaret Thatcher's determination to inject private-sector disciplines and personnel policy into Whitehall in the eighties was driven by her admiration of the capitalist buccaneers of that era. The notion of 'downsized' or lean government owed a lot to the efficiency-mania of the arrival of a global market in financial services. So it is not surprising that Blair has picked up the new company thinking.

The other source for stakeholding is the writing about civic society and social capital as an important component in economic success. The idea that such things as a country's propensity to obey its own laws, to trust its public institutions and to enjoy a rich mix of community, church and sub-political activity are related to its ability to create wealth is hardly surprising or new. It has been discussed earlier in this book; some readers may think it banal. Yet, rediscovered by such gurus of the right as Francis Fukuyama in his second book, *Trust*, it has helped push back the neo-liberal tide and reassert the need for social and political action of however humble a nature.

What might stakeholding mean in practice? At a basic level, it means well-known Labour policies like a basic minimum wage and the worker-protection provisions of the European social chapter. More interestingly, though, it would justify a shift in welfare provision to funded personal pensions for all: if the idea is for everyone to have a stake, a sense of belonging and ownership in the economy, then possession of one's own pot of money for illness or retirement clearly helps. It must mean more vigour in trying to bring people off benefit and back into work; no 'stakeholder economy' could consign millions of people to life without that most basic stake in the country, a role to play. These jobs might come through better training and a reformed tax and welfare regime or from tax-funded public employment; but stakeholding would not absolve a new government of concentrating on the victims of globalization. Does stakeholding link to the political reform programme itself? Though I haven't used the word, it has been part of my purpose to show that it must. If people don't have any faith in their local politics; if they are governed by secretive quangos; if cities or countries don't have the ability to act for themselves; if the central political institutions are discredited or disregarded – then politics increases the sense of rootlessness rather than curing it. A stake is also a political stake, a voice, a vote that influences the real world.

A Journalist's Reply to Just Criticism (and the other sort)

It must be clear by now that 'second thoughts' about the issues raised in Ruling Britannia are not retractions. There were a couple of factual errors in the first edition and they have been corrected here; no doubt other errors have been inserted. (There are some deliberate errors too. Having hunted in vain for suitable poetic epigraphs for chapters two, three and four, I eventually gave up and faked them, attributing them to some current and eminent members of the parliamentary press gallery. Pleasingly, no one noticed.) In general, the critics were more kind than not. The attacks that stung were not those directed against my argument or prose, but against my jokes. Such people will not be easily forgiven. They will be hunted down.

More seriously, though, some critics have argued that the reforms proposed here are too sketchy and timid, asking why I had not provided a more detailed and radical blueprint for the overthrow of our failed politics, and its replacement by a new system, complete with written constitution, different institutions, and so on. Why could I not be braver and go the whole hog? Because, in brief, the whole hog won't go. It is a phantom hog, a hog with wings, flying across a rose-tinted sky. While it is possible that our entire political economy will collapse, either because of environmental catastrophe, or because the demands of the global economy are too destabilizing, that collapse does not seem imminent or to be desired. Yet it would require some such radical breakdown, with all its attendant dangers and miseries, for there to be the kind of political revolution the architects of absolute reform await. In its absence, there is no mechanism for the upending of our institutions and culture. The Commons would have to suspend its activity and start again. But Britain is a place where we live, not a blank sheet of paper. To draw up detailed plans for a new regime may feel satisfactorily thorough and rigorous, but it is to misunderstand how change happens. Reformers must work with the parties, politicians and social forces that exist now and urge them forward.

And now is a good time to do it. The electoral weakness of the Conservatives, who mostly oppose political reform, and the agenda of both Labour and the Liberal Democrats are bringing the prospect of radical change nearer than at any time since the Liberals took power early in the century. Tony Blair's mixture of stakeholding and political reformism is nearer to Gladstonian and Asquithian Liberalism than to the managerialism of Labour in the sixties or seventies. Paddy Ashdown's Liberal Democrats have a reform agenda which goes even further; in many respects they are the true philosophers of reform, and Labour has been following behind. As I write, both of these Opposition parties have been talking privately about the remaking of our politics.

Journalists are constitutionally suspicious and negative, expecting always in our guts that we will be let down, sold out, lied to and hoodwinked. This is our professional vice, our necessary evil. So I not only expect but assume that the Opposition parties will betray some of their bold words and brave intentions if they come to power. The elected reformers need to be kept under constant pressure by voters, the press, civic institutions and their own activists to go further and avoid inadequate compromise. It is still unclear whether Labour truly understands the need to rebuild local democracy or whether Blair will go far enough on voting reform to clear out the abuses and absurdities of the current system. There will be a backlash against the proposed Scottish parliament, attempting to limit its powers and push it back to the status of large local authority. The House of Lords should be abolished, not tinkered with.

But the Opposition reform agenda is hardly minimal or bland; let those who think it so pause until the parties try to fight it out in the Commons and Lords. How is it possible to regard as timid a looming package of change which, on paper, includes the creation of a Scottish parliament, a Welsh assembly, local government reform, a Bill of Rights, a referendum on voting reform, changes to the House of Lords and consideration of a new and more democractic agenda for Europe – all within the first few years? However suspicious we are about whether all of this agenda would actually be implemented, it is there, and must be taken seriously.

These have been a pretty miserable few years for politicians and many of the rest of us. I return at the end to Dr Johnson, who in his typically Tory fashion felt that subordination to rulers was a good thing: 'There is a reciprocal pleasure in governing and being governed.' Having watched the governors and experienced the being governed, it seems to me that neither pleasure has been much in evidence in the 1990s – not a bad definition of political decay. But in writing this I remain an optimist. There is a change in the national mood. It isn't merely the passing intellectual breeze that signals a coming change of government, a gust of goodbye to the Conservatives, after which the old constitution will stagger miserably on. It is a wind of change. There! A clear prophecy at last. I hope that there will be no more editions of this book, because its time will soon have passed and some of the more dramatic failures it chronicles will be history. We are living in interesting times. And that is not a curse but a blessing.

April 1996

Notes

INTRODUCTION

1. Evidence to the Nolan Committee, February 1995.
2. The issue of Scottish Home Rule is not discussed in this book, first because it remains something potential, not actual; and, second, because it has been covered in my previous book, *The Battle for Scotland*, Penguin, London, 1992/1995.
3. This is my calculation based on OPCS figures for school-age children of social classes 1,2 and 3n – the children of professional, managerial and skilled non-manual heads of household, and on Department of Education figures on children at private schools. There are around 740,000 of the former and 560,000 of the latter. The figures do, however, underline the class nature of British schooling.
4. And, according to the most reliable scientific research, clearly unavailable in Thoreau's day, every woman too.
5. From *Resistance to Civil Government*, first published in 1849.
6. *Aneurin Bevan* (vol. 1) by Michael Foot, MacGibbon and Keen, London, 1962. Also quoted in *Whitehall* by Peter Hennessy, Secker & Warburg, London, 1989.
7. Cobbett's 'First Letter to the Electors of Westminster', August 1806. It is quoted here at length so that nobody may say that this volume contains nothing said well.
8. H.L. Mencken.

CHAPTER ONE: THE BRITISH VOTER

1. Poll on democracy, ICM Research; 1,427 adults interviewed on 11–12 March 1994.

2. Quoted in *Attlee* by Kenneth Harris, Weidenfeld & Nicolson, London, 1982, p.33.

3. Quoted in *A History of Parliamentary Elections* by Joseph Grego, Chatto & Windus, London, 1892.

4. Michael Foot, op. cit.

5. *The Journey not the Arrival Matters* (an ironic title, given what he concluded) by Leonard Woolf, Hogarth Press, London, 1969, p.158.

6. *Tom Driberg: His Life and Indiscretions* by Francis Wheen, Chatto & Windus, London, 1990, p.334.

7. *Westminster Blues* by Julian Critchley, Elm Tree Books/Hamish Hamilton, London, 1985.

8. *True Blues: The Politics of Conservative Party Membership* by Paul Whiteley, Patrick Seyd and Jeremy Richardson, OUP, Oxford, 1994.

9. Ibid., p.17.

10. See *Labour's Grass Roots* by Patrick Seyd and Paul Whiteley, OUP, Oxford, 1992.

11. See, for this and the following page, *British Political Parties Today* by Richard Kelly, Manchester University Press, Manchester, 1993.

12. 'Back to Greece' by Andrew Adonis and Geoff Mulgan, *Demos Quarterly*, Issue 3, 1994.

13. *Coming to Public Judgement* by Daniel Yankelovich, Syracuse University Press, New York, 1991.

14. See Andrew Adonis and Geoff Mulgan, op. cit., upon which this article heavily depends.

15. This information comes from an essay by Kris Kobach in *Referendums Around the World*, ed. David Butler and Austin Ranney, Macmillan, London, 1994.

16. Ibid.

17. See essay by David B. Magleby in *Referendums Around the World*.

18. *What Are People For?* by Wendell Berry, Rider Books, London, 1991, p.202.

CHAPTER TWO: DOWN THE LOCAL

1. From *A History of Local Government in the Twentieth Century* by Brian Keith-Lucas and Peter G. Richards, Allen & Unwin, London, 1978, p.30.

2. *Democracy in America*, A. de Tocqueville, Fontana Press, London, 1994, pp.62–3.

3. *Conditions of Liberty* by Ernest Gellner, Hamish Hamilton, London, 1994.

4. *English Local Government from the Revolution to the Municipal Corporations Act* by Sidney and Beatrice Webb, London, 1906–1929, quoted in *The British Political Tradition* by W.H. Greenleaf (vol.3, part 1), Methuen, London, 1987, p.31.

5. Cf. W.H. Greenleaf, op. cit. (vol.1), p.87.

6. Cf. Ken Young, chapter 11 in *The Conservative Century*, ed. Seldon & Ball, OUP, Oxford, 1994.

7. *Socialism in England* by Sidney Webb, Gower, Aldershot, 1987.

8. Translated by Kevin Crossley-Holland in *The Anglo-Saxon World*, The Boydell Press, 1982.

9. Cf. 'A Critique of the Ageing Hypothesis' in *Interests and Obsessions*, Macmillan, London, 1993.

10. *Honest Opportunism* by Peter Riddell, Hamish Hamilton, London, 1993, pp.104–5.

11. Cf. *Failure in British Government* by David Butler, Andrew Adonis and Tony Travers, OUP, Oxford, 1994, pp.272–73.

12. *Unfinished Business* by Norman Tebbit, Weidenfeld & Nicolson, London, 1993.

13. *The View from Number 11* by Nigel Lawson, Bantam Press, London, 1992.

14. Evidence to Treasury and Civil Service Select Committee, 28 January 1985.

15. Ibid.

16. *The Downing Street Years* by Margaret Thatcher, HarperCollins, London, 1994.

17. Lecture to the Public Finance Foundation, July 1993.

18. Both quotations come from *Public Bodies 1994*, published in January 1995 by the Cabinet Office.

19. Democratic Audit of the UK; paper 2, 'Ego-Trip', Human Rights Centre, University of Essex/Charter 88 Trust, 1994.

20. *The Quango Explosion* by Holland and Fallon, Conservative Political Centre, 1978.

21. *Review of Guidance on Public Appointments* from the PAU, published by the Cabinet Office, 1995.

22. Ibid.

23. See the report by Jonathan Foster in *The Independent on Sunday*, 5 February 1995.

24. *The Independent on Sunday*, 3 April 1994.

25. By Simon Jenkins, columnist for 'The Wapping Times'.

26. *My Style of Government* by Nicholas Ridley, Fontana, London, 1991, p.80.

27. Interview with *Scotland on Sunday*, June 1994.

28. See Audax/Demos report.

29. W.H. Greenleaf, op. cit. (vol.1).

30. Margaret Thatcher, op.cit., p.71.

31. *Schools and the State* by Evan Davis, the Social Market Foundation, 1993.

32. House of Commons Education Committee, First Report, Session 1992–93, HoC paper 305: 'The Department of Education's Expenditure Plans 1992–93 to 1994–95'.

33. Norman Tebbit, op. cit.

34. Simon and Schuster, London, 1994.

35. *Radical Regeneration* by Peter Hain, 1975.

36. IPPR 'Building Social Capital' by Mai Winn, January 1995.

37. IEA Health & Welfare Unit, 'Reinventing Civil Society' by David Green, 1993. It should, however, be pointed out that, while Green sees Friendly Societies as representing a sturdy pre-Welfare State era of working-class self-help, in their day they too were often regarded as institutions which sapped initiative. In his classic work, *Resistance to Civil Government*, Thoreau inveighs passionately against them.

38. Demos pamphlet, 'The Common Sense of Community' by Dick Atkinson, 1994.

39. Cf. Chris Blackhurst, the *Observer*, October 1994.

CHAPTER THREE: WESTMINSTER

1. *The Diary of Benjamin Robert Haydon*, ed. W.B. Pope (vol.4), OUP, Oxford, 1963.

2. *England's Case* by A.V. Dicey, quoted by Ferdinand Mount in his *The British Constitution Now* (Heinemann, London, 1992), which is, despite the unpromising title, a ripping read and much recommended for anyone who wants to pursue these matters further.

3. *Citizens and Subjects* by Tony Wright, Routledge, London, 1994.

4. *The English Constitution* by Walter Bagehot, *Collected Works* (vol.5), ed. Norman St John Stevas, *The Economist*, London, 1974, p.268.

5. Article in *The Economist* by Walter Bagehot, 1871, *Collected Works* (vol.6), p.36.

6. 'Dull Government' in *The Saturday Review*, February 1856. Republished in Bagehot's *Collected Works* (vol.6), p.81.

7. Quoted in *Westminster: Does Parliament Work?* by John Garrett MP, Gollancz, London, 1992, p.25.

8. *Phineas Finn* by Anthony Trollope, Penguin, London, chapter 2.

9. *The Party System* by Hilaire Belloc, 1911. Cf. A.N. Wilson's biography, *Hilaire Belloc*, Hamish Hamilton, London, 1984, chapter 8.

10. *Hansard*, 17 November 1994, col.185.

11. *The Decline in Press Reporting of Parliament* by Jack Straw MP, researched by Benjamin Wegg-Prosser, October 1993.

12. Quoted in *Stick it up your Punter!* by Peter Chippindale and Chris Horrie, Heinemann, London, 1990.

13. *The House Magazine* (vol.19), No.632.

14. Ibid.

15. *Hansard*, 24 June 1994, col. 522.

16. See Peter Hennessy, second Gresham Lecture, November 1994.

17. *The Eclipse of Parliament* by Bruce P. Lenman, Edward Arnold, Sevenoaks, 1992, pp.17–18.

18. *The Decline and Fall of the British Aristocracy* by David Cannadine, Yale, London, 1990, pp.191–93.

19. *Can Parliament Survive?* by Christopher Hollis, Hollis & Co., London, 1949.

20. *The Passing of Parliament* by Professor G.W. Keeton, Benn, London, 1952.

21. Bruce P. Lenman, op. cit.

22. Butler, Adonis and Travers, op. cit., pp.116–17.

23. *Hansard*, 20 June 1994, Col.28.

24. Nigel Lawson, op. cit., p.368.

25. Written evidence to Hansard Society Commission, published in 'Making the Law', Hansard Society, p.263.

26. John Garrett, op. cit., p.107.

27. *Parliament: Functions, Practices and Procedures* by J.A.G. Griffiths and Michael Ryle, Sweet & Maxwell, London, 1989, p.430.

28. Austin Mitchell in *The House Magazine*, 23 May 1994.

CHAPTER FOUR: THE DECLINE AND FALL OF THE FREE STATE

1. The Council for the Protection of Rural Idylls has recently reported that only 2.4 idylls are left in unspoilt condition in the whole of southern and south-western England (CPRI annual report, 1993).

2. Quoted in *The Rise and Fall of the Great Powers* by Paul Kennedy, Fontana Press, London, 1989, p.575.

3. 'Homage to a Government' by Philip Larkin, *Collected Poems*, The Marvell Press/Faber & Faber, London, 1988.

4. Quoted by Christopher Hitchens in *Blood, Class and Nostalgia*, Farrar, Straus & Giroux, New York, 1990, which doesn't make happy reading, despite being well written.

5. See *The Diary of Virginia Woolf* (vol.1), 18 September 1918, Penguin, London, 1979.

6. *Reinventing Civil Society* by David Green, The IEA Health and Welfare Unit, 1993.

7. *Satan's Children* by Alan Duncan and Dominic Hobson, Sinclair Stevenson, 1995, p.113.

8. *The Mad Officials* by Christopher Booker and Richard North, Constable, London, 1994, p.201.

9. *The Politics of the Judiciary* by J.A.G. Griffiths, Fontana Press, London, 1977, p.319.

10. *Freedom Under Thatcher* by K.D. Ewing and C.D. Gearty, OUP, Oxford, 1990, p.115.

11. *Preparing for the Twenty-first Century* by Paul Kennedy, HarperCollins, London, 1993, p.123.

12. 'The Diminished Nation State' by V. Cable, *Daedalus* Paper, The Royal Institute of International Affairs, Chatham House, London, 1994.

13. Quoted by Paddy Ashdown in his 1994 Hugh Gaitskell memorial lecture.

14. 'Prospect for European Disintegration' by George Soros, speech to Aspen Institute, Berlin, September 1993.

15. Lords Official Report, 25 May 1994, col. 763.

16. *The World in 2020* by Hamish McRae, HarperCollins, London, 1994.

17. Hamish McRae, op. cit., p.153.

18. These figures come from the 'Fortune 500' in *Fortune Magazine*, 25 July 1994, and from the 1994 *Europa World Handbook*, mostly based on World Bank statistics.

19. Andrew Jay Schwartzman of Media Access Project, quoted in *Murdoch* by William Shawcross, Chatto & Windus, London, 1992.

20. *Sex, Economy, Freedom and Community*, Pantheon Books, New York, 1992–93, p.24. In general, Berry writes as well and as angrily against globalism as anyone you can find. He is one of the most important people to read on politics, as well as farming, literature and other things, and it is a complete national disgrace and source of shame that his writing is largely unknown and unavailable here. Grr . . .

21. 'Sense and Sovereignty' by Noel Malcolm, CPS Autumn Address, 1991.

22. Essay by Nico Colchester in *The Independent*, 20 February 1995.

23. For this and following quotations see *Britain and European Unity: 1945–1992* by John W. Young, British History in Perspective Series, Macmillan, London, 1993.

24. 'Fine, Remarkable, Dirty and Devious' by Boris Johnson in the *Spectator*, 9 April 1994.

25. Powell speech at Aldridge, March 1988, quoted in *Enoch Powell on 1992*, ed. Ritchie, Anaya, London, 1989.

26. From 'Literature, Dialogue, Democracy' in *Reports From the Present*, Jonathan Cape, London, 1995.

27. *The European Union: Creating the Single Market* by Lord Cockfield, Wiley Chancery Law, Chichester, 1994.

28. Private conversation with senior State Department official.

CHAPTER FIVE: IN A BIT OF A STATE

1. *Collected Works* by Walter Bagehot (vol.5) p.243.

2. A self-conscious Scotticism, meant jocularly: one of this writer's most irritating traits. Most of these facile attempts at 'humour' have been caught by Mr Michael Joseph, working late into the night. Not this one, though.

3. In his first lecture as Gresham Professor of Rhetoric, University of London, 25 October 1994.

4. I am indebted to Charles Clarke, the former adviser to Mr Kinnock, for these thoughts.

5. *Public Service and the Future* by William Waldegrave, Conservative Political Centre, 1993.

6. Keith Middlemas, cited in his essay 'The Party, Industry and the City' in *Conservative Century*, ed. Seldon and Ball, OUP, Oxford, 1994.

7. 'The Sources of the New Right' by Maurice Cowling in *Encounter*, November 1989.

8. See *John Major* by Bruce Anderson, Fourth Estate, London, 1991, pp.286–87.

9. All this information was collated and reported by Chris Blackhurst, then Westminster Correspondent of *The Independent*, during 1994.

10. *Beyond Next Steps* by Sir Peter Kemp, Social Market Foundation, 1993.

11. From 'The Labour Party's preliminary evidence to the Nolan Committee', 1995.

12. John Wilman, 'Labour and Public Services', Social Market Foundation, March 1994.

13. 'Where do we Point the Finger?', *The Times*, 16 January 1995.

14. Comments by Professor Eric Caines, Vernon Bogdanor, Professor

Fred Ridley and Brian Thompson to the Treasury and Civil Service Select Committee, quoted in its fifth report, 1993–94, para.165.

15. Ibid., para.171.

16. Vernon Bogdanor, 'Can Government be Run Like a Business?', Public Finance Foundation, 1994.

17. Institute of Historical Research seminar, March 1994, quoted in Peter Hennessy's third Gresham College Lecture, 22 November 1994.

18. Peter Hennessy, Second Gresham College Lecture, 8 November 1994.

19. 'The Secret Garden of the Crown', the *Spectator*, 2 April 1994.

20. TCSC, Fifth Report 1993–94, para.102.

21. Ibid., Annex 1.

22. TCSC, minutes of evidence, Fifth Report (vol.2), p.132.

23. Ibid., p.99.

24. From 'English Judges as Lawmakers', *Public Law*, summer 1993. This section relies heavily on Anthony Lester's writings, as well as official government commentaries and the work of his adversary in such matters, J.A.G. Griffiths.

25. See J.A.G. Griffiths, op. cit., p.116.

26. Ibid., pp.272–73.

27. *Judicial Review Handbook* by Michael Fordham, Wiley Chancery Law, Chichester, 1994.

28. Interviewed on *News at Ten*, 19 December 1994.

29. Lord Lester in *The Changing Constitution*, ed. Jowell and Oliver, Clarendon Press, Oxford, 3rd edn, 1994.

30. Ibid., pp.35–36.

31. Ibid., p.37.

32. Quoted in Ferdinand Mount, op. cit.

33. Ibid., p.223.

34. Government evidence to Treasury and Civil Service Select Committee, 26 April 1994.

35. *The Independent on Sunday*, 13 November 1994.

36. See Mervyn Jones's biography of Michael Foot, Gollancz, London, pp.130–31.

37. *The New Yorker*, 12 December 1994.

38. But often don't: remember the disaster of the polls on election

night, 1992, and the red-facedness of many pundits. The present author was not one of those who publicly predicted a Labour victory then. But this was only because I happened to be working for *The Economist*, which was able to wait for the result and pronounce then: on the basis of a decade of intense study of political trends, and a naive faith in polls, I was pretty clear that Neil Kinnock was on his way to Downing Street. Perhaps I shouldn't have relegated this revelation to the notes. I am but human.

39. Butler, Adonis and Travers, op. cit., pp.106, 116.

40. Though it should be pointed out that, had he ordered the Home Secretary to be banged up, Howard would probably have managed to escape from the prison system within weeks: everybody else seemed able to.

41. *The Spirit of Community* by Amitai Etzioni, Crown Publishing Group, New York, 1993.

42. An achievement, according to researchers from East London University, only managed by a Mr Anthony Bevins of the *Observer*.

43. The Following descriptions of the history of the Transport Department draw heavily from an excellent and well-researched history of the subject published in 1992 by the Council for the Protection of Rural England, *Where Motor-Car is Master*. The CPRE is, of course, a partisan organization, but its account of the facts has not been challenged by either the department or (so far as I have discovered) by anyone outside the DoT itself.

44. Quoted in the above document, page 54.

45. CPRE paper cited above, p.18.

46. Most are listed in the 1994 edition of *The Directory of British Political Organizations* by Paul Mercer, Longman, Harlow.

47. Dr Phil Goodwin, Linacre Lecture, Oxford, 13 October 1994.

CHAPTER SIX: CULTURE AND ANARCHY

1. See *The Principle of Duty* by David Selbourne, Sinclair Stevenson, London, 1994. See it, but don't necessarily read it; it is extraordinarily long-winded and repetitious.

2. *The Undoing of Conservatism*, Social Market Foundation.

3. *Reinventing Civil Society* by David G. Green, IEA, 1993.

4. *Civic Conservatism*, Social Market Foundation.

5. Interview with the *Sunday Times* magazine.

6. See *The Age of Unreason* by Charles Handy, Arrow Books, London, 1989; and *The Empty Raincoat*, Hutchinson, London, 1994.

7. *Scenarios for the Shape of the New World Order*, The Royal Institute of International Affairs, Chatham House, London, 1994.

8. See, above all, *The Future of Welfare* by John Hills, Joseph Rowntree Foundation, 1993.

9. See, for example, *After the Gold Rush* by Stewart Lansley, Henley Centre for Forecasting, 1994.

10. 'Alone Again' by Zygmunt Bauman, *Demos* Paper No.9 1994.

11. Amitai Etzioni, op. cit., p.15.

12. White Horse Press/Centre for Citizenship Development, Verulam House, 3 Orchard Close, Risby, Bury St Edmunds IP28 6QL.

13. Bauman, op. cit.

14. Wendell Berry, op. cit., p.135. And p.136 is pretty good too.

15. Ernest Gellner, op. cit., pp.47–48.

16. McRae, op. cit., p.186.

17. *The Revolt of the Elites and the Betrayal of Democracy* by C. Lasch, Norton, New York, 1995.

18. *The Culture of Anxiety: The Middle Class Crisis* by Matthew Symonds, Social Market Foundation, 1994.

19. Charles Handy, op. cit., p.119.

20. See Peter Hennessy, op. cit.

21. 1994 Disraeli Lecture.

22. See *The Times* magazine, 12 March 1994.

23. See 'Centre for Policy Studies' by Simon Burgess and Geoffrey Alderman in *Contemporary Record*, November 1990.

AFTERWORD: SECOND THOUGHTS

1. *The Empty Raincoat: Making Sense of the Future* by Charles Handy, Arrow Business Books, London, 1996, p. 157.
2. Tony Blair, speech to the Keidanren, Tokyo, 5 January 1996.

Index

READ MORE IN PENGUIN

In every corner of the world, on every subject under the sun, Penguin represents quality and variety – the very best in publishing today.

For complete information about books available from Penguin – including Puffins, Penguin Classics and Arkana – and how to order them, write to us at the appropriate address below. Please note that for copyright reasons the selection of books varies from country to country.

In the United Kingdom: Please write to *Dept. EP, Penguin Books Ltd, Bath Road, Harmondsworth, West Drayton, Middlesex UB7 ODA*

In the United States: Please write to *Consumer Sales, Penguin USA, P.O. Box 999, Dept. 17109, Bergenfield, New Jersey 07621-0120*. VISA and MasterCard holders call 1-800-253-6476 to order Penguin titles

In Canada: Please write to *Penguin Books Canada Ltd, 10 Alcorn Avenue, Suite 300, Toronto, Ontario M4V 3B2*

In Australia: Please write to *Penguin Books Australia Ltd, P.O. Box 257, Ringwood, Victoria 3134*

In New Zealand: Please write to *Penguin Books (NZ) Ltd, Private Bag 102902, North Shore Mail Centre, Auckland 10*

In India: Please write to *Penguin Books India Pvt Ltd, 706 Eros Apartments, 56 Nehru Place, New Delhi 110 019*

In the Netherlands: Please write to *Penguin Books Netherlands bv, Postbus 3507, NL-1001 AH Amsterdam*

In Germany: Please write to *Penguin Books Deutschland GmbH, Metzlerstrasse 26, 60594 Frankfurt am Main*

In Spain: Please write to *Penguin Books S. A., Bravo Murillo 19, 1° B, 28015 Madrid*

In Italy: Please write to *Penguin Italia s.r.l., Via Felice Casati 20, I–20124 Milano*

In France: Please write to *Penguin France S. A., 17 rue Lejeune, F–31000 Toulouse*

In Japan: Please write to *Penguin Books Japan, Ishikiribashi Building, 2–5–4, Suido, Bunkyo-ku, Tokyo 112*

In South Africa: Please write to *Longman Penguin Southern Africa (Pty) Ltd, Private Bag X08, Bertsham 2013*

BY THE SAME AUTHOR

The Battle for Scotland

A nation without a parliament of its own, Scotland has been wrestling with its identity and status for a century. But the dominance of English Conservatism at Westminster has closed off the option of Home Rule. Scottish politics has entered uncharted waters and its course will matter for all of Britain.

Scots have tried unfamiliar political tactics as they struggle with the dilemma of being a minority inside a centralized state and their experience is now being studied by opposition leaders in England. Yet for many Scots their own political history is a dim mystery; and outside Scotland it is almost unknown. Here, Andrew Marr provides an excellent and up-to-date account of the distinctive story of Scottish politics, from the collapse of Liberalism, the rise of radical Labour and of the Scottish National Party, to more recent Tory agonies and the complexities of contemporary Nationalism. Now published with a new afterword which discusses recent significant events, *The Battle for Scotland* is a book no well-informed European can afford to ignore.

'Excellent, precise, but never dry . . . He writes with a refreshing light-ness of tone and absence of rhetoric . . . It is rare to find a political book which deploys its evidence so deftly, yet which, at the same time, injects real conviction, even passion' – Magnus Linklater in *The Times Literary Supplement*

05127962

Robert Ludlum is one of the world's bestselling authors and there are more than 300 million copies of his books in print. He is published in 32 languages and 50 countries. As well as blending sophisticated plotting and extreme pace, Robert Ludlum's novels are meticulously researched and include accurate technical, geographical and biological details. In addition to the popular titles in the Covert-One series, Robert Ludlum's best-known books include *The Scarlatti Inheritance*, *The Chancellor Manuscript* and the Jason Bourne series – *The Bourne Identity*, *The Bourne Supremacy* and *The Bourne Ultimatum* – among others. Visit Robert Ludlum's website at www.orionbooks.co.uk/Ludlum.

Also Available

The Bourne Series
The Bourne Identity
The Bourne Supremacy
The Bourne Ultimatum
The Bourne Legacy
The Bourne Betrayal
The Bourne Sanction
The Bourne Deception
The Bourne Objective
The Bourne Dominion
The Bourne Imperative

The Covert-One Series
The Hades Factor
The Cassandra Compact
The Paris Option
The Altman Code
The Lazarus Vendetta
The Moscow Vector
The Arctic Event
The Ares Decision
The Janus Reprisal
The Utopia Experiment

Road To . . . Series
The Road to Gandolfo
The Road to Omaha

The Janson Series
The Janson Directive
The Janson Command

The Matarese Series
The Matarese Circle
The Matarese Countdown

Standalone Novels
The Scarlatti Inheritance
The Osterman Weekend
The Matlock Paper
Trevayne
The Rhinemann Exchange
The Cry of the Halidon
The Gemini Contenders
The Chancellor Manuscript
The Holcroft Covenant
The Parsifal Mosaic
The Aquitaine Progression
The Icarus Agenda
The Scorpio Illusion
The Apocalypse Watch
The Prometheus Deception
The Sigma Protocol
The Tristan Betrayal
The Ambler Warning
The Bancroft Strategy